Eccentric France

THE BRADT GUIDE TO MAD, MAGICAL AND MARVELLOUS FRANCE

Piers Letcher

Bradt Travel Guides Ltd, UK
The Globe Pequot Press Inc, USA

Published in 2003 by Bradt Travel Guides Ltd,
19 High Street, Chalfont St Peter, Bucks SL9 9QE, England
Published in the USA by The Globe Pequot Press Inc,
246 Goose Lane, PO Box 480, Guilford, Connecticut 06437-0480

British Library Cataloguing in Publication Data
A catalogue record for this book is available from the British Library

ISBN 1 84162 068 8

Photographs
Cover Neil Setchfield (photograph), Dave Colton (cartoon)
Text Piers Letcher (PL), Peter Letcher (RPL), Jean-Marc Demars (JMD), N Soury (NS)

Cartoons Dave Colton (www.cartoonist.net)
Illustrations Carole Vincer
Maps Alan Whitaker
Regional maps compiled from Philip's 1:3,200,000 base, and Paris area from Philip's
Paris approach map, both found in Philip's *Multiscale Europe Road Atlas*
(www.philips-maps.co.uk)

Typeset from the author's disc by Wakewing, High Wycombe
Printed and bound in Italy by Legoprint SpA, Trento

Author

Born and educated in the UK, Piers Letcher has been permanently based in France since 1984. As an independent writer and photographer he has published 14 books, more than a thousand newspaper and magazine articles, and hundreds of photographs. From the mid-nineties he spent several years as a speechwriter at the United Nations in Geneva, before once again taking to the road, in 2002, to write *Croatia: The Bradt Travel Guide*, and *Eccentric France*, his sixth and seventh travel books. He's not half as eccentric himself as people would have you believe.

DEDICATION
To Sarah Parkes –
and to French eccentrics, past, present and future.

Contents

Acknowledgements   VIII

Introduction   x

Chapter 1   **The Eccentric Year – Festivals and Fairs**   1
                    All year round 1, January 7, February 9, March 11,
                    April 13, May 15, June 18, July 20, August 24,
                    September 28, October 28, November 30, December 32

Chapter 2   **Eccentric Pioneers**   34
                    Eccentric aviators 34, Eccentric seafarers 48, Eccentric
                    montagnards 52, Eccentric scientists 58, Eccentric
                    engineers 62, Eccentrics in a class of their own 65,
                    Travel information 73

Chapter 3   **Historical Eccentrics**   74
                    Abélard & Héloise 74, Brittany's Arthurian forests 76,
                    The Cathars 77, Charlemagne 79, Cyrano de Bergerac 80,
                    Sainte Enimie – saved by leprosy 80, Henry IV 81, Joan
                    of Arc 83, Lenin 84, Louis XIV – the Sun King 86, Louis
                    XVI & Marie Antoinette 87, Mata Hari 89,
                    Napoleon 90, Nostradamus 92, Papal Avignon 93,
                    Tournemires and d'Anjonys – centuries of family
                    rivalry 94, Travel information 96

Chapter 4   **Artistically Eccentric**   97
                    Luis Buñuel 97, Camille Claudel 98, Salvador
                    Dalí 100, Paul Gauguin 101, Alberto Giacometti 103,
                    Fernand Legros 104, Victor Lustig 105, Lee Miller 105,
                    Amedeo Modigliani 106, Henri 'Douanier' Rousseau 107,
                    Henri Toulouse-Lautrec 108, Suzanne Valadon 110, Vincent
                    Van Gogh 112, Fashion victims 114, Travel information 117

Chapter 5   **Eccentrically Musical/Eccentric Performers**   119
                    Eccentrically musical 119, Eccentric performers 130, Travel
                    information 136

Chapter 6   **Writerly Eccentric**   138
                    Historically eccentric writers 138, Eccentrically modern
                    French pens 148, Expatriately eccentric writers 160,
                    Travel information 177

Chapter 7   **Eccentric Food and Drink**   179
                    Eccentric food 179, Eccentric drink 187, Travel
                    information 191

Chapter 8	**Eccentric Collections**	**194**
	Eccentric Parisian 194, Eccentric provincial 202, Travel information 215	
Chapter 9	**Eccentric Edifices**	**219**
	Art becoming life 219, Eccentric architecture 228, Travel information 234	
Chapter 10	**Eccentric Towns, Parks and Gardens**	**237**
	Eccentric towns 237, Eccentric parks 242, Eccentric gardens 245, Travel information 249	
Chapter 11	**Eccentric Hotels and Restaurants**	**252**
	Eccentric nights in – hotels 252, Eccentric nights out – restaurants 257	
Chapter 12	**Nuts and Bolts**	**262**
	Getting around 262, Hotels, restaurants, bars and cafés 265, Practical information 267	
Chapter 13	**Eccentric Itineraries**	**270**
	Paris/Ile de France 270, Northwest 271, Northeast 271, Southwest 278, Southeast 279	
Appendix	**Further Reading/References**	**284**
Index		**290**

THE REGIONS OF FRANCE

Mainland France is administratively divided up into 94 *départements*, which are grouped into 21 *régions*. The départements are numbered according to their alphabetical order, so for example Ain is 01, Alpes Maritimes (Nice) is 06, Dordogne is 24, Gironde (Bordeaux) is 33, Rhône (Lyon) is 69, Savoie is 73, Seine (Paris) is 75, and Vaucluse is 84. The last two digits of a car's number-plate tell you where it's from.

The 21 regions have been divided into five zones for the sake of convenience in this book, which correspond roughly to the areas denoted by the five different two-digit telephone prefixes – 01 for Paris, 02 for the northwest, 03 for the northeast, 04 for the southeast, and 05 for the southwest (though you need to dial the full ten-digit number wherever you are).

The five zones used in this guide comprise the following regions: Paris/Ile de France; Northwest (Bretagne, Basse Normandie, Haute Normandie, Pays de la Loire, Centre, Poitou-Charentes); Northeast (Nord-Pas-de-Calais, Picardie, Champagne-Ardenne, Lorraine, Alsace, Bourgogne, Franche-Comté); Southwest (Aquitaine, Limousin, Midi-Pyrénées, Auvergne, Languedoc-Roussillon); and Southeast (Rhône-Alpes, Provence-Alpes-Côte d'Azur).

France also has nine administrative DOM (Départements Outre Mer) and TOM (Territoires Outre Mer) regions, which include Corsica, as well as Martinique, Réunion, New Caledonia, French Polynesia, French Guiana and Wallis and Fortuna. There hasn't been room, unfortunately, to include these French territories in this edition of *Eccentric France* – but send in your ideas, and we'll see what we can do for the next one.

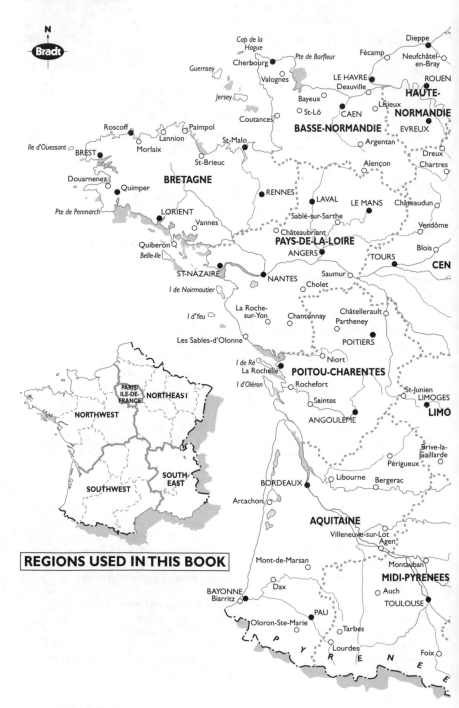

REGIONAL MAP OF FRANCE

Acknowledgements

A book like this is the result of speaking to hundreds and hundreds of people, writing thousands of emails, sending endless faxes, and reading half a tonne of books – not to mention living in France for 20 years. But it could never have been written without the help of a whole army of people, to whom I am deeply grateful.

First of all I'd like to apologise, however, to the dizzying mass of local tourist offices who were only trying to help when they recommended the annual jazz festival, a look at the local church, and a visit to the charming old town. I'm sorry, they didn't make it. The Bradt rules are very strict, and only genuine eccentrics get in.

In order of thanks, first mention must go of course to those people who died before I could get to them, and I'm grateful to their widows, former companions, and families for speaking to me and showing me round. Special thanks to Caroline Bourbonnais, Madame Chomeaux, Jean Ducuing's widow, Serge Tekielski's widow, the long-time companions of Irial Vets and Jacques Warminski, and the family of Léopold Truc.

In Paris, I'd like to give special thanks to Ornella Volta, Bernard Marchois, Alain Plumy, Ronald Kenyon, Arnaud and Laurent the whisky tasters, the cheerful copper at the police museum, Catherine Pécheux and Christian Le Bras, David Applefield and last but not least Lauren Davis. Working clockwise round the provinces from the northwest, sincerest thank yous to: Jacques Lucas, Pierre Arnoux, Cardo's wife, Yves Humblot's long-time companion, Eric Sleziak, Henri Vastine, Philippe Anginot, Alain Bardo, John Berger, Didier Bovard, Roland Dutel, Jacques Filliettroz, Luc Fougeirol, my ever-hospitable godparents, Max Manent, David and Patrick at Paddy's; Claude Reynaud, Yves Rousset-Rouard, Gabriel Santucci, François Siohan, Raymond Vuillemenot, Hervé Rofritsch at La Boule Bleue, fellow Bradt-pack author Paul Ash and his wife Fiona, Gérard Buisset, André Forget, Yvette Charvet, Wynford Hicks, Sue Tudor and her team at the Imperial Tobacco press office, Bernard Lafon, Gilbert Launet, Madame Martinet, Daniel Ponceau, and last but not least Yvan and Mary-France Quercy. Also, across France, a heartfelt thank you to all those people whose names I never quite caught, who offered help, hospitality and pointers in new directions.

At home, I'd like to single out Cyrille Roussel, who was a fount of inspiration all year, and to thank Patricia Benoit-Guyot, Viki Knight, Lisa Winters and Michèle Young for their help. Sylvia Petter did her bit in getting me into writing official speeches (and out again the other side); Patrice at Rhizone did more than just cut my hair; Eric and Isabelle upstairs provided welcome sustenance and encouragement; Dylan minded the dog; Shirley Parkes flew over all the way from Australia to help out when the going got tough; Charlotte Stimpson kept an eye on the children when deadlines were looming; and Stuart Panes kept reminding me that there's more to life than just working. Thanks to you all.

In the UK, I'd like to thank Hilary Bradt, for being the wonderful person she is, Tricia Hayne as my editor, Adrian Phillips for keeping the process going, and the rest of the staff at Bradt Travel Guides, who make it all possible. A quick thank you too, to Benedict le Vay, who started off the Eccentric series, and to Laurence Phillips, who wrote the *Bradt Guide to the Eurostar Cities*. My father, Peter Letcher, proved at the age of 78 that it's never too late to become a first-rate research assistant, and helped me deal with the vast and wonderful repast served up by the Quercys, while my mother, Virginia, provided characteristic support. It was left to my brother, Peregrine, to bail me out when funds ran out. Thank you.

Finally, I remain forever indebted to Sarah Parkes, who has shown more kindness, fortitude and thoughtfulness (not to mention proof-reading, childminding, meal-making and bread-winning) than anyone could deserve. And thanks too, to Brice and Alec, for being so understanding, and indeed loveable – I owe you both.

FEEDBACK REQUEST

At Bradt Travel Guides we're well aware that any guidebook starts to go out of date on the day it's published – and that you, our readers, are out there in the field, doing research of your own. There's a good chance you'll find out before us when a wacky new museum opens up or an old favourite shuts its doors for the last time – so why not write to us and tell us about your experiences for the next edition? We'll send you the Bradt Travel Guide of your choice and include you in the acknowledgments of the next edition of *Eccentric France* if we use your feedback. We look forward to hearing from you!

For personal correspondence and feedback, please feel free to email me at eccentricfrance@yahoo.co.uk.

Introduction

When I was four, I was taken to Brittany for the first time, and I was delighted to see a dog calmly sitting up at table in a restaurant. The experience was trumped during the very same meal by being served *moules marinières* and trying my first oyster – the start of a beautiful relationship with both mussels and oysters which has continued unchecked to the present day.

By the time I reached my teens we had holidayed along the Loire, ventured down the Atlantic coast, dipped into Provence and camped along the blustery cliffs of the Cotentin. We all loved France, and my parents bought a ruined house in the southwest to prove it. Summers were spent doing it up, and I quickly learned that my building talents were never going to keep the wolf from the door, let along provide a roof over my head. Indeed, in the early 1980s, when I finally moved to France and took over the family homestead, the barn roof promptly collapsed, terminally crushing the caravan inside. I paid the local roofer to fix up the house, and started to write to pay the bills.

By this time I'd already seen more of France than most French people ever will, spending the summers of 1978 and 1979 bumming round the country by LandRover, and when that expired, putting in more than 10,000km by bicycle through 1981 and 1982. I slept in barns when it rained and in the woods when it was fine, and delved deep into La France Profonde.

It was a fine moment, therefore, when I went to Hilary Bradt in the summer of 2001 with a proposal to write a book about Croatia (which happily did happen), and she came back with another idea: to write about French eccentrics. I dashed off a sample section to Tricia Hayne, the commissioning editor, as requested, and saw it bounce back, equally swiftly, rejected (not unfairly, I should add). After a shuttlecock rally of proposals and counter-propositions we agreed on a structure and a schedule, and here you are: *Eccentric France*. I hope you enjoy reading it as much as I enjoyed researching and writing it.

AN IMPORTANT NOTE TO FRENCH READERS

The word 'eccentric' in English isn't a good translation at all of the word *excentrique* in French; whatever the dictionary says, in reality they are *faux amis*. Because in English – and indeed throughout this book (and series) – we have included events, people and places because they're eccentric in the sense that they're interesting, original, unusual, intriguing, fascinating or exceptional, and never because they're just plain *fou*.

The Eccentric Year – Festivals and Fairs

France is a country astonishingly rich in social, cultural and sporting events, and in total around 20,000 are organised annually – that's an average of more than 50 a day, year round. Amongst them you'll find a wealth of theatre, film, comedy, folklore, music and dance festivals, any number of more or less successful replays of historical events (from the medieval to the revolutionary), a whole range of sporting activities, and plentiful excuses to eat and drink more than might strictly be considered good for you. Regional fare and regional fairs still come very high on the French agenda.

Be warned, however, that not everything is quite as it may seem – the *Défilé des Sans Culottes*, in Mutzig, near Strasbourg, isn't a panty-free occasion at all, but instead a colourful re-enacting of the storming of the Bastille in 1789. Equally, something billed interestingly as the *Frairie des culs noirs* (literally the black-bottomed brotherhood), which struts its stuff every year at Saint Yrieix la Perche, near Limoges, is actually only celebrating the wonderful flavour of the local saddleback pigs.

ALL YEAR ROUND...

The sections in this chapter go through the 100 or so most unusual events, on a month-by-month basis, but whatever time of year you come to France, and almost wherever you go, there's always something interesting going on.

Manifestations

The French word *manifestation* doesn't have a simple translation into English – depending on the context it can be a special occasion, an event, or a demonstration.

TRAVEL INFORMATION

Please note that while the *Travel Information* in the rest of the book is given at the end of each chapter, in this section you'll find the information given with the event being described. Next to town names you'll find the telephone number for the local tourist office (or town hall, where there isn't one), as well as details for event organisers where appropriate. When you call you'll find these days that many respondents will have a reasonable command of English – but far from all, especially at the town halls.

THE ECCENTRIC YEAR – FESTIVALS & FAIRS

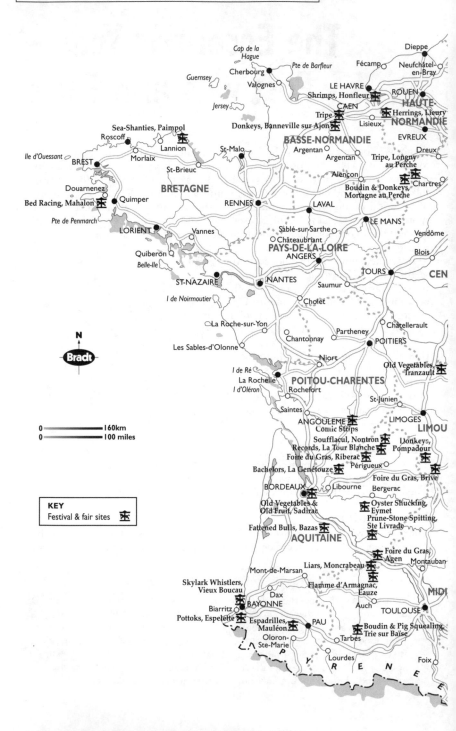

Cap de la Hague

Dieppe

Pte de Barfleur

Fécamp

Neufchâtel-en-Bray

Cherbourg

Guernsey

LE HAVRE

Valognes

Shrimps, Honfleur

ROUEN

HAUTE

CAEN

Herrings, Lieury

Jersey

Tripe

Lisieux

NORMANDIE

Donkeys, Banneville sur Ajon

EVREUX

Sea-Shanties, Paimpol

BASSE-NORMANDIE

Roscoff

Argentan

Dreux

Lannion

St-Malo

Argentan

Tripe, Longny au Perche

Ile d'Ouessant

Morlaix

Alençon

Chartres

BREST

St-Brieuc

Boudin & Donkeys, Mortagne au Perche

Douarnenez

BRETAGNE

RENNES

LAVAL

LE MANS

Bed Racing, Mahalon

Quimper

Vendôme

Pte de Penmarch

Sablé-sur-Sarthe

LORIENT

Vannes

Châteaubriant

Blois

Quiberon

PAYS-DE-LA-LOIRE

ANGERS

TOURS

CEN

Belle-Ile

TOURS

ST-NAZAIRE

NANTES

Saumur

I de Noirmoutier

Cholet

La Roche-sur-Yon

Châtellerault

Parthenay

Chantonnay

POITIERS

Les Sables-d'Olonne

Niort

I de Ré

Old Vegetables, Tranzault

La Rochelle

POITOU-CHARENTES

I d'Oléron

Rochefort

St-Junien

Saintes

ANGOULEME

LIMOGES

LIMOU

Comic Strips

Soufflaçul, Nontron

Donkeys, Pompadour

Records, La Tour Blanche

Foire du Gras, Ribérac

Périgueux

Foire du Gras, Brive

Bachelors, La Genétouze

BORDEAUX

Libourne

Bergerac

Old Vegetables & Old Fruit, Sadirac

Oyster Shucking, Eymet

Prune-Stone Spitting, Ste Livrade

Fattened Bulls, Bazas

AQUITAINE

Foire du Gras, Agen

Liars, Moncrabeau

Montauban

Mont-de-Marsan

MIDI

Skylark Whistlers, Vieux Boucau

Flamme d'Armagnac, Eauze

Dax

Auch

TOULOUSE

Biarritz

BAYONNE

Pottoks, Espelette

Espadrilles, Mauléon

PAU

Boudin & Pig Squealing, Trie sur Baïse

Oloron-Ste-Marie

Tarbes

Lourdes

Foix

P   Y   R   E   N   E   E

Bradt

N

0 ——— 160km
0 ——— 100 miles

KEY
Festival & fair sites

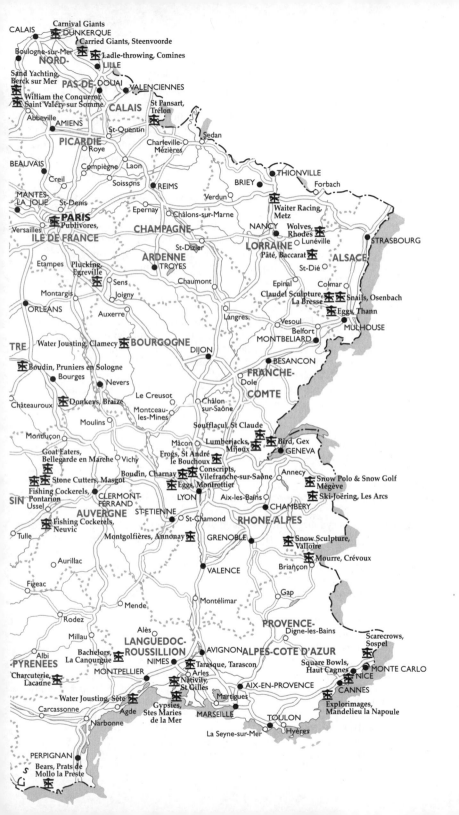

With the latter in mind, you should keep an eye out for local *manifestations*, as the French remain the most politicised nation in Europe, frequently favouring direct action and a public demo or six.

Hardly a day goes by, it seems, without a French farmer dumping a trailer-load of produce outside the local *mairie* or government offices, or setting fire to a load of condemned carcasses in the middle of a busy town square. Most French people have close ties to the land, and still rely on family contacts for their own supplies of wine or local produce – so while they may have let the French Franc disappear without a murmur of protest, they're still highly supportive of the small French farmer. Witness the enormous popularity of a man like José Bové (see page 66).

But it's not just the farmers. Truck drivers (whose working conditions and pay are pretty awful everywhere) take to the streets – and indeed *autoroutes* – when things get too much; air traffic controllers close the skies at the drop of a hat; bus and taxi drivers bring public transport to a halt if one of their number is attacked; schoolteachers lock classrooms and doctors shut surgeries if pay and conditions aren't improved in line with demands; and fishermen are quite happy to blockade ports with their boats if the fishing quotas aren't up to expectations.

It's not all hostile stuff, either. The police will close the roads in a trice if there's a *course cycliste* or a marathon being run anywhere in the vicinity, and local weddings tend to disrupt the traffic, with cavalcades of revellers playing tunes of a sort with their car horns, and forming circles on the roundabouts on Saturday afternoons.

Personally, I'm glad to live in a country where protest is not just tolerated but is also effective, and where a cycle race or a wedding is deemed to be more important than the regular throughput of traffic – but be warned that it can affect your holiday plans.

Food and drink

The French don't just love their food, they adore it. We're not talking here about *Croque Monsieur-Frites* in the more touristy bits of Paris, or *Le Fast Food* springing up wherever teenagers are to be found, but about *La France Profonde* – the heart of France. And the way to a French person's heart is of course through his or her stomach.

So you'll find every ingredient celebrated with its own festival or fair, and people spending far more time (and vastly more money) on food than you might expect. Come Christmas, you need to order your fresh *foie gras* a fortnight before you need it, to avoid disappointment, and at cheese stalls in markets around the country people think nothing of spending a small fortune on the week's supply. If you're in the market for the best fresh truffles, you'll need to be in the marketplace within minutes of its opening.

There are separate fairs and festivals around the country celebrating apples, lemons, apricots, tomatoes, plums, bilberries, cherries, melons, pumpkins, prunes, walnuts, chestnuts, violets, mushrooms, onions, garlic, truffles, olives, olive oil, honey, lavender, saffron, gourds, capons, turkeys, chickens, ducks, geese, guinea-fowl, pigs, cows, sheep, ham, *boudin noir, boudin blanc, andouillette*, tripe, frogs, snails, crayfish, scallops, oysters, herrings, shrimps, trout, tuna, perch, pike and literally scores of different cheeses.

Towards the end of the year, practically every market in southwestern France holds a **Foire du Gras** (fat fair), where the best fattened fowls are available, along with the finest *foie gras* – particularly good *foires* are held in Agen (tel: 05 53 47 36 09), Brive (tel: 05 55 92 39 39) and Riberac (tel: 05 53 90 03 10), though there are several score more to be discovered.

Vegetarians, however, may want to eschew the fat and concentrate instead on the humble truffle, which is available across the southwest and in Provence in winter. In the southwest the truffle markets are often hard to find (and in any case can be over in a matter of moments), but in Provence there are a number of popular truffling events.

There are **truffle markets** on Mondays in Chamaret (no tourist office), Tuesdays in Grignan (tel: 04 75 46 55 96), Thursdays in Nyons (tel: 04 75 26 10 35), Fridays in Carpentras (tel: 04 90 63 00 78) and Saturdays in Richerenches (tel: 04 90 28 05 34), while Lalbenque (tel: 05 65 31 50 08) has a truffle afternoon every Tuesday – in the aptly named rue du Marché aux Truffes.

Grignan (see above) also has a truffle and wine festival the weekend before Christmas, complete with a truffle-hunting contest; Uzès (tel: 04 66 22 68 88) has a special truffle day at the end of January, with tastings; and Saint Paul Trois Châteaux (tel: 04 75 96 61 29) goes the whole hog on the second weekend in February, with truffle-based meals served from ten in the morning until eight at night. Finally, in Richerenches (see above), in mid-January, there's a truffle-mass held at the local church, with the area's truffles being blessed, and truffles being put in the collection plate instead of cash.

None of these events would be complete – and France wouldn't be France – without a splash of **wine**. Anywhere wine's made (and that's pretty much everywhere except Brittany) there are festivals and fairs at the end of the grape harvest, and wine tastings are held pretty much all year round. The biggest, of course, are in the major wine regions (Bordeaux, Burgundy, Côtes du Rhône, Beaujolais, Champagne, Alsace), but there are scores of minor wines across France, and minor festivals for each. You can also drop in at the vast majority of wine producers around the country, have a taste of the local production, and stagger off with a case or two (be)for(e) laying down.

Cycling

If the French adore their food, they're also mad about cycling, and there are hundreds of local, regional and national cycling events. Every town and village has its own cycling club, and whenever there's an event on, half the populace comes out to watch. Thousands of amateurs now take part in each of a wide variety of so-called *cyclo-sportifs*, which are organised on a (supposedly) non-competitive basis throughout the season.

There's also a packed calendar of major pro-races, which gets underway with the Paris–Nice eight-stage race in the second week of March and hots up with Paris–Roubaix on the second Sunday in April. In May you can follow the Quatre Jours de Dunkerque (actually a five-day race with six stages); in June you can sign up with the 1,500 amateurs who take part in the Bordeaux–Paris event (a 622km course which has to be covered in under 28 hours); and in July you can join the whole country as it comes to a complete halt to watch the Tour de France.

Of all the events, **Paris–Roubaix** is probably the toughest, partly because it's almost always cold, wet, windy and muddy in early April in that part of the world, but mostly because of the appalling course, with just over 50 of the 260-odd kilometres being ridden on 27 sections of narrow pathway paved with huge cobblestones. It's not known as 'the Hell of the North' for nothing. The race was

instigated in 1896, and run for the 100th time in 2002 – the winner completing the course in just six and a half hours. But the fastest man to date was the Dutch rider Peter Post, who won Paris–Roubaix in 1964 at an average speed of over 45km/h! True grit – or plain madness?

The **Tour de France**, for its part, dates back to 1903 and remains the most important event on the global cycling calendar. Raced clockwise in odd years and anti-clockwise in even ones, Le Tour starts on the first Saturday and ends on the last Sunday in July. On its way, it covers around 3,000km in 20 stages, with two rest days, and takes in both the Pyrenees and the Alps. It usually dips into one or more of France's neighbouring countries – even spending two days in southern England in 1994.

The event is without question the biggest feat of human endurance in the regular sporting calendar, with the riders spending an average of over four hours a day in the saddle over a three-week period, and it brings out the best and worst in men. Typical of the attitude of the riders is that of the Englishman Tommy Simpson, one of the very few riders to die in the Tour, whose last words before expiring on the vicious slopes of the Mont Ventoux in 1967 were 'Put me back on the bloody bike'.

You certainly need to be tough to win – and to win more than once you need to be an iron man. For example, take Jacques Anquetil. In 1965, having already been the first to win the Tour de France on five occasions, he went on to win the Dauphiné Libéré stage race on the afternoon of 29 May, and the 550km Bordeaux–Paris race (which started at 2am) the following day – a feat not even matched by the other five-time Tour winners (Eddy Merckx, Bernard Hinault and Miguel Indurain – and quite possibly Lance Armstrong in 2003).

For more about French cycling check out web: www.letour.fr, www.velo101.com and www.velo-club.net – while in the UK there's also the excellent www.cyclingnews.com.

Penitents' processions

If you're in France during a religious festival (especially during Lent, at Easter, or on 15 August, the Feast of the Assumption of the Virgin Mary) don't be alarmed if you see a Penitents' Procession – it's perfectly normal, and nothing whatsoever to do with the Ku Klux Klan.

Confraternities of Penitents were established in France from the 13th century onwards, defining themselves by the type of penance being performed (fasting, hair shirts, caring for the dying, that kind of thing), and often having their own churches and even their own cemeteries. Members wear heavy robes, drawn in with a rope belt, and topped off with a pointed hood with only slits for the eyes (though that particular restriction is often now waived).

Different coloured robes originally identified the different confraternities' penances, though these days most of them perform broadly similar work, caring for the poor, the sick and the dying. But you'll still find processions of White Penitents, Black Penitents (who originally looked after condemned criminals and accompanied them to their executions), Grey Penitents, Blue Penitents, Red Penitents and even Green and Violet Penitents.

Carnival giants

Ever since the 16th century there's been a solid tradition of giant puppets in Flemish towns on both sides of what's now the Belgian–French border, and at most carnivals in the region the giant's a key participant. Originally the giants (anything from 3 to 10m tall) were heroic Biblical figures, carried through town on the local saint's day, but after the French Revolution the emphasis turned away from the Bible and towards more mythical and legendary figures.

Purists rightly insist that the giants should be carried by a human crew, rather than by a mechanical float, so that they can 'dance' to the carnival music (the giants have a certain amount of flexibility, being made of wicker), and it makes for a fantastic spectacle. Altogether there are around 300 of the enormous figures spread across both sides of the border, and although they usually stay in their home towns, there are (very) occasional giants' meetings, which are well worth getting to see. The biggest, by far, is the **European Procession of Carried Giants**, which only happens every six or seven years (the next one is planned for April 2006, see page 14, in the town of Steenvoorde).

Meanwhile, almost every French town along the Belgian border, especially from Dunkerque to Lille, has at least one annual giants' outing, and Dunkerque (tel: 03 28 66 79 21) itself has a procession every weekend from mid-January to early March, featuring different giants every time.

JANUARY
International Snow Sculpture Competition

Where better to start the Eccentric Year than up in the snowy French Alps? Here, in the ski resort of Valloire (1,400m), during the third week of January, France's only snow sculpture competition takes place. The artform was born in Canada (apparently they have plenty of raw materials there), but has since been taken up in the USA, Russia, Sweden, Finland, Austria and Switzerland – although Valloire is the smallest community in the world to offer a competition.

Over a two-week period after Christmas, the Valloire snowploughs head up towards the Galibier (a name you'll be familiar with if you're a Tour de France fan) and bring back enough snow to fashion 17 enormous blocks, each one measuring 3.5m x 3.5m x 4m, and therefore requiring a staggering 50m³ of pressed snow apiece.

The teams of sculptors – three to a cube – are then let loose on the 17 blocks, which are strategically placed all the way along Valloire's main drag, l'Avenue de la Vallée d'Or. There are eight French teams who take part in the national contest, and nine foreign teams, who participate in the international competition. One year there was even a team from Burkina Faso, where the artists had never even seen snow, let alone sculpted it.

The rules are simple enough: anything goes, but you can only use manual implements (shovels, picks, saws, chisels and knives are popular) and you only have 72 hours to complete the job. The teams sculpt right through the night, as the snow's often easier to work when it's *really* cold, and on the morning of the third day the results are judged. Plenty of prizes are dished out, so nobody goes away empty-handed, and around 15,000 visitors a year come and enjoy the spectacle – the 20th edition took place in January 2003.

After a few weeks – depending of course on the weather – the sculptures simply melt away, as if they'd never been.

For more information – or if you're interested in spending 72 hours of your life fashioning a snow sculpture – contact the **Valloire tourist office** (tel: 04 79 59 03 96; web: www.valloire.net).

International snow polo

While we're in the mountains, there's another great event which also takes place in the third week of January, this time at Megève (1,100m). Over a four-day period, six international teams with more than 150 horses come together and engage in polo matches on the snow. *Vin Chaud* plays the part of Pimm's, five acres of freshly flattened snow plays the part of the polo ground, and there's none of that unpleasant fuss with divots to worry about – though the horses do have to be shod with special studded rubber horseshoes to improve their grip.

The event, which has been running since 1995, is increasingly popular, and is sure soon to overtake the rather *passé* world championship skiing which Megève is more famous for. So if you fancy a winter chukka next year, contact the **Megève tourist office** (tel: 04 50 21 27 28; web: www.megeve.com).

International Comic Strip Festival

The French take comic strips – and we're not just talking Asterix and Tintin here – rather seriously, and bookshops have whole aisles full of them. Grown-ups are as passionate about the *BD* (*bande dessinée*) as kids or adolescents. So it's hardly surprising that there's a **Festival International de la Bande Dessinée** (tel: 05 45 97 86 50), or that the venue, Angoulême, is also home to the **Centre National de la Bande Dessinée et de l'Image** (CNBDI, tel: 05 45 38 65 65; web: www.cnbdi.fr).

The festival, held at the end of January every year, is enormously popular, attracting a staggering 200,000 visitors and more than 3,000 comic-strip industry professionals. The events are spread across the whole town of Angoulême, from the CNBDI itself to local exhibitions and themed pavilions, and businesses and shops tend to join in the comic-strip theme. There's also a series of workshops available for budding cartoonists. But if you want to go to the festival at all, book well ahead.

The Pottok Fair

The last Tuesday and Wednesday in January sees the annual Pottok Fair take place in Espelette (tel: 05 59 93 95 02), a small town nestled into the foothills of the Pyrenees, just 20km inland from Biarritz.

Pottok (pronounced Potiok) simply means 'little horse' in Basque, and that's exactly what pottoks are: ponies (though it was only recognised officially as a breed in 1971). Small, hairy and tough (I won't say 'like their Basque owners'), pottoks have long been employed as working horses on farms, and a number were unfortunate enough to be used as pit ponies, but for the most part they've remained semi-wild, living in the foothills of the mountains. Given their kind disposition, they're also increasingly popular as horses for riding or pony-trekking.

Once a year, then, the pottoks are herded up and brought to Espelette, where they're branded for identification, and either sold on or returned to the hills as breeding stock. The fair itself is your classic Basque animal event, with plenty of bargaining going on, the Basque language much in evidence, and festivities continuing on well into the small hours.

If you want to ride a pottok in Espelette, get in touch with the **Ixtaklok Pony Club** (tel: 05 59 93 82 13).

Conscripts' Festival

Drop in to Villefranche sur Saône (tel: 04 74 07 27 40), just upriver from Lyon, on the last Sunday in January and you'll find an extraordinary festival taking place: the **Fête des Conscrits**.

In the 19th century, conscription was effected amongst each year's 20-year-olds by means of a lottery. In Villefranche, in 1850, two young men turned up for the conscription wearing black tie (which the French endearingly call *en smoking*) and top hats, and the following year a whole group copied the idea. The outfit soon became *de rigueur*, and a tradition was born.

In 1880, a local man called Charles Hugand wanted to celebrate the 20th anniversary of his own conscription, and joined in the festivities with that year's 20-year-olds. Soon, anyone celebrating a new decade in their lives became part of the event – and in spite of conscription being abandoned in 1905, and obligatory military service itself being dropped in 1998, the party goes on.

Each year, therefore, the participants comprise the 'class' of that year – so in 2002 the event was open to men born in 1982, 1972, 1962, etc, with the 'class of 3' taking over the following year. The festivities are planned years in advance (you only get to take part once a decade, after all), and there are strict rules about the comportment of participants (drawn up in a very formal charter), but it's still an astonishingly good knees-up.

There's also a charming little **Conscription Museum** (tel: 04 74 60 39 53, open Tuesday to Saturday) in Villefranche, upstairs in the Musée du Patrimoine, complete with original lottery urns.

FEBRUARY
Ski-joëring

You love to ski, and you have a horse, so what could be more fun than to get the horse to pull you along on skis at high speed? No more tiresome queuing for lifts, or tramping home at the end of the day in heavyweight ski-boots. So inevitably it's become all the rage in the French Alps, and notably in Les Arcs, which holds the main ski-joëring jamboree of the year on the first weekend in February.

It's not for the faint-hearted or the unskilled. In one hand you hold the traces, which are covered over with a board to help prevent you from being showered with snow and ice-fragments from your horse's hooves, while in the other you hold both the reins *and* the whip. Obviously you need a well-disciplined horse and nerves of steel.

The tradition dates back over 4,500 years, when *shörekjöring* was first used in Sweden simply as a means of locomotion. At the end of the 19th century, it became a competitive winter sport in Switzerland and France, only to die out completely after World War II, when horses themselves became a rarity. Today the French Ski-Joëring Federation, in conjunction with the national riding federation, organises championships, of which the Les Arcs days in February are the mainstay on snow (it also organises ski-joëring events on grass and on sand, with the entrants on wheeled skis).

You can choose to enter in one of two categories, slalom or speed ski-joëring. In the slalom event, you have to pass with your horse through a series of gates, and then do the course in reverse, this time keeping the horse off to one side, so only you get dragged through the gates. It's not easy. On the other hand it's arguably less frightening than the speed contest, where it's simply a question of who can get round the 400m course the quickest.

The **Les Arcs/Bourg Saint Maurice tourist office** (tel: 04 79 07 12 57; web: www.lesarcs.com/fr/skijoering.htm) can provide you with more detailed information.

Bear Festival

Down in the charmingly named Catalan town of **Prats de Mollo la Preste** (tel: 04 68 39 70 83), 50km southwest of Perpignan, and almost on the Spanish border, they re-enact a local bear legend every February, the **Fête de l'Ours**. Originally the date was set for February 2, the day after bears traditionally rouse themselves from their long winter nap, but these days the festival happens whenever it fits best into the February school holidays, and then segues seamlessly into the local pre-Lent carnival.

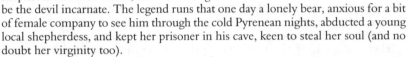

Back in the middle ages, bears weren't just a threat to shepherds and their flocks, but were thought to be the devil incarnate. The legend runs that one day a lonely bear, anxious for a bit of female company to see him through the cold Pyrenean nights, abducted a young local shepherdess, and kept her prisoner in his cave, keen to steal her soul (and no doubt her virginity too).

A rescue party was sent out to find the beauty (whoops; shepherdess), and after a long search they finally found her safe and sound, if terrified. But the beast (whoops; bear) wasn't keen for them to steal his treasure, and put up a terrific fight, killing many of the party before eventually being subdued and brought back to the town in chains. A great festival ensued, and the bear was shaved with an axe, and tamed, and in due course became something of a local handyman, doing odd jobs around town (bear with me).

In celebration of this somewhat implausible scenario, the Fête de l'Ours features three young men from Prats de Mollo dressing up as (black) bears in the Lagarde Fort, overlooking town, while down below others set themselves up as (white) hunters and barbers. The 'bears' have sheepskins sewn on to their clothes and then have their hands and faces daubed with soot and oil, so as to be able to blacken the 'whites'.

The 'bears' then charge down into town, being shot at by the 'hunters' (using blanks) and chased by the 'barbers', and trying to smear people's white clothes. After some time and a great deal of noisy confusion, the 'bears' are caught, and ceremoniously sheared of their sheepskins in the main square – using an axe as the razor and a blood sausage dipped in wine as the shaving brush – thus demonstrating how the evil bear can be made human.

Needless to say, all of this is followed by much revelry and some fine Catalan dancing. A certain amount of wine is usually imbued.

Fattened Bulls' Festival

For more than 900 years, without a single break, the town of **Bazas** (tel: 05 56 25 25 84), 50km southeast of Bordeaux, has played host to **La Fête des Boeufs Gras** – the Festival of the Fattened Bulls. The event takes place on the Thursday before Shrove Tuesday, and celebrates the ancient custom of allowing the local butchers to parade their finest beasts through town as part of the carnival festivities.

At around 1.30pm, the bulls' procession starts, with each animal crowned with flowers and wearing ribbons. The poor beasts are serenaded in front of each butcher's shop in town, and then blessed in front of the cathedral in the main square, before being judged.

For the first nine centuries or so only one prize was awarded, essentially for the best-bred and fattest animal, but in 1988 a new prize was also given, for the bull best suited to the butcher's trade. In 1993, obviously clutching at straws somewhat, a third prize was added to the list, for the bull with the best muscle-tone. What was once a noble animal, judged mainly on its ability to produce tallow, has simply become a muscle-bound bodybuilder.

After the bulls have been led off to their fate, there's a gastronomic feast, featuring beef consommé, Pot-au-feu, and steak, one after the other. It's a vegetarian's nightmare.

MARCH
The egg in its finery

As Easter approaches, most people (Penitents notwithstanding, see page 6) come over all pagan and start getting obsessive about fertility symbols like Easter bunnies and Easter eggs. And while most of us have neither the time, energy nor hard cash to go the Fabergé way, there's something quite endearing about decorating eggs for Easter, as an old-fashioned complement to the mass-produced chocolate and tinfoil numbers.

A couple of weeks before Easter, in Thann (tel: 03 89 37 96 20), just west of Mulhouse, there's a fine decorated egg market, l'Oeuf en Habit de Fête, which bills itself as the biggest in Alsace. Close to 100 exhibitors from around the world come to Thann to display their wares, ranging from your standard chicken egg done up in pearls, embroidery, lace, paper cut-outs or painted with watercolours, to chocolate eggs, wooden eggs, toy eggs and even musical-box eggs.

The event was launched in 1990, and has since gone from success to success – though when I was in town you couldn't get an omelette for love nor money.

L'Oeuf en Habit de Fête – the egg in its finery – is organised by the Relais Culturel Régional de Thann (tel: 03 89 37 92 52; web: www.relais-culturel-thann.asso.fr). Contact them with your decorative eggy ideas – but be warned that painting eggs with cuddly cats has already been done to death.

Snow golf

If you're skiing in Megève in the middle of March, don't be alarmed by cries of 'Fore!' – it's just the Megève Winter Golf Cup, the only French golfing competition to be played on snow. The event's a new one, having been launched only in 2001, but it's quickly taken root in the popular imagination. It's highly weather-dependent, though. If it's miserable, you can be up to your plus-fours in slush, but if it's fine (as it was, magnificently, in 2002) it makes a great spectacle for the fans, and a tough challenge for the players.

The nine-hole snow tournament is created on top of Megève's famous Mont d'Arbois golf course, one of France's oldest and most prestigious, and is played to Saint Andrew's rules, over two rounds. There are also driving and putting contests – though you don't want to make the mistake of using standard white golf-balls, as they're the very devil to find in the snow.

The competition is open to serious golfers with a maximum handicap of 35.5, and is played in two-person teams. If you're interested in tee-ing off on the snow next year, contact the **Mègeve tourist office** (tel: 04 50 21 27 28; web: www.megeve.com).

International Boudin Contest

If you like *boudin noir* (blood sausage), you'll love Mortagne au Perche (tel: 02 33 85 11 18) near Alençon, in Normandy, which is the *boudin*'s undisputed capital. You can get *boudin noir* all year round, of course, but in the third weekend in March it's especially worth coming for the international competition, which brings together scores of contestants, and enough visitors to munch their way through four to five *kilometres* of the stuff.

The competition was started in the early 1960s by the Confrérie des Chevaliers du Goûte-Boudin (the confraternity of the knights of the blood-sausage-tasters), who keep a keen eye on the quality control, and award prizes to the world's finest *boudins*, after multiple tastings. There's also a contest to see who can eat the most *boudin* – the amount being of course a great deal more than can possibly be good for you.

There are plenty of other, smaller, *boudin* festivals in France, as you'd expect, including one in **Pruniers en Sologne** (tel: 02 54 96 60 53), near Blois, on the third weekend in June, which features a contest to see who can eat a metre of *boudin* the quickest (!), and one in **Trie sur Baïse** (tel: 05 62 35 50 88), not far from Tarbes, which is held in conjunction with the national pig-squealing championships in August (see page 24). Finally, there's a festival in **Charnay** (04 78 43 90 69), just north of Lyon, on the last weekend of March, where about a tonne of *boudin* is served up.

(Should you be interested in making a tonne of *boudin* for yourself, you'll need 440 litres of blood, 65kg of fat, 65 sets of intestines, 120 litres of milk, 90 dozen eggs, 110kg of spinach, 65kg of onions and 90 litres of cream, along with an *extremely* large saucepan.)

Saint-Pansart's Carnival

Many, many years ago, according to legend, an apprentice glassworker was so greedy that he became enormously fat, and when he opened his mouth his cheeks covered his eyes. His paunch (*panse*, in French) was the size of a large animal's. During a fast, one year, he refused to abstain, and died of indigestion. Ever since there's been a curious Saint-Pansart Carnival in Trélon (tel: 03 27 57 08 18), right up in the north of France, just across the Belgian border from the beer-brewing monks at Chimay.

The carnival, held usually at the end of March, features a Saint-Pansart straw puppet, dressed in black and wearing a white headscarf. The locals then dress up as *Pansartistes*, with a costume consisting of a white apron and white hat, and a black mask. A 'devil' dressed in red carries a trident to poke Saint-Pansart with, and after parading through the town, the effigy is placed on a tarpaulin and then tossed up into the air by the crowd. The festivities end with Saint-Pansart being burned on the top of a huge bonfire. It's all very odd.

La Nuit des Publivores

Very often the trailer's more interesting than the film, and the ad breaks are better entertainment than the programming in between. So, at least, must have reasoned the organisers of the first Nuit des Publivores (*publicité* being French for advertising, and *vore* as in carnivore, herbivore etc), which took place in 1981.

The event was a huge success, and today it's spread out across time and space, starting off every year in March in Paris and then going out on tour across France and abroad, and attracting some 200,000 viewers annually. It consists of 500 ads and film trailers culled from television and the cinema around the world, dating from the dawn of film to the present day, and the programme is created afresh every year.

The show starts at 9pm and runs until 4am, with three intermissions – except in Paris where it starts at midnight and finishes up at 7am. It's an excellent idea, although you may find it all becomes a bit of a blur after the first couple of hours.

See www.publivores.com (or tel: 01 44 88 98 00) for more information.

APRIL
Soufflacul festivals

Soufflacul festivals were once widespread across France, but there are now only two major events, one in Nontron, in northern Périgord, and the other in Saint Claude, in the Jura – and neither quite manages to capture the fundamental spirit of the original merriments.

In the past, the Soufflaculs were masked men who dressed in nightshirts, nightcaps and clogs on Ash Wednesday. Armed each with a pair of bellows, they would wander the streets for three days inflating ladies' dresses, thereby chasing away the evil spirits lurking therein (*soufflet* being bellows; *cul* being an impolite word for bottom).

The history of the Soufflaculs is somewhat obscure, though it seems to be a corruption of the processions held before Easter by White Penitents (see page 6). According to tradition one of the penitents' prayers calls for the devil to be chased from wherever he's hiding. It's thought that medieval secular jokers may have taken advantage of the imprecation to dress themselves up as White Penitents, and charge around 'putting the wind up' the local noblewomen.

In an era of political correctness (and, frankly, fewer billowing dresses) today's festivities tend to focus more on the traditional carnival parade, with decorated floats and a party in the evening. Even the date's been changed, to fit in with the school holidays.

In **Nontron** (tel: 05 53 56 17 28), the **Fête des Soufflaculs** takes place on a weekend in early April, and features a big parade of night-shirted locals. An effigy called Bouffadou is tried, condemned, and burned on the bonfire, and the revelries continue late into the night.

In **Saint Claude** (tel: 03 84 45 34 24), the festival is celebrated on either a Saturday or Sunday at the beginning of April (depending on the calendar). There's a big procession of floats, accompanied by pretty much the whole populace in nightshirts, followed by the traditional burning of a carnival effigy, around which the Soufflaculs perform a ceremonial dance.

Egg festival/egg hunt

All over France, on Easter Sunday, children and adults go out on a traditional Easter egg hunt – but since the early 1960s, at **Montrottier** (tel: 04 74 70 13 07), a village in the hills 40km west of Lyon, the egg hunt's been a full-blown festival.

At 9am sharp, the hunt is on for a staggering 32,000 fresh eggs, which have been hidden by the locals – in hedgerows, tree-trunks, dry-stone walls, along country paths, and in fields and meadows. You can keep any eggs you find, or contribute them to the small mountain which is needed to make the giant omelette served up as part of a communal meal taken in the sports hall. Fifty specially marked eggs are the equivalent of lottery tickets with a winning number, and can be exchanged for all manner of prizes.

There's also a parade with flower-bedecked floats and children in fancy dress, street acrobats, jugglers and musicians, pony-riding, food and drink stands, and stalls selling local produce – if egg-hunting alone isn't enough to tempt you to Montrottier.

Bachelors' fairs

Rural depopulation has left the French countryside with a surfeit of older singles, so it's no surprise to find there are two bachelor's fairs held annually, one in La Canourgue, north of Millau, towards the end of April, and the other at La Genétouze, 50km northeast of Bordeaux, at the end of the third week in August.

Both events are decidedly low-key, aimed more at finding long-term partners for bachelors, spinsters, widowers and widows than replicating glitzy urban cattle-markets. So the **Foire aux Célibataires** at **La Canourgue** (tel: 04 66 32 69 50), in the heart of France's least populous *département*, the Lozère, prides itself on offering traditional meals, a gentle ambience, and an old fashioned *bal-musette* – and has been successful in bringing scores of couples to the altar since its inception in the early 1980s. The fair at **La Genétouze** (tel: 05 46 04 82 33) is broadly similar, having been held for the first time in 1977, with the main difference being the symbolic release on the first day of a flock of doves.

Festival of the Forgotten Vegetables

The last weekend of April sees forgotten vegetables celebrated at the **Château de Belloc** (tel: 05 56 30 62 00), just outside the village of Sadirac, 10km east of Bordeaux. The festival is organised by Bernard Lafon, who created the museum, gardens and preserving factory which is **Oh! Légumes Oubliés** (see page 187), and features a busy programme of events all centred on vegetables which are no longer commonly used but which used to be staples of French provincial cooking.

The 2002 festival, for example, was dedicated to the stinging nettle, and dubbed **La Fête Nationale de l'Ortie** – National Nettle Day. A giant vat of nettle soup was prepared, and the local restaurant created a special gastronomic menu featuring only dishes with different nettle sauces. Hints and tips on cultivating the much maligned nettle were available, along with a guided tour through the countryside to demonstrate a wide variety of edible wild plants.

(See also the *Festival of the Forgotten Fruits*, on page 30.)

Fishing cockerels' competitions

Two of Europe's three fishing cockerels' competitions take place in France (the third is in Leon, in Spain). The first is in the middle of April, at Pontarion, just south of Guéret in the Creuse, while the second is on May 1, at Neuvic, just south of Ussel, in the Corrèze.

Having made the journey deep into the heart of rural France, I was heartily disappointed to find out that in spite of the *coqs de pêche* tag, you can't actually teach cockerels to fish. Instead it's the name given to chickens which have been specially bred to provide the perfect hackles for making the flies used in fly-fishing.

Pontarion (tel: 05 55 64 51 41) is the smaller of the two events, with around 100 cockerels in competition to see which has the finest neck feathers, while at **Neuvic** (tel: 05 55 95 93 79) you'll find closer to 200 of the temperamental creatures being judged for their finery. Both contests come with fly-tying demonstrations, and fishing flies are usually on sale. If you're in Neuvic you may also be lucky enough to catch one of the temporary *coqs de pêche* exhibitions at the **Maison de la Pêche et de l'Eau**.

The European Procession of Carried Giants

There are giants all over Flanders, and at least once a year they come out on parades or carnival processions (see page 7). But there's one event which is head and shoulders above the rest (so to speak), and that's **La Ronde Européenne des Géants Portés** – the European procession of Carried Giants.

Created by Les Amis de Fromulus, a society in **Steenvoorde** (tel: 03 28 42 97 98 or 03 28 48 10 27) which wants to keep up the giant-carrying tradition, it was staged for the first time in 1989, to celebrate the 75th birthday of the local giant Jean le Bûcheron (Yan den Houtkapper, in Flemish), and featured 31 giants from France, Belgium and Spain.

The event was held for the second time in 1993, and this time 102 giants from six countries came to the spectacular festival. More than 1,500 people in fancy dress joined in, along with over a thousand musicians, and 40,000 spectators. Jan Turpin, the biggest giant in Europe (at 11.40m – 37ft!), from Nieuwpoort, in Belgium, participated for the first time, along with his 24-man crew of carriers. A (jolly) green London giant, Bertilak of the High Desert, came too, carrying his severed head in one hand.

In 2000, celebrating the millennium, the third edition was held, and repeated the enormous success of the 1993 version – the number of giants was limited to 100 (Steenvoorde is a small town), but this time they came from 10 countries.

The European procession of carried giants will be held for the fourth time in April 2006.

MAY
Snail Festival

The village of **Osenbach** (tel: 03 89 47 00 26), between Colmar and Mulhouse, has put on a minor snail festival every year since 1969. The event is organised in rotation by the local fire brigade, football club, and music society, and takes place over two or three weekends around 1 May. New members are inculcated into the local snail order (motto: *Escargol Gloriam, Degustate Fratres In Aeternum*), snails are eaten in abundance, and there's even snail racing (and serious betting), with some nail-biting performances as the gastropods charge hastily along the runnels in their specially built racecourse.

Tripe Contest

For more on the tripe contest which takes place at Longny au Perche on May 1 (and indeed the world tripe championships, in Caen, in October) see page 29.

The 'Camille Claudel' Sculpture Festival

Since 1990, the small town of **La Bresse** (tel: 03 29 25 41 29), in the Vosges, west of Colmar, has staged an annual Festival International de Sculpture 'Camille Claudel'. The event is held during the week of Ascension (which usually falls in May), and attracts 20 to 30 international sculptors and around 4–5,000 visitors.

The sculptors choose whether they want to work with wood, stone or metal, and are then given a week to create a work of art from the raw material (stoneworkers are given a few days' head start), based on a different theme each year. In 2002 the works were inspired by the John Lennon song *Imagine*, while recent years have included 'movement', 'games' and 'the storm' as themes.

As a visitor, you can watch the sculptors at work, and at the end of the week vote for the one you like most. You'll also find sculpture for sale, as well as a range of artefacts from the Musée Rodin in Paris – for there is of course a Camille Claudel (see page 98) connection: her father, Louis Prosper Claudel, was born in La Bresse in 1826, and lived in the town for many years.

Bird Festival

Back in the 13th century, a wealthy woman called Léonète, from Gex (in the Jura, not far from Geneva), married a prince, Simon de Joinville, and a huge banquet was ordered, with roast capercaillies as the main dish. Impatient for the leftovers, one of the servants made the mistake of asking de Joinville whether he'd finished eating, and the prince immediately condemned the scallywag to be hanged for his impudence.

Feeling the sentence to be somewhat harsh – and no doubt thinking of the bad karma attached to having your servants strung up on your wedding day – Léonète pleaded clemency. De Joinville agreed, but in a bid to save face he ordered the leftovers put up on tall spikes, only to be given to those archers who could successfully shoot them down. Fortunately for the hungry servant, his aim was true, and he was one of the first to spear a carcass with his arrow – though whether he'd have had much of an appetite by then is debatable.

The whole thing has been the subject of an annual festival for more than 500 years (complete records are available since 1608), which now takes place in the village of Gex over the long weekend of Ascension, and then again a week or so later in the village of Saint Genis Pouilly, just 10km down the road (information on both events from the **Pays de Gex tourist office**, tel: 04 50 41 53 85).

There's a big procession, with floats, one of which is a giant capercaillie (*grand tétras*, in French), led by the king and queen of the carnival, representing Simon de Joinville and Léonète. Bird carcasses are shot out of trees (using rifles, these days, rather than bows and arrows), with the winner becoming next year's king, and the whole festival goes on for three or four days in each location.

Waiter racing

Waiters haven't raced on the streets of Paris with trays full of drinks since the summer of 2000, when the 22nd edition of the famous **Course des Garçons de Café** took place. Since then, the street leading from la République to la Bastille has been free for ever-increasing amounts of traffic, which may be one reason why the race is no longer run; another might be the overwhelming dominance of the then 44-year-old Marc Fabre, who notched up his sixth victory in 2000, ahead of more than 300 other waiters.

Fortunately there's another waiters' race you can go and see (or indeed participate in, if you're in the trade). This one's at Metz, and is organised every May by **l'Union Professionnelle de l'Industrie Hôtelière de la Moselle** (tel: 03 87 32 55 21).

Around 150 participants, including both waiters (and waitresses) and students from the Lycée Hôtelier Raymond Mondon, run the 5km course with a tray containing a full bottle and two glasses, with the winner being the first to arrive with everything intact. Everyone prays for fine weather, as the cobbled streets of Metz are particularly slippery when wet.

Gypsies' pilgrimage

The town of **Saintes Maries de la Mer** (tel: 04 90 97 82 55), in the Camargue, hosts one of Europe's most important gypsy gatherings in the month of May, when more than 10,000 Roma from all over the world (but especially the French Gitans, Manouches, Sinti and Roma) come together to pay homage to their patron saint Sara-la-Kâli.

How Sara became the patron saint of the gypsies – or even a saint at all (she's not officially sanctified) – is something of a mystery. Clearly associated with the two Maries who give Saintes Maries de la Mer its name (Marie Jacobe the sister of the Virgin Mary and Marie Salomé the mother of the apostles John and James), Sara is said variously to have been their black servant, a local gypsy woman who rescued the Maries from a storm at sea, an Egyptian abbess or a Persian martyr.

Whatever, the statue of Sara-la-Kâli (Kâli is a gypsy word meaning both 'black' and 'gitane') is one of the holiest objects in the gypsy world. In the weeks leading up to May 24, thousands of gypsies descend on the town, their children are presented to the statues of the saints, and a great number of baptisms and weddings are arranged. The streets echo with the music of their guitars and violins. In the crypt housing the statue of Sara, hundreds upon hundreds of candles are lit and votive offerings of children's clothes, simple jewellery, and scribbled notes are left behind.

On May 24, the shrines of the two Maries are brought down and carried in an enormous procession to the sea, and on the 25th Sara is brought out of the crypt by the gypsies, chanting an endless round of '*Vive Sainte Sara!, Vive Sainte Sara!*'. The two Maries meanwhile are paraded along the shore by boat, immersed in the water, and returned to their niches for another year. It's a splendid event.

Mourre Championship

The village of **Crévoux** (tel: 04 92 43 18 11), a small alpine resort south of Briançon, holds France's only mourre championship at the end of May every year.

Mourre is an extremely old game (it's thought that Roman soldiers may have brought it back from Egypt) requiring neither cards, nor markers nor dice. Two players simply sit opposite one another, with one fist closed on the table. At the same time, each then opens his (it's not much of a ladies' game) hand, displaying one to five fingers, and shouts out a number between one and ten, ideally very noisily, and in *patois*. If the number is the same as the combined number of digits shown by both players, then a point is scored. For example if you shout out six, show two fingers, and your opponent shows four, then you win a point.

Today mourre is only played in France by a few shepherds high in the mountains along the French–Italian border, and in Corsica, where it's called mora – although there are also a few handfuls of people in the Caucasus mountains who play the game.

Crévoux, for its part, is working hard to keep the game alive by hosting the annual championships, which prove that mourre is both demanding and a good deal harder than you'd expect. It's played deafeningly and at immense speed, and even if patois isn't being used it's almost impossible to keep up. Spend any length of time watching the game and the best you can hope for is to understand that *dur* is patois for one, *touta la mana* and *cinque la mourra* both mean five and *baraca* means all ten fingers. At least I think so.

Transhumance festivals

Throughout the Alps, the Pyrenees and the Jura, cattle spend the summer season up in the *alpages* (the mountain pastures), where the best cheese can then be made from their summer milk. The herdsmen spend months with their cows in almost complete isolation from the rest of the world, so it's only natural that they want to party before they go up, and party again when they come down.

As a result there are dozens of transhumance festivals around the end of May and the beginning of June, which commemorate their departure for the mountains. Cows are decorated with wreaths of flowers and ribbons, and have their summer bells ceremoniously attached. The men who accompany them on foot wear traditional dress, with embroidered waistcoats, and the villages along the route to the mountains celebrate their passage with special events and communal meals.

In September the whole thing happens in reverse, with the tired, sunburned herdsmen leading their cattle back down to the autumn pastures in the valleys and on the plains. If you're stuck in traffic on a mountain road in May or September, you could be unwittingly taking part in a transhumance festival.

JUNE
Montgolfier Festival
The town of **Annonay** (tel: 04 75 33 24 51; web: www.mairie-annonay.fr), south of Lyon, has a major annual celebration at the beginning of June, commemorating the world's first balloon flight, which took off from the town's main square in 1783.

The Montgolfier brothers' (see page 34) historic feat is recreated in the Place des Cordeliers by around 100 people in 18th-century costume, usually on the Sunday closest to June 4, the actual anniversary of the original flight. Since 1983, the festivities have also been combined with a three-day international ballooning festival, which brings together 40 to 50 hot-air balloons. It's an event not to be missed by fans of the Montgolfiers or balloonists in general.

The **Annonay Club des Montgolfières** (*montgolfière*, feminine, is the French word for hot-air balloon) can be contacted by balloonists looking for more information (tel: 04 75 67 57 56; web: www.ima7.com/MA/index.html).

William the Conqueror Festival
William the Conqueror, bastard son of Robert the Devil, Duke of Normandy, set sail with his fleet from Dives sur Mer, between Caen and Le Havre, in September 1066. Unfortunately a big storm blew up, and he and his ships had to seek refuge 150km up the coast at Saint Valéry sur Somme (just south of the eternally amusing Berck Plage).

So it was from **Saint Valéry** (tel: 03 22 60 93 50), nowhere near Normandy, that the last successful invasion of Britain was launched, and it's there that you'll find the annual jollifications celebrating *Guillaume le Conquerand*'s departure from France.

The festivities are usually held in June (why not September, one can't help wondering?) though in 2002 they were held in July because of the football World Cup. Being this far north in France, they feature a giant puppet (see page 7) called Guillaume, who gets paraded around the old town, and there's the usual range of food and drink stalls, fancy dress and street music. In certain years (call ahead to find out) they also stage a dramatic jousting tournament on the beach. Wear sensible shoes.

Eat a metre of boudin...
For more details of the contest in Pruniers en Sologne, on the third weekend in June, along with other *boudin*-related festivities, see page 11.

Water jousting (Sète)
Water jousting has been a tradition at the ports around Sète (tel: 04 67 74 71 71) for centuries, and the tradition continues. Each year, there's a league which plays off the various teams against each other, and you should keep an eye out for jousts from June onwards in **Agde** (tel: 04 67 94 29 68), **Balaruc les Bains** (tel: 04 67 46 81 46), **Béziers** (tel: 04 67 76 47 00), **Frontignon** (tel: 04 67 48 33 94), **Mèze** (tel: 04 67 43 93 08), **Palavas** (tel: 04 67 07 73 34) and **La Grau du Roi** (tel: 04 66 51 67 70).

In Sète itself, there's a preparatory tournament at the end of June, and then the major championships take place during the last week of August, centred on the 25th, the **Fête de la Saint Louis**, the local patron saint.

The aim is easy enough – you simply need to stand on the raised prow of your boat (known as a *tintaine*), dressed all in white and carrying a special shield, and then knock the other guy off into the canal using your lance to destabilise him as your two boats (one red, one blue) pass each other. The champions are invariably Sète's fishermen and dockers, but they say you can't really consider yourself a *Sètois* unless you have yourself jousted.

If you want to see the Saint Louis jousting, you should reserve well ahead, and be at the canal-side several hours before the tournament commences – 20,000 people show up every year. And if you don't know what all the fuss is about, drop in at **La Maison des Joutes** (tel: 04 67 19 09 93), the small museum in Sète dedicated to Languedoc jousting. It's open all year round.

Tarasque Festival

Long ago, a monster called the Tarasque took up residence near the town of Nerluc, on the river Rhône, between Arles and Avignon. The monster had the look of an over-sized armadillo, with a huge spiked carapace covering its back to protect it from any attack, and would devour its victims whole after breathing fire on them. The locals were naturally terrorised, but could do nothing to protect themselves or their livestock, which the Tarasque was using as bite-sized snacks.

Into this scene arrived Saint Martha, having arrived from the Holy Land on the same boat as the two Saint Marys (see page 16), apparently. She went into the woods alone to find the Tarasque, and quickly overpowered it (as one does) with the sign of the cross. Martha then led the monster back to town, using her girdle (or her braided hair; there's some confusion at this point) as a collar for the now-docile beast, which subsequently disappeared into the Rhône, never to be seen again.

Saint Martha became the town's patron saint, and her remains are said to be in the 12th-century church of Sainte Marthe, in the town of Nerluc – which was re-christened Tarascon, in honour of the vanquished monster. Towards the end of the 15th century, the Provençal King René then ordained an annual Tarasque festival, which has taken place ever since in **Tarascon** (tel: 04 90 91 03 52) – though it's now held at the end of June, rather than Whitsun, the original date.

The event features a big parade, with a young girl representing Saint Martha, who leads the Tarasque around town, and there's much in the way of folk music, dancing, and street merriment. The event has been confused somewhat, however, by the more recent arrival of Tartarin, the hero of Alphonse Daudet's 1872 novel *Tartarin de Tarascon* which brought the town great fame in the late 19th century. Tarascon's **Maison de Tartarin** has been created in a period property in the middle of town to celebrate the fictional character's life, and Tartarin is now also paraded around during the Fête de la Tarasque.

Charcuterie Festival

There are more pigs than people in the rural *département* of Aveyron, in the south of France, so it's hardly surprising that it's here, in the small town of **Lacaune** (tel:

05 63 37 04 98), that you'll find the **Grande Fête de la Charcuterie** on the last Sunday in June. Close to a quarter of a million pigs are raised every year by Lacaune's farmers, translating into over 20,000 tonnes of dried and salted pork, ham and sausages – including, a couple of years ago, the world's largest ever dried ham (25.65kg, since you ask).

The festival includes a prestigious competition not just for the best local ham but for the best ham in the whole of France, as well as a parade of the Confrérie des Mazeliers – *mazelier* is an old Occitan word for pork butcher; they were later called *chaircuitiers* (producers of cooked meat), which finally evolved into today's *charcutiers*. As you'd expect, there's plenty of the local produce on show and on sale, and there's also an excellent piglet race, complete with betting.

If you miss the festival, you can still take a guided tour round Lacaune's *Maison de la Charcuterie* (open every day in summer, weekends only from April to October), where you'll find out everything there is to know about the art of salting pork and making hams and sausages.

JULY
Howling at the moon
There are plenty of animal parks large and small in France, but only one where you can go and hear wolves howling at the moon on clear nights in summer. Through July and August, the **Parc Animalier de Sainte Croix** (tel: 03 87 03 92 05; web: www.parcanimalier.com), at Rhodes, between Metz and Strasbourg, arranges night visits to hear the wolves (reserve well in advance). It's really the most primeval of sounds, touching some dark place in the human psyche which is still very, very afraid of what might happen out in the woods at night.

If the wolves whet a primitive passion in you, you can also go and hear the troat of the stag in rutting season, during September and October nights (also by advance reservation only), as the park has a herd of around 60 deer which take the mating season just as seriously as anyone else.

The park also has bears, lynx, beavers and 80 other species of European animals roaming semi-free in its 100ha, so it's a good place to visit even if you're not a night bird. The annual festival of star animals, who've been in advertisements and films, which the park used to hold in August, seems however to have been abandoned.

Frog Festival
If you like frogs (to eat), you'll love the annual **Grande Fête de la Grenouille**, which usually takes place on the second Saturday in July, at **Saint André le Bouchoux** (tel: 04 74 42 50 77 for the date, which can vary), a small village surrounded by lakes, southwest of Bourg en Bresse.

During the afternoon there's an enormous line-fishing contest out at the frog ponds, with a prize for the biggest catch (by weight). The fresh frogs' legs are then cooked up by a local chef and served to the 400 to 500 people who come to celebrate the event every year.

There's a *bal dansant* which goes through to the small hours, and does its bit in helping you digest your dinner if you've had one frog too many.

(And we'll pass on the opportunity to remark that actually *all* of the festivals in this chapter are frog festivals, if you don't mind.)

National Donkey Day

The 14th of July is better known as France's *fête nationale*, but it's also national donkey day (**la journée nationale de l'âne**), which is celebrated annually (*âne-ually?*) in the Pays de Pompadour, 30km north of Brive la Gaillarde, in the southwest of France.

The event is held at the Pompadour racecourse, one of France's most attractive, sitting as it does at the foot of the splendid 15th-century Château de Pompadour. Between 300 and 400 donkeys make the journey to **Arnac Pompadour** (tel: 05 55 98 55 47), where they take part in all manner of activities, including dressage, flat racing, breeding contests, jumping, harness events, donkey-riding and steeplechasing – and more than 10,000 people come to enjoy the fun every year. If you want to bring your donkey to the fair, contact Francis Pecout (tel: 05 55 73 67 23) well in advance.

National donkey day is just one of a dozen or more fairs and festivals dedicated especially to donkeys. Try the Cotentin donkey rally at **Banneville sur Ajon** (tel: 02 31 77 07 51), just outside Caen, which takes place on the first Sunday in July, where breeders have to show just how well they can handle their donkeys, or the donkey fair at **Braize** (tel: 04 70 06 12 73), just south of Bourges, and bang in the middle of France, where you'll see some excellent donkey racing on the last Sunday in August.

Also at the end of August are the world donkey championships, held in **Mortagne au Perche** (tel: 02 33 85 11 18), which is even more famous for its *boudin* (see page 11). The championships judge donkeys from around the world in a wide range of categories, and there's plenty of donkey-related entertainment – though you should of course refrain from trying to pin tails on any of the animals.

Water jousting (Clamecy)

As Paris expanded in the middle ages, it began to use more firewood for heating and cooking than it could easily replace, and by the 16th century the situation was critical. People therefore set their sights on the vast forests of the Morvan, southeast of Paris, although it was clear that overland transport would be impossible for the quantities needed – the Morvan was over 200km away, and up to 500,000 tonnes of firewood a year was required.

Fortunately, wood may be heavy (a cubic metre weighs between 500 and 750kg), but it doesn't sink, so the idea was born of floating logs down the river Yonne until it joined the Seine, and then steering them on downstream to Paris. As a result, Clamecy, 40km south of Auxerre, on the river Yonne, became one of the most important small towns in France. It was here that the Yonne became easily navigable, and it was therefore the obvious starting point for the flotillas of log rafts which would keep Paris warm and fed through the winter.

For more than 400 years, from the middle of the 16th century until the beginning of the 20th, three quarters of all Paris's firewood transited through Clamecy, and the town was synonymous with the log-floating trade.

During the winter and spring, logs would be floated down to Clamecy's 22 harbours, and sorted and taken out of the water to dry during the summer. In the autumn, huge rafts would be put together (75m long and 4.5m wide, they comprised up to 240m³ of wood apiece) by raftsmen, and then steered downriver as part of a 'wood train' comprising 50 to 100 rafts. For the first 50km or so, until the last narrows had been passed, near Auxerre, each raft had a boy on board, at the back, to help steer, but from there to Paris each raft had a crew of just one. As they travelled day and night, rafts were coupled together in pairs so one of the two raftsmen could take turns to sleep.

The journey to Paris took 11 days, after which it was a 200km *walk* back to Clamecy for the raftsman – only to start out all over again. Some 500 raftsmen from Clamecy were employed in the log-floating business, along with more than 4,000 other people in the community, showing how important the town then was (the total population now is under 5,000).

Today, all that's left to commemorate the enormous log-floating trade is an annual water jousting tournament which takes place on the river at Clamecy (tel: 03 86 27 02 51), in the Nièvre, on July 14. Two boats, a blue one called *Tu Iras* ('you'll go in') and a red one called *Toi Aussi* ('you too'), face up to each other, and two chaps on raised wooden platforms do their best to push their opponent into the water using a large barge-pole, while their crews jockey for the best position on the water. It makes for an excellent spectacle.

The jousting tournament is repeated 8km downriver at Coulanges sur Yonne, on August 15 – and as Coulanges is across the inter-departmental border, the contest is naturally billed as the Nièvre vs Yonne championships.

World Bed-Racing Championships

If donkeys and water-jousting aren't your thing, but you're stuck for entertainment on the national holiday, how about a spot of bed-racing? If you're interested, head over to the little village of **Mahalon** (tel: 02 98 74 52 76), west of Quimper, in the Finistère peninsula, which hosts the world championships every July 14.

Events start with registration of the 20 to 30 teams at 2pm (each team consisting of a bed on casters, two pushers and one 'patient'), after which there are elimination rounds on a 345m circuit to be completed in well under two minutes.

Before the finals at 5pm (which consist of a last race around the village church) there's a procession of comic beds, with prizes for the most original and inventive, while afterwards there are attempts on a number of important world sporting records, three of which have already been broken in Mahalon. In 1987, Serge Fougère (see also page 23 and page 26) managed to spit an apricot stone over 15m; in 1992, a man called Cormier managed to throw a beret over 52m; and in 2000, a local lad, Fabien Le Coz, achieved the world's long-distance crêpe-throwing record, with a 7.45m fling.

Lumberjacks' Festival

If you're in the village of Mijoux, at the head of the Vallée de Valserine in the high Jura, on the third Sunday in July, don't be alarmed if you see a bunch of tough-looking, mostly bearded men, coming towards you with axes on their shoulders – it's only the local **Fête des Bûcherons**.

The event has been organised annually since 1975, and celebrates the work and life of woodcutters. A special open-air church service starts off the festivities, followed by the main entertainment, a wide range of competitive lumberjacking events. These demonstrate the strength, speed and dexterity of your average woodsman, as they wield handsaws, chainsaws and axes. It's all stirring stuff, and ends with a parade led by the lumberjacks with their axes over their shoulders, and followed by carnival floats and a herd of cows decked out as if they're in the transhumance festival (see page 17). Contact the **Monts Jura tourist office** (tel: 04 50 20 91 43) for more information.

Masgot's stonecutting days

The hamlet of Masgot, in the commune of **Fransèches** (tel: 05 55 66 67 04), just south of Guéret, in the middle of France, would be entirely unremarkable, were it not for the extraordinary work of the self-taught granite sculptor François Michaud.

Born in 1810, Michaud was a local farmer, but like most of the locals he also turned his hand to stonecutting when there was work on offer. He nurtured a prodigious talent as a sculptor, in the naïve style, and put his granite works all over the village, creating several score by the time of his death at the age of 80. His work is mostly of animals, though there are also representations of a seated man, a female nude, the then president Jules Grévy (who resigned in 1887, following a scandal involving the sale of *Légions d'Honneurs*), and the ubiquitous Marianne (the symbol of the French Republic, and still to be seen in every town hall in France, as well as on the stamps and coins).

What's extraordinary is that Masgot (and Michaud's sculptures) managed to remain unremarked upon until the last decades of the 20th century. But since 1985, when the association Les Amis de la Pierre de Masgot was set up, the village has welcomed both visitors and budding sculptors, who can take part in professional stonecutting and sculpting workshops and training courses.

In July each year, the village hosts the **Journées de la Pierre** (Stone Days), during which sculptors and stonemasons from all over France come and work in public, creating new works of art, or demonstrating the mason's craft. Accordion music and the excellent local cider help things along a treat.

You can also visit François Michaud's house, which has been turned into a small museum – it's open every afternoon in July and August. Call the stone association for more information on stonecutting courses, the open days in July, and the **Michaud house** (tel: 05 55 66 98 88/05 55 67 86 76).

Prune-Stone Spitting World Championship

Most of the country's – indeed a good chunk of the world's – prunes come from the *département* of Lot et Garonne, in the southwest of France. So it's inevitable that there are various prune fairs and even a prune museum (see page 184) in the area, but less predictable that there would be a world championship for prune-stone spitting.

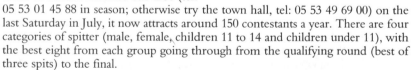

The event was started in 1995, and has gone from strength to strength. Organised in the small town of **Sainte Livrade sur Lot** (tel: 05 53 01 45 88 in season; otherwise try the town hall, tel: 05 53 49 69 00) on the last Saturday in July, it now attracts around 150 contestants a year. There are four categories of spitter (male, female, children 11 to 14 and children under 11), with the best eight from each group going through from the qualifying round (best of three spits) to the final.

The world record holder, Serge Fougère, who spat a prune stone an unbelievable 17.81m in 1996 at the **records' festival** in La Tour Blanche (tel: 05 53 91 13 78, see page 26) in the Dordogne, failed dismally at Sainte Livrade in 2001 and 2002. In 2001 he managed to produce the championship's current record spit of 13.10m during the qualifying round, but was disqualified in the final for overstepping the mark twice and spitting outside the 3m-wide sandy *piste* on the third occasion. And in 2002 he didn't even qualify for the final – for though he's a world-class stone-spitter, Fougère isn't a particularly accurate one. (He's also been seen taking part in the national pig-squealing world championships in **Trie sur Baïse**, tel: 05 62 35 50 88, which must say something.)

André Forget, organiser of the world championship in Sainte Livrade, is pleased with the way the event has smoothed the prune's somewhat wrinkled image. It's not only tourists who come and discover how delicious the semi-dried fruit can be, either, he says. 'To be honest, it's the one sure way of getting the local kids round here to eat prunes.'

AUGUST
Sea-Shanty Festival
As you might expect, the biggest global sea-shanty festival takes place in Brittany, home to the world's widest variety of maritime songs. Staged in Paimpol, on Brittany's north coast, the **Fête du Chant de Marin** takes place during August in odd-numbered years (August 15–17 in 2003).

Over a three-day period you can hear concerts on board and on shore, along the quays and on the decks of the tall ships which assemble for the festival. Hundreds of musicians and more than a thousand singers from around the world take part, celebrating the maritime life, whether it be on square-riggers, ocean-going trawlers, fishing boats, merchant ships, sailing yachts or just plain skiffs. Bell-bottom trousers and 'Ahoy there matey!' or 'Hello Matelot!' T-shirts optional.

For more information on the 2003 and 2005 sea-shanty festivals, contact the organisers (tel: 02 96 55 12 77) or **Paimpol tourist office** (tel: 02 96 20 83 16).

Liars' Festival
The picturesque little village of **Moncrabeau** (tel: 05 53 65 10 34), just north of Condom (see page 238), is the self-proclaimed 'World Capital of Liars'. So it's only natural that they should hold an international liars' festival each year on the first Sunday in August, which elects a new Liar King. (As an aside, if I were the one to tell you that the food and drink in the region's no good, I'd be lying. Check out the superb melons, goats' cheese, *foie gras* and *confit de canard* – fatty duck cooked in duck fat; excellent – and wash it all down with the hearty local red wines, topped off with a fiery glass of Armagnac.)

According to legend, the festival originated after a facetious monk from Condom (well, you'd have to be facetious, wouldn't you?) travelled around the local area in the 18th century, telling tall tales – though quite how that helped create the 40-strong Academy of Liars in Moncrabeau isn't clear. (Or indeed why the village had a long-running face-pulling contest, which has now been sadly abandoned.)

The rules for participating in the **Fête des Menteurs** are simple enough – you simply have to spin a good yarn, actively misrepresenting the truth (the whole truth, and nothing but the truth), while avoiding the subjects of sex, politics and religion. The winner, who gets to be crowned as the year's Liar King, is the one whose fib has the most verisimilitude.

In 2002, the laurels were won by a local man, which came as something of a relief to the organisers, as it had been won unexpectedly the previous year by a German from Düsseldorf, who lamented that he'd had a dreadful year since winning, as his wife wouldn't then believe a word he said.

A dozen contestants are selected by the organisers from texts submitted in advance, and are limited to speaking for five to six minutes each. To enrol as a potential liar, contact Gilbert Launet, the President of the **Liars' Academy** in **Moncrabeau** (tel: 05 53 65 43 27).

National Pig-Squealing Championships
The small town of **Trie sur Baïse** (tel: 05 62 35 50 88), 30km east of Tarbes, was famous for over half a century as Europe's biggest piglet market, with up to 6,000

of the little chaps changing hands every Tuesday morning, right up until the early 1980s. Celebrating the region's biggest cash-sow (so to speak), therefore, is **La Pourcailhade**, an annual pig festival held on the second Sunday in August.

The highlight for visitors is undoubtedly the French national pig-squealing championships, which have been held under the auspices of La Pourcailhade for the past 25 years or so. Contestants have to imitate the noise a pig makes at various stages in its life – starting off as a piglet, then suckling (with all the grunting that entails from the sow), followed by noisy lovemaking, and finally ending up with the last moments before going under the knife. And the prize for the lucky winner? A whole pig, of course, ready prepared, including the head and feet.

Between 10 and 15 people usually take part, though anyone is free to get up and have a go in front of a crowd of a thousand or more, and inevitably some out-of-town TV crews. Only a handful, however, can hold it together well enough to perform the full ritual, and for the last few years it's been a closely fought contest between Jean-Claude Sarran, a five-time champion, and Michel Dauvin, who came first in 2000, 2001 and 2002.

In the 2002 event, Sarran wore a fabulous pink silk suit with plastic nipples sewed on, and he plans to add pig's feet for 2003 – but he was trumped by Dauvin, a winemaker from Langon, near Bordeaux, who brought along a bottle of his own red wine and a basin for the dramatically realistic death scene.

If you fancy a flutter, there's a piglet race you can bet on in the afternoon, and there's also a *boudin*-eating contest (see also page 11), with the winner in 2002 putting away over a metre of the stuff in just five minutes. The all-time record, however, is 1.68m (that's five and half *feet!*) of *boudin* consumed in under ten minutes. Now that is piggish behaviour.

Oyster Shucking Contest

The small town of **Eymet** (tel: 05 53 23 74 95), in the southwestern corner of the Dordogne, more than 100km from the nearest seashore, seems a strange place for an oyster festival, especially on August 15 when most of the rest of the country is shunning rather than shucking the little beauties. For oysters (except where they're actually grown) are generally given a rest in the months when there isn't an 'r' (May, June, July, August) – ostensibly because hot summer weather makes them dodgy, but actually to allow stocks to replenish.

But Eymet holds its annual **Fête de l'Huître et du Vin Blanc** regardless, and if you're feeling competitive you can try your hand at the shucking contest. To be in with even a chance you'll need to be able to cleanly open a dozen oysters in comfortably under four minutes, and that without driving the oyster-opener bloodily through the palm of your hand (which is known as a shucking disaster).

It's also an excellent occasion, as you'd imagine, to scarf down oysters by the dozen, and to wash them down with a selection of crisp local white wines. At the 2002 festival, the participants managed to see off over three tonnes of shellfish during the one day, which ends as you'd imagine, with a *bal populaire*.

Espadrille Festival

The small town of **Mauléon** (tel: 05 59 28 02 37), 50km west of Pau, in the foothills of the Pyrenees, is the espadrille capital of France, and still meets nearly three quarters of the country's annual demands. That's nothing like as many pairs of shoes as used to be manufactured – in 1911, there were nine espadrille factories in Mauléon alone, employing 1,600 workers – but the 'cool' rope-soled and canvas-uppered espadrille has proved remarkably durable all the same.

On August 15 every year there's an **espadrille festival**, celebrating the town's most famous export. You can see espadrilles being made, and there are exhibitions on the history and tradition of the rope-soled shoe – as well as more generic festivities, like the local version of boules, *pelote basque*, and dancing late into the night. Keep an eye out for the world's largest espadrille (as acknowledged in the *Guinness Book of Records*), which was created by Armand Perez of Armaïté Espadrilles in 1992. At around three metres long, it's a European size 500 espadrille (UK size 310).

Water jousting

For more details on the water jousting which takes place at Coulanges sur Yonne on August 15, along with the reason why they do it at all, see page 21.

For more on the spectacular water-jousting finals which take place at Sète during the last week of August, see page 18.

Scarecrow summer

The village of **Sospel** (tel: 04 93 04 15 80), up in the hills above Menton, on the French Riviera, and right on the Italian border, has always had a thing about scarecrows. So much so, that each summer it organises a **scarecrow festival**, attracting around 150 entrants.

The scarecrows (*épouvantails*, in French) are gathered together in the main square, in front of the church (usually in the first week of August), and judged by a local jury, which then dishes out prizes. They then stay in the village all summer long (the scarecrows, not the jury) and a further prize is awarded at the end of the season for the scarecrow the holidaymakers liked best.

They're most endearing (the scarecrows, not the holidaymakers) – so I was alarmed when I rang the Sospel town hall about next year's dates to find out that the scarecrows may soon be written out of the picture, to make way for younger, more attractive talent, in the quest for tourist euros. So check if the festival's still happening before you make the journey.

Records' Festival

Not, as you might have expected, anything to do with obscure white-label indie 12-inch singles or rare Presley promos, but instead a festival at which records (as in *Guinness Book of Records*) – ideally eccentric ones – are tilted at.

Organised by **Daniel Ponceau** (tel: 05 53 91 13 78) in the village of **La Tour Blanche**, in the upper Dordogne, halfway between Angoulême and Périgueux, the festival takes place in even-numbered years over the last weekend of August. Throughout the summer, alternate Wednesdays are also dedicated to trying to break world records, and the summer of 2000 saw some 27 records shattered.

So don't be surprised to find Philippe Pujolle trying to beat his own world record for producing distinct separate vocal noises in the shortest possible time (the record stands at 12.8 seconds for 26 separate imitations, from a variety of animals to a train), or to catch Serge Fougère (see also page 22 and page 23) trying to improve on the spitting records he achieved here – 17.81m for a prune stone and 19.36m for an olive pip.

The record for a *lanceur de crêpes* was also taken here, when Jean-Marie Livonnen tossed a pancake 8.60m into the air and caught it again successfully in the pan, as was the record for the number of separate cheese packets, which is held by André Dubreuilh, who has over 1,000 different varieties. For its part, the festival committee built the world's largest cork, which is 3m tall and weighs over half a tonne (work is still on hold on the bottle it's due to stopper).

It's a huge amount of fun, and well worth attending even if you're not tossing, spitting, hurling or building anything yourself. You might even get to see one of Didi Senft's extraordinary bicycles, which make occasional appearances. The German, better known to anyone who's ever seen the Tour de France on TV as the Red Devil (*le diable rouge*), not only follows the world's major cycle tours dressed as a devil, but also designs and builds wacky bikes. In total he has produced more than 100, including the world's largest (7.80m long and 3.70m tall!).

La Tour Blanche also has a **records museum**, open all year round, where you can see the giant cork, the world's largest stamp, a 3m-high baby chair, and other colourful but useless objects. Contact Daniel Ponceau or the **town hall** (tel: 05 53 91 11 98) for information on both the museum and the 2004 and 2006 records' festivals.

World Square Bowling Championships

There's practically no limit to human ingenuity – so when confronted with the irritating reality that the national pastime, *boules*, was a non-starter on the precipitous streets of **Haut Cagnes** (above Cagnes sur Mer, just west of Nice, on the Riviera), the locals soon came up with a brilliant way of stopping the bowls running away: square balls.

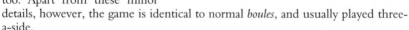

They also had to make them smaller and lighter than traditional *boules*, so settled eventually on coloured wooden cubes, 7cm³, to allow for a certain amount of rolling – and the *cochonnet* (the jack) had to be made square too. Apart from these minor details, however, the game is identical to normal *boules*, and usually played three-a-side.

It's popular all year round, but things reach fever pitch during the annual **Championnat du Monde de Boules Carrées**, which is organised by the **Cercle des Amis du Haut Cagnes** (tel: 04 93 73 53 72) over the third weekend in August. Taking place on the Montée de la Bourgade and the roads nearby, the championship attracts more than 300 players, with the first day being used for eliminatory games and the Sunday being dedicated to the world championship itself, followed by a major party on the Place Grimaldi, at the top of the town.

If you want to take part, contact the Cercle des Amis in advance (they can supply you with square *boules*), and get there by taking the free shuttle up from the bottom of town which runs every 15 minutes, as there's no parking whatsoever in the old town. The Cercle is 150m downhill from the Château.

Bachelors' Fair

For more information on the Bachelor's Fair at La Genétouze, held annually at the end of the third week in August, please see page 13.

SEPTEMBER
Skylark Whistlers' World Championship
In the past, being able to imitate the sounds of gregarious birds and animals was one of the surest ways hunters had of bringing dinner to the table. Today, for most of us, it's more of a curiosity than a hunter's lure, but in the southwest of France, at **Vieux Boucau** (tel: 05 58 48 13 47), 30 km up the coast from Biarritz, the traditional birdcalls are still being used by people keen to take a pot-shot at skylarks, buntings, thrushes and woodpigeons. It's logical, therefore, that the skylark whistlers' world championship should be held here.

Vieux Boucau's low-key annual festival is on the first weekend of September, and the championships are held on the Saturday afternoon. ('We call them the world championships,' says the disarmingly honest local tourist office, 'but we have no idea if there are any other world championships.')

A dozen or so *chioulayres* (the Gascon word for hunters who can make the skylark's call) then compete either using whistles or simply imitating the skylark's trill with voice alone. The winners walk away with hampers and other local produce. Skylarks themselves, meanwhile, are suspected of holding their own world championships, to see which one can best imitate a gascon hunter. It's all a bit of a lark, apparently.

Lorraine Pâté Festival
Lorraine is rightly famous for its pâtés (the *pâté Lorrain* is actually a delicious slab of pork and veal pâté wrapped in puff pastry), so you'd expect there to be a Lorraine pâté festival, and indeed there is, held on the second weekend in September, in the small town of **Baccarat** (tel: 03 83 75 13 37), between Nancy and Colmar. (Baccarat is also where the eponymous glass company was founded in 1764, by the Bishop of Metz, if you were wondering.)

The festival celebrates the production of the pâtés, and there are plenty of opportunities for tasting and buying them, along with a busy street market featuring bric-à-brac and the occasional bargain antique. However, the real draw of the **Fête du Pâté Lorrain** isn't the chance of picking up a cheap set of old wineglasses, a nightstand or an unusual coffee table, but the pâté eating competition.

Up to 20 contestants sit down to eat, and the winner is the one who's stuffed away the most pâtés in ten minutes. The 2002 winner managed to force down a stonking eight and a half entire puff-pastry-wrapped pâtés before the time was up. A magnificent achievement (one of the pâtés is about as much as you'd want for lunch), but still well off the record established more than ten years ago by a Mr Masselot, who managed to stuff down 13 of them in just ten minutes. A triumph – but please don't try this at home.

OCTOBER
Shrimp Festival
Honfleur (tel: 02 31 89 18 90/02 31 81 88 00), on the Normandy coast, is the French shrimp capital, specialising in *la petite grise*, a delicious if fiddly food item, so it's only natural that the town should organise a **Fête de la Crevette** annually on the first or second weekend in October.

The event actually has more to do with latter-day maritime life than with the preoccupations of the prawn, though there are shrimp-tastings, and there's an excellent shrimp-shelling contest, with the winner being the one who can produce the greatest weight of cleaned shrimps in a short space of time. It's more fun to watch than to take part.

Otherwise, enjoy the 40-odd rigged vessels which tie up for the event in the old port, and take lessons in how to furl sails, mend nets, splice ropes, tie knots, and sing sea-shanties.

Ladle-throwing Festival

According to legend, many centuries ago the *seigneur* of Comines (a town now straddling the Belgian border, near Lille) was being held prisoner by unnamed baddies, who were then able to make use of his assets. Fortunately, the *seigneur* was able to alert his loyal townspeople to his plight by carving the Comines coat of arms on to his cutlery (made of wood, in those days) and by throwing it out of the window at passing workmen. He was rescued, and in gratitude created an annual festival with ladle-throwing as the dominant theme.

Or so the story goes. What we do know is that for at least 500 years the town of **Comines** (tel: 03 20 14 58 58) has celebrated a **Fête des Louches** and it's still going strong. The hugely popular festival is held on the second weekend in October, with the main event being a big Sunday parade through town, with participants dressed in medieval costume, and 40-odd floats carrying replicas of long-gone monuments. From time to time wooden ladles are thrown into the eager crowd.

The last float, based on a giant ladle motif, carries the Damoiselle de Comines, who is elected the night before, along with a couple of courtiers, and more ladles and wooden spoons are distributed. It being this part of the world, there are also a couple of carnival giants (see page 7) to be seen, called Grande Gueuloutte and P'tite Chorchine, who parade with the Brotherhood of the Giant Ladle.

When the procession reaches the town hall, hundreds of larger wooden ladles are rained down into the throng from the balcony – but don't worry if you don't get one in the crush, as practically every shop in town also sells them as souvenirs.

Old Vegetables' Fair

The village of **Tranzault** (tel: 02 54 30 81 05), southeast of Châteauroux, in the Indre, celebrates old vegetables on the second Sunday in October, and is a particularly good place to pick up unusual gourds and calabashes. Special dishes are prepared on the spot, making use of rare and ancient greens, and you can take away the raw ingredients and recipes to practise on at home – where, sadly, nothing ever tastes quite as good.

World Tripe Championships

In French there's no amusing connotation to the word 'tripe' at all. So it's not considered the least bit strange to have a tripe competition, a tripe brotherhood, or indeed tripe trophies. You can even be a Grand Master of the Tripe – although it takes years of training. As the professionals point out, in all seriousness, tripe is good for you. It's gelatinous, rather than fatty, and an excellent source of protein.

There's an annual competition held every October in Normandy, to find the world's best *tripe à la mode de Caen*. The event is organised by la Confrérie de la Tripière d'Or (the Brotherhood of the Golden Tripe Butcher) and was held for the 50th consecutive year in 2002. It generally attracts between 200 and 300 *tripiers* (tripe butchers), *charcutiers* and *restaurateurs*, who come with the hope of having their tripe voted the best in the world – or at least of winning one of the other coveted tripe prizes at the international or national level.

Find out more about tripe, and the contest held annually in Caen, from the **Caen tourist office** (tel: 02 31 27 14 14; web: www.ville-caen.fr/tourisme/decouvrir/tripiereor).

There's another fine tripe contest held at **Longny au Perche** (just east of Mortagne au Perche, *boudin* heaven, see page 11) which is organised in conjunction with the traditional May Day festivities in the town. Call the **tourist office** (tel: 02 33 73 62 51) for more details.

Festival of the Forgotten Fruits

Two weeks after the old veg (see page 29), the last Sunday in October sees forgotten fruits celebrated at the **Château de Belloc** (tel: 05 56 30 62 00), just outside the village of Sadirac, 10km east of Bordeaux. The festival is organised by Bernard Lafon, who created the museum, gardens and preserving factory which is **Oh! Légumes Oubliés** (see page 187), and features an interesting programme of events centred on fruits which are no longer commonly available.

It's your chance to try (and buy) various species of melons, marrows and pumpkins (cucurbitaceous plants), Jerusalem artichokes (*topinambours* in French), elderberries, ground-cherries or Périgord verjuice. There are also tastings and celebrations of delicious forgotten vegetables including nettles, dandelions and sorrel – which have their own festival in the spring (see page 14).

Sand-yacht endurance racing

Sand-yachts have been around for an awful long time – one of the Egyptian pharaohs was buried with his – but only at the end of the 19th century did the sporting potential become apparent, when various Belgian designers perfected vehicles which could be raced along the beach. In France it was Louis Blériot (see page 42), the first man to fly across the channel, who invented the *aéroplage* in 1911 (*'non, non'*, it's not *supposed* to fly…'), and the first major races were held at Berck sur Mer in 1913.

Berck was also the venue for Bertrand Lambert's 1991 world speed record in a sand-yacht of 151.55km/h (close to 100mph) – simply terrifying when you think of lying on your back in a three-wheeler extremely close to the ground with no brakes.

So it's hardly surprising that **Berck sur Mer** (tel: 03 21 09 50 00; web: www.berck.com) hosts the European sand-yachting community's toughest challenge, the so-called **6 heures de Berck**, which takes place annually on the last weekend of October or the first weekend of November.

The race, started back in the 1960s by Berck's prestigious Eole Club, is the oldest endurance sand-yachting event in Europe, and arguably the hardest, too. It takes place on Berck's wonderful beach, and features 40 sand-yachts, each with two pilots who race alternately around the six-kilometre course, trying to clock up the greatest distance in the six hours between 08.30 and 14.30.

It's extraordinarily difficult, with the slightest pilot-error spelling failure, and the race being won not necessarily by the fastest pilot but by the one with the best technique, skill, and above all endurance – which is why it's frequently referred to as the Paris–Roubaix (see page 5) of the sand-yachting world. If you want to sign up as a contestant, get in touch with the **Eole Club** in Berck (tel: 03 21 09 04 55; email: eole.club@libertysurf.fr).

NOVEMBER
Explorimages Festival

There's something charmingly quirky about a whole festival dedicated to images which only have one thing in common: they have to come from underground. That's the only rule – they can come from anywhere in the world, and can be in the form of film, video, photographs, paintings, drawings, or mixed media, and they can come from natural settings (such as caves, grottoes and canyons) or man-made ones (like mines, quarries, military works, sculpted caverns, or troglodyte shelters, houses, villages or cities), but they have to come from below the ground.

The festival was born of the merging together of two earlier events, the International Caving Film Festival, which was started in 1977, and an underground photography festival, which was created in parallel in 1980. With new resources, the combined event has been known as Explorimages since 2001, and now takes place annually in **Mandelieu la Napoule**, just outside Cannes, in the second week of November. It attracts its fair share of speleologists, mining experts and scientists (and the occasional troglodyte), but it's also keen to bring in the general public – and to be honest, the images are simply fabulous. It's a whole different world down there.

For further information contact Explorimages (tel: 04 92 97 19 85; web: www.explorimages.com).

Herring Fair

The small town of **Lieurey** (tel: 02 32 56 34 29), situated 20km or so from the sea, in rural Normandy, seems like an unlikely place to hold a herring fair, but hold a herring fair they do, every November 11 (handily a public holiday in France).

The event dates back to the Hundred Years War, which as you'll no doubt already know was a particularly herring-rich period of history (see Joan of Arc and the Battle of the Herrings on page 83). According to the story, a herring convoy (one assumes they were loaded on to carts, rather than making their own way across country) was on its way inland from the port of Pont Audemer, when it was caught in a violent snowstorm. Rather than let the herrings rot, the haulage company sold off the cargo at bargain prices so they could be kippered by the locals.

A tradition was born, naturally, and today you'll find several tonnes of herrings changing hands each November 11 in Lieurey, along with herring tastings, and the inevitable contest to see who can dispose of the largest quantity of herring at a single sitting. In 2001, with a field of 27 contestants, the competition was won by a fishy fellow who put away almost two kilograms in under an hour. The prize? Your weight in herrings. Lovely. (It's a pity my grandfather isn't on hand, as he claimed once to have triumphed in an eating contest in World War I, by dispatching 37½ pairs of kippers.)

The Flame of Armagnac

France's oldest spirit, Armagnac, has been seen as a cure-all for centuries, and around nine million bottles of the stuff are now consumed every year – two thirds of that in France, and around 5% in the UK (Armagnac's single largest export market). It's made by distilling the current year's wine in big alembics (copper stills), and then maturing the resulting clear *eau-de-vie* (known as Armagnac blanche, and fearsome stuff, at 52–72% pure-alcohol) in the oak barrels which give it its distinctive colour and flavour.

The moment the distillation process begins is a period of great celebration in the Armagnac region, which is centred on the towns of Condom (see page 238) and Eauze, spread across three *départements*, and sub-divided into the Bas Armagnac, Ténarèze and Haut Armagnac classifications.

When the wine is ready for distillation, a ceremonial flame, the **Flamme de l'Armagnac**, is carried from producer to producer, and used to light the wood fire under the alembic. (Smaller producers, of which there are hundreds, make use of a mobile still.) The *flamme* ceremony is followed by dinner at the foot of the still, and tastings not just of matured Armagnac but also of Armagnac blanche and Floc d'Armagnac (an aperitif made of Armagnac mixed with unfermented grape juice). Not surprisingly, there's usually a certain amount of singing involved.

It's difficult to predict exactly when the *flamme* is going to happen, as everything depends on when the grapes are ready for harvesting. Come at the beginning of November and you can be too early; come at the end of the month and you may be too late. Your best bet therefore is to call the **Bureau National Interprofessionnel de l'Armagnac** (BNIA), in Eauze, in October, and see what's cooking (tel: 05 62 08 11 00; web: www.armagnac.fr – there's also www.armagnac.org, though at the time of writing it was still trapped in 1999).

You can also find out which producers are organising special events from the tourist offices in **Eauze** (tel: 05 62 09 96 09) and Condom (tel: 05 62 28 00 80; web: www.condom.org – which was still in development in late 2002, though 'Rockin' Condom' sounds interesting). Finally, the **Montréal tourist office** (tel: 05 62 29 42 85), between Eauze and Condom, organises walks through the vineyards and tastings at various properties in conjunction with the *flamme*.

Brotherhood of Goat Eaters' Festival

In the village of **Bellegarde en Marche** (tel: 05 55 67 65 27), in the heart of France, between Limoges and Clermont Ferrand, they're not *kidding* when they say they like goats. Indeed, so much so that they have a brotherhood, presided over by a 'Great Goatherd', called the **Confrérie des Mangeurs de Chèvres**, who must eat goat flesh at least once a year.

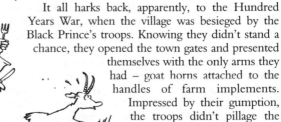

It all harks back, apparently, to the Hundred Years War, when the village was besieged by the Black Prince's troops. Knowing they didn't stand a chance, they opened the town gates and presented themselves with the only arms they had – goat horns attached to the handles of farm implements. Impressed by their gumption, the troops didn't pillage the village, but instead paved a street with goat horns in honour of the moment. (More than 600 years later, there's still a small street, the Rue des Cornes de Chèvre, with vestiges of goat horn in the paving.)

Back in the 14th century, goats were a good deal more common in the area than they are now, and – either salted down or boiled up – formed the main source of meat. By the early 1960s, however, there was barely a goat to be seen in the fields, let alone on the menu, so a brotherhood was founded in Bellegarde. Since then, the fraternity has held an annual procession on the last Sunday in November, accompanied by accordion music, to celebrate the induction of new recruits, who swear fealty to the kid (by eating one). The celebrations culminate in a communal feast with a goaty theme.

DECEMBER
Fat Poultry Fair and Plucking Contest

If you really want to see feathers fly, then **Egreville** (tel: 01 64 29 21 66), between Paris and Auxerre, is the place to come, on the first weekend in December, when they hold the annual **Concours de Volailles Grasses et de Plumage**, a fair which has been running continuously since the 1920s.

The event takes place in Egreville's superb 16th-century market hall, an unusual building with a vast triangular gable and tiled roof supported by 24 solid wooden pillars on stone bases, which slopes almost down to the ground at the sides. On the Saturday of the fair, you'll find a dozen contestants here with their sleeves rolled up, ready to pluck a duck.

Whilst they're for the most part local farmers, anyone can take part (sign up with the tourist office), and even the owner of the local château's been known to have a go. The rules are simple enough: you simply have to pluck and clean a duck in the minimum time possible, to the satisfaction of the local judges. What's astonishing is the speed at which the professionals work – most of them can do the job in well under ten minutes, and the best in under five. There are feathers everywhere.

The following day is positively tame by comparison, with geese, guinea-fowl, chickens, capons and ducks (live, this time) being traded in the market hall, and competitions to judge the best-cooked farmhouse chickens.

Living Nativity scene

For those who find Christmas cribs just that little bit dull and lifeless, a trip to **Saint Gilles** (tel: 04 66 87 33 75), in the Camargue, just west of Arles, is in order. Here, on the Saturday before Christmas, you'll find a fabulous living nativity festival, featuring more than 200 actors and actresses, and plenty of animals too.

The event takes place on the square in front of l'Abbatiale de Saint Gilles, a church with a superb 12th-century Romanesque façade hiding a spacious interior, with an enormous triple-naved crypt underneath (where you'll find the remains of Saint Gilles himself).

Although the cast aren't paid, it's a highly professional show, with full sound and lighting, featuring real-life versions of the arrival of the shepherds, the adoration of the magi (and rather more hangers-on than I remember being in the Bible), along with the nativity scene itself, centred on Mary, Joseph and the baby Jesus. Winged angels are much in evidence, as are sheep, donkeys and dromedaries.

It ends with a medieval horseback procession of Provençal-costumed nobles, accompanied by drummers, jugglers, fools and other folkloric types, who are all blessed by the local priest before climbing up the steps into the church for a fine midnight mass. Whether or not you have strong religious convictions, it makes for a great spectacle.

Eccentric Pioneers

If you're going to be a pioneer you're doing two things at once: you're facing potential failure (someone else might get there first; the task's impossible; or you're not up to it), and you're taking your life in your hands (lots of pioneers end up prematurely dead). But then the stakes are high – if you succeed, your name goes down in history. That said, posterity doesn't seem to be the reason why most pioneers go pioneering after all…

ECCENTRIC AVIATORS

The quest for the skies was fraught with mishaps, accidents, spectacular successes and eccentrics – and nowhere more so than in France. Once the Wright brothers had abandoned their cycle shop for the joys of powered flight, it was the French who took up the challenges of being the first to fly higher, further and faster than anyone else.

Higher, further, and faster, perhaps, but often with disastrous results – from the unfortunate who was first filmed flapping haplessly down to his death from the Eiffel tower in the late 1890s, to the dramatic misfortunes of the early pioneers of powered flight, who plunged one after another into the English Channel in vain attempts to win the *Daily Mail's* thousand pound prize. Cash for foolish daring sound familiar? It's been around and selling papers for at least a century.

Montgolfiers and other balloonists

Featherless flight really took off for mankind in November 1782, when Joseph and Etienne Montgolfier surprised their parents (not to mention their 14 siblings) by sending a smoke-filled envelope made of taffeta ('a closely woven, lightweight silk with a subtle sheen and a distinctive rustle') up to the ceiling. The hot-air balloon was in the process of being born.

Within six months the juvenile 30- and 40-something brothers had sent a number of increasingly large inflatables up into the air, and were ready for their first serious public display, the launch of the 12-metre aerostat *Seraphina*. In spite of their ingenuity, however, the Montgolfiers hadn't realised that hot air and not smoke provided the lift for their contraptions, so their increasingly popular and grandiose experiments were characterized by wet straw and damp wool bonfires – and much choking, fainting and eye-watering amongst the assembled spectators.

On June 4 1783, in front of a huge crowd in Annonay, 70km south of Lyon, the brothers finally lit the bonfire that was to inflate their balloon and spread their reputation across France and around the world. The noisome, pungent wool-and-straw smoke soon began to fill the *Seraphina*, and before long it was tugging alarmingly at the wooden stakes securing it.

The enormous aerostat – constructed of wrapping fabric lined with paper (the Montgolfiers' family business was paper manufacture), and held together with more than 2,000 buttons – soon became untenable in rising winds, and the orders

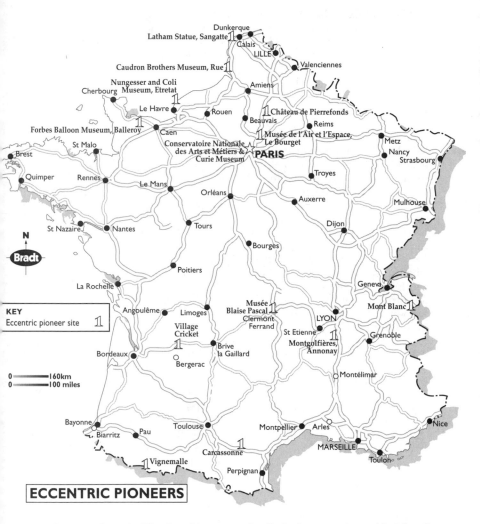

Dunkerque
Latham Statue, Sangatte
Calais
LILLE
Valenciennes
Caudron Brothers Museum, Rue
Amiens
Nungesser and Coli Museum, Etretat
Cherbourg
Le Havre
Rouen
Château de Pierrefonds
Beauvais
Reims
Forbes Balloon Museum, Balleroy
Caen
Musée de l'Air et l'Espace
Le Bourget
Metz
St Malo
Conservatoire Nationale
des Arts et Métiers &
Curie Museum
PARIS
Nancy
Brest
Strasbourg
Quimper
Rennes
Troyes
Le Mans
Orléans
Auxerre
Mulhouse
N
St Nazaire
Nantes
Tours
Dijon
Bradt
Bourges
Poitiers
Geneva
La Rochelle

KEY
Eccentric pioneer site
Angoulême
Limoges
Musée
Blaise Pascal
Clermont
Ferrand
LYON
Mont Blanc
Village
Cricket
St Etienne
Grenoble
Montgolfières,
Annonay
Bordeaux
Brive
la Gaillard
Bergerac
Montélimar

0 ———160km
0 ———100 miles

Bayonne
Toulouse
Montpellier
Arles
Nice
Biarritz
Pau
MARSEILLE
Carcassonne
Toulon
Vignemalle
Perpignan

ECCENTRIC PIONEERS

were given to release it. The *Seraphina* promptly climbed to an estimated height of 2km before gradually losing its heat and landing in a vineyard a short distance away.

Hearing the news, in Paris, the less inventive but vastly more scientific Jacques Charles immediately set to work on the world's first hydrogen balloon – reportedly thinking he was copying the precocious Montgolfiers. His first balloon to be publicly launched, on August 26 1783 – from the Champ de Mars, the site today of the Eiffel Tower – was filled with hydrogen made by pouring nearly quarter of a tonne of sulphuric acid on to half a tonne of scrap iron, and was made of silk covered with rubber solution. It was a remarkably modern device for the times.

The small balloon (capable of lifting a mere 9kg) ascended rapidly and flew off to the north, pursued by balloon-chasers on horseback. In the crowd watching on the Champ de Mars was the 77-year-old American Minister to France, Benjamin Franklin, no doubt reflecting on the giddying pace of technological change since he'd performed his famous kite experiments 31 years earlier.

The hydrogen balloon proved dramatically more airworthy than the Montgolfiers' *Seraphina*, flying for three quarters of an hour before coming down 16km away, just outside the village of Gonesse – a village which tragically hit the news again in 2000 when a Concorde bound for New York crashed there two minutes after take-off, killing 113 people. Charles' unmanned hydrogen balloon didn't cause any damage in 1783 – but it was a casualty itself, being attacked and destroyed by pitchfork-wielding locals, terrified by the arrival of a monster from the heavens.

Just over three weeks later the Montgolfiers were back in style, launching the first balloon with living beings aboard. A sheep, a duck and a rooster made up the first payload on the eight-minute flight from the gardens of the Palace of Versailles, watched over by Louis XVI and Marie-Antoinette (see page 87). By surviving their ascent to 500m and the trauma of take-off and landing, the animals proved once and for all that the skies were safe for mankind, and set the way for ballooning's first manned flight, on November 21, 1783.

On that day Pilâtre de Rozier, a physicist, and his close friend the Marquis d'Arlandes, took off from the Château de la Muette in a balloon built by Joseph and Etienne Montgolfier and powered by a straw-burning brazier. Together they made a 25-minute flight over Paris, astonishing the populace and only narrowly averting total disaster, as some of their ropes caught fire.

Just ten days later, on December 1, it was once more Jacques Charles' turn to be in the spotlight. Charles and his companion Nicolas Robert took off from the Tuileries Gardens in Paris in a hydrogen balloon, flying more than 25km to Nésles la Vallée. Robert abandoned ship at that point (for reasons unrecorded), leaving Charles to fly alone to an astonishing altitude of over 2km. And once more Benjamin Franklin was on hand as a spectator.

Within just six months ballooning had ... well, ballooned, from a mere flight of fancy to fully-fledged flight. Six months later, on the first anniversary of the Annonay spectacle, a French opera singer, Mme Thible, became the first woman to take to the skies.

De Rozier, the first man into the air in 1783, sadly went on to make more ballooning history in 1785, by becoming aviation's first fatality. He perished in a daring attempt to cross the English Channel in a hybrid balloon, combining a lethal mixture of naked-flame heated air and a cell filled with hydrogen. Ironically, it was a balloon based on the de Rozier hybrid design – the Breitling *Orbiter 3* – which completed the first non-stop flight around the world in 1999.

Back in October 1797, it was André-Jacques Garnerin's turn to make history, by being the first person to fall from the skies – safely. For performing the world's first successful parachute jump, from a balloon over 2,000m up in the air, he was awarded the honorific title 'Official French Aeronaut of the State'.

Every June, the town of Annonay, 70km south of Lyon, recreates the first balloon flight on the Place des Cordeliers, and since 1983 it's been held annually in conjunction with a three-day **international ballooning festival** (see page 18).

For a more eclectic look at the life of the Montgolfiers you can visit the **Musée des Papeteries Canson et Montgolfier**, which is at their birthplace at **Vidalon**, two kilometres from the town centre. It's a rare opportunity to learn how to make handmade paper.

More serious enthusiasts will want to go to the world's first Balloon Museum, housed at the **Château Balleroy**, in Normandy. Founded by Malcolm Forbes in 1975 at the Forbes-owned château, the museum documents the history of ballooning from its beginnings, and has a great series of models collected by Forbes, himself a world-record breaking balloonist, and the first to fly coast-to-coast across America.

French birdmen of the 1900s

The 19th century was a relatively quiet time for aviation in Europe, but once the Wright brothers had got off the ground, at Kitty Hawk in North Carolina in 1903, things really began to take off in France – with former balloonists becoming some of the keenest (and most unusual) pioneers of 'heavier-than-air' machines.

Alberto Santos-Dumont (1873–1932) – a 'Father of Aviation'

Wealthy, diminutive, Brazilian-born Alberto Santos-Dumont was one of early aviation's most striking pioneers. After a fall from a horse left his father a paraplegic, the family moved from Brazil to Paris in 1891, and Alberto pursued his education – and his passionate interest in all things technical and mechanical – there. It is said that by the age of ten he had read the entire works of Jules Verne, and one of the first things he did on arrival in Paris was to build himself a motorised tricycle.

Backed by the considerable resources of the family's vast coffee plantations in Brazil, Santos-Dumont soon reached for the skies, and by 1898 he was aloft over Paris in the world's first gasoline-powered airship, *Santos-Dumont #1*. He continued inventing, building, flying and refining his dirigibles over the next three years, and became a familiar sight over the rooftops of the capital. He even ate his meals at a table ten feet up in the air, to acclimatise himself to high altitudes.

On October 19 1901, Santos-Dumont won the Aero Club's Deutsch prize with his #6 dirigible. The prize was to be awarded to the balloonist who could take off from Saint-Cloud, fly around the Eiffel Tower and return to the starting point – all in less than 30 minutes; Santos-Dumont achieved the feat in 29½, narrowly avoiding crashing into the Eiffel Tower. Whether he made the flight dressed in his customary pin-striped suit and stacked shoes (he was only five feet tall) is not recorded.

At the celebrations afterwards at Maxim's, Santos-Dumont complained to his friend Louis Cartier about the struggle he'd had in checking his pocket watch to monitor his progress during the flight. Cartier set to work on the problem right away, and finally came up with an ingenious solution: a watch with a leather strap and a buckle. From 1904 onwards, Santos-Dumont never flew without his personal Cartier – the world's first wristwatch.

After winning the Deutsch prize, Santos-Dumont divided up almost the entire prize money of 100,000 francs – along with another 100,000 francs from the Brazilian government – between his workers and the beggars of Paris; gifts worth more than half a million pounds (close to € 800,000) in today's money.

After building yet more dirigibles – including #9, in which he overflew the military parade for Bastille Day in 1903, firing his revolver repeatedly (and dangerously, one can't help thinking) into the air – Santos-Dumont turned his attention to heavier-than-air flight. Between September and November 1906, in the *14-bis* (an aircraft of his own design, and the first known plane to feature a wheeled undercarriage), he made Europe's first successful powered flights, and by November 1907 he had claimed the world speed record for a 220-metre flight, achieving the distance in just 21 seconds.

He went on to produce – and fly – many other innovative and successful designs for aircraft, including the world's first sports plane, the Demoiselle, in 1908, and the delta wing, more than 30 years ahead of its time, before tragically falling ill in 1910 with what has now been diagnosed as multiple sclerosis. He returned to Brazil in 1916, and lived out the rest of his life there in an unusual house of his own design. Three days after his 49th birthday (and ill and depressed over seeing aircraft used in warfare), he committed suicide.

While the Wrights can rightly claim the prize for being the first men to master heavier-than-air powered flight, Santos-Dumont solved the problem of making a heavier-than-air machine take off by its own means – a feat the Wright brothers, with their slipways and catapults had singularly failed to achieve. Which explains why, even today, many (especially in Brazil) still consider Santos-Dumont to be the 'Father of Aviation'.

The Voisin Brothers

Gabriel Voisin's closest friend in the world was his younger brother Charles, and together, in 1906 (at the tender ages of 26 and 24 respectively), they proved their passion for flight by founding the world's first aviation company – Les Frères Voisin.

With only a limited understanding of what the Wrights had been up to in America – mostly based on hearsay rather than any detailed first-hand knowledge – the brothers' first aeroplane was almost impossible to turn, even though it was pretty good at staying airborne. The plane was built for the aviation-mad artillery captain, Ferdinand Ferber (see opposite), but neither the Voisin brothers nor Ferber understood the principles of wing warping which the Wrights had innovated stateside. As a result they tried to use vertical box-kite-like curtains between the wings to provide stability and prevent rolling – although this almost entirely prevented lateral control (ie: steering).

The brothers soon improved their techniques, however, and went on to build a whole range of successful aircraft – so successful, in fact that Gabriel went on to become the youngest *Chevalier de la Légion d'Honneur* in France in 1909, at the age of just 29 years old. His brother Charles never achieved the same level of recognition, and was killed in a car crash in 1912.

In 1918, horrified at his planes having been used as engines of war, Gabriel quit the aviation industry, and proceeded to spend the next 42 years designing and building fast cars. Sadly, he was too innovative – and too quick to innovate – to be able to compete with the nascent French car industry giants, Citroën, Peugeot and Renault. Voisin's problem was that he was never entirely happy with any of his cars – so he would immediately withdraw them from the market and produce a superior model, often in only a matter of months. His engineering and design skills were no match for his lack of understanding of the product cycle.

Voisin was easily the longest-lived of the early French aviation pioneers, surviving until Christmas Day 1973, six weeks before his 94th birthday.

Captain Ferdinand Ferber

Ferber (1862–1909) was an artillery commander whose interest in flying had been piqued by the experiments undertaken by the father of modern hang-gliding, Otto Lilienthal, in the early 1890s (gliding experiments which were cut terminally short by a crash near Berlin in 1896), and he himself built and flew a number of gliders from 1901 onwards.

As a founder member of the French Aero-Club, Ferber was among those who first heard Octave Chanute, a French-born engineer living in the USA (and, more importantly, friend and advisor to the Wright brothers), speak in Paris in 1903 about the latest developments abroad. Soon afterwards he persuaded Earnest Archdeacon, a rich French sporting lawyer of Irish descent (and would-be aviator himself), to encourage French aviators by launching a prize. This Archdeacon did, with the industrialist Henry Deutsch de la Meurthe, putting up prize-money between them of 50,000 francs to go to the first person to publicly fly a heavier-than-air machine around a one-kilometre course – and land it safely.

Even though the Wrights had made a 39km flight in America by 1905, the Deutsch–Archdeacon prize remained unclaimed in Europe. The Wrights, disdainful to the end of what they called 'circus-flying', and more interested in drumming up business with the US government, let the prize stand until it was finally claimed in 1908 by the French pilot Henri Farman (see below).

Ferdinand Ferber, meanwhile, made great progress with various Voisin-built biplanes – until fatally crash-landing one into a ditch near Boulogne sur Mer in 1909.

Captain Marchal

Ferber was pre-deceased a year earlier by French army captain Marchal and three of his crewmen, in aviation's first 20th-century accident leading to multiple fatalities. When a propeller spun free and ripped through the shell of their 51.5m airship, *La République*, the dirigible plummeted to the ground – though this didn't stop Paul and Peter Lebaudy, the constructors, from building ever larger and faster ships, including an 80-metre monster in 1911 named after the luckless Captain Marchal.

Henri Farman

English-born Henri Farman (1874–1958) was a popular racing cyclist and racing-car driver long before he took up the cause of aviation. He learned to fly with his younger brother, Maurice, in a Voisin-built machine, and on January 13, 1908 won the Deutsch–Archdeacon Prize, completing the one-kilometre circuit in one minute and 28 seconds. Already popular, he became hugely famous in Europe for this feat – even though the Wrights had already flown a kilometre in 1904 and 39km in 1905.

Henri and Maurice went on to open a flight training school, and founded the Farman Aviation Works (which were to provide France with more than 10,000 military aeroplanes during World War I) and Farman Lines, the precursor to Air France.

Baronne de Laroche

The young actress, Elise Deroche, better known by her extravagant stage sobriquet of Raymonde, Baronne de Laroche, made instant history on October 22 1909 by becoming the first woman to fly solo. The 300m hop in a Voisin aircraft was trumped the following day by a 6km flight, and marked the beginning of a brief but extraordinary career as an aviatrix for the 23-year-old Elise.

Having flamboyantly wooed both the Paris theatre and the world of fashion, as well as being an accomplished painter and sculptress, Elise went on to become the first licensed woman pilot in the world on March 8, 1910, obtaining *brevet* #36 from the French Aero-Club. That spring and summer she flew everywhere she could, and took part in showy flying displays and competitions at Heliopolis, Saint-Petersburg, Rouen and Budapest – where she was fined two pounds by the organisers for flying over the crowd. But on July 8, at the Reims meeting – an event which saw Louis Blériot break the world speed record – Elise had a terrible crash during the Ladies' Prize event, and suffered multiple fractures.

Her injuries left her handicapped but indomitable. Indeed, hardly was her convalescence over before she was back in the air again, competing and winning prizes – including the first 'Coupe Fémina' in 1913. She went on to win the Fémina twice more, before specialising in numerous attempts on the women's altitude record. In 1918 she finally took this by climbing to 4,800m, and in the same year she also broke the women's distance record by flying non-stop for 323km.

Not content to rest on her laurels, Elise started serious preparations for the next Fémina – but fatally crashed her new plane at Crotoy in 1919 during a test flight. She was five weeks short of her 33rd birthday.

Pierre Marechal – Lifeboat Aviator

Luckier by far was the French aviator Pierre Marechal, business partner to the more famous Louis Paulhan, who won a £10,000 prize for flying from London to Manchester in under 24 hours in 1910.

One evening in April 1912, Marechal was playing cards with three friends on a transatlantic crossing when they heard a loud bump. The ship was the Titanic. Fortunately for Marechal and his card-playing pals, they were first class passengers, and were therefore among the first to get to the lifeboats; all four were safely rescued. It's reported that throughout the entire drama Marechal never removed his monocle – even when taking a turn at the lifeboat's oars.

Harriet Quimby

And while we're on the subject of Titanic tie-ins, it shouldn't be forgotten that the first woman to fly solo across the Channel, from England to France, was the American pilot Harriet Quimby. She was the first American woman to get an aviator's licence, in 1911, and wanted to be the first woman to pilot a plane across the Channel.

On April 16, 1912, in great secrecy and using a borrowed Blériot monoplane, she flew successfully from Dover to Calais, in 59 minutes. But the pioneering flight barely made the inside pages of the newspapers; the Titanic had sunk two days earlier, drowning 1,523 passengers and crew.

Ten weeks later, on July 1, 37-year-old Harriet and her passenger, William Willard, died on the mud flats of Boston Bay, abruptly terminating Harriet's 11-month flying career. First Willard and then Harriet plunged to their sticky ends from 400m up, when they fell out of her brand new two-seater Blériot monoplane – probably as a result of Willard leaning too far forward to look out, and then losing his grip. They should have buckled up – but seatbelts hadn't yet been invented.

Channel crossing – the great prize

First across the Channel, of course, was not the ill-fated Harriet Quimby, but the French pioneering aviator Louis Blériot. That it was Blériot, and not Hubert Latham, the favourite for the prize, changed the course of history.

Hubert Latham – the unlucky contender

Hubert Latham had everything it takes to be a popular hero – wealth, good looks, talent and courage – and he already had a reputation as an outstanding sportsman by the beginning of 1909, when he succumbed to the temptation of aviation.

Born in Paris in 1883, Latham made his first aerial crossing over the Channel in an airship in 1905, while completing his military service. He and his cousin, Jacques Faure, an experienced aeronaut, intended to set off from Dover on 10 February, but insufficient gas supplies meant they had to set off from Crystal Palace instead on the following day.

With the airship gassed up and ready to go, Faure and Latham finally set off at 6.45pm from Crystal Palace. By 8pm they were at Hastings, and enough ballast was thrown out to lift the airship to an altitude of 700m for the Channel crossing. As they flew across the water they lost so much height that the balloon's guide rope started trailing through the sea below. But finally they reached the French coast at 10pm, and jettisoned the remaining ballast, allowing the intrepid pair to fly all the way to Paris, arriving three hours later.

In March 1909, having returned from several years on safari, Latham bought a stake in the Antoinette Company and soon became their Chief Pilot. He perfected his aviator's look with a jaunty checked cap and a distinctive ivory cigarette holder – no-smoking flights were still decades away.

Latham spent the spring of 1909 learning to fly, and on June 6 set a new monoplane endurance record of 77 minutes and 37 seconds. For the last 20 minutes of the flight it poured with rain, and on landing Latham was soaked through but still puffing away at a cigarette. On the following day he claimed the Ambroise Goupy prize by making a flight of more than 5km across country. The four-and-half-minute flight was made with bravado, and delighted the crowd – at the time only the Wright brothers had flown further.

What really pleased the onlookers, however, was Latham's showy – you might even say rash – flying style. Through June 1909 Latham had been practicing stunts, including the reckless one of cutting the ignition off and gliding down to within a few metres of the ground before restarting the engine. He took passengers up for short flights, including a correspondent from London's *Daily Mail*, who described Latham afterwards in his newspaper column as 'a man compact of steel and whipcord, without any nervous system at all.'

Latham was clearly ready to fly the English Channel. The challenge to do so had first been made the previous year by Lord Northcliffe, the owner of the *Daily Mail*, who offered a prize of £1,000 for the first Channel crossing by a heavier-than-air aircraft in 1909. Whether Northcliffe was more interested in aviation (he had met Alberto Santos-Dumont in Monte Carlo in 1902) or simply increased newspaper circulation isn't clear, but the prospect of a pioneering exploit and a decent cash prize drew interest from across the continent (£1,000 in 1909 was about £60,000 today).

Northcliffe was surprised to discover Wilbur Wright wasn't interested – though he should have remembered that the Wright brothers had also eschewed the Deutsch–Archdeacon prize back in 1905. One of Wilbur Wright's first three pupils, ex-pat Russian aristocrat Count Charles de Lambert, was keen, however, and set up camp with his Wright aeroplane at Wissant, near Boulogne sur Mer. He announced he would be ready to make an attempt after July 23.

That gave Latham his chance. Installing himself not far away, near Sangatte, he took advantage of the disused buildings and equipment left behind by the Channel Tunnel Company (see page 64) 25 years earlier, and started readying his Antoinette plane. After a moderately successful test flight on July 13 he was ready – but was then held up for several days by bad weather.

Media interest in the event was at fever pitch, so it was with some relief all round that Latham was able to make his historic first attempt on Monday July 19. He took off and headed out across the Channel towards Dover. Everything was near perfect – he had flown both further and longer before, and he was confident he could make it. But before he was even half way across, his engine stopped. His plane glided down and landed in the water – fortunately for Latham it floated. Latham put his feet up, lit a cigarette and waited for the rescue ship to arrive.

Count Charles de Lambert was no more fortunate, crashing his biplane a few days later on a test flight and injuring himself sufficiently badly to put himself right out of the contest, leaving Latham time to get his plane fixed for a second attempt. Before he could make it, however, he was beaten to the mark by Louis Blériot, who didn't even enter the contest until after Latham's first attempt.

Both Latham and de Lambert continued flying after their attempts to cross the Channel, and both broke records and won numerous prizes – but neither achieved anything like the glory (or indeed riches) of Blériot. De Lambert eventually emigrated to America and became close friends with Orville Wright, surviving into his late 70s.

Latham, for his part – and characteristically, it should be said – went out more dramatically. In 1912 he was shooting big game near Fort Archambault, in the Congo, when he was fatally gored by a wounded buffalo. He was only 29.

Louis Blériot – snatched from the jaws of bankruptcy

By rights, Louis Blériot should have been confined to the more obscure annals of early powered flight, but instead, by snatching the *Daily Mail*'s Channel crossing prize, he became one of the most famous of all aviators.

Born in 1872, Blériot made a small fortune in manufacturing acetylene lamps for the nascent motor industry, and from 1901 proceeded to spend the proceeds on building, flying and all too frequently crashing planes of his own design.

By 1909 – with the substantial assistance of hired craftsmen and engineers – he was having more luck and had managed to make several flights in his Blériot X and Blériot XI aircraft. But he was also facing financial ruin, having spent his way through not just most of his business, but also through his wife's impressive dowry. In total he had blown 780,000 francs (nearly £2 million at today's prices), and he was too broke to even make the Channel attempt – effectively his last chance for success as an aviator.

But on 1 July 1909 – Blériot's 37th birthday – his luck changed, when his wife, Alice, happened to save the young son of a wealthy Haitian planter friend from falling to his death. You can understand the grateful parents offering to advance the Blériots enough funds, in recompense, to finance the attempt on the Channel, but it's harder to imagine Alice Blériot being happy to see yet more money going into hare-brained aircraft. Then again, women didn't win the right to vote until 1945 in France.

Even with the money problem fixed (temporarily), the odds were still firmly stacked against Blériot. For one thing, he was still on crutches through July 1909, having badly burned his foot on the exhaust pipe of the Anzani engine powering the Blériot XI, and could barely walk, let alone fly. For another, the Anzani engine was a far cry from Latham's beautifully crafted fuel-injected Antoinette, and tended to spray hot oil on to Blériot's face and into his splendidly waxed moustache. Once he arrived at Calais, however, Blériot was quick to set up camp at Les Baraques (today known for its military cemetery), and his aircraft was ready to fly in no time at all – though bad weather then kept both Blériot and Latham grounded for days.

During the night of July 24 1909, the wind finally dropped, and by 2am on the 25th, Blériot and his camp were up and ready for the attempt. A short test flight – the first time the XI had been off the ground since being reassembled in Calais – was marred for both pilot and victim when a small dog ran into the propeller of Blériot's plane on take-off, but otherwise all went smoothly.

Not so over at Latham's camp, however, where in spite of having left instructions to be woken if the weather improved (not to mention the noisy commotion going on at the Blériot camp nearby), Latham slept on.

At 4.41am, having been told that dawn had officially broken, Blériot took off, pausing only to ask his engineer the immortal question 'Where is England?' – not as crazy as it sounds, as Blériot was flying instrument-free.

Just 37 minutes later, having got lost only once on the way, Blériot crash-landed on top of the white cliffs of Dover, guided in by the tricolour-waving French journalist Charles Fontaine, assigned by the Paris daily *Le Matin* to do everything possible to scoop the *Daily Mail* for the story.

Not far behind Fontaine came British soldiers, followed by a policeman with the requisite customs form for Blériot to fill in. With no box to check for arriving flights, Blériot was registered as the 'Master' of a yacht called 'Monoplane'.

Latham, for his part, had (to mix a metaphor) once more missed the boat. By the time his camp were aware of what was going on, it was too gusty to fly after Blériot. It would have been a brave-faced man who composed the short telegram to Blériot: 'Cordial Congratulations. Hope to follow you soon.'

Two days later Latham was as good as his word. This time, he flew to within a mile of the English Coast before engine failure. Without the fortuitous arrival of a ship's boat from the British battleship *Russell*, Latham would certainly have drowned.

With the possible exception of the author's great-grandmother, Louise Fenn-Smith, the public gave Blériot a rapturous reception. The recently widowed Mrs Fenn-Smith claimed to her dying day (more than 60 years later, at the age of 104), that she had been in Dover on that day in 1909 and had been asked to congratulate Blériot on his feat. 'Don't be so preposterous, young man,' she said, 'it can't be done.' In an ironical twist, her youngest son, Warren, was killed while flying a combat mission for the Royal Flying Corps in January 1918.

The public acclaim for Blériot was far out of proportion to the feat achieved or the prize on offer – people including both Latham and the Wrights had already flown further and for longer – but Blériot was fêted by huge crowds on his arrival in London as the first person to breach British airspace. As HG Wells said at the time, 'England is no longer, from a military point of view, an inaccessible island.' When the Blériot XI was put on display in Selfridges, more than 10,000 people queued to see it.

Blériot went on to make a fortune from the aircraft factory bearing his name, but he stopped flying not long after his Channel crossing – reportedly at the behest of the long-suffering Alice. He died in Paris on August 2 1936, 137 years to the day after the death of the pioneering balloonist, Etienne Montgolfier.

The actual Channel-crossing Blériot XI monoplane is now in Paris at the **CNAM** (Conservatoire Nationale des Arts et Métiers). It's suspended up in the top of the nave of the Saint Martin des Champs church, itself one of the high points of the museum. Blériot's plane is the one in the middle – walk up the metal ramps for a close-up, and marvel that Blériot ever got off the ground, let alone across the channel. The CNAM also houses a vast range of other science-related exhibits, ranging from early clocks and watches to exhibitions of manufacturing materials ancient and modern, to pioneering bicycles, tricycles and automobiles.

There's a good bronze **statue of Hubert Latham** on the coast road from Wissant to Sangatte, near the original (19th-century) Channel Tunnel works. Latham stands on a stone plinth with one hand in his pocket and his trademark flat cap and flying scarf. The cigarette holder is presumably in his jacket pocket. The monument marks the take-off point for Latham's two failed attempts at crossing the Channel.

World War I – French flying aces, and the Atlantic challenge

Blériot's successful flight across the Channel in 1909 paved the way for two important developments in aviation – the use of aircraft in warfare (the Wright Brothers had cottoned on to this early on, and were forever lobbying governments at home and abroad to buy their aircraft) and the potential of ever greater aerial exploits, culminating in the challenge of flying across the Atlantic.

Roland Garros – the first fighter pilot

Famous these days mainly for having a tennis club and tournament named after him, Roland Garros was a famous exhibition flyer before World War I (he was taught to fly by Alberto Santos-Dumont) and in 1913 was the first Frenchman to fly non-stop across the Mediterranean. When war broke out the following year, Garros signed up with the French Air Service, on the Western Front.

When his best friend, Armand Pinsard, was shot down in February 1915, Garros decided it was high time to implement the brilliant (if eccentric) idea of firing a machine-gun through his propeller – up until then pilots had only been able to fire ineffectively at each other with pistols or rifles. What Garros hoped was that most of the bullets would miss the propeller blades – and those that didn't could be deflected by metal plates. One can only presume that Garros and Raymond Saulnier, the manufacturer of his monoplane, did plenty of tests on the ground before risking shooting away the whole propeller in mid-air.

The invention was a great success, first seeing action on 1 April 1915, when Garros shot down two German biplanes. Over the next couple of weeks he downed another three, making him the first Ace Fighter Pilot and earning him the *Légion d'Honneur* – as well as a fearsome reputation amongst the Germans.

But his success was short lived. Within days he was forced to make a landing behind enemy lines after a rifleman on the ground managed to shoot through his fuel pipe. Infuriated, Garros tried to burn his plane to protect the secret of his success, but it was too wet and wouldn't catch fire.

Garros was made a prisoner-of-war, while his plane was taken to Berlin, for examination by Anthony Fokker, the Dutch pilot and aircraft designer. Using the basic Garros/Saulnier template, it took Fokker just three days to design a superior forward-facing machine-gun, which only fired when the propeller blades were out of the way. The Allies had lost their advantage.

Garros managed to escape from his POW camp at Magdeburg in early 1918, by the simple expedient of walking out of the main gate wearing a German uniform. After a quick refresher course to catch up on three years of new dogfighting strategy, he went straight back to his beloved combat flying. But on October 5, just five weeks before the Armistice, the 36-year-old pilot was shot down by a German Fokker D-7. Garros had been hoist by his own petard.

The main monument to Roland Garros is of course the **Roland Garros tennis stadium**, in Paris, which hosts the French Open every year. But for more on the Air Ace than the Tennis Ace go to the **Musée de l'Air et l'Espace** at **Le Bourget**.

Charles Nungesser

Charles Nungesser was one of the most colourful Frenchmen to make his mark as an Ace during World War I. Born and educated in France, he had gone to Brazil to work on his uncle's plantation – but by 1909, at the age of 17, he was popular as a boxer, rodeo-rider and professional racing driver in Argentina.

Returning to France when war broke out, Nungesser started off in the Hussars, only transferring to the Service Aéronautique in 1915 after a number of daring raids behind enemy lines – returning from one escapade with a stolen German staff car, which he was allowed to keep.

For shooting down his first enemy plane, Nungesser was given eight days under house arrest – he'd left the airfield without permission – and the Croix de Guerre. Not content with this, he proceeded to do stunt flying over the local town. After the residents complained, Nungesser was told by the squadron commander that if he wanted to do aerobatics he should do them over the German lines – which he promptly did, only to be re-arrested on his return.

Whether brave or plain foolhardy, Nungesser must have been a hell of a pilot, and he eventually notched up more than 40 victories in aerial combat – along with a horrific tally of injuries sustained, including broken legs, ruptured organs, loss of teeth, a skull fracture, dislocated wrists and ankles, and cuts and bruises beyond number. Even when he was unable to walk he would be carried from his hospital bed to his plane by his crew, and then carried back again after the flight.

Predictably, Nungesser was quick on the ground too, loving fast cars and faster women. While on leave in Paris he had a well-publicised fling with Mata Hari (see page 89), and (suspecting she was a spy) fed her a juicy story about a new super-plane the French were building.

After the war Nungesser continued to live hard and fly hard, and also flirted briefly with Hollywood, playing himself in the 1925 silent classic, the Sky Raider, before being tempted to have a go at winning the Orteig prize in 1927. The prize had been on offer since 1919, when Raymond Orteig, a wealthy Frenchman who owned two hotels in New York, put up US$25,000 for the first person to fly non-stop from Paris to New York (or from New York to Paris). The original offer had been good for five years, but with nobody having even attempted the flight, Orteig renewed it in 1926.

By the late spring of 1927 Nungesser and his co-pilot, François Coli (another World War I veteran), had outfitted their Levasseur biplane, and called it *Le Oiseau Blanc*. On the side was painted Nungesser's famous World War I insignia of a black heart containing a skull and crossbones, a coffin and two candles. On 8 May they took off from Le Bourget airfield ... and were never seen again. Although it's assumed they perished in the Atlantic, there are some who believe the Atlantic crossing was successful, and that the White Bird crashed in Newfoundland. The search continues.

You can find out more about Nungesser and his partner Coli and their failed transatlantic attempt at the **Nungesser and Coli Museum** in Etretat – the last place the two pilots were ever seen. TIGHAR (The International Group for Historic Aviation Recovery) started a big project in 1985 to find the missing plane – see www.tighar.org/projects/pmg.html.

Le Bourget airport – the departure point for Nungesser's last flight and the arrival point for Charles Lindbergh's solo transatlantic crossing – is now home to the **Musée de l'Air et l'Espace** (Air and Space Museum) which houses a superb collection of nearly 200 historic aircraft, including originals or replicas of almost all the aircraft mentioned in this chapter.

Lindbergh's arrival in Paris

Less than two weeks after Nungesser and Coli took off on their final flight from Le Bourget, a vast crowd swarmed to Le Bourget to await the expected arrival of Charles Lindbergh. When the *Spirit of St Louis* landed, the crowd went mad. Lindbergh's first (and only) words on arrival, before being bodily dragged out of his plane, were: 'Well, I made it.'

Fortunately for Lindbergh, two French aviators rescued him from the frenzied mob, pushing the exhausted American into a car and driving him to the commandant's office. *The Spirit of St Louis* wasn't so lucky, becoming a target for zealous souvenir hunters; if something could be removed from the plane it was, including bits of the wings. The rest was saved, and shipped back to America.

Maryse Bastié – crossing the South Atlantic

Surprisingly little is known about the early life of Maryse Bastié, one of France's most stubborn aviators. Born Marie-Louise Bombec in Limoges, in 1898, her father died when she was 11 and she was sent to work in a shoe factory.

After a failed early marriage, which left her with a small son, she appears to have first adopted the young Louis Bastié, an orphan of World War I, and then subsequently to have married him. As a military pilot, Louis wasn't allowed to give her lessons though, so she learned to fly instead with a civil pilot, during 1925. The following year Louis was killed in a flying accident.

Maryse herself then became a teacher at flying school. Within two years she was breaking records: in 1928 she flew 1,058km, a distance record for a female pilot; in 1930 she broke a new endurance record with a 37-hour and 55-minute flight; and in 1931 she dramatically improved her distance record by flying 2,976km non-stop.

It was in 1936, however, with nine international records already under her belt, that Maryse really made headlines, by being the first woman to fly alone across the South Atlantic. She made the flight in a single-engined plane without a radio, from Senegal to Brazil, a distance of 3,173km, in a record time of 12 hours and five minutes.

During World War II, Maryse Bastié became France's first female Air Force Captain, clocking up over 3,000 flying hours and winning the *Légion d'Honneur* on a purely military basis. She continued to fly after the war, often in test aircraft, until her untimely death at an air display in 1952, when she and four other passengers crashed their test cargo plane outside Lyon.

Great pictures and flying ephemera can be seen at the **Belltower and Caudron Brothers Museum** in the small town of Rue, between Le Touquet and Abbeville. The Caudron brothers made the planes that gave Bastié her records – and which Saint-Exupéry crashed (see below).

Maryse Bastié herself is buried in an impressive grave in the **Montparnasse Cemetery** in Paris.

Antoine de Saint-Exupéry

France's most notorious literary aviator, Antoine de Saint-Exupéry, was born into a *nouveau pauvre* aristocratic family in 1900. His father, Comte Jean-Marie de Saint-Exupéry, died of a stroke (aged only 41) when Antoine was barely four years old, leaving his mother, Marie Boyer de Fonscolombe, with five children to bring up on her own. This she seems to have done with her extended family in a series of huge country houses, surviving herself to the age of 97 (she died in 1972).

Ill-disciplined and a dreamer at school, the young but brilliant Antoine managed to make his maiden flight at the age of 12, when he lied his way into a plane at the local aerodrome, insisting that his mother had ordered him to be taken up. At the age of 14, Saint-Exupéry won a school prize for a story he had written, but although he then passed his baccalauréat at 17, he subsequently failed his university entrance exams – passing maths and science with ease but being let down by his literature papers. He went on to study architecture at the Beaux-Arts in Paris, and while there fell for the 16-year-old beauty, Louise de Vilmorin.

In 1921, Saint-Exupéry learned to fly, as part of his military service, and stayed on in the Air Force, but two years later, in 1923, had a particularly bad year, when he managed to break both his head and his heart. His skull was fractured in what was to be the first of many plane crashes, resulting in his being demobbed, while his heart was broken when Louise de Vilmorin broke off their engagement after just six months. (De Vilmorin went on to live a full and interesting life, becoming a prominent poet, song-smith and screenplay writer, as well as having famous affairs with both Orson Welles and Duff Cooper, the British Ambassador to Paris and father of the writer John Julius Norwich. She started writing in 1933, after a fling with the novelist and historian André Malraux, and also spent her last months with him before her death in 1969. Malraux, for his part, spent the rest of his life with de Vilmorin's niece, Sophie.)

Condemned to civvy street, Saint-Exupéry settled in Paris and started writing, supporting himself first as a bookkeeper and then as a truck salesman. He finally landed a job as a pilot, however, flying the mail to North Africa. He proved so good at it that in 1928 he was made director of an airfield in one of the remotest parts of the Sahara.

While in the desert, Saint-Exupéry wrote his first novel, *Southern Mail*, which paints an extraordinary picture of the loneliness and bravery of the early mail pilots, and was published to great acclaim in 1929. In the same year, he moved to South America, flying mail across the Andes with fellow pioneers Mermaz and Guillaumet, both of whom were to end up dead in plane crashes.

In Buenos Aires, in the summer of 1930, Saint-Exupéry was introduced to the beautiful Salvadorian journalist and artist Consuelo Suncin, who had recently been widowed for the second time at the age of 29 (in a small coincidence, her husband, Enrique Gomez Carillo, had been a close friend of Oscar Wilde's). Saint-Exupéry insisted on taking Consuelo and her friends immediately on a flight over the Rio de la Plata, and – once airborne – threatened to drown them all if she didn't kiss him. After cutting the engine several times and performing a series of acrobatics, she complied – and he, apparently, proposed. Her friends were all violently sick (presumably from the turbulent flight rather than the immodest proposal) but Antoine and Consuelo were indeed married the following year. The bride wore black, and carried red carnations.

Marriage for the Saint-Exupérys was a stormy affair, and their life was a continuous series of break-ups and reconciliations, though both continued to send each other love letters until Saint-Exupéry's death. Consuelo loved artists, and counted André Breton, Max Ernst, Pablo Picasso and Salvador Dalí amongst her friends. (She died in Provence in 1979, only seven years and a few miles away from Antoine's mother, Marie.)

Meanwhile, Antoine's Andean flying exploits formed the basis for his 1931 bestseller, *Night Flight*, which was made into a box-office smash starring Clark Gable in 1933. But throughout the 1930s, Saint-Exupéry lived a double life, never quite fitting in with the literary world or the flying one. He worked as a test pilot for Air France, and had many minor and two major plane crashes. He also wrote – on the advice of André Gide – *Terre des Hommes* (published in English as *Wind, Sand and Stars*), about a pilot's life, which won prizes on both sides of the Atlantic.

In 1940, with France having fallen, Saint-Exupéry went to America, where he lived first in New York and then in California. Unable – or unwilling – to learn a word of English, he was a hostage to his American publishers, but it was in America that he was to write and illustrate the work which is arguably his best-loved, *Le Petit Prince*. A children's book for adults, it remains one of the classics of the 20th century.

In 1943, unfit, unhealthy and depressed, Saint-Exupéry returned to the fray in Europe, but it was with great difficulty – compounded by age, injuries and his inexperience with modern aircraft – that he found his way back into the air.

Allowed eventually to pilot reconnaissance flights, Saint-Exupéry flew several missions in a Lockheed Lightning, before taking off from Bastia in Corsica for the last time on July 31 1944. His plane is thought to have crashed into the sea near Marseille (his bracelet was recovered by a fisherman in 1998) but his body has never been found.

It's unlikely we'll ever know for sure what happened on that day, and whether Saint-Exupéry was shot down, had an accident, or committed suicide. What we do know is that both he and *Le Petit Prince* made it on to the French 50 franc note, only to be disenfranchised by the arrival of the Euro. At least he's still got Saint-Exupéry airport in Lyon to be grateful for.

Saint-Exupéry has a major website at www.saint-exupery.org, where you can find out everything you need to know (in French), along with details of the numerous activities organised by the Saint-Exupéry Foundation. There's also a nice site dedicated to *Le Petit Prince*, at (you guessed it) www.lepetitprince.com, and a Little Prince Museum, too – but that's in Japan, not France. There's a campaign underway to create a Saint-Exupéry museum at his birthplace in Lyon, but it's no more than a campaign so far.

ECCENTRIC SEAFARERS

It's one thing to go swimming in summer, or out sailing with the family on the weekend – or even to get into ocean-going racing – but it's quite another to decide you're going to swim across the Atlantic, row across the Pacific, sail around the world backwards, or pedal your way from Lake Geneva to Memphis, Tennessee.

Gérard d'Aboville

Gérard d'Aboville was born in Paris in 1945, and loved the sea even as a child. Once his military service was over he spent his twenties sailing the seven seas, before deciding it would be a great idea to row alone across the Atlantic. In the summer of 1980, after two years of preparation, he set off from Cape Cod in the USA, and turned up 72 days and 5,200km later in Brittany, swearing 'Never again!'

Notwithstanding that, 11 years later, approaching his 46th birthday, Gérard was off again, this time in an attempt to row solo across the Pacific, a hugely harder undertaking. He set off on July 11 1991 from Japan at just about the worst time of year, in a 26-foot rowing boat, with 10,000km of empty ocean ahead of him.

D'Aboville rowed for up to 12 hours a day, and faced appalling weather with no hope of landfall – he recorded 12m waves and 150km/h winds. For two weeks he made no progress at all, pushed back by headwinds as fast as he could row forwards. Even worse, his boat capsized more than 30 times – once for almost two hours, with the oxygen running out fast, before he could right it.

But after 134 days, on December 21, he came into shore in Washington State, becoming the first person to row across the Pacific Ocean alone. As he said memorably afterwards, 'I didn't conquer the Pacific – it let me go across.'

Alain Bombard

As a young doctor in Boulogne sur Mer, Alain Bombard was on duty one night when the drowned bodies of 21 sailors were brought in. It got him thinking about how to survive a shipwreck, and in 1951 he tested his own resistance by swimming across the Channel.

The following year, at the age of 28, after studying sea-water at the Oceanography Institute in Monaco, he set off in an inflatable rubber dinghy to test his theory that you could survive at sea with no stored supplies. The 15-foot dinghy (an early model Zodiac) was fitted out with a small sail, a sextant, a plankton net, a fishing line and hooks, and a couple of harpoons – but no motor, no radio, no food and most importantly no fresh water.

An English friend, Jack Palmer, accompanied him during the first few weeks at sea, which took the couple as far as Tangiers, before jumping ship ('Enough plankton, Doctor!'). Bombard, meanwhile, set off down the Moroccan coast, and then cast off into the Atlantic from Casablanca, alone, on October 19 1952.

Guided only by the wind and the sea currents, Bombard lived on plankton and raw fish for three weeks, during which it didn't once rain. Rough seas constantly flooded his dinghy, and he had only his hat and shoes to bail with. Desperately enfeebled by sea-sickness and diarrhoea, he finally stopped a passing cargo ship, and accepted an egg, an apple and some vegetables – but refused to give up.

After 65 days alone at sea – and 113 days after leaving Monaco – Bombard washed up in Barbados on December 23, in a shocking state, and was promptly hospitalised. But he had survived, and proved that despair rather than physical deprivation is the real killer when you're lost at sea. Today, all ships carry life-rafts, and Zodiac has an entire Bombard range of inflatables – excellent even if you're not planning on a two-month diet of plankton, unprepared fish, and rainwater.

Didier Bovard

As a 32-year-old lorry driver and failed pro-footballer, Didier Bovard was cruising along the Swiss–French border in the cab of his truck in early 1995, when he heard that Guy Delage (see opposite) had just successfully swum the Atlantic.

Delage's exploit gave him a brilliant idea. Being a keen cyclist, and an even keener Elvis Presley fan, why not pedal from his home town of Evian, on the shores of Lake Geneva, to Memphis, home of the King? The overland parts could by cycled, and the Atlantic could be crossed … in a pedalo. Cool.

With no money to speak of, and no seafaring experience whatsoever, Bovard was off to a sticky start. But he's nothing if not persistent, and he set about building himself a customised pedalo called *My Way*. A boat-builder across the lake, on the Swiss shore, gave him some useful tips on how to make a pedalo self-righting and unsinkable, and Bovard got to work, hampered somewhat by being allergic to epoxy resin.

Towards the end of 1996, *My Way* was ready. The local media came to see the launch, and were impressed as Bovard demonstrated its speed and versatility – all in reverse, as the cranks had been set back to front. A quick fix, and Bovard was off, almost failing to make it as far as Geneva, down at the end of the lake.

From Geneva, with a friend towing *My Way* on a trailer, and Bovard sleeping in the pedalo at night, it was a fearsome and snowy 2,000km cycle ride over the Pyrenees to Cadiz, in Spain. Once there, Bovard made a series of attempted departures, and ended up badly shipwrecked and suffering from tendonitis. Even worse, the Spanish coastguard impounded *My Way*, and Bovard didn't have the resources to redeem it.

Indomitable, and after a series of further adventures, Bovard finally managed to set off from the Portuguese coast 18 months later, and after 27 days of hard pedalling, arrived in the Canary Islands. Except that until then, he hadn't realised he also suffered from terrible sea-sickness.

After a winter of yet more administrative and fiscal bother, Bovard pedalled off alone in *My Way* in February 1999, without even a radio, only to be plagued by El Niño. Half his daily progress was wiped out while resting at night, and it was to take him 117 days to reach the island of Guadeloupe, pedalling for an average of nine and a half hours a day. On arrival he was down to his last half packet of spaghetti. But he had made the first Atlantic crossing by pedal power alone – even if he had to be towed into harbour at the end.

Out of money, Bovard returned home to Evian, until in April 2001 he was able to continue the journey – except this time, resolved to make landfall under his own steam. He started from the Canaries again, and pedalled over to Martinique, covering over 5,000km in 88 days. Broke once more, he returned to France, determined nonetheless to make it to Memphis in time for the 25th anniversary of Presley's death in August 2002.

PEDALO SURVIVAL KIT

If you're planning an ocean-going pedalo journey, take Didier Bovard's advice and get seriously fit before you go. Onboard, take dehydrated food, fresh water (and a desalination pump and filter to generate more – count on needing 5–8 litres of water a day), a small medical kit and antibiotics, a CB radio and a GPS system, earplugs for the night, and flares (not bell-bottoms). You'll also need two buckets, one for washing and the other for your toilet – don't mix them up.

With new funds and a book about his earlier trips published at the beginning of 2002, Bovard set off to Martinique in February, with a new responsibility as a champion in the fight against Cystic Fibrosis. On April 7, after weeks of bad weather, he pedalled out of the Caribbean port, and arrived in America 76 days and 4,000km later, after enduring tropical heat, huge seas and violent storms. The hardest part was over.

Fit as a butcher's dog, Bovard took a mere nine days to cycle up to Memphis, where he promptly checked into the Heartbreak Hotel. He'd made it from Evian to Memphis, under pedal-power alone, in seven and a half years, arriving just one week before the big Elvis anniversary.

When I rang him up to congratulate him, back home in September 2002, he was over the moon – but coy about his next project, which would depend on sponsors, he said. Watch this space.

Peggy Bouchet

Like Didier Bovard (see above), Peggy Bouchet was born in Evian, on the shores of Lake Geneva. Unlike Didier, however, Peggy was all for the sea from an early age, and even made a career of it, studying maritime logistics first in Plymouth and then in Brest. Keen to be the first woman to row solo across the Atlantic, and finding herself living in rue d'Aboville in Brest, she contacted the famous oarsman – d'Aboville (see page 49) had been the first man to row solo across the Pacific. He agreed to help her plan her trip, and gave her useful hints and tips for the journey ahead ('Now, Peggy, you may find it rather lonely out there…').

In March 1998, aged only 23, she set off from the Canaries, and after an exemplary voyage lasting 79 days and covering nearly 5,000km, she found herself within 120km of Guadeloupe – only to capsize disastrously. It took 15 dives into the flooding hull of her upturned boat to recover emergency flares, and Peggy nearly drowned.

Fortunately, she did succeed in rowing solo across the Atlantic in January 2000 – though she was pipped for the title of the first woman in the world to do so by the American Tori Murden (who was also trained by d'Aboville), who sculled in the previous month, and by the British oarswoman Diana Hoff, who rowed into Barbados on the very same day that Peggy Bouchet arrived in Martinique.

Guy Delage

Impassioned by the sea as a child, Guy Delage went on to design, build and sail some of the world's fastest boats. In his early thirties he then trained as a microlight pilot and instructor, and in 1991 became the first person to fly a microlight across the South Atlantic, requiring him to stay awake for over 26 hours.

He then turned to swimming, and spent two years training for an attempt on the Atlantic. Setting off from Cape Verde in December 1994, just after his 42nd birthday, Delage was armed only with super-strength flippers, a revolutionary mask giving near-180 degree vision, and a 15ft raft with his supplies aboard.

For the first days in the water he was so sea-sick he could neither swim nor eat, but things improved rapidly, and he was soon putting in six and seven hour days in the water. After 26 days, however, he was attacked by a shark, and only narrowly repelled it. Three days later he was stung by a large jellyfish, and temporarily paralysed.

On January 21, after five weeks at sea, he had an especially bad day, when firstly one of his flippers broke, and secondly the lifeline connecting him to his raft snapped. You can imagine the sheer panic which dominated the two and a half hours it took him to recover the raft. But all was well, and three weeks later, on February 9 1995, he swam into Barbados, after 55 days in the water. He had swum (and drifted) a total of nearly 4,000km. For someone like me, who finds the local pool a bit of a challenge, it's an inconceivable achievement.

Benoit Lecomte

Three years after Delage's epic swim, a young pretender in the shape of Benoit Lecomte took up the challenge. Lecomte had emigrated from France to Texas at the age of 23, in 1990, but when his father died of cancer two years later he decided he should swim home to Europe.

For two years, under the supervision of the Human Performance Laboratory at the University of Texas, Lecomte trained hard, and effectively turned himself into a swimming machine.

In July 1998, he set off from Cape Cod, accompanied by a support boat and protected from dangerous fish by electronic shark repellent. Each day he swam for up to eight hours and fuelled himself with a diet amounting to between 7,000 and 8,000 calories.

After 73 days and 5,600km in (and on) the water, Lecomte waded ashore at Quiberon. His family were waiting for him, along with his girlfriend, who finally accepted his third proposal of marriage – the first had been made in Cape Cod and the second when he was half way through the swim.

Philippe Monnet

The champion sailor Philippe Monnet was born in the French Alps in 1959, but has spent much of his life on or near the sea. As a skipper he's absolutely fearsome, having broken several of the world's toughest records – sailing single-handedly around the world in 130 days in 1987, from New York to San Francisco in 81 days in 1989, and from Hong Kong to London in 67 days in 1990.

He's also a formidable sportsman off the water, being a keen skier, rider, skydiver and rally driver – with 11 titles under his belt, including the 1992 race from Paris to Cape Town, and the 1999 rally from Paris to Dakar. But the reason he's here (in this book) is for spending 152 days in the first half of the year 2000 single-handedly sailing backwards around the world.

The reverse route, against the prevailing currents and winds, is always notoriously difficult, and the previous record, set by the English sailor Mike Golding, had stood unchallenged since 1994.

By heading south to the Antarctic and braving the vast seas 70° south, Monnet knocked ten days off Golding's record time – though to do so he had to confront endless icebergs and hurricanes, deal with a bout of malaria, and (in his own words) 'live like an animal'. It takes all sorts.

All seven seafarers in this section are still alive (which makes a nice change). There's nothing special to do or see, but details of their books and websites appear in the Appendix: *Further Reading/References.*

ECCENTRIC MONTAGNARDS

There's clearly a strong human instinct to get to the top of whatever it is, but most of us sensibly resist it (unless there's a cable car, of course). Those who can't resist donning crampons and wielding ice-axes fall into two categories: the regular guys, and the true pioneers.

Jean-Marc Boivin – extreme sportsman

With hindsight it's pretty obvious that Jean-Marc Boivin wasn't ever destined for a pipe-and-slippers retirement. Born in Burgundy in 1951, he took to rock climbing as a teenager, and as soon as he'd left school he worked in menial jobs with the sole aim of taking two months a year off for mountaineering.

After completing his military service, in 1974, he added the brand-new sport of hang-gliding to his existing ice-climbing and extreme skiing, and also took up diving and sailing. He then trained as a ski instructor, high mountain guide, hang-gliding instructor and film maker, describing himself as an all-round professional adventurer.

In 1979, having already achieved a number of firsts in the descending-ridiculously-steep-ice-slopes-on-skis department, he claimed his first world record by climbing the world's second-highest mountain, K2 (8,613m) – and then jumping off from an altitude of 7,600m, suspended from his hang-glider.

During the next decade he became a pioneering parachutist, para-glider, and base-jumper – base-jumping being any parachute jump where you start off from the ground (BASE stands for Buildings, Antennas, Spans and Earth).

In 1988, he made the ultimate para-glide, by jumping off Mount Everest, breaking not only the para-gliding altitude record but also achieving the fastest descent – he was down in a breathtaking 12 minutes.

A year later, Boivin went to the world's tallest waterfalls, the Angel Falls (949m) in Venezuela, and made a base-jump off the top. But on 17 February 1990, while making a programme for French television, he made a jump too far. On trying to reach a fellow para-glider in trouble, in remote Venezuela, he crashed into a tree-top and suffered multiple fractures. When the helicopter rescue arrived he asked them to help the other para-glider pilot first. By the time they returned, Boivin was dead.

Apart form an impressive list of world records and first descents, there's not much to see or do relating to Jean-Marc Boivin, though if you ever get the chance to see any of his film footage, do – it's truly terrifying (I went to a lecture he gave in 1987, and resolved right there and then that extreme sports weren't for me. Not ever).

If you want to take up base-jumping, bear in mind it's illegal in the USA and most of Europe – though you can sign up to be one of the 300 or so people who get to base-jump during the annual 'Bridge Day' high jinks in Fayetteville, West Virginia. Register online at www.bridgeday.info.

Christine Janin – pole star

Christine Janin was born in 1957, and skied from infancy. She qualified as a doctor in 1982, and has dedicated her life since then to the marriage of medicine and mountaineering.

Janin's expeditions have been legendary. In 1981 she became the first Frenchwoman to reach 8,000m without oxygen, in 1987 she crossed the Himalayas on a mountain bike, and in 1988 she toured Baffin Island by kayak.

In 1990 she then became the first Frenchwoman to reach the summit of Mount Everest, and two years later was the first European to complete the 'Seven Summits' – the highest peaks on each continent (which are Everest, 8,848m; Vinson, 4,897m, Antarctica; McKinley, 6,194m, Alaska; Elbrus, 5,642m, Russia; Kilimanjaro, 5,895m, Africa; Carstensz, 4,884m, West Papua (Indonesia); Aconcagua, 6,962m, Argentina – since you ask).

In 1994, increasingly interested in the parallels between climbing mountains and making a full medical recovery, Janin created an association called *A Chacun son Everest* (Everest for Everyone – the name is a quote from the great mountaineer Maurice Herzog, who was the first person to climb Annapurna, in 1950).

The association takes children and teenagers with cancer, or in remission, out for a week in the mountains, ending in a summit, and has been a huge success – more than a thousand patients from 15 hospitals have participated so far, and the association now has its own centre in Chamonix.

In 1997, Janin spent 62 days on skis with her Russian partner Serguei Ogorodnikov, travelling more than 1,000km overland from Siberia, and becoming the first woman ever to reach the North Pole unassisted. Nine children were helicoptered up from hospital to the ice-floe, to celebrate the occasion.

Christine Janin has a number of books out in French, but you can do much more by supporting her excellent association. Send donations to *A Chacun son Everest*, BP 101, F-74941, Annecy-le-Vieux Cedex, France – bank account number: CCP 3.147.35L (Grenoble). There's a good website (French only) at www.achacunsoneverest.com.

Mont Blanc – the first ascents

Mont Blanc, dominating the Chamonix Valley and straddling the border between France and Italy, isn't the hardest mountain to climb in western Europe, but it is the tallest – and that's always a challenge.

Until 1760, however, nobody seems to have thought of making the attempt. It wasn't until the 20-year-old Horace Bénédict de Saussure (see opposite), the Geneva naturalist, offered a 'considerable reward', that people started thinking about the climb. Even then, the first attempts weren't made until 1775, and de Saussure would be nearly 50 by the time he actually saw the summit.

The race to be first up was dominated by three men: Marc-Théodore Bourrit (1739–1819), the choirmaster of Geneva cathedral, and a notoriously unlucky (indeed cowardly) mountaineer, Jacques Balmat (1762–1834), a somewhat reckless mountain guide, crystal gatherer, and chamois hunter, and Michel-Gabriel Paccard (1757–1827), a Chamonix doctor.

In 1775, Paccard (aged only 18) made the first serious attempt on Mont Blanc, in the unlikely company of the famous Scottish landscape gardener Thomas Blaikie (see page 62). They reached the Grands Mulets, at 3,000m, and then had to turn back.

It was to be eight years before the next endeavour, which featured Paccard – now a qualified doctor – and Marc-Théodore Bourrit, along with local guides. Bad weather, however, prevailed. The following year, a party of hunters reached the summit of the Aiguille du Goûter, at over 3,800m, and Paccard and two guides made yet another failed attempt.

In 1785, de Saussure and Bourrit, along with a team of 16 guides, reached the summit of the Aiguille du Goûter, but had to turn back because of abundant fresh snowfalls. The same year saw the appearance of Jacques Balmat, who made it up to the 4,000m Grand Plateau on his own. The 4,800m summit was almost within reach.

The following June, two parties of guides – featuring members of both the Paccard and Balmat families – found two different routes up to the Dôme du Goûter, at 4,300m. Following some way behind, alone, was Jacques Balmat, who continued onwards after the others started descending. As a result he was caught by nightfall, and had to camp in a crevasse, thereby becoming the first known person to bivouac out on the glacier. The following day, frozen half to death, he popped into Paccard's surgery for a bit of warmth, and the two men were quick to see the advantages of forming a partnership.

As a result Balmat and Paccard slipped quietly out of Chamonix in perfect conditions on August 7 1786, and bivouacked under a full moon. At 4am the following morning they set out, and 14 hours and 23 minutes later they arrived at

HORACE BÉNÉDICT DE SAUSSURE AND THE HAIRY HYGROMETER

Born into the Geneva aristocracy in 1740, Horace Bénédict de Saussure showed early academic promise, and had already graduated at the age of 19. By 22, he was Professor of Physics and Philosophy at Geneva University, a post which gave him plenty of opportunity for primary research, and which he held until 1788.

In 1760, de Saussure went to Chamonix for the first time, and offered a bounty (not the chocolate and coconut bar) to anyone who could find a route to the summit of Mont Blanc. Meanwhile he pursued his groundbreaking research in the fields of mineralogy and geology (which actually does involve ground-breaking), as well as botany and meteorology. He even introduced the term geology into the language.

In 1783, he invented the hygrometer, an instrument to measure humidity. The essential ingredient was human hair, which de Saussure noticed contracts in dry weather and grows longer when it's damp. The following year he travelled over to Lyon, to see the Montgolfiers (see page 34) demonstrate their new travel sensation, the hot air balloon. Disappearing into the smoky interior, he insisted on staying inside the balloon as it was inflated, to take measurements.

A year later, at the age of 45, he came very close – with Bourrit (see facing page) to being the first person to climb Mont Blanc, but finally had to settle for third place, after Balmat and Paccard took the prize in 1786. He was however the very first of several thousand tourists to arrive at the summit.

the summit, exhausted. Just 34 minutes later they started heading downhill for the return journey.

The truth of how the ascent really went, and whether it was Balmat or Paccard who made the running, will probably never be known. Paccard's account of the marvellous exploit was never published, as Bourrit sprang straight to the offensive, claiming it was Balmat who deserved the glory, and not Paccard – in what may well have been nothing more than a particularly bad attack of sour grapes.

In spite of Bourrit's writings being (according to the 1911 *Encyclopaedia Britannica*, anyway) 'naïve, sentimental and rather pompous', he nonetheless swayed the public opinion of the day. The anti-Paccard feeling was only reinforced when Alexandre Dumas interviewed Balmat in 1832 – by which time Paccard had already been dead for five years and was in no position to defend himself.

As soon as Paccard and Balmat had come down from the top of Mont Blanc's first ascent, Balmat nipped down to Geneva to claim the reward from de Saussure. The naturalist was keen to scale the mountain himself, however, so rushed back with Balmat to Chamonix, but the weather had closed in, and they had to wait until the following year.

On July 5 1787, Balmat climbed Mont Blanc a second time, with two other guides, before the great expedition which went up on 3 August, comprising de Saussure, his manservant, and no fewer than 18 guides. They spent more than four hours on the summit. After another ascent that year and one in 1788, it was to be 14 years before Mont Blanc was climbed again.

In 1808, a local girl from Chamonix, Maria Paradis, became the first woman to reach the top, while in 1851, the English comedian, Albert Smith, and his party,

ANNE LISTER

If she hadn't written an enormous diary (four million words or so), and if that diary hadn't been coded to keep her lesbian relationships secret, Anne Lister would probably have sunk into obscurity as just another 19th-century lady landowner.

But her diaries were discovered, and deciphered, and revealed a woman who was way ahead of her time. Born in 1791, she inherited a sizeable property, Shibden Hall, near Halifax, when her younger brother died in a boating accident in 1813 (or is that boating 'accident'?). She turned out to be an excellent estate manager, and was a keen horsewoman and a good shot. The locals – although presumably not to her face – referred to her as 'Gentleman Jack'.

After a series of moderately scandalous liaisons in the 1820s, Anne settled down with the heiress next door, Ann Walker, and they merged their equally prosperous estates. They even had a marriage ceremony, apparently, in a church in York in 1834.

Lister and Walker travelled widely across Europe together, living in Paris for a while, and found themselves in the Pyrenees in the summer of 1838. What could be more obvious, then, for a 19th-century English lesbian couple in their late forties, than a successful summit attempt on the highest mountain in the French Pyrenees, Vignemale?

Two years later, in 1839, the couple went on a journey to Russia, and Anne contracted the fever there which was to be the unexpected death of her, the following year, at the age of 49. She was initially buried in Moscow, but was re-interred in Halifax Parish Church the following year.

Anne Lister's diaries have been published in various formats by various publishers – and even though they came out only in 1988, they're nonetheless easiest to find secondhand.

took 115 bottles of wine with them up Mont Blanc and scarfed the lot. He went back to London a happy man, and spent the next few years talking nightly at London's Egyptian Hall about his feat, backed up with a series of tableaux showing the somewhat drunken ascent.

Jacques Balmat, for his part, became a gold prospector, and Chamonix valley lore still holds that he discovered a serious trove. He died mysteriously, it's said, while deep in the mountains, perhaps at the hands of someone who knew too much (although to be fair, he was in his early seventies). There's no-one left to ask in Chamonix, however, as his family sold up after his death and emigrated to America.

There aren't many firsts left in the Chamonix valley, but it's still a major experience to climb up Mont Blanc, even though people have been doing so for more than two centuries. If you do want to go, however, a few words of warning: be fit, be prepared, and hire a professional guide. The Mont Blanc massif kills plenty of people every year, and you really don't want to be one of them.

For more information on the valley as a whole, check out the official website at www.chamonix.com, or go straight to www.ohm-chamonix.com, the site of the Office de Haute Montagne. And if you do get to the top, you'll be higher up than Balmat, Paccard or de Saussure ever were – Mont Blanc was a mere 4,807m tall back then, but these days, according to the latest GPS measurements, it's a whopping 4,810m and 40cm, give or take a bit.

In the middle of Chamonix itself you can't miss the statue of Balmat and de Saussure. Poor old Paccard doesn't even get a look in.

Count Henry Russell

Count Henry Russell was a great Pyrenean pioneer in the second half of the 19th century, and a wonderful eccentric to boot. He was born in 1834 in Toulouse, of a noble Irish father and a French mother. After exploring the Pyrenees as a teenager, he set off on a long voyage to America in 1857, at the age of 23, but the following summer discovered mountaineering, his true passion, and climbed the highest peak in the Pyrenees, le Mont Perdu (3,355m), three times, once solo.

The following year, however, he was off on his travels once more, and didn't return home until 1861. In the intervening two years he covered an astonishing 65,000km, from St Petersburg, Moscow and Siberia, to Peking (crossing the Gobi Desert twice), and on to Shanghai, Hong Kong, Melbourne and Wellington. He returned to Europe from New Zealand via Calcutta, Ceylon, Cairo and Constantinople (apparently eschewing anywhere which didn't begin with the letter 'C').

In September 1861, Russell made his first ascent of Vignemale (3,298m), the highest mountain on the French side of the Pyrenees, and he dedicated the rest of his life to exploring the area. Although he went on to be the first to summit more than thirty Pyrenean peaks, Russell was far from the first to climb Vignemale. That honour had gone in 1837 to two local guides, with the first recorded tourist ascent coming a year later, when Miss Anne Lister (see opposite), a 'spinster from Halifax', made it to the top.

In spite of all the other mountains he climbed, Vignemale became Russell's obsession, and he made a total of 33 ascents to the summit, the last one at the age of 70. During the winters he was a bastion of Pau society, but the moment summer arrived he was off up into the mountains. Unable to access the deeper reaches of the Pyrenees on a single-day hike, he started bivouacking at altitude, using a lambs-wool sleeping bag, but soon realised a more durable solution was needed.

Unwilling to deface his beloved mountains with mountain huts, he decided instead to dig grottoes into the mountainside. The first (called the Villa Russell, naturally) was completed in 1882, and followed by the Grotte des Guides in 1885 and the Grotte des Dames in 1886. By 1893, there were a total of seven, one of which, up on the Glacier d'Ossoue, became Russell's summer home. He would entertain lavishly there, inviting princes and kings for splendid dinner parties, and laying out a red carpet on the ice.

At the end of 1888, Russell managed to persuade the local *préfet* to lease him the summit of Vignemale, along with the 200ha of ice and rock surrounding it, for 99 years, for the princely sum of one franc per year. He built a three-metre cairn on the top, to break the symbolic 3,000m barrier, and spent his summers on the mountain until his death, in 1909.

There's lots of Russell trivia around Vignemale, his beloved mountain, including the Russell refuge, and several local peaks feature his name, the ultimate accolade for a mountaineer. Outside the village of Gavarnie – the traditional starting point for ascents of Vignemale – there's also a fine bronze statue of Russell. The one you see here today is a 1952 replica; the original, put in place in 1911, was requisitioned during World War I to make gun barrels.

Russell wrote a dozen books, including *Souvenirs d'un Montagnard*, and *Seize Mille Lieues à Travers l'Asie et l'Océanie*, though they're in French only, and devilishly hard to find.

ECCENTRIC SCIENTISTS

There's a lot of leeway for eccentricity in science, from the opportunity to invent madcap propeller-driven vehicles to diverting your knowledge of industrial chemistry into your home-made wine production. If that's not enough, how about inventing experiments to make monks leap in the air?

Marie Curie

Born in Warsaw in 1867, to parents who were both respected teachers, Marya Sklodowska was a brilliant pupil herself, but financial constraints meant she ended up working for seven years as a governess, so her sister could study medicine in Paris.

In 1891, at the age of 24, it was her turn, and she set off for the Sorbonne, enrolling for a physics degree under the name of Marie. For four years she studied hard and lived a miserably poor existence, unable even to heat her room. But she earned her degree (and one in mathematics, for good measure), and in 1895 met and married Pierre Curie, a young French physicist.

The next decade was to be the most eventful and perhaps the happiest of her life. She and Pierre worked together from 1897 with Henri Becquerel, who was studying X-rays, and Marie pursued a doctorate in physics – unheard of for women at the time. While doing so, she discovered polonium (named in honour of her native Poland) and then radium, and coined a new term, dubbing the new elements 'radioactive'.

In 1903, Becquerel and the Curies were awarded the Nobel Prize for Physics, but neither Pierre nor Marie felt well enough to make the journey to Stockholm – both were already ill from radiation poisoning, though the sickness wasn't yet known as such.

The Nobel Prize brought them huge fame, but the Curies stayed poor, refusing to patent the process only they knew about, for producing radium, which was suddenly in huge demand. Curie-therapy, as it was then called, became the treatment of choice for cancerous tumours, and the French government created a special facility for the Curies, the Radium Institute.

In 1906, however, weakened and exhausted by radiation poisoning (and probably feeling delirious), Pierre Curie stepped into the path of an oncoming horse-drawn wagon, and was instantly trampled to death. Marie then became the first woman professor at the Sorbonne, and ran the Radium Institute, but also had to take charge of an ageing father and her two small daughters. Undaunted, she went on to win a second Nobel Prize (the first person to do so), this time in Chemistry, for the discovery and isolation of radium.

During World War I, Marie and her daughter Irène travelled along the front, teaching doctors how to use mobile X-ray vans, and installing X-ray equipment in hospitals. For the rest of her life she ran the institute tirelessly, although suffering increasingly from the results of massive overdoses of radiation. She died in 1934, at the age of 67.

Her daughter Iréne married Frédéric Joliot, and the couple continued the Curies' work at the institute, earning a Nobel Prize for themselves in 1935 for the discovery of artificial radiation. But Iréne, like her mother, was also fatally irradiated, and died of leukaemia at the age of 59.

In 1995 (better late than never) the ashes of Pierre and Marie Curie were transferred to the Panthéon in Paris, making Marie the only woman to be buried there on her own merits. (The other woman in the Panthéon is Sophie Berthelot, who only snuck in by dint of being married to the famous chemist and politician Marcellin Berthelot. Curiously enough, under the inscription to Sophie is one to the physicist Paul Langevin, who had a scandalous fling with Marie Curie in 1911. It can't be a coincidence.)

One of the most interesting little museums in Paris is the **Musée Curie** situated just a couple of blocks away from the Panthéon, where Marie and Pierre are buried. The museum was created from Marie Curie's original laboratory and office in 1964, but was only decontaminated in 1981, and then opened to the public in 1996. It's a touching place, all porcelain, enamel, wood, glass and brass, with neat handwritten labels on jars and vials in the laboratory, and a solid desk, old-style telephone and battered leather chair in the office.

The Curies also found fame in the 1990s on the last French 500 franc note, before being disenfranchised (like St Exupéry on the 50 franc note) by the introduction of the euro in 2002.

Marcel Leyat

Not a great deal is known about the engineer and inventor Marcel Leyat, but he well deserves a place in this book for inventing one of the most preposterous road vehicles known to man, the Leyat Helicycle.

The principle is an ingenious (if, frankly, ridiculous) one: take an early aeroplane (the first Helicycle prototype was built in 1914), lop off the wings and tail, don a flying cap and goggles, and then drive like the clappers down the public highway.

The first models were tricycles, with a big engine, an enormous wooden propeller and a pair of wheels at the front, but only a single wheel at the back. It was notoriously unstable and accident prone, but amazingly fast. Leyat added stability and a certain amount of respectability to the ludicrous vehicle by turning it into a four-wheeler, and it went into production in 1919. By the time it was decommissioned, in 1925, a total of only 30 had been built.

It was a spectacular failure. In spite of the Helicycle's ability to accelerate rapidly up to speeds of 70km/h or more, the wind generated straight into the driver's face meant it simply had no future. An interesting diversion nonetheless.

There's an original Leyat Helicycle (l'Hélica) on permanent display in Paris at the **CNAM** (Conservatoire Nationale des Arts et Métiers). It's on one of the metal ramps leading up to the actual monoplane Blériot used on the first Channel crossing.

Luberon Lubrication

My godparents, Jenna and Richard, bought a house in Provence in 1980 – though it wasn't so much of a house then as an uninhabitable ruin. But it had potential, and it had land. More importantly, it had vineyards.

The first season's *recolte*, once bottled, matured and tasted, turned out to be just filthy. The whole lot went down the drain. Fortunately, however, Richard's not just an indomitable spirit, he's also an industrial chemist. While Jenna got on with sorting out the house – the novelty of going up the hillside with a bucket and spade instead of nipping into the en-suite had soon worn off – Richard experimented with his wine.

The Côtes de Luberon began to improve. Guests no longer politely wrinkled their noses and pushed their wineglasses away, with a muttered '*très intéressant*' as the latest batch was uncorked. Given authority not just by his steadily improving wine, but by his chemist's credentials, Richard even became something of a local wine oracle.

Worries in the early 1990s that the wine would become too commercial – and might need (heaven forbid) to be regulated, labelled or even taxed – proved unfounded, and the production these days just about matches the consumption.

In spite of property prices which have gone through the roof (since the 1989 publication of Peter Mayle's *A Year in Provence*), and most of the neighbours now being Belgians, Dutch, Austrians, Germans and Americans (*Gladiator* director Ridley Scott has an enormous place a few miles away), the essence of the place remains unchanged – especially after a couple of bottles of Richard's wine.

The peace and quiet of a summer evening is still remarkable in Provence, with just the upper branches of the great chestnut tree creaking in the tail-end of the evening breeze to disturb the silence. That, and the hornet-like buzzing of the local lads burning up and down the road on their defiantly un-silenced mopeds.

Jean-Antoine Nollet

Jean-Antoine Nollet was an abbot as well as being one of the finest physicists of the 18th century. Born in 1700, he was the inventor of an early electrometer called the electroscope, which measured electric charge, and was the author of many important scientific papers, describing processes as arcane as electrostatics and osmosis. He was also a member of London's Royal Society, and went on to become a famous physics teacher and lecturer (he taught the Duke of Savoy, in Turin, and the king's children in Versailles), as well as inventing presses, fire-pumps and testing and measuring instruments.

But it's Abbé Nollet's work with electricity which brings him on to these pages, and in particular two marvellous experiments he performed in 1746. In the first, he persuaded 180 Royal Guards to hold hands ('No, go on, it'll be a bit of fun'), and then discharged a powerful Leyden jar (an early battery, or capacitor) through the whole parade, in front of King Louis XV. Not surprisingly, all 180 soldiers leaped into the air at once, proving Nollet's theory about the rapid speed of electricity.

The king was delighted, and ordered a repeat of the experiment in Paris. This time (and why not?) Nollet used 200 Carthusian monks in white robes, strung out in a line more than a kilometre long, and connected them to each other with 25-foot iron wires. True to form, when the Leyden jar was discharged, all the monks jumped in unison. Marvellous!

(In an interesting aside, the old Nollet gag was still being practised more than two centuries later in some English schools, according to a friend who was at Tavistock Comprehensive in the 1980s. She was one of the unamused subjects in the hilarious copycat experiment, though she really ought to be grateful for not having being made to dress up as a Carthusian monk – or indeed a Royal Guard – as well.)

Blaise Pascal

Blaise Pascal, mathematical genius and religious philosopher, was born in Clermont Ferrand in 1623. His mother died while he was still a small boy, and his father brought him and his sisters up to Paris, largely to encourage Blaise's prodigious intellect, already apparent at eight years old.

By the age of 12, he was working on geometrical proofs, and at 16 he wrote a prolonged essay on conic sections. Two years later he invented the world's first calculator, an arithmetic machine originally intended to help his father, who was now the tax collector in Rouen. It took four years and more than 50 designs before he perfected the eight-column machine, which he charmingly called the *Pascaline*, and eventually some 50 or so were produced and sold. It wasn't a huge commercial success, however, largely because it cost more to produce the calculator than to pay the mathematicians it was built to replace. (It would be another 300 years before calculators would really become commercially viable.)

Pascal moved on to natural sciences, and his studies of hydrostatics soon led to his inventing both the syringe and the hydraulic press. Meanwhile his experiments with barometers proved they could indeed be used as altimeters, given that the mercury changed with altitude as well as with changes in the weather.

Continuing to suffer from the poor health which had afflicted him since childhood – and which was exacerbated by over-taxing his brain – Pascal took the advice of friends and settled briefly into a more frivolous existence in Paris, studying gambling and working out the odds at various games of chance. As a result he used his newly developed probability theories to prove that it's rational to believe in God.

Pascal's Wager runs like this: If you bet on God, and he exists, then you have infinite gain; if you bet on God and he doesn't exist, then there's no loss; if you bet against God, and he exists, then you have infinite loss; and if you bet against God and he doesn't exist, then you neither win nor lose. Put more simply, if God exists and you don't believe, then you've had it, whereas if he doesn't exist and you do believe, then there's no harm done.

Pascal's next stroke of genius was to invent Pascal's Triangle, for working out the odds in gambling. Each row in the triangle is calculated by adding up the numbers above it (the first row is 1; the second 1, 1; the third 1, 2, 1; the fourth 1, 3, 3, 1; the fifth 1, 4, 6, 4, 1; etc), and it's a remarkably versatile tool, having uses far beyond gambling, in statistics, higher mathematics and physics.

After a dramatic accident on the Pont de Neuilly in 1654, where the horses pulling his carriage plunged off the parapet to their deaths (Pascal was only saved when the traces broke) he retired from the world and took to religion, joining an order of Jansenists. For the rest of his life he carried a parchment account of the near-fatal accident next to his heart. He also took to wearing a cincture of nails around his waist, to mortify himself further.

He only produced one further bit of maths, a devastating essay on the geometry of the cycloid (whatever that is), but he also wrote a marvellously fragmented book, called *Pensées*, which does nothing more nor less than 'contemplate the greatness and the misery of man'. By this time, however, he was sick and exhausted, increasingly dyspeptic, and probably suffering from cancer. In 1662 he finally expired at the age of only 39.

(A personal favourite from *Pensées* is his pre-existentialist paean: 'When I consider the short duration of my life, swallowed up in the eternity before and after, the little space I fill, and even can see, engulfed in the infinite immensity of space of which I am ignorant, and which knows me not, I am frightened, and am astonished at being here rather than there, why now rather than then.')

When it finally re-opens as the **Musée Blaise Pascal**, you'll be able to see a fine pair of Blaise Pascal's *Pascaline* calculators at the former **Musée Ranquet**, housed in one of Clermont Ferrand's finest renaissance palaces. Don't hold your breath, however, as restoration work still hadn't got underway at the time of writing.

ECCENTRIC ENGINEERS

Engineers on the whole are a sober bunch, more concerned with stress- and strain-ratios than making their mark as eccentrics, but cast the net a little wider and you can haul in Scottish gardeners who won't learn French, people who dedicated their whole lives to Chunneling, and influential architects who were let loose on the *patrimoine national.*

Thomas Blaikie

Thomas Blaikie, the Scottish landscape gardener, lived most of his life in France. Born in 1751, near Edinburgh, he was sent off to the Alps in April 1775 by two doctors, in order to look for Alpine plants for their botanical gardens. He was never to return. At the beginning of September, he spent six days in the Chamonix mountains with the 18-year-old Michel-Gabriel Paccard (see page 54), in a joint attempt to be the first to climb Mont Blanc, Western Europe's highest mountain (an ascent eventually achieved by Paccard 11 years later).

Blaikie next shows up in Paris the following year, as gardener to the Comte de Lauraguais, after which he entered the service of King Louis XVI's brother, the Comte d'Artois (who would much later become King Charles X). As a result he got caught up in a bet between d'Artois and Marie-Antoinette (see page 87) that a mansion fit for royalty in the Bois de Boulogne couldn't be built in two months.

By the expedient of recruiting 900 workers and requisitioning incoming convoys of stone to the capital, the Comte won his bet, and the Bagatelle (a *mere* bagatelle, apparently) was finished in November 1777. Blaikie was commissioned to landscape the gardens, but he wasn't one for a rush job, spinning out the work until 1784.

Blaikie became the gardener of choice for the French aristocracy, renovating the Parc Monceau, and becoming a confidante of Marie-Antoinette, who apparently found his Scottish directness charming. The French Revolution, however, was just around the corner, and Blaikie found himself out of a job – but luckily enough kept his head. The closing entry for his diaries, published in the 1930s, is a first-hand account of the bloody massacre of the Swiss Guards, on August 10 1792.

In spite of being out of business, Blaikie seems to have made a remarkable recovery, and by 1800 was landscaping the vast gardens at Malmaison for Napoleon's first wife Josephine (see page 90). He went on to work for Napoleon's favourite marshal, Marshal Ney, and lived to the age of 87, dying only in 1838. It's said that during more than 60 years on the continent, he never mastered the French language.

The only work of Thomas Blaikie's still visitable is the **Bagatelle**, in the Bois de Boulogne, just outside Paris – though what you see today owes as much to the expansion and replanting of the gardens in 1835 as to Blaikie's original work.

Chunnelers

Ever since France and Britain were separated by the English Channel (or *La Manche*, as the French prefer to call it), 13,000 years ago, people have dreamed of ways of reuniting the two countries. It wasn't until 1751, however – when the French engineer Nicolas Desmaret came up with a totally impracticable plan for a tunnel – that anyone started taking the idea even remotely seriously.

Albert Mathieu-Favier

Half a century later, it was Albert Mathieu-Favier's turn to come up with a scheme for a tunnel, which might almost have worked.

Mathieu-Favier's concept was an ingenious one. Firstly, the Varne Bank, in the middle of the Channel, would be built up into an island, allowing for a place where you could change horses (and presumably stop for a cheeseburger and a pint). The tunnel itself would then be built, with an upper  level for stagecoaches and a lower one for the inevitable seepage, which would be continuously pumped out. Lighting would be provided by regularly spaced oil lamps, and ventilation by chimneys up to the surface of the Channel.

In 1802, Mathieu-Favier showed his plans to Napoleon, who was apparently keen to go ahead. Unfortunately, France then spoiled things by going to war with England for the next decade or so, and the plans were shelved.

Aimé Thomé de Gamond

The civil engineer Jean-Pierre Louis-Joseph-Aimé Thomé de Gamond (Aimé Thomé de Gamond for short) was next up. Over a 34-year period in the middle of the 19th century he proposed any number of schemes, from a submerged tube-tunnel to a fixed bridge, to a pontoon. He even suggested filling in the Channel altogether to create a land isthmus.

In his early forties, in 1851, Thomé de Gamond finally came up with the more realistic proposal of a rail tunnel, strangely enough situated pretty much exactly where today's tunnel lies. Like Mathieu-Favier, he reckoned an artificial island would be needed mid-Channel for the relief of sooty passengers, and even planned a hotel there for overnighters. But he also added another 12 islands for good measure, to provide stable air supplies, and to allow for the tunnel to be flooded if England and France were ever to go to war.

Realising that much more would need to be known about the geology of the sea bed before a tunnel could be built, Thomé de Gamond spent years taking soundings from an open boat, and even did some dangerously unaccompanied dives to the sea bed, over 30m below the surface, with neither suit nor oxygen tank to help him.

In 1856, he took his proposal to Emperor Napoleon III, who – like his uncle Napoleon I before him – was keen on the concept, and agreed to set up a commission to evaluate its viability. The commission reported favourably, but raised the inevitable question about relations with Britain, so Thomé de Gamond went on a roadshow to the UK to canvass support. Isambard Kingdom Brunel was all in favour, having successfully put a tunnel under the Thames, and Queen Victoria – notorious for her sea-sickness – was ecstatic. But Lord Palmerston, the

Prime Minister, is reported to have said 'What? You wish to make us contribute towards a scheme, the purpose of which is to reduce the distance we find already too short!'. (Palmerston would clearly have been right at home amongst the Eurosceptics.)

Plans came grinding to a halt once again, however, in 1858, when there was an assassination attempt on Napoleon III (one charming web resource refers to it as an 'assignation attempt' – then again, the Napoleons always were an evasive family). But the ball was now rolling, albeit slowly, and in 1867 a plan backed by a number of key players (William Gladstone, Prince Albert, and others) and favoured by many engineers of the day was put forward and accepted in principle by parliament.

The Channel Tunnel Company

In 1872 the Channel Tunnel Company was formed with the intention of building a pair of parallel rail tunnels, and in 1880 digging finally got underway. By the end of 1882, 1,839m of tunnel had been dug from the French side, and 1,883m had been dug from the English side. But the following year work was suspended on the orders of the British government, and the tunnels and outbuildings fell into disrepair (though Hubert Latham was to use the property at Sangatte, at the French end, as a base for his cross-Channel flight attempts in 1909, see page 41).

In 1917, the original unlined tunnels began to flood, the suspected cause being the enormous shock wave resulting from setting off mines under the German trenches at Ypres. In 1924, the subject came up for discussion once again when five former British prime ministers met to discuss the tunnel – only to vote unanimously to oppose it.

By 1955, however, the government had changed its tune, renouncing its opposition, and just thirty years later tenders were sent out to potential bidders. Eurotunnel, a project based on twin rail tunnels, won the contest, and in 1994 the Channel Tunnel finally opened for business – only two years late.

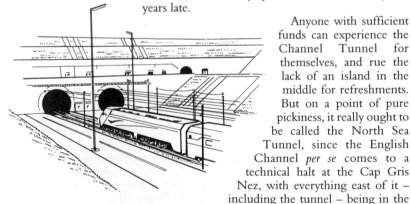

Anyone with sufficient funds can experience the Channel Tunnel for themselves, and rue the lack of an island in the middle for refreshments. But on a point of pure pickiness, it really ought to be called the North Sea Tunnel, since the English Channel *per se* comes to a technical halt at the Cap Gris Nez, with everything east of it – including the tunnel – being in the North Sea.

Viollet le Duc

Eugène Emmanuel Viollet le Duc was the greatest French architect and expert on architecture and archaeology in the 19th century, and being a close pal of the emperor, Napoleon III, was given a free rein in restoring some of France's most famous treasures, including Sainte Chapelle, Vézelay Abbey, Notre Dame, Amiens, Chartres, Laon and Reims cathedrals, and the citadel at Carcassonne.

Over a 20-year period he wrote (and beautifully hand-illustrated) two of the most influential works in architecture: the ten-volume *Dictionnaire Raisonné de l'Architecture Française du XI au XVI Siècle* (Dictionary of French Architecture from the 11th to 16th Centuries, 1854–69) and the *Dictionnaire Raisonné du Mobilier Français de l'Epoque Carolingienne à la Renaissance* (Dictionary of French Furnishings, 1858–70).

As the leading exponent of the Gothic revival and the most famous architect of his day, Viollet le Duc was at the heart of a fierce debate on what it meant to actually 'restore' monuments. His feeling was that buildings didn't necessarily need to look like they may have looked at any one time, but that they should end up, post-restoration, with a 'unity of style'. In England, however, Viollet le Duc was attacked by the art critic John Ruskin and the writer William Morris, among others, who believed in protection rather than restoration.

While Viollet le Duc's approach was doubtless marvellously successful in some cases (Chartres and Laon cathedrals spring particularly to mind), in others it was disastrous. The ancient citadel at Carcassonne, which had fallen into disrepair, was pretty much entirely rebuilt by Viollet le Duc, largely as a product of his fertile imagination rather than as any kind of historical reconstruction. Even more drastic is the medieval fantasy he fabricated for Napoleon III in the shape of the Château de Pierrefonds. Which is not to say that both Carcassonne and Pierrefonds aren't worth visiting. They are – just as long as you don't think you're seeing anything medieval.

ECCENTRICS IN A CLASS OF THEIR OWN

Some people simply won't be categorised – whether they dedicate their lives to the homeless or to the emancipation (or liberation) of garden gnomes, spend their time running ultra-marathons, or stand up for the small farmer in the face of agri-business.

L'Abbé Pierre

L'Abbé Pierre, with his distinctive beret, cape, walking stick, spectacles and white beard, is one of the best known and most popular figures in France.

Born Henri-Antoine Groués in Lyon in 1912, he became a Capuchin monk at the age of 18, taking the name Brother Philippe. In 1938 he was ordained and went to work in Grenoble, just as the war was breaking out, and from 1942 to 1944 he was a pillar of the French Resistance. He helped Jewish families across the border into Switzerland, and was given the codename which has stuck ever since, l'Abbé Pierre.

In May 1944, after being denounced, he was arrested by the Gestapo, but was fortunately able to escape the following month, and managed to join General de Gaulle in Algeria. By the end of the war he was serving as a naval chaplain, and when peace broke out, de Gaulle asked him to stand for parliament. Even though he was anti-Gaullist, l'Abbé Pierre agreed, and from 1945 he represented the mining constituency of Meurthe et Moselle.

Increasingly preoccupied with the plight of the poor and the homeless, he set up an international youth hostel in his own presbytery, in Neuilly, just outside Paris, called the Auberge de Jeunesse Internationale Emmaus. (The name comes from Luke 24:13, where the resurrected Jesus first reappears to the disciples: 'And, behold, two of them went that same day to a village called Emmaus, which was from Jerusalem about threescore furlongs.')

By 1949, there were 18 homeless men living at the presbytery, and l'Abbé Pierre was spending his entire salary on war-surplus materials, so that shelters could be built in the garden. The result was the first Emmaus community, which soon became self-supporting, via the sale of recycled and refurbished goods.

With new Emmaus communities springing up, l'Abbé Pierre resigned his parliamentary seat in 1951, and became an early media activist, badgering the government incessantly in his crusade to provide adequate housing for all. During the exceptionally harsh winter of 1954, he asked the government for a billion (old) francs for urgently needed housing, and was turned down. But three weeks later – after a media blitz – parliament universally approved not one billion francs but ten, for the construction of 12,000 emergency lodgings for the poor. L'Abbé Pierre then became the driving force behind France's excellent council housing programme, the HLMs (*Habitiations à Loyer Modéré*).

For the past 50 years, l'Abbé Pierre, in spite of increasing old age and failing health, has continued to campaign ceaselessly, and in 2001 was made a *Grand Officier de la Légion d'Honneur.*

Since its foundation in 1949, Emmaus has grown to comprise more than 100 communities in over 40 countries, operating under the basic credo of helping the homeless to help themselves. For the most part Emmaus is self-sufficient, though some international public funding is involved in the start-up of new communities.

For a pretty good dramatisation of the events of the winter of 1954, look no further than the 1989 biopic *Un Hiver 54*, staring Lambert Wilson as l'Abbé Pierre.

José Bové

Right up with l'Abbé Pierre in terms of popularity in France, though in a completely different line of work, is the farmer and activist José Bové. With his trademark moustache and pipe, and his championing of the little guy against agro-industrial giants, most French people are sympathetic to his causes, and speak of his jail sentences with regret.

Bové was born in Bordeaux in 1953, the son of two university researchers, and as a child he followed them to Paris and then on to Berkeley, California (to which he owes his impeccable English).

Back in France in 1972, he refused to do his military service, and in 1973 found himself caught up in a local battle to prevent the extension of a military base on the beautiful Plateau de Larzac, near Millau. As part of a back-to-the-land movement, Bové and his wife started farming sheep on the edge of the plateau, and making Roquefort cheese (see page 181). Eight years later, in 1981, the farmers won their case against the army.

Six years on, in 1987, Bové co-founded *La Confédération Paysanne* (The Peasant Confederation), a radical farmers' union dedicated to protecting the interests of small farmers, local produce and good food against the increasing industrialisation of agri-business. But it wasn't until 1999, when Bové and his supporters took apart a McDonald's burger joint under construction in Millau that he really hit the international headlines – in spite of having already organised the ploughing of the Champ de Mars, underneath the Eiffel Tower, in 1988, in protest against the EU's Common Agricultural Policy.

Millau's McDonald's was targeted as a protest against the USA putting huge tariffs on Roquefort, in response to France refusing to import hormone-treated beef. As a result, Bové's bail was paid by supporters from across the whole country, and the court hearings attracted crowds of up to 30,000 people. He eventually lost the case, though only served a short prison sentence in 2002. He drove himself to jail by tractor, at the head of a large convoy of farmers.

Bové's biggest crusade in the early years of the new decade has been against the use of genetically modified crops – which his father, ironically, helped pioneer. In

April 2000, he and his supporters destroyed a field of GM oilseed plants, asserting that the government has consistently underestimated the risks of cross-pollination with other crops. In his defence Bové uses the 'state of necessity', which compels French citizens to act even if it means breaking the law. At the trial in September 2002, Bové and his co-defendants wore white frocks, in reference to a centuries-old dispute between local peasants and the taxman.

Meanwhile there are more court cases on the horizon. In 2001, Bové led an invasion by more than 1,000 Brazilian farmers on plantations and offices belonging to the agri-business giant Monsanto. So he's not a popular man in America.

Garden gnome societies

France is particularly fortunate in having not just one but two societies dedicated specifically to the freedom of the (common or) garden gnome.

The first is MENJ, the *Mouvement d'Emancipation des Nains de Jardin* (the Movement for the Emancipation of Garden Gnomes), a peaceable organisation dedicated to allowing garden gnomes to achieve their full potential and to trying to observe their nocturnal habits (for we all know that gnomes are only active at night).

The second organisation, FLNJ, the *Front de Libération des Nains de Jardin* (the Garden Gnomes' Liberation Front), is much more of a hard-line outfit, which aims to release gnomes from the awfulness of their garden lives and set them free in forests.

MENJ does not approve. Forests, they say, are totally unnatural settings for what are, after all, *garden* gnomes. It feels sorry for the homeless gnomes, deprived of their tools, cold and miserable, and lost in the woods. So it's no surprise to find the FLNJ castigated by MENJ, who (like so many gnome-owners) consider garden gnomes to be amongst their closest friends. The MENJ management committee tells sorry stories of how – when out on photo safari, as is their wont – they sometimes run into the bereft owners of garden gnomes 'liberated' by the FLNJ.

FLNJ for its part makes it clear that whilst it knows garden gnome theft is illegal, liberation shouldn't be, and it campaigns (albeit not very vigorously or effectively) for the laws concerning garden gnome liberation to be changed. Given that gnomes have souls (runs the FLNJ party line), a life of enslavement in a garden is no life at all. In gardens, gnomes are urinated on by dogs, and they're not even allowed to drink alcohol or smoke weed (I'm not making any of this up). Worse, a certain number of garden gnomes every year are subjected to sexual abuse (gnome-ophilia, a seriously taboo subject if there ever was one).

The FLNJ rules for being able to count yourself a true gnome liberator are strict and seven-fold: you must leave a letter of explanation; you mustn't grass up your gnome-liberating friends; you must be against bourgeois attitudes; you must keep the FLNJ webmaster informed of your activities; you must publicise the FLNJ; you must free garden gnomes (good to see that's right down there at number six); and you mustn't have sexual relations with gnomes at any time.

Suggestions are also made as to how you should go about your nocturnal liberations (ideally wearing green trousers, a red shirt, and a bonnet – but an anorak will do), and gives helpful tips on pitfalls to watch out for (dogs, automatic lights, booby-trapped gnomes, police on their rounds, and gnomes which have been alarmed).

Both MENJ and FLNJ have a web presence (see *Appendix*: *Further Reading/References*). The FLNJ obviously has good legal counsel, as it goes to some lengths to stress it cannot be held responsible for gnome thefts or for inciting people to liberate. It even says the FLNJ management committee is only there to compile statistics. So while we're on the subject, please note that we at Bradt Travel Guides can neither encourage nor condone garden gnome liberation in any form.

Fernand Meyssonnier

Fernand Meyssonnier became a pioneer only in October 2002, when he became France's first and last executioner to speak out in public about his professional career, lopping the heads off convicted criminals. Perhaps, at the age of 72, with liver cancer himself, he felt he had nothing left to lose.

Meyssonnier was born and brought up in Algeria, where his father worked as an executioner from 1928 to 1962. So it was hardly surprising that Meyssonnier himself ended up first of all as an apprentice, and finally as an executioner, assisting in the guillotining of some 200 victims during his career. Most of the time, he had the unpleasant job of first assistant, the guy who has to drag the 'guillotinee' through the *lunette* by his head and hold him steady while the blade comes down. It's an important job – and one in which you can lose your fingers if you hesitate for an instant. What's worse, if you don't execute your work properly, cleanly and quickly, you have to finish it all off with a butcher's knife.

Three cheers, then, for the abolition of the death penalty in France in 1981.

With no apparent regrets, Meyssonnier left Algeria in 1962, and went to Tahiti, where he ran a successful bar for thirty years. He then retired to Fontaine la

WHY GUILLOTINE?

There's a common misperception that a) the guillotine was invented by Dr Joseph Guillotin, and b) that he himself perished under its blade. As it happens, however, all Guillotin did, as a member of the Assembly, was to lobby hard for the ending of all torture, and to insist on equality, efficiency and as little pain in death as possible for all condemned criminals, from whatever class. A bit of a humanist, really – as until that point only the nobs had been entitled to a speedy death.

Before Guillotin's pleas to the Assembly, in fact, the infernal machine had been known as a Louison or Louisette (after the surgeon Antoine Louis, who refined the existing machines by introducing a far more efficient sloping blade). The actual method of execution dates back far earlier, however, and was even used in Scotland in the 16th and 17th centuries (there's a primitive guillotine in Edinburgh called the 'maiden'). It was also used in Halifax, where it was known as the 'Halifax gibbet'.

But once the French penal code was changed (at Guillotin's instigation) in 1791, and with the Revolution in full flow, it became Guillotin's fate to be forevermore associated with the fabled instrument of death, which was last used in France in 1977, in Marseille. Guillotin himself, however, died at the age of 76, in 1814, of natural causes.

Vaucluse, in Provence, in 1992, where he briefly opened up a controversial but unsuccessful executioner's museum (the boxes with the bits of his full-scale guillotine and the occasional head are still in his basement today).

François Siohan

The European Laboratory for Particle Physics (that's CERN) runs from France to Switzerland and back again, and is home to hundreds of eccentrics; physicists with flowing beards who only work at night; budding (and failed) musicians; any number of men with cardigans unevenly buttoned up; and François Siohan, whose passion is a simple one: cycling. Over a lifetime on the bike, he's pedalled something like 400,000km.

I cycled over to meet Siohan at the CERN cafeteria on a wet weekday in March, and found an irrepressibly cheerful man bearing just a passing resemblance to a fit Albert Einstein, complete with a shock of white hair and a grizzled moustache.

Born in Brittany in 1941, Siohan started cycling seriously while studying physics at Rennes University, successfully racing for the prize money. After completing his degree, he went to Bolivia, where he taught physics as an attractive alternative to French military service, and stayed on there until the end of 1967. With plenty of spare time, he entered local races, and enjoyed the challenge of cycling on rocky dirt roads up to the world's highest all-year-round cosmic ray observatory (Chacaltaya, near La Paz, at 5,220m).

Before leaving Bolivia, Siohan was the 1967 winner of the La Paz–Copacabana race, one of the highest in the world, climbing up to 4,200m. Of 170km, only 10km was paved, and Siohan won the race in under six hours – of which he was alone in the lead for all but the first 30 minutes.

By 1981, having realised he was never going to make it as a top-flight physicist, Siohan started working instead as a scientific translator at CERN, just outside Geneva, and that's what he's been doing ever since.

The job leaves him time to cycle 200–300km a week on average, and to set unusual records. The first one was in 1984, when he wanted to see if he could effectively climb Everest from sea-level on a bike, between sunrise and sunset. There being no handy Everest nearby, he cycled up and down the local mountain pass in the Jura instead (La Faucille), a climb of 700m or so, 13 times in 13h29, thereby comfortably making the grade (the climbing part, a total of 9,243m, took 10h01. Objections that it's harder to climb at altitude than it is in the Jura can be dismissed when you remember that Everest ascents start at 5,400m, for a total climb of only 3,500m).

In 1986, the old Bordeaux–Paris race was resuscitated as a pro-amateur event, as too few pure pros were willing to ride it. The race took off in total confusion and pitch darkness at 11pm, with around 1,000 starters, and Siohan found himself in the second group, with 100 riders or so (including a good 50 pros) in the first group having slipped off ahead into the night. Of the 900 or so not in that first group, he was the only one to finish, and one of only 61 in total to make it to Paris. He had cycled 590km in 19 hours. Two years later he rode the complete race again, this time on a 623km course, and took part in a 350km breakaway, finishing 41st in 19h08.

In 1991, Siohan wanted to confirm the theory that you could climb faster on foot than you could on a bike. To do this, he first measured a cycle ride featuring 10,000m of climb (Everest, remember, is a mere 8,848m), which took him 11 hours of climbing time. He then descended just over 100m into one of the CERN particle accelerator wells at 7am, and climbed up the stairs to the surface 100 times. To get back down he used the lift – leaving a note inside saying he would donate ten francs to charity for each time he found it waiting for him at the top. It took him 10 hours and 20 minutes, eight hours of which were actual climbing time (ie: three hours quicker than cycling). Most importantly, however, he found it far easier than cycling, and says he wasn't even tired at the end.

Finally, in 1996, in his mid-fifties, Siohan set the world record for the amount of altitude gained without assistance in a 24-hour period. He cycled up and down La Faucille a staggering 21 times, logging 15,000m of climbing, from 2pm on one day to 2pm on the next. The current world record, held by a young Italian who cycled up 16,000m in 24 hours in 2001, would be even harder to beat.

I asked Siohan what his longest day ride had been, and he said it was a 24-hour time-trial he did in 1975, in which he came second. And the distance? The winner clocked 687km, while Siohan managed a mere 681.5km (officially – he'd also missed a turning and added another unofficial 3–4km to the journey). Both distances were new US 24-hour records at the time. But he's confident he could do a great deal better now, being much fitter at 60 than he was at 33.

So what *would* be his ambition now, I asked? He replied that he might just have a crack at the 'Race Across The Alps', the toughest single-stage bike ride in the world, covering 525km and featuring 12,600m of climb over 12 of the hardest mountain passes in Austria, Italy, and Switzerland. At 62 he would be easily the oldest entrant – but then he has high hopes for a long cycling career ahead. After all Maurice Garin, the winner of the first-ever Tour de France, in 1903, crossed the USA by bicycle at the age of 83, in 1954.

Bernard Tapie

Bernard Tapie is one of the most charismatic and colourful people in France, with a career spanning sport, big business, politics, film, stage and TV – and even time in the clink. You couldn't make it up.

Born in Paris in 1943, Tapie didn't arrive in the limelight until some 36 years later (after having spent 15 years as an engineer) when he created the Groupe Bernard Tapie. The empire grew quickly, with new acquisitions paid for by collateral from earlier ones, and by 1990 Tapie was able to buy the German shoe company, Adidas.

In the meantime he had become enormously well-known in France, from 1986 onwards, as the manager of the hugely popular Olympique Marseille (OM) football team, and as the presenter of an appropriately named show, *Ambitions*, on the nation's main TV channel, TF1.

For a few years, Tapie lived the life of a true high-roller, learning to fly, sailing his vast yacht and dipping into rally-driving. In 1989 he was elected to parliament as the representative for Bouches du Rhône (ie: Marseilles), and in 1992 President Mitterrand brought him into the cabinet as the Ministre de la Ville. Tapie was on top of the world.

But his empire was already creaking at the seams. 1992 also saw Adidas disposed of in a fire-sale, and although 1993 saw Tapie re-elected to parliament, it was also the year in which he resigned from the cabinet and in which news of the OM match-fixing scandal broke. By the end of the year, Tapie was stripped of his political immunity, and on trial on any number of counts.

He tried to dodge the flak by getting successfully elected to the European Parliament in 1994, but was then arrested, fined and bankrupted – owing the Crédit Lyonnais a whopping 1.3 billion francs (which we French taxpayers are still coughing up for, I might add). After a protracted series of high-profile court cases, Tapie finally went to jail for five and a half months in early 1997, convicted of match-fixing and financial fraud.

He was already bouncing back, however. In 1996, he had his first major film role, in the Claude Lelouch film *Hommes, Femmes, Mode d'Emploi*, and in 1999 he took to the Paris stage as Patrick McMurphy in *One Flew Over the Cuckoo's Nest*, proving himself unexpectedly good as an actor in both roles. For the last couple of years he's also had a chat programme on the cable TV channel RTL, and in 2001 even made a triumphant return to Olympique Marseilles as manager. By September 2002, he was back on TF1 with a new show. All he needs now is a return to politics – but don't hold your breath.

In the excellent *Hommes, Femmes, Mode d'Emploi*, Bernard Tapie more or less plays himself, and it's worth catching if you get the chance. There's also a quirky film from 2001 called *Who is Bernard Tapie?* which traces Marina Zenovich's attempts to track down the loveable rogue (she succeeds – after a four year hunt).

Village cricketers

Dig a little into the development of English cricket in the southwest of France and it won't be long before you come across the name of Wynford Hicks, captain for 21 years of the Saint Aulaye Cricket Club in Périgord. Having enjoyed the game over the length of a whole lifetime (Hicks turned 60 in 2002) he wasn't going to let a mere move to France spoil anything, and he soon put together a local team. For a while, they played on the municipal football fields, but with space limited, Hicks eventually bought his own field and prepared the ground himself. It's hardly Lords or the Oval – but then again the weather's consistently better.

With other cricket clubs in the region well-established, a league championship was started a few years ago, featuring three teams in the Dordogne (Eymet, St Astier and St Aulaye), one in the Lot et Garonne (Damazan) and one in Bordeaux. On Sundays throughout the season you'll find the matches well attended, and a new club in the Gers may well be the next to join the league.

So far, and not surprisingly, cricket has largely been an Anglophone affair in France (there's a strong complement from the Commonwealth), but there are signs of change on the horizon. Cricket has finally been brought into the school curriculum in Chauny, in the north of France (near St Quentin), where cricket-mad Daniel Beneyt is chairman of the local club and teaches English at primary level and cricket at both primary and secondary levels. Chauny is one of the 36 cricket clubs which now take part in the French Cricket Championship. (That's not 'French cricket' by the way, which is neither French nor cricket.)

Wynford Hicks, founder, groundsman and secretary (and captain, until 2002) of the St Aulaye Cricket Club, was a journalist, then taught journalism and now writes textbooks for budding hacks – *English for Journalists*, *Writing for Journalists*, and *Subediting for Journalists* are all available.

Hicks has also written a history of cricket in France (not yet published), and if you talk to him for any length of time you'll find him brimming with cricket anecdotes. Ask him about the 1789 English cricket tour of France, which was organised by the Duke of Dorset (cancelled; Revolution stopped play) or why his *alma mater*, Stonyhurst College, founded in 1593, spent 200 years in France instead of England.

Roland Vuillemenot

As someone who can't even run to catch a bus, I can only swoon in the presence of Roland Vuillemenot, a champion runner with a houseful of around 400 trophies to his name, along with – at the time of writing – 92 marathons and 60 completed 100km races under his belt. That would all be impressive enough, but Vuillemenot is not a young man. Born in 1946, he eschewed sport of all kinds until he was 31 years old. He didn't run his first race, a marathon, until he was 34, and was 44 (a veteran) when he became world champion over the 100km distance.

Vuillemenot moved to the French Jura, near Geneva, in the early 1970s, when his wife found work at GATT (now the World Trade Organisation), and it was he who stayed at home to look after the couple's three children. He built a fine house with his bare hands, and studied at night school.

But in 1977, he couldn't help notice the growing numbers of cyclists coming past his front door (he lives half way up the Col de la Faucille, the biggest local mountain climb) in the surge of enthusiasm which greeted a spate of Tour de France wins by wiry French blokes called Bernard (Bernard Thévenet won in 1975 and 1977, while Bernard Hinault triumphed in 1978, 1979, 1981, 1982 and 1985). On an impulse he jumped on a bike and found himself overtaking the lot.

So began a short career as an amateur racing cyclist – though he makes a point of saying he only raced, but never trained. After a couple of years he took up cross-country running in winter, when it was too cold to cycle, and so found himself accidentally signed-up for a local marathon. Vuillemenot was 34, and had never trained for a long-distance run, and yet he won, posting a very respectable time of 2h33.

Over the next two years, obsessed by this new diversion, he trained like mad, ran many races, and found he simply couldn't beat his own maiden time. Only when he stopped worrying about the training programme did he find he could better himself, and eventually became the second fastest marathon runner in France.

Turning 40, in 1986, Vuillemenot was now able to race as a veteran, and in that year he came fifth overall in his new discipline, the 100km race (try imagining running from London to Brighton, and then some), in the French championships. Four years later, in Duluth, Minnesota, he became the world champion, running 100km in 6h34 – and that just after having run a string of marathons in Paris, Berlin and Nice.

In 1991, he won the French 100km championships, coming first in Millau in a field of 3,687 starters, and in 1993 he posted his personal best time of 6h30, after leading the field from start to finish. In 1996, at the age of 50, he made his first run of more than 100km, by taking part in the Spartathlon, a shocking 236km single-stage race from Athens to Sparta, celebrating the famous run by Pheidippides in 490BC. With a 36-hour time limit (Pheidippides' time, apparently), Vuillemenot was comfortably home first, an hour and twenty minutes ahead of his nearest rival, in 26h21.

I drove up to meet Vuillemenot two days after the 2002 French 100km championships (he came seventh overall, third amongst the veterans and first in his age group – aged 56!), and found him picking walnuts in his ample garden. We repaired to his trophy-filled house, which doubles as the editorial offices of *l'ultramarathonien*, the French ultra-marathon journal, and I asked him if the Spartathlon was the hardest thing he'd ever done? Not at all, he replied – that was the Tasmania stage race in 1994, where they covered 620km in seven days, with Vuillemenot coming 13th.

And what of the future, I ask? He dissembles, briefly. 'It's harder to suffer, as you get older – after 40km the glycogen runs out, and after that it's all pain.' But then he admits, as I'm leaving, that he'd like to do another big race. He's clearly tempted by the TransAmerica, a 3,100-mile run which takes around 70 days…

Sign up for any 100km ultra-marathon in France and the chances are you'll be running against Roland Vuillemenot. The chances are also pretty high that he'll be far higher up the final *classement* than you are.

TRAVEL INFORMATION

Belltower and Caudron Brothers Museum Rue, between Le Touquet and Abbeville; tel: 03 22 25 69 94; open Feb–Oct, closed Mon mornings and Wed, open every day in Jul and Aug; free.

Château de Pierrefonds near Compiègne; tel: 03 44 42 72 72; open every day; € 5.50

CNAM (Conservatoire Nationale des Arts et Métiers), 60 rue Réamur, Paris, 75003; M̄ Arts et Métiers, Réaumur-Sébastopol; tel: 01 53 01 82 00; web: www.arts-et-metiers.net; closed Mon; € 5.50.

Forbes Balloon Museum Château Balleroy, between Caen and St Lô, Normandy; tel: 02 31 21 60 61; web: www.chateau-balleroy.com; open mid-Mar–mid-Oct; closed Tue; € 4.50.

Musée de l'Air et de l'Espace (MAE) Le Bourget airport; tel: 01 49 92 71 99; web: www.mae.org/n_index.htm; open every day; € 5.

Musée Blaise Pascal (the former Musée Ranquet) Clermont Ferrand; tel: 04 73 37 38 63 for more information, currently closed for restoration.

Musée Curie 11 rue Pierre et Marie Curie, Paris 75005; M̄ Luxembourg (RER B), Saint Michel, Maubert Mutualité; tel: 01 42 34 67 49; web: http://musee.curie.fr; open Mon–Fri afternoons only; closed Aug; free.

Musée des Papeteries Canson et Montgolfier Vidalon, 2km from the centre of Annonay, 70km south of Lyon; tel: 04 75 69 88 00; open Wed–Sun afternoons, every afternoon in high summer; € 3.

Nungesser and Coli Museum, Etretat; tel: 02 35 27 07 47, open spring weekends, daily in summer; € 2.

Historical Eccentrics

France has a long history, and a long list of historical eccentrics, from the leprous Sainte Enimie (one way of getting out of a wedding) to Joan of Arc and her voices, and from the big-nosed Cyrano de Bergerac to the pint-sized but gallon-ego'd Napoleon.

Royalty gets a look in, as always, with most of the amusing names clocking in between the 8th and 15th centuries. Lucky winners would be Louis the Debonair, Charles the Great (Charlemagne), Philip (and Charles) the Fair, Charles the Wise, John the Good, Charles the Victorious, Philip the Bold, Philip the Tall and Charles the Affable – while unlucky losers would include Louis the Indolent, Charles the Simple, Charles the Bald, Pepin the Short and both Louis and Charles the Fat.

ABÉLARD & HÉLOISE
There's nothing like a medieval romance – and the sad truth is that the tale of Abélard and Héloise, medieval romantics *par excellence*, is… well, nothing like a medieval romance. Moonstruck lovers standing at the couple's grave in Père Lachaise cemetery in Paris don't know the half of it.

By the early 12th century, Pierre Abélard was one of the most combative theologians of his day, and pupils flocked to Paris from across Europe to be taught by him. Popular, articulate and charismatic, he was nonetheless an inveterate fight-picker, and managed to upset many of the great figures of the day, including his dialectics and rhetoric teacher, William of Champeaux, the venerable Anselm of Laon, and even Saint Bernard of Clairvaux, arguably the most powerful man in the church at the time. He even published a controversial book, *Sic et Non*, which listed the 158 most divisive religious issues of the day. Little surprise, then, that such an illustrious figure should be brought so low by the all-too-often lethal combination of arrogance and lust.

Lust was first on the scene, with the arrival of the lovely teenager Héloise – and it's easy to see what Abélard saw in her, as she was not just attractive (and more than 20 years his junior), but also amongst the most intelligent and best-read girls of her day. Persuading her uncle, Canon Fulbert, that he should become her private tutor, Abélard was soon teaching Héloise more than just mere dialectics, and it can't have come as any great surprise when Héloise fell pregnant.

Abélard spirited Héloise away to his sister's house in the country to have the baby, and when she returned they conspired to a secret wedding ceremony. Canon Fulbert and some friends were invited, but neither Abélard not Héloise would publicly admit the marriage, as it would have meant Abélard losing his prestigious position at the cathedral.

Career-minded as ever, Abélard persuaded Héloise to retreat to a nunnery, and it was this, rather than any sins of the flesh, which was his downfall. Retribution from Canon Fulbert and friends was swift and awful – and best described in Abélard's own words:

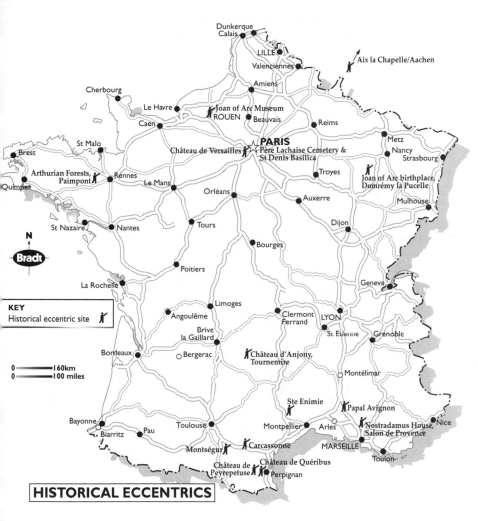

HISTORICAL ECCENTRICS

When her uncle and his kinsmen heard of this, they were convinced that now I had completely played them false and had rid myself forever of Héloïse by forcing her to become a nun.

Violently incensed, they laid a plot against me, and one night while I, all unsuspecting, was asleep in a secret room in my lodgings, they broke in with the help of one of my servants whom they had bribed.

There they had vengeance on me with a most cruel and most shameful punishment, such as astounded the whole world; for they cut off those parts of my body with which I had done that which was the cause of their sorrow.

This done, straightway they fled, but two of them were captured and suffered the loss of their eyes and their genital organs. One of these two was the aforesaid servant, who even while he was still in my service, had been led by his avarice to betray me.

Rough justice indeed. As Abélard himself pointed out: 'in comparing your sorrows with mine, you may discover that yours are in truth nought, or at the most but of small account.' Well, quite.

Certain he would be mocked for the rest of his days if he stayed in public life, and citing Deuteronomy in a poorly argued defence (Chapter 23, Verse 1: 'He that is wounded in the stones, or hath his privy member cut off, shall not enter into the congregation of the Lord'), Abélard quit academia and retired to a monastery for the rest of his days – though he continued his famous correspondence with Héloise until his death, in 1142.

In a twist of irony, Héloise went on to become far more successful than Abélard, gaining fame in the twenty years after his death as an abbess and as one of the most literate women of the 12th century. Separate for most of their lives, Abélard and Héloise finally shared a grave at the monastery after her death in 1164, before being transferred to Père Lachaise cemetery in 1817.

You can go and see Abélard and Héloise, together at last, in Paris – but you'll get a much better flavour of 12th-century life by reading their letters to one another, or any of Abélard's other works. My personal favourite is *The History of My Misfortunes*, which is hard to find in print but available at various academic locations on the Internet.

BRITTANY'S ARTHURIAN FORESTS

Head west out of Rennes, and within half an hour you're firmly into Arthurian territory – or at least the last remnants of the once vast **Forest of Brocéliande**, as likely a setting as any for the legendary antics of Arthur, Merlin, Sir Lancelot and the Lady of the Lake.

Within a 10km radius of the village of Paimpont, you'll find plenty of supposed Arthurian sites, but not much in the way of authentic Arthurian sights. The **Fontaine de Barenton**, northwest of Paimpont, is supposedly the site of Merlin's first encounter with Vivian, the Lady of the Lake, while the **Fontaine de Jouvence**, a few kilometres northeast, is where she's said to have bewitched him with his own spells, returning his youthful good looks quicker than the nippiest plastic surgeon.

Between the two springs you'll find the **Château de Comper**, which sits attractively on **L'Etang de Comper**, a lake fit for any lady, and perhaps the last resting place of Excalibur, the world's most famous sword. South of Paimpont, meanwhile, you can get sentimental with your loved one on the **Pont du Secret**, just possibly the bridge on which Lancelot finally realised he had a major crush on the boss's wife, Guinevere.

Most famous of all the Arthurian sites, however, is **Le Tombeau de Merlin**, Merlin's Tomb. A rival to the various other Merlin sites in England, Scotland and severally in Wales, all that's left here now, sadly, is a couple of standing stones – which is a pity, as pictures from the late 19th-century show a substantial Neolithic tumulus.

(So why is he called Merlin anyway? I'll tell you. It's that Geoffrey of Monmouth again. In his instant bestseller, *History of the Kings of Britain, to 689AD*, published in 1136, Geoffrey was the first person to refer to Arthur's wizard companion as Merlin, having apparently only Latinised the original Myrddin for fear that delicate readers might confuse the name with the French word *merde*. So there you go: Latinise, sanitise.)

Finally, over to the west of Paimpont, near the tongue-twisting village of Tréhorenteuc, there's the **Val Sans Retour** – the Vale of No Return. This is where Arthur's wicked half-sister Morgane Le Fay lured and trapped knights in search of the Holy Grail, and indeed there's a **Church of the Holy Grail** at Tréhorenteuc – actually dedicated to Saint Onenne, but Arthurianised by the local priest, Abbé Gillard, during the 1940s and 50s (so successfully, in fact, that the locals put up a good-sized statue of the Abbé outside the front porch).

It's hardly surprising, then, that the entire area is regularly over-run with druids, cults, and witches' covens, and home to all manner of covert rituals.

There's little to beat a trip to Paimpont and the surrounding area, 30km west of Rennes. The Paimpont tourist office (see *Travel Information* section at the end of this chapter) even does spooky guided tours on foot through the woods.

THE CATHARS

Largely forgotten from the 14th to the 19th centuries, the French Cathars have since been held up for retrospective admiration by liberals, pacifists and even feminists – so who were they, really?

It's hard to tell. As a religious offshoot from Christianity in the 12th and 13th centuries, the Cathars were spread widely across Europe, though they were never especially numerous. Even the name is something of a mystery – is it derived from the Greek *katharos* (meaning pure) or the German *ketter* (meaning heretic)?

We'll never know. But the Cathars did come to be influential in the region of Languedoc (literally 'the language of Oc', which was spoken here rather than the French used further north), and particularly in the area centred on Albi (hence Albigensians), at the end of the 12th century.

The Cathars called themselves Christians (and said the Lord's prayer and used the New Testament as their Bible), but had one major breach with Christianity, in believing that good and evil were opposed equals – thus denying forever the possibility of absolute redemption, or even of an all-powerful God.

Beyond this schism, most Cathars, who called themselves simply *croyants* (believers), led ordinary lives. Being a *parfait* (priest) on the other hand meant leading an ascetic life, with marriage and meat-eating off the menu. There were both male and female *parfaits*, though it would be a mistake to think that women priests were treated as anything like equals, in spite of the Cathars' egalitarian creed – or indeed that many women ever became *parfaits*.

Apart from dressing in black and preaching a lot – common enough behaviour at the time – what singled out the Cathar *parfaits* from other priests was their insistence on people's equality and their refusal to buy in to the feudal hierarchy or to be bound by secular laws. It's surprising, then, that they were largely tolerated by the local aristocracy – and not at all surprising that the Pope was soon on to their case.

By 1209, Pope Innocent III had had enough, and launched the Albigensian Crusades. Like most of the crusades before and since, this one was as much about power as it was about religion, and the armies who headed into southern France were more interested in the possibilities of a decent land-grab than they were in converting *parfaits* to Catholicism.

This was especially true of the main champion of the crusade, Simon IV de Montfort l'Amaury, who had only recently been disinherited from the family estates in England by King John I, and was looking for new fiefdoms. (Ironically, years later, the Leicester estates were restored to Simon's youngest son by Henry III – though that didn't stop Simon the younger being killed at the Battle of Evesham in 1265, fighting *against* Henry's forces...)

Simon IV led his army first to Béziers, which fell quickly – and violently. The crusader knights slaughtered Cathars and Catholics alike, with at least 10,000 people being massacred, even though barely 200 Cathars lived in the town.

TREASURE-HUNTING AT RENNES LE CHÂTEAU

South of Carcassonne, off the road to Quillan, you'll find the little village of Rennes le Château. It ought to be a sleepy, forgotten place, but instead it's a magnet for treasure hunters. Because there's really treasure to be found? Or because of some carefully managed tourist-attracting tittle-tattle in the 1950s? Perhaps both.

Rennes le Château has been around forever – the Visigoths had an important settlement here, and the church dates back to the ninth century (notwithstanding the gaudy 19th-century refit). So it's a plausible place to hide away your medieval stash.

Indeed, the legends are legion. Was this the hideaway for the Cathar riches from Montségur? Was this where Blanche of Castille hid the treasures of France, at the beginning of the 13th century? Could this have been where the Visigoths buried the gold sacked from the Temple of Jerusalem? Did the Knights Templar bury untold riches here?

Well, maybe. It's certainly true that at the end of the 19th century the local priest, Abbé Saunière, somehow found enough money to renovate the church and build himself a nice villa – which you wouldn't necessarily expect in a poor parish like Rennes le Château. But it's difficult now to unravel gossip from fact. Did Saunière really refuse to disclose his source of income to his bishop, but tip the wink to the Pope instead? Who were the wealthy and famous people who came to dine at the villa?

It could all be more prosaic. In the 1950s, the villa was turned into a restaurant, and the owner seems to have drummed up trade by telling people about Saunière, and his having found a huge hoard of treasure. The gambit worked – in fact it was so successful that within a few years people's houses were beginning to collapse, undermined by tunnelling treasure-hunters.

The mayor put a stop to the digging – but still the treasure hunters (an arcane, secretive crowd, believe me) come in droves.

The next stop was the massively fortified city of **Carcassonne**, which would probably have survived a siege forever, except that the town had no access to water (why didn't they think of that earlier, you wonder?). The thirsty inhabitants soon gave up, but were spared the Béziers bloodbath – counting themselves lucky, no doubt, to merely lose their homes and livelihoods.

And so it went on, from town to town across southern France, with people capitulating more or less slowly, and the Cathars gradually being eliminated. When Simon de Montfort was killed in 1218, the leader's mantle passed to his son Amaury, who followed in his father's bloody footsteps the following year by having the 5,000 'heretic' inhabitants of Marmande killed after a six-month siege – hardly the most 'cathartic' of experiences.

In 1229 political peace was achieved and the crusade was officially over, though the Cathars held out in a number of places – notably at the huge fortress of **Peyrepertuse**, which wasn't captured until 1240; the stronghold of **Montségur**, which fell in 1244 after a five-month siege (after which 210 Cathars were burned alive for refusing to recant, singing to their fiery deaths apparently – now that's what I call faith); and finally **Quéribus**, which was taken only in 1255 (though for some reason no effort had been made to attack it until then).

The Cathars were finished – though there is a record of one last *parfait* being burned at the stake in 1321.

The Cathar castles, in their various states of ruin and restoration, are well worth visiting – **Peyrepertuse** is the largest and most evocative, perhaps because it's the least-restored. **Montségur** is excellent, but entirely post-dates the Cathars – for more authentic medieval defences go to **Quéribus**. And **Carcassonne**, while never a Cathar stronghold, is always a bit of fun.

CHARLEMAGNE

We know a great deal more about Carolus Magnus (that's Charlemagne, to you and me) than we do about most 8th-century rulers, mainly because of a man called Einhard, who not only knew him well but also wrote everything down, in *Vita Caroli Magni* – unquestionably the best biography of the early Middle Ages.

So we know, for example, that the most powerful and influential man of his era wore local Frankish costume (a tunic and leggings) and despised foreign fashion; that he was a champion horseman and swimmer; that he mastered not just his native Frankish but Latin and some Greek as well (though he never really got on with writing in any language); and that doctors were hateful to him – mainly, it seems, because they wanted him to give up his cherished roasts, and eat boiled meat instead.

Like most great rulers of ancient (and possibly even modern) times, Charlemagne could be utterly ruthless when he thought it necessary, and on a single day in 782 he ordered the execution of 4,500 Saxon prisoners – just part of a phenomenal military campaign which lasted for three decades from the year 772. By the year 800, Charlemagne's domain stretched across all of France (except a small corner of Brittany; sound familiar to Asterix fans?), Switzerland, Belgium and the Netherlands, most of northern and central Italy, most of Germany and parts of Hungary, Austria and Spain.

In the same year, Charlemagne went to Rome to meet Pope Leo III, whom he had helped both politically and financially. Leo owed Charlemagne a favour not just for the help he'd had, however, but also for the support following an ugly scene on April 25 799 when an armed mob had tried to tear out the Pope's tongue and rip out his eyes – unsuccessfully, remarkably. Charlemagne's troops had taken the entire mob into captivity, leaving the Pope to make a full recovery. As a result, on Christmas Day, 800, the Pope surprised Charlemagne at prayer in Saint Peter's, by crowning him Holy Roman Emperor – Charlemagne, with typical down-to-earthness, is said to have declared that if he'd known, he'd never have gone into the church in the first place.

When he died, in 814, Charlemagne was embalmed (by Egyptians, apparently), and buried in the Imperial Tomb at Aix-la-Chapelle, seated on a throne with the Gospels open on his lap and his sword by his side. It's said that when King Otto III opened up the tomb, in the year 1000, he found Charlemagne in a state of perfect preservation, looking asleep rather than dead.

If you're in the vicinity of Aix-la-Chapelle (also called Aachen) on the Dutch/Belgian/German border, it's worth visiting the cathedral. Although it's been greatly expanded since Charlemagne's day, you can still see the marble columns

Charlemagne brought over from Rome and Ravenna in the closing years of the eighth century, as well as the famous throne which was used by him and his successors. It's a boxy, stone affair, and you'd want plenty of cushions.

CYRANO DE BERGERAC

As a buck-toothed, speccy teenager, I loved the story of Cyrano de Bergerac – the idea that the pretty girl might be interested in something more than the merely handsome. But I had no idea there were two Cyrano de Bergeracs: the Cyrano of Edmond Rostand's smash-hit play of 1897, and the real Cyrano, a larger than life minor aristocrat from the early 17th century, who achieved fame as a soldier, a duellist and a writer of satirical science fiction.

Let's deal with Rostand's Cyrano first. In the play (and indeed the many filmed versions, from the 1950 original, to Steve Martin's *Roxanne*, to Gérard Depardieu's magnificent 1990 performance), Cyrano is a sensitive, brave and intelligent man, in love with Roxanne, but certain she could never love him on account of his huge nose. His best friend, Christian, gets the girl through being handsome and using Cyrano's poetic penmanship as a prop, only to be killed in battle. In a truly poignant ending, it's only on his deathbed that Cyrano confesses his lifelong love to Roxanne, and admits it was he and not Christian who wrote the letters and poems.

The real Cyrano – Savinien Cyrano de Bergerac – was born in Paris in 1619, and then spent his early childhood years in Périgord, before coming up to the capital to complete his studies. Contrary to the Rostand rendition, his hooter wasn't horrendous, and indeed contemporary engravings show a man with a generous but not astonishing nose – though it must have been something of a sore point for him to have said 'a large nose is the mark of a witty, courteous, affable, generous, and liberal man.'

Cyrano joined the army in 1639, and quickly established himself as a dashing and courageous fighter, even on one occasion single-handedly fighting off the major ambush of a fellow poet. But he was twice-wounded – once during a heroic fight at the siege of Arras in 1640 – and soon left the army. The pen being mightier than the sword, he naturally turned to literature, but seems forever to have been involved in duels and spats with men around town, including the famous actor, Montfleury.

As a free-thinker in a restricted time, Cyrano turned from writing plays to crafting satire and fantasy instead, as a way of expressing his more radical opinions. In the posthumously published *Voyage dans la Lune* and *Histoire comique des états et empires du Soleil*, he took on the church, the state, the justice system, the army and family values – all the while arguing for a more just world. He'd never have got away with it, had it not been dismissed as science fiction – a technique which later went on to inspire the likes of Swift and Poe.

In 1653, Cyrano was hit on the head by a piece of falling timber (did it fall or was it pushed?) as he was going into his patron's house, and he was never the same again, dying tragically young in 1655 at the age of just 36 – reconciled apparently with God, if not his patron.

With very little available about the real Cyrano, you're best off with Rostand's play, either at the theatre or cinema. If you speak French you'll find the experience hugely rewarding – the couplets are wonderful, though they don't really translate well into English. The charming town of Bergerac, in the Dordogne, doesn't make a great deal of Cyrano – probably because he never lived there.

SAINTE ENIMIE – SAVED BY LEPROSY

Tucked into one of the narrower stretches of the Gorges du Tarn, behind the Cevennes, is the medieval town of Sainte Enimie. It's a touristy but pretty place, with narrow lanes, cobbled streets and ancient houses – but you're reading about it here because of Enimie, the 7th-century saint the town's named after.

Enimie was your classic princess, the daughter of Clotaire II, the Merovingian king, and sister to the future King Dagobert (love that name). Clotaire ruled from 613 to 623 over large tracts of what was to become France and bits of what were to become Germany; so he can't have been in the least bit amused to see his daughter caring for the sick, the blind and even lepers – daughters being major tradable assets.

It can't have helped that Enimie was pretty as … well, a princess. With the entire court at her dainty feet, all Enimie wanted to do was to serve God. But Clotaire, knowing which side his *pain* was *beurred* on, wasted no time in betrothing her to one of his most powerful barons.

Enimie wasn't having any of it, and on the eve of her wedding managed to contract leprosy, an off-putting disease to even the most arduous suitor. The court physicians could do nothing, but fortunately for the young princess an angel appeared to her (as they do) and suggested she went to Gévaudan, in the Tarn (then as now a remote part of the country), and bathe in pure waters.

With a small army of retainers, servants and maids-in-waiting, Enimie set off on the long journey. Bathing at the baths at Bagnols les Bains had little effect, so the troupe trooped along to the even remoter Tarn gorges, and it was here, at the source of the river Burle, that Enimie's leprosy, after a ritual thrice-washing, was miraculously cured.

The party headed for home, no doubt sending messengers ahead to warn the thwarted husband-to-be to gird himself for the occasion, only to find on arrival that poor Enimie was suffering from leprosy again. Sending away the wedding caterers for the second time, Enimie and her retinue returned to the magical waters of the Tarn, where she was miraculously cured once more.

You can see this coming, can't you? On going home again, the healthy princess was smitten with leprosy a third time; on returning to the Tarn she was cured a third time. Clearly, this was a message from God: Enimie must stay near wholesome waters and far, far away from beastly barons.

Enimie became a nun and founded a monastery on the site of what's now the town of Sainte Enimie, and worked the occasional miracle to keep her hand in. When she died, she was buried in a silver coffin in the Grotte de l'Ermitage, a couple of kilometres out of town. Several years later, her brother, King Dagobert, wanting some relics for his newly built basilica at Saint-Denis, came to dig up his sister, but through some monastic chicanery ended up with the bones of her niece instead – allowing the local monks to 'rediscover' Enimie a few centuries later.

And that's quite possibly where the whole story originates – the monks who came here in the 10th century hadn't got much in the way of stuff to venerate, and some miracle-working relics can't have done them any harm. By the time the bard Bertrand de Marseille first put the whole thing into verse in the 13th century, it was as good as true.

There's nothing to see of Sainte Enimie in Sainte Enimie, though the medieval town is pretty and the **Gorges du Tarn** are wonderful – especially if you're into hiking or biking. If you want to get authentic, you can go and see the tomb of King Dagobert, Sainte Enimie's brother, in the wonderful **Saint-Denis Basilica**, just outside Paris – the world's first Gothic building.

HENRY IV

Henry IV was the third French King Henry in a row to die an unnatural death – Henry II died in a jousting accident in 1559, Henry III was assassinated by a Catholic priest in 1589, and Henry IV was stabbed to death by a religious fanatic in 1610.

Henry's mother was Jeanne d'Albret (1528–72), Queen of Navarre, who was one of the leading lights of the French reformation, providing shelter for Huguenots from across Europe. As the niece of the French king François I, she had been married off as a political pawn at the age of 13 to the Duke of Cleves, though apparently she literally had to be dragged to the altar. When the Duke's importance waned, the marriage was annulled, and Jeanne was married off again, this time by the new king, Henry II, to Antoine de Bourbon – who was the first in line to the throne at the time, should Henry II and Catherine de Medici fail to produce heirs.

Jeanne seems to have been happier with Antoine, and the couple had five children, including Henry, who was born in 1553. With the outbreak of the first civil war in 1560, Jeanne, an avowed Calvinist, stayed in the Béarn, in the south of France, to rule Navarre, while Antoine and Henry took up residence in the Château de Vincennes, outside Paris. (It can only be assumed that the place had been given a thorough spring cleaning, after King Henry V of England had died there of dysentery back in 1422, and been boiled up in the kitchen downstairs, prior to being shipped back to the UK for burial).

The French civil wars – over religion, what else? — raged on, and in 1570 Paris was captured by the Huguenots, under the command of Gaspard de Coligny. Hoping to secure peace, Catherine de Medici, Henry II's widow and mother of the current king, Charles IX (whose childhood physician had been none other than Nostradamus, see page 92), proposed that her youngest daughter, Marguerite, marry Jeanne d'Albret's son, Henry.

With the wedding plans well underway, in the summer of 1572, Jeanne d'Albret died of tuberculosis, leaving Catherine de Medici free to instigate a hideous plot – the massacre of the Huguenots on her daughter's wedding day.

On August 24, Saint Bartholomew's Day, it came to pass. Coligny, along with thousands of Huguenots, was brutally murdered. Henry was spared, but imprisoned, leaving the way free for the war of the three Henrys – the Catholic Henry of Guise, the Protestant Henry III, and Henry of Navarre. Henry III finally succeeded in having Henry of Guise assassinated in 1588, only to succumb to the same fate the following year, leaving Henry of Navarre as his successor.

For four years Henry IV stayed a Calvinist, but in 1593, with the *seventh* civil war underway, he converted to Catholicism, with the dry phrase *'Paris vaut bien une messe'* ('Surely Paris is worth a Mass'). Entering Paris the following year, not a shot was fired, and the Spanish garrison departed, leaving the way free for the coronation in 1594. Four years later, Henry IV made history – and created lasting peace – with the Edict of Nantes, which granted Protestants the freedom to worship as they wished, in perpetuity (until it was revoked in 1685 by Louis XIV, anyway).

A Good Man, then – but apparently a dreadful soap-dodger, too, with washing consisting at best of a rare splash of water, and both wives and mistresses complaining about the shocking BO, which overpowered even the heaviest applications of scents and perfumes.

In 1607, Henry IV was the first person to ride across the newly completed Pont Neuf, just three years before a young man called François Ravaillac jumped up onto the king's carriage and stabbed him swiftly and fatally in the side. Ravaillac was promptly convicted of regicide, and received the standard punishment for the crime – being tortured appallingly and then pulled apart by four horses in front of a huge crowd.

Ravaillac's parents were exiled from France and his family was forbidden to use the name forevermore – which makes it all the more cheeky that the controversial student magazine at the prestigious Henri IV school in Paris today bears the assassin's name.

Henry IV's widow, Marie de Medici, had a statue of her husband put up on the Pont Neuf, though the original was toppled and melted down in 1792 to make canons for the revolution. In 1818, the new bronze statue of Napoleon in Place Vendôme was itself melted down to cast a second Henry IV. The man who did the melting couldn't bear to see his hero entirely forgotten, however, so look out for the small statue of Napoleon being carried by Henry. This is the statue you see today – which must have still looked spanking new when Berlioz used to eat his lunch on the steps here in 1825 and 1826.

JOAN OF ARC

Born into a farming household on January 6 1412 (probably), in the village of Domrémy, in the Vosges (now Domrémy la Pucelle, or Domrémy the Virgin, after the Maid of Orleans) Jeanne d'Arc was the youngest of five children. Apart from knowing she could sew, spin and weave but couldn't read or write – few people could, at the time – Joan's early years are a historical blank.

The next we hear is her first encounter with the 'voices' in the summer of 1425, when she was 13½ (presumably coinciding with the frightening onset of puberty). But for nearly three years she kept the voices to herself, until May 1428, when she found she could suppress them no longer – insistent instructions were coming in a blaze of light from Saint Michael, Saint Margaret and Saint Catherine that she must help the king, Charles VII. Not only that, she must also go to the local army commander, Robert Baudricourt, and tell him so.

It's not hard to imagine Baudricourt's reaction to the 16 year old's demands – he threw her out on her ear. The following January, having turned 17, Joan of Arc was back, and this time she was determined to be heard. Baudricourt was still highly sceptical, but Joan had a breakthrough on February 17, when she announced the defeat of the French at

the Battle of the Herrings. (I thought you'd ask – 300 wagonloads of herrings, on their way to Paris for Lent, were attacked outside Orleans by Burgundians in a fish-frenzy.)

Although the defeat had occurred five days earlier, outside Orleans, it wasn't public knowledge, so Baudricourt agreed to take Joan to meet the king. Dressed as a soldier – probably just for pragmatic on-the-road-with-soldiers reasons – Joan was finally granted an audience with Charles VII on March 8, recognising him immediately even though he hid amongst his courtiers ('Easy, Your Majesty! Your royal features grace every note and coin in the realm!').

Joan told the king he would be crowned at Reims that summer (the kind of thing kings just love to hear) and he agreed to let her lead an army into battle. Joan refused the sword he offered her, insisting on the one buried behind an altar in a nearby church which no-one knew was there, and within weeks she was raising the siege of Orleans with a small army. By July her military campaigns had been so successful that she was indeed able to be at the king's side for his coronation in Reims.

Unfortunately it all went downhill for Joan from here. Now 18, she started suffering military defeats – and more importantly started losing the support of

Charles, who reckoned he could sue for peace rather than fighting for it. In May 1430, Joan was captured by the Burgundians, and sold to the English for the princely sum of 10,000 pounds (well over a million at today's rates), who wanted to try her for witchcraft – on the reasonable grounds that 18-year-old girls don't normally lead (let alone defeat) armies.

Charles VII did nothing to save her, and she was tried for sorcery, adultery and heresy, though the first two were dropped after it became clear just how squeaky clean Joan's life had been. After months in prison, weakened and ill, and confused into tripping herself up, Joan agreed to sign a confession of sorts, and to stop wearing men's clothes – clearly the greater of the offences on trial.

But she seems to have been tricked – some accounts say she wasn't granted the right to attend church (the one thing she had asked for) and so reverted rebelliously to men's clothing; others that the women's clothes were taken from her cell and there was nothing else to wear. In either case the English had her bang to rights, and she was quickly convicted and burned at the stake in the marketplace in Rouen, on May 30 1431, aged just 19. Her ashes were thrown into the Seine.

In a bizarre postscript, a young shepherd called Guillaume, from Gévaudan (Sainte Enimie country – see page 81), came along soon afterwards with a remarkably similar claim to Joan of Arc's – God had commanded him, he said, to go to the king and raise an army to see off the Burgundians and the English. With copiously bleeding stigmata on his hands, side and feet, what could Charles VII do but lend him a horse and send him into battle at the head of his army? Guillaume was immediately captured, sewn into a sack, and drowned in the Seine.

Charles VII (too little, too late) tried to have Joan of Arc's guilty verdict overturned, and within 25 years Joan had received a pardon from the Pope. In 1920, she was canonised.

You'll find most of the Joan of Arc memorials where she was born and where she died. At **Domrémy la Pucelle**, there's Joan of Arc's birthplace, bought enterprisingly by the state in 1818 and a tourist attraction ever since, while there's an impressive neo-Gothic basilica at the spot where she heard her voices, just out of town. You can also see the church she was baptised in – check out the **statue of Saint Margaret** (one of the famous 'voices'), and the Arc family tombstone near the font. As one of the first commoners to speak out for French nationhood, however, it's worth noting that Joan of Arc has recently been hijacked by far right politicians, and in particular the National Front. Avoid her birthplace on 30 May, her saint's day.

In **Rouen** there's a Joan of Arc Museum within a few metres of the spot where she was burned to death in 1431, which features some extraordinary waxworks documenting her short life.

Finally, there are any number of films from 1895 onwards; the 1954 Roberto Rossellini version (with Ingrid Bergman in the title role) is my personal favourite.

LENIN

Vladimir Ilyich Lenin and his wife, Nadezhada Krupskaya, (and her mother) moved from Geneva to Paris at the end of 1908, and took an apartment on Rue Beaunier, not far from the Parc Montsouris. In her memoirs, Krupskaya describes the brand new flat as having mirrors over the fireplaces and being different from what they were used to, with the concierge being scornful of their crappy furniture (though she doesn't actually use the word 'crappy').

While Lenin was pursuing the bourgeoisie in his writings, Krupskaya was pursuing the authorities in search of the requisite permit to get the gas switched on ('The red tape in France is unbelievable,' she moans, in her 1933 *Reminiscences of Lenin*, in a remark which wouldn't be far out of place in 21st-century France). She was also concerned about her husband getting worn out on his cycle rides up to the Bibliothèque Nationale, a harder ride than anything he'd had to cope with in Geneva, apparently, and about his ire at the bureaucracy he faced there ('Ilych swore at the library, and while he was at it, at Paris in general.').

Lenin's passionate loathing of the petty-bourgeoisie was probably honed at the library, in fact, when he found his bicycle stolen one day from its spot on the stairs of the house next door – Lenin had been paying the concierge ten centimes a day to mind it for him, but when it was nicked, she claimed she'd taken the money for the parking spot, and not for the minding duties. It's not recorded whether he actually said to her 'When the revolution comes, you'll be the first against the wall,' but he surely must have thought it.

Cycling played a big part in Lenin's life, and after the initial Paris-fatigue he seems to have got as fit as the proverbial butcher's dog. By the summer of 1909, when the family took the cheapest summer lodgings they could find for a month at Bombon, just southeast of Paris, he and Krupskaya were cycling out every day to the Clamart woods, 15km away – and the couple thought nothing of pedalling out to see Marx's daughter, Laura Lafargue, a round trip of more than 50km.

Bombon was the perfect place for spying on the awfulness of the petty-bourgeois holidaymakers, and Krupskaya lost no time in snooty note-taking ('a downright practical crowd … they ape the gentry … this mediocrity was rather boring … a good thing we were able to keep aloof from them').

After the summer break, they moved three blocks up the road to Rue Marie Rose. With just two rooms and a kitchen for the next three years, and endless visitors, things must have been pretty cramped. Over the next year Lenin worked harder than ever, going to the library every day to study, and working through the night on his philosophies.

It wasn't all drab manifesto-writing, though – in the summer of 1910, they got away to Pornic, in the Vendée, for three weeks of eating crabs, cycling and sea-bathing. Back in Paris, Lenin was frequently to be seen at the Dôme (though the version you see today is the 1923 refurbishment), until it was over-run with Americans, at which point he moved across the street to the Rotonde – not a smart move, as the owner was an informer, passing on Lenin's *bon mots* to the police.

The following summer, Lenin set up a secret Party School (not as much fun as it sounds, with a notable lack of balloons and streamers) in Longjumeau, just south of Paris. After long days of lecturing the faithful, he and Krupskaya would cycle over to an aerodrome 15km away for a quiet hour or two of plane-spotting ('Ilyich was able to watch the evolutions of the aeroplanes to his heart's content').

The year 1911 was also marked by the collective suicide of Laura Lafargue and her husband, who killed themselves because they were 'too old and had no strength left for the struggle'. Lenin wrote a eulogy for them and read it at the funeral, visibly moved by such self-sacrifice.

In 1912, aware of increasing surveillance by the French police, Lenin moved to Krakow, and the rest, as they say, is revolutionary history. On leaving, the new tenant asked Lenin how much goose and veal cost. But neither Lenin nor Krupskaya had the first idea – as Krupskaya said later, they'd lived on horse-flesh and lettuce for three years, and never eaten such luxuries in Paris.

You used to be able to visit **Lenin's flat** at 4, rue Marie-Rose, in the 14th arrondissement, a short walk from the Alésia metro stop, but it's been shut for ages, and the Lenin plaque's now been removed from the wall, probably implying that someone's living there and doesn't want to be bothered by rubberneckers like you and me. When I spoke to the tourist office, they said the flat was closed for 'an unspecified length of time'.

LOUIS XIV – THE SUN KING

Someone else who certainly never knew how much goose or veal cost – though enough of it would have passed his greasy lips – was King Louis XIV, the Sun King, who came to the throne in 1643, at the age of five.

His father, Louis XIII, had himself come to the throne as a child, aged nine, when Henry IV (see page 81) was assassinated in 1610. Power in the reign of Louis XIII rested first in the hands of his mother, Marie de Medici, and then with the arch-royalist Cardinal Richelieu.

Richelieu handed over the reins to Cardinal Mazarin on his death in 1642, only a year before Louis XIII was himself to die of tuberculosis, thus ensuring that until Mazarin's death in 1661, it was he who was firmly in charge.

When Mazarin died, Louis astonished everyone by announcing that he would rule the country alone, and he proceeded to do so, convening ministers on a daily basis. He also took on the 'Sun King' sobriquet. Originally a quip following his adolescent performance as the sun in a ballet – in which the young composer Jean-Baptiste Lully (see page 123) also performed – it soon became a self-fulfilling prophecy of Louis XIV as Apollo, the Sun God. It wasn't long before Louis was exclaiming 'L'Etat, c'est moi!' – 'I am the State!'

Louis was not an unintelligent man, but he seems to have been fatally in love with flattery – as his vast court was quick to discover. The more preposterous the plaudit, the greater the king seemed to love it, proving that if he was a master of anything, it was self-deception.

He was also a lifelong lover of the pleasures of the flesh, and it's said there was barely a woman at court he hadn't seduced – in a court of 7,000 in total, that's really saying something. But he also had serious (official, even) mistresses, and he had the decency to legitimise his growing army of illegitimate children.

His first true love was Marie Mancini, Mazarin's niece, but Louis then pragmatically married his cousin, Marie-Therese, the daughter of King Philip IV of Spain, in 1660. By 1661 he was pursuing a long and public affair with Louise de Vallière, trading her in for the Marquise de Montespan in 1667. In 1680, however, after 13 years, the Marquise's luck ran out when she was implicated in the 'Affair of the Poisons', a mysterious business of witchery, black magic and murderous plots.

The Marquise was pensioned off, and Louis XIV came over all pious, returning his affections to his wife – who died (presumably of shock) soon afterwards. Suddenly, the court was a sober, formal place, with strict rules for public behaviour but plenty of hypocrisy behind closed doors. The king took his illegitimate children's governess, Mademoiselle de Maintenon, as his next mistress, secretly marrying her in 1683, and is said to have lived faithfully with her until his death in 1715 – apparently insisting on his marital rights twice a day to the very end.

The Sun King was also responsible for introducing and sustaining new fashions – from the widespread adoption of the high heel on shoes (it had been invented earlier, but Louis popularised it) to increasingly preposterous hairstyles (nearly 50 wig-makers were employed at Versailles). He's also the man who can be blamed for the way most women in the western world still give birth today.

Above The Pompidou Centre, Paris, with the infrastructure on the *outside* of the building (PL)

Right The Grande Arche de la Défense, Paris (PL)

Below Notre Dame du Haut, Ronchamp, reflects Le Corbusier's fabulous church architecture from the 1950s (RPL)

Above Marcel Leyat's fast if extremely windy Helicycle, at the CNAM, Paris (PL)

Below Coming up on 'Top Gear': a Porsche tractor, at the Museum of Factory Machinery, Cazes Mondenard (PL)

Below left Cycling for softies – the smart way to travel, on the Ile de Ré (PL)

Below right François Siohan adds extreme altitude to France's most popular sport, on his way up the famous Col de la Faucille (PL)

HOW NOT TO GIVE BIRTH

Louis XIV, like so many proud fathers today, wanted to see his (many) children being born, but back then it wasn't the done thing – so Louis took to spying from behind the curtains. Not getting the full picture, with birthing stools obscuring his line of sight, he had a 'viewing table' built instead. The mother-to-be was then placed on it, on her back, leaving Louis an uninterrupted view.

Unfortunately word soon got out that the king's children were benefiting from a new birthing technique, and before long everyone was insisting on the table method – oblivious that it was merely for viewing convenience, rather than helpful in any way to mother or child.

It would be amusing if it weren't tragic – more than 300 years later, the majority of women in the western world are still giving birth, and defying the laws of gravity, on variants of the Sun King's viewing table.

Louis XIV's other contribution to the world was of course **Versailles**. The original hunting lodge here had been built by the Sun King's predecessor, Louis XIII (or more accurately by Cardinal Richelieu), but from 1661 onwards Louis XIV gave his monster ego free rein. Not content with mere embellishments, he embarked on a fifty-year programme of such enormity that it's still one of the world's top tourist attractions.

The 414m frontage of the palace beggars belief, and it's hardly surprising that it took an army of 35,000 craftsmen nearly three decades to do the main work, or that the building of Versailles was so expensive that it practically bankrupted France.

The **Hall of Mirrors** alone, opened in 1684, is over 70m long and more than 10m wide, and is illuminated with 17 vast windows onto the gardens, and 17 equally vast mirrors on the other side of the room. The solid silver tables, lamps, and pots for orange trees must have been extraordinary, but they were melted down to pay for the Sun King's later wars. As the ultimate symbol of absolute monarchy, it's perhaps fitting that the Hall of Mirrors was the room used for the signing of the Treaty of Versailles between Germany and the Allies in 1919.

The palace may have been (and indeed is) the last word in magnificence, but before you envy it too much bear in mind how uncomfortable you'd find it today – there's no plumbing at all. Commodes were the only lavatories, and there are no bathrooms. This wouldn't have been a problem for Louis, of course, as he apparently only bathed twice in his whole life.

Taxes to pay for Versailles were raised by Louis XIV's astute treasurer, Colbert, who's gone down in history for saying *'L'art de l'imposition consiste à plumer l'oie pour obtenir le plus possible de plumes avec le moins possible de cris'* — or 'The art of taxation consists in so plucking the goose as to obtain the maximum feathers with the minimum hissing.'

LOUIS XVI & MARIE-ANTOINETTE

History has not been kind to Louis XVI and Marie-Antoinette – but then history isn't generally written by the losers.

When Louis was 15 and Marie-Antoinette (daughter of the Austrian Empress Maria Theresa) was 14, the couple were wed – though the marriage apparently went unconsummated for seven years. By the time they were 20 and 19 years old respectively, in 1774, they were on the throne of France – declaring at the coronation, in Reims cathedral, 'Protect us, Lord, for we reign too young.'

LET THEM EAT CAKE

Believe it or not, Marie-Antoinette never said 'Let them eat cake.' The phrase actually comes from Jean-Jacques Rousseau's *Confessions*, which were completed in 1768 (when Marie-Antoinette was only 12), although not published until after his death, in two parts, in 1782 and 1789. Towards the end of book six of the *Confessions* (published in 1782), which covers the period from 1736 to 1740, you'll find the phrase *'je me rappelai le pis-aller d'une grande princesse à qui l'on disait que les paysans n'avaient pas de pain, et qui répondit: Qu'ils mangent de la brioche.'*

In the official translation, this comes out as 'At length I recollected the thoughtless saying of a great princess, who, on being informed that the country people had no bread, replied, "Then let them eat pastry!"'

It's possible Rousseau just invented this, but he may have been referring to Marie-Therese, the wife of Louis XIV, a century or so earlier. In any case it has nothing to do with Marie-Antoinette.

What's more, it's not the thoughtless throwaway remark you think. At the time, if bakers ran out of cheap bread – which was subsidised – they were obliged to sell off their more expensive products (which included *brioches*) at the lower price. So 'Let them eat cake' is in reality nothing more than an exhortation to bakers to feed the poor at subsidised rates.

And their task, as king and queen, was an impossible one. They'd inherited a kingdom which had been bled dry of its entire wealth over the previous 130 years by the opulent lives of Louis XIV and Louis XV. It certainly didn't help that neither Louis nor Marie-Antoinette had much of a brain between them, or that both had led lives so sheltered from the real world they simply had no idea what was going on. But ignorance is as dangerous as arrogance.

Inevitably (particularly with Marie-Antoinette being a foreigner) they came to symbolise everything that was worst about the aristocracy – power, conceit, wealth and indifference. But in reality, as the situation deteriorated year by year, it was the nobility which heaped abuses on the people and not the royal family *per se*. In the face of the financial crisis, Marie-Antoinette even trimmed the royal household, and both she and Louis were strongly in favour of financial reform – with the nobility firmly against.

That doesn't excuse the lavish balls, the expensive clothes, the extravagant parties, or living in a place the size of Versailles – and you can see how real peasants, living the horribly authentic rustic village life, would hate the queen for dressing up as a *paysanne* and playing at the same thing in her reconstructed medieval hamlet ('It's just like the real thing, dear, only a lot less dirty') within the safety of the vast Versailles gardens.

The crisis grew rapidly worse when crops failed and the price of basic foods sky-rocketed, and in 1788, Louis was obliged to reinstate the National Assembly – which immediately reined in the king's powers.

By July 1789, the people had had enough, and the mob stormed the Bastille, the state prison (creating the national holiday, 14 July, in the process). The king's diary for the day unfortunately records *'Rien'* — nothing. By October, the rioters were at Versailles, and Marie-Antoinette narrowly escaped with her life by using the secret passage from her chambers to those of the king. It was for nought – the couple were brought to Paris and put under house-arrest.

In 1791, Louis nearly escaped, but was brought back to Paris, and the following year was put on trial for treason. The result was a foregone conclusion, and he was sent to the guillotine on January 21 1793. His last words were drowned out by the beating of drums, but his penultimate words were: 'I die innocent of all the crimes laid to my charge; I pardon those who have occasioned my death; and I pray to God that the blood you are now going to shed may never be visited on France; and you, unfortunate people…'

The moment the king was dead, the crowd went crazy, pressing on the execution site to dip their handkerchiefs and hands in the royal blood, and smearing it on their faces, in one of the ugliest scenes of the revolution.

The next nine months were miserable ones for Marie-Antoinette. Her children were taken away from her, and in September her best friend, the Princesse de Lamballe, was executed and her mutilated body was paraded around town – her severed head being waved past Marie-Antoinette's window on a pike. It's no wonder her hair went white in the final weeks before she too was executed.

On October 16 1793, Marie-Antoinette had her head shaved and her hands tied behind her, and was then paraded around Paris in an open cart for more than three hours, to be booed, jeered and spat upon. She walked unassisted up the steps to the guillotine, and met her fate there bravely. She was 37.

Versailles is well worth a visit, both to see the **State Apartments** and the incredible **gardens**. You can also see the *faux-village* which Marie-Antoinette had built, and the **Trianons**, large and small, which anywhere but Versailles would be impressive in their own right.

MATA HARI

Margaretha Geertruida Zelle, better known as Mata Hari, was born in the Netherlands in 1876 to a Dutch businessman and his Javanese wife. A precocious, cheerful child, we hear little more from her until she's 16 – when she has to be removed from school, as the headmaster has fallen embarrassingly in love with the provocatively dressed adolescent.

With a lifelong love of authority-figures and uniforms (which would eventually be her downfall), two years later she answered a small-ad from an officer on leave from the Dutch East Indies, and within months was married to Rudolph Macleod, 20 years her senior. The couple had a stormy relationship, with the young bride attracting unwelcome attention from Rudolph's fellow-officers, and Rudolph himself increasingly turning to prostitutes, drink and violence.

Their two children, Norman John, and Jeanne Louise (known as Non) were born in the Dutch East Indies in 1897 and 1898, but in 1899 were tragically poisoned – in Norman John's case fatally. With an increasingly strained marriage, the couple agreed to separate, and Mata Hari was granted custody of Non and a hundred guilders a month. Rudolph the red-nosed drunk never paid up, however, and even placed an ad in the local paper asking people not to help his estranged wife.

With no money and no obviously marketable skills, Mata Hari found herself penniless and hopeless, and returned her daughter to Rudolph. She moved to Paris, and became a model, though at first her unfashionably small breasts meant she nearly starved, even at modelling – until she adopted the jewelled breast-cups which would soon become her trademark.

Having taken up an interest in oriental dancing while in the Dutch East Indies (and even having danced for Dutch officers on occasion) she finally found her metier, adopting the style and attitudes of a Javanese princess, and taking the name Mata Hari – the Eye of the Dawn.

At a time when even a finely turned ankle was considered an erotic come-on, Mata Hari's dances were electric. Performing at first in private, in wealthy salons, her 'dances' were really nothing more than elaborate strip-teases – though the skin-coloured body-stocking and the oriental bra meant she never actually went naked.

Her fame spread rapidly, and she was soon in demand across Europe, performing in Monte Carlo, Spain and Germany as well as in France. But she was spending faster than she was earning, and not getting any younger – and increasingly it was her role as a courtesan rather than her gifts as a dancer which kept her in the lifestyle she loved.

She was reputed to have an astonishing sexual technique (probably studied if not learned in the East Indies) and was enormously popular with the richest men of the era – though even for them she wouldn't go topless, claiming somewhat preposterously that Rudolph had bitten off her nipples. With both French and German lovers, the outbreak of war in 1914 was always going to be problematic for Mata Hari, and it was inevitable that she would be asked to spy for one or both sides.

The only evidence we have for her spying, however, is when she agreed to do a job for the French – something she only accepted in order to visit the one true love of her life. In Paris, she had fallen hopelessly in love with a Russian officer, Vadim Maslov, who was nearly 20 years her junior, but was currently wounded, and laid up in a forward hospital. More to the point, to be with Maslov she wanted to ditch her job as a courtesan, so she was hoping to be able to retire on the million franc fee on offer from the French.

It wasn't, of course, to be. On her way to neutral Holland, via Spain, she was arrested by the British in Falmouth – MI5 had been keeping tags on her from 1915 onwards – and sent back to Spain after questioning. Having an affair in Spain with the German military attaché there must have been the unwisest decision of her life. The attaché sent a message in a code widely known to have been cracked by the Allies, saying that agent H21 had been most useful, and when Mata Hari returned to Paris, at the beginning of 1917, she was promptly arrested as a spy.

Having taken money from the Germans – only as a courtesan, insisted Mata Hari – her case was always a weak one, and she was found guilty and condemned to death. At dawn on 15 October 1917, Mata Hari – one of the greatest spies of the century (not) — faced the firing squad. Refusing a blindfold, her last act was to blow a kiss at her executioners. With nobody claiming Mata Hari's body, she went straight to one of the Paris medical schools for dissection. There's really nothing left of her to see.

In a sad ending to a sad story, Mata Hari's beloved daughter Non died suddenly in her sleep only two years later, on the eve of setting sail for the East Indies to take up a post as a teacher. She was 21.

NAPOLEON

French sources claim Napoleon is the most written-about person in history, saying he features in 200,000 books (make that 200,001, then), though I can't find any hard evidence to support this at all – a cursory drift round the Internet dragged up many more web pages about Churchill, Hitler, Jesus, Mandela, Nostradamus or even Jacques Chirac (though I'm sure even Chirac wouldn't claim to be as famous as Napoleon. Or then again, am I?).

Famously born a Corsican in 1769 (and rather less famously sharing a birthday with this author), Napoleon Bonaparte must have been one of the most charismatic men in history (which is where the comparisons between us must end, I fear). As a young soldier it was already clear he was brilliant, but few of his army colleagues would have seen the 'Little Corporal' as their next Emperor.

He rose rapidly through the ranks, being promoted to Brigadier-General in 1793 at the age of 26 for successfully booting the British out of Toulon. After two years serving on the coast, he was offered the command of the Army of the West. His refusal to take the post ('I simply can't stand the setting sun') was nearly the end of Napoleon as we know him, and he was punished by being relegated to the army's map-making department.

As a result he was in Paris in 1795 when royalists tried to take the city, and he was given the job of putting down the uprising. This he did ruthlessly, by turning his artillery on the insurgents in the Tuileries, earning himself command of the Army of the Interior in the process.

Within months he had met and married Josephine, and was on his way south to invade Italy. It took a year or so, but by the middle of 1797, Napoleon was installed in Monbello castle, near Verona, with Josephine, as de facto rulers of Italy. Perhaps it was here that he took up the curious habit of insisting on eating a meat course followed by a dessert at every meal. Followed by another meat course, followed by a second dessert.

Napoleon's next command was of the Army of England, but after looking at the English Channel on a choppy day he changed his mind and relinquished the post, and went off towards Egypt instead, at the head of an army of 35,000. In early June 1798 he conquered Malta, and by the end of the month he had captured Alexandria and was on his way to Cairo to win the Battle of the Pyramids. In August he was unfortunate in having Horatio Nelson sail in and destroy his fleet, cutting him and the army off from France, but by October 1799 he was back in Paris, just in time to overthrow the government.

As the 30-year-old First Consul, he was a virtual dictator, and Napoleon wasted no time in putting things to rights. He sorted out France's minor civil war going on in the Vendée, before leading his army over the Grand Saint Bernard pass to retake Italy (the Austro-Hungarians had snuck in while he was in Egypt). In spite of the massively heroic painting by Jacques-Louis David, of Napoleon crossing the Alps on a fearsome charger, he actually went over on a mule. When he got to the top, he became the only person in the monastery's thousand-year history ever to lock himself in (terrified of soft dogs with brandy barrels, perhaps?).

Back at home, he pushed through sweeping reforms of pretty much everything, from the way maps were drawn to the entire legal system (creating the Code Napoleon, which is still used in France today). As a man of letters he was unrivalled, dictating – as dictators will – up to a hundred letters a day to his secretaries, even in the midst of eating, drinking, campaigning, or (it's said) lovemaking.

He was hugely popular, so it must have seemed logical to convert himself from Consul to Emperor, and to have himself crowned (in 1804) by no lesser personage than Pope Pius VII. The dramatic effect was spoiled somewhat when he greedily snatched the crown out of the Pope's hands and crowned himself.

Two years later, Napoleon took on Prussia and won, and by 1808 he controlled the whole of Europe – except, of course, for Britain. By keeping large numbers of French troops occupied during the Peninsular War in Spain, from 1808 onwards, Britain pretty much guaranteed the eventual downfall of Napoleon – though his real ruin was assured by the disastrous decision to take on Russia.

Napoleon made it to Moscow, and occupied the city for a month in 1812, but came home with only a fragment of his Grand Army of half a million men. After fighting his new father-in-law (he had dumped Josephine and married Marie Louise, the daughter of the Austrian Emperor, in 1810) brilliantly but unsuccessfully in 1813, Napoleon finally lost Paris in 1814, and was forced to abdicate. He was exiled to Elba, at last allowing the world's favourite palindrome to be penned ('Able was I ere I saw Elba').

He wasn't there for long. The French weren't happy with the newly installed royalists, so Napoleon left Elba in February 1815 and marched unopposed to Paris, where he reinstated himself as Emperor. The Allies weren't thrilled about this, however, so Napoleon was forced to go to war again, and this time it was to be his … well, Waterloo.

The Duke of Wellington was victorious, of course, and Napoleon was exiled to the island of Saint Helena, far away in the South Atlantic, where he lived until his early death, at the age of 51. The cause of death has been variously stated as being anything from cancer to scurvy to syphilis, but my favourite explanation is that he was killed by his wallpaper. Tests on bits of the wallpaper from his room revealed that it contained large amounts of arsenic (common in paint, back then), and arsenic is present, too, in locks of Napoleon's hair. Then again, he could simply have been poisoned.

Napoleon was exhumed in 1840, and returned to France, where he now lies in state under the giant memorial to him at the Hôtel des Invalides, in Paris.

Amazingly enough, apart from a small museum in Cap d'Antibes and the Emperor's tomb in the Hôtel des Invalides, in Paris, I haven't found many places you can actually visit to find out more (I can just see the letters flooding in) but there are vast amounts of books and thousands of websites (see *Appendix: Further Reading/References*).

NOSTRADAMUS

Michel de Nostredame was born in 1503, but we don't know very much about his life until he enrolled in medical school in Montpellier 26 years later, having apparently already sold his services as an apothecary in the meantime, during various plague epidemics.

In Montpellier he met fellow medical student François Rabelais, and it seems quite plausible that the two renaissance men learned as much from each other as they did from the school. Afterwards, Nostradamus set up in practice as a doctor in Agen, married, and fathered two children. So far, so good. But in 1535 both wife and children died in an epidemic, and Nostradamus seems to have gone off the rails, spending most of the next decade on the road 'wandering through many lands and countries' until turning up in Marseille in 1544, where he was to be found again studying the plague.

By this time he apparently had quite a reputation as a doctor, and was much in demand whenever the plague broke out – though he later confessed to not having the first idea how to cure it. In 1546 he was called to Aix en Provence, and then to Salon de Provence, and the following year he settled down once again, remarrying, and this time siring no fewer than six more children.

In 1550 he took up his quill and penned his first almanac, which turned into a runaway success – as did his 1555 publication *Traité des Fardemens et des Confitures* (*Book of Cosmetics and Jams*, literally). Both the *Traité* and the annually published almanac were far better sellers in his lifetime than the prophecies, which were written and published from 1555 to 1558. The almanac in particular was hugely popular – which is odd, given that it was far more often wrong than right, and that random guesswork would generally prove more accurate.

He was nonetheless sufficiently famous to be called to court to pronounce a horoscope for Catherine de Medici and her children, and it was his success with her – he allegedly forecast correctly that all her sons would become kings, and that she would outlive them all – that he had the royal seal of approval for the rest of his days, even becoming the official physician of the young King Charles IX.

Today it's his prophecies rather than his recipes which are most famous, and which are pored through for relevance any time there's a major human drama. Designed to be ten volumes of 100 quatrains (hence the 'centuries', so often mistaken for chunks of 100 years), there are actually only 942 verses, though 58 sixains were published after his death, to fill the gap. Most scholars suspect these weren't actually written by Nostradamus.

The quatrains are a collection of prophecies forecasting all of history through to the year 3797, and are cyclical, working essentially on the principle that history repeats itself. The language used is vague and obscure, with a mixture of Latin, Provençal and French, and there are any number of possible translations for any particular quatrain – even before you start getting into what they might actually mean.

Which is probably the whole point. Keep the number of meanings as wide as possible and before you know it everything that's ever happened can comfortably be found in the writings of Nostradamus. It seems the only certifiably accurate prediction he made in his whole life, in fact, was on the evening of July 1, 1566, when he told his secretary he wasn't going to make it through the night. He didn't.

It's a rare and unusual treat to be able to wander round the house of someone so famous who lived 500 years ago – so if you're anywhere near **Salon de Provence**, take the time to visit the **Nostradamus house**, where he lived from 1547 until his death in 1566. It's now a charming little museum dedicated to the prophet's life – perhaps a little too credulous on the predictions, but sound on what it was like to be a 16th-century physician.

PAPAL AVIGNON

When Clement V came to Avignon in 1309, looking for somewhere more peaceful than riot-ridden Rome to rule from, it wasn't the first time a Pope came to live in France – Innocent IV had spent several years in Lyon half a century earlier – but it was the first permanent installation of the papacy abroad. It was to mark the beginning of a full century of papal upheaval.

From 1309 to 1378, seven popes – Clement V, John XXII, Benedict XII, Clement VI, Innocent VI, Urban V and Gregory XI – lived in Avignon, and the city grew dramatically in size, wealth and importance. When Clement V arrived, there were around 5,000 inhabitants in town, but within 20 years Avignon had more than 40,000 residents, and had become one of the most important cities in Europe.

Clement V wasn't just avoiding trouble in Rome – he also wanted to stay in France to try and unite the French and English (always a troubled enterprise) and to launch a new crusade, this time against the uppity Templar order. Never a well pope, Clement V died on April 20 1314, supposedly after swallowing a dish of crushed emeralds prescribed to him as a curative ('Come on Your Worship, this'll cheer you up – it's just like broken glass, but more expensive.').

The vast fortified Papal Palace complex, which still dominates Avignon today, was started a couple of popes later, in 1335, and was largely completed within an amazingly short 20-year period. At the same time numerous and lavish cardinals' residences were built.

The reign of Pope Clement VI, from 1342–52, marked the apotheosis of the Avignon papacy. Clement VI was both a *bon vivant* and a big spender, and he loved vast receptions and banquets – so much so that he even increased the frequency of the Holy Year (in 1348) from every century to every half century, so that the next one could fall in 1350, well within his reign. In 1348 he also bought the freehold of Avignon from the Kingdom of Naples, for a very reasonable 80,000 florins (whatever they are).

Popular as a pope – largesse always goes down well – Clement was also unusually tolerant for the era, insisting on providing a haven for Jews (who were widely accused of being responsible for the plague), and a keen patron of the arts.

Munificent to a fault, Clement left his successor, Innocent VI, empty coffers and an insufficient tax-base, but the papacy continued in Avignon until the reign of Gregory XI, who announced in 1375 that it was time to return to Rome. His departure was delayed until the following year, and he didn't actually arrive until the beginning of 1377, after an appalling three-and-a-half- month journey. In poor health, and complaining feebly to the end about the Italian weather, he died in the Vatican a year later.

The year 1378 was a busy one for the cardinals. As a French majority they elected a French pope, but then unelected him in the face of a Roman furore, putting the Italian, Urban VI, on the throne. The French cardinals however weren't satisfied, and re-assembled to appoint Clement VII as pope, marking the beginning of the Great Schism. Clement ruled from Avignon, and had the allegiance of France, Spain and Naples, while Urban ruled from Rome, with the support of England, Flanders and Central and Northern Italy.

Enormous rivalry sprang up between the two papacies with insults traded ('I'm the Pope, and you're the Anti-Pope!') and many a Bull issued ('You're excommunicated!' 'No I'm not, you're excommunicated!'), only exacerbating the problem.

In Avignon, Clement was succeeded by the Spaniard, Benedict XIII, while the death of Urban in Rome led to the election of Boniface IX. Benedict wanted to re-unite the church, but both popes would have had to stand down, and neither was keen to do so. An epistolary mission from Benedict to Boniface in 1404 seems to have led to an apoplectic fit of mortal proportions on the part of the latter, who was then succeeded by the short-lived Innocent VII.

When Innocent died in 1406, everyone hoped that Benedict would finally stand down, but instead he sued for the right to return to Rome, as the sole incumbent. The Vatican elected Gregory XII instead, who finally convened the Council of Pisa in 1409, to end the schism. The Council only made things worse, however, by electing Alexander V as the one true pope – making three popes in all.

Alexander died the following year, and was succeeded by John XXIII, but when both John in Pisa and Gregory in Rome died in 1415, the Council of Constance finally made a serious attempt at ending the schism – electing Martin V as pope in 1417. Benedict never accepted the decision, though, ruling over an ever-tinier papacy and with ever-fewer cardinals at his side, until his death in 1423.

Avignon is a lovely city (especially during the busy festival, in July) and the **Papal Palace** is well worth a visit at any time. If you can't get to Avignon there's a remarkably good 360-degree virtual tour of the palace complex available at www.palais-des-papes.com.

TOURNEMIRES AND D'ANJONYS – CENTURIES OF FAMILY RIVALRY

In the middle of the Auvergne, north of Aurillac, the medieval village of Tournemire is famous for the Château d'Anjony – and thereby lies a tale.

The village is named after the ancient Tournemire family, who lorded it over the area from the 10th century on. By the 13th century, however, having overspent on crusading, the Tournemires were in decline, and even had to give up a quarter of their estate, including, crucially, a corner of their fortified château.

This was inherited in 1351 by the d'Anjony family, who became de facto co-*seigneurs* of Tournemire, and they moved in, far too close for comfort for the Tournemire family. Things can't have looked too bad when Bernard d'Anjony married Marguerite de Tournemire in 1368, but the rivalry was stronger than the marriage-bond – and the Tournemires made the fatal mistake of picking the wrong side in the Hundred Years War, opting for Plantagenet cousins, while the d'Anjonys cosied up to King Charles VII of France.

By 1435, the Tournemires were heavily in debt to the d'Anjonys, and losing influence fast. Louis d'Anjony, who had fought alongside Joan of Arc, received a commission from Charles VII to protect the local surroundings, and he did so by building a defensive castle – the main keep of this is what you see today.

The Tournemires, suffering from classic cuckoo-in-the-nest syndrome, were livid, and lost no time in doing anything they could to fuel the feud between the two families. With their complaints about the d'Anjonys falling on deaf ears at court ('Weren't they that family that supported the other side during the war?'), the Tournemires took matters into their own hands, and the next two centuries saw an endless series of increasingly violent disputes.

At one point the d'Anjonys managed to introduce a spy into the Tournemire household, only for him to be caught, and sent back with his ears cut off and stitched to his buttocks. A bailiff sent from the capital to try and enforce a judgement against the Tournemires was sent back with his thumbs cut off, and the two families lost no opportunity in sniping at one another – or even in knocking one another off. There are even stories about rival graves being dug up, and the remains of the recently dead being fed to the wolves.

In 1590, the d'Anjonys were finally given equal political status to the Tournemires, in an attempt to calm things down, which seems to have worked – eventually. In 1623, the two families fought their last pitched battle together in the square in front of the church, and three members of each family met their death. Twenty years later, Michel II d'Anjony married into the Tournemire family, and the centuries-old vendetta was finally over.

Or was it? A quick visit to www.tournemire.net will show you that some members of the Tournemire family are still harbouring a major grudge against what happened more than 500 years ago. On the main page there's an irritated complaint that an old drawing, showing the village in the 15th century, and which was given to the d'Anjony family, isn't on display. You can also find a complete list of all the male descendants to the present day, along with no opportunity missed to carp on about the d'Anjonys.

Today, the château is owned – and indeed lived in – by the Comte de Leotoing d'Anjony. It features the original keep and a rather more comfortable 18th-century wing beneath it, and you can see some interesting 16th-century frescos, as well as a tapestry, recalling the life of a certain Mademoiselle de Fontanges, who was related to the d'Anjonys.

De Fontanges was a famous beauty, who was introduced to Louis XIV (see page 86) at the age of 17, and went on to become one of his most important mistresses – though her most valuable contribution to court life was an unkempt-looking hairstyle which followed a riding accident, and which took the King's fancy. It lasted decades, though she herself died at the age of 20 – at the time poisoning was widely suspected (she had usurped another mistress or two), though it's now thought she died instead of an unpleasant combination of tuberculosis and the complications of post-pregnancy.

All that's left of the Tournemire fortress is a few ruins, though the 12th-century church in the village below still shows off the Sacred Thorn, brought back from the crusades by one of the Tournemires. And in a fine twist of irony the d'Anjony owners of the château suggest that anyone wanting to visit, could stay overnight in Aurillac. At the Auberge de Tournemire…

TRAVEL INFORMATION

Carcassonne tel: 04 68 11 70 77 (tourist office); citadel open every day; free.

Château d'Anjony Tournemire, 20km north of Aurillac; tel: 04 71 47 61 67; open afternoons Feb–Nov, mornings also in summer; ∈ 3.

Château de Versailles tel: 01 34 84 74 00; web: www.chateauversailles.fr; M̲ Versailles-Château (RER C); state apartments open Tue–Sun (long queues at any time of year, and especially in summer), ∈ 7, gardens open every day of the year, ∈ 3.

Domrémy la Pucelle Joan of Arc birthplace; tel: 03 29 06 95 86; open every day except Tue in winter; free.

Gorges du Tarn near Millau, tel: 05 65 59 74 28 (Rivière sur Tarn tourist office); web: www.ot-gorgesdutarn.com; free.

Hôtel des Invalides 129, rue de Grenelle, 75007 Paris; tel: 01 44 42 37 72; web: www.invalides.org; M̲ Invalides; open every day except Mon and public holidays; ∈ 6.

Joan of Arc Museum 33 place du Vieux Marché, Rouen; tel: 02 35 88 02 70; web (with music on every page): www.jeanne-darc.com; open every day; ∈ 4.

Montségur Castle 60km south of Avignonet-Lauragais; tel: 05 61 03 03 03; open every day except Mon in Dec and Jan; wear sensible walking shoes; ∈ 4.

Napoleon Museum (Musée Naval et Napoléon) Cap d'Antibes; tel: 04 93 61 45 32; open Mon–Fri, Sat mornings every day except public holidays, closed Oct; free.

Nostradamus house rue Nostradamus, Salon de Provence; tel: 04 90 56 64 31; open year-round, Mon–Fri; ∈ 4.

Paimpont 40km west of Rennes; tel: 02 99 07 84 23 (tourist office).

Papal Palace Avignon; tel: 04 90 27 50 73; web: www.palais-des-papes.com; open every day of the year; ∈ 9.50.

Peyrepertuse Castle 35km northwest of Perpignan; tel: 04 68 45 03 26; open every day from Feb–Dec; wear sensible walking shoes; ∈ 4.

Quéribus Castle 60km south of Lézignan-Corbières; tel: 04 68 45 03 69; open every day from Feb–Dec; wear sensible walking shoes; ∈ 4.

Saint-Denis Basilica 1 rue de la Légion d'Honneur, Saint-Denis, north of Paris; M̲ Saint-Denis (RER D), Saint-Denis-Basilique; tel: 01 48 09 83 54; open every day except public holidays; ∈ 5.

Artistically Eccentric

Most artists live on a different plane from you and me, driven by pure emotion and ungoverned by the conservative instincts which keep the rest of us grounded – but even amongst artists, some stand out for being truly eccentric. From the ear-splitting antics of Van Gogh to the naïvety of Douanier Rousseau, and from the ludicrous moustaches of Señor Dalí to the absinthe-minded behaviour of Modigliani, Toulouse-Lautrec or La Goulue – not to mention Paris's fashion-conscious, fashion victims – artists are a strange lot (and especially the con-artists).

There's also Eugène Boudin, of course, the only painter known to have been named after a blood sausage (with the possible exception of the obscure 18th-century British watercolourist Jack 'Black' Pudding, who I just made up), and the first artist to work exclusively outdoors – though that, and his name, are unfortunately as eccentric as he gets.

LUIS BUÑUEL

Luis Buñuel, the greatest of the surrealist filmmakers, was born into a wealthy Spanish family in 1900. After a Jesuit upbringing which would usefully nurture his lifelong hatred of the Catholic Church, he went to Madrid university in 1917 to study engineering, and while there he met Salvador Dalí (see page 100) and Federico García Lorca – though he refused to accept Lorca's homosexuality.

In 1925, Buñuel went to Paris, where he studied film and worked with the experimental director Jean Epstein. He also learned to play banjo. In 1929, with funding from his mother and creative input from Salvador Dalí, he made the world's first surrealist film, *Un Chien Andalou*. Although under 20 minutes long, the film is still an extraordinary one, more than 70 years after being made, full of disjointed and shocking images – the film opens with Buñuel cutting open a woman's eye with a razor. It caused a scandal; but the surrealists loved it.

Two years later, again with Dalí's collaboration, Buñuel made *L'Age d'Or*, a full-length feature stuffed with nonsensical scenes – some morbid and amoral, others hilarious – aimed at upsetting the bourgeoisie. It was hugely effective, causing riots in Paris when it opened, and was banned for years.

With the outbreak of civil war in Spain, Buñuel went to America, where he made documentaries and anti-Nazi films, but when Dalí labelled him an atheist and a communist in his autobiography, Buñuel lost his job. He moved to Mexico, where he spent most of the rest of his life, though from 1955 onwards he frequently worked in France, and ended his career with half a dozen French masterpieces.

These include *Belle de Jour* (1967), in which Catherine Deneuve plays a housewife who works as a prostitute while her doctor husband's at work, *The Discreet Charm of the Bourgeoisie* (1972), where a group of diners find themselves unable to finish a meal, and the wonderful, final, *That Obscure Object of Desire* (1977), where a wealthy older man finds himself ensnared by a virginal beauty (played by two different actresses).

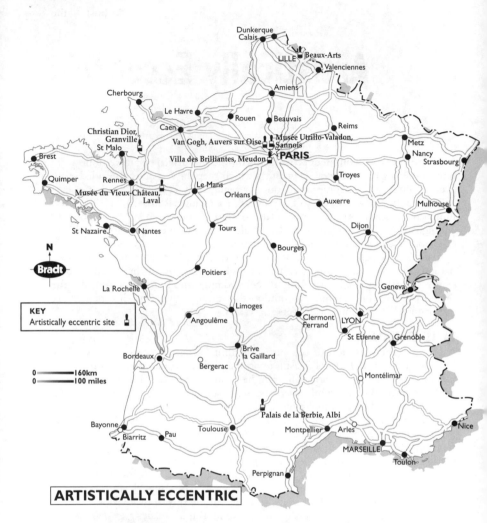

ARTISTICALLY ECCENTRIC

Buñuel was a committed atheist to the end ('Thank God I am an atheist', he would quip), and a ready wit. In his later years, he said he wanted to stage a final surrealist joke for his deathbed scene – he would convene all his atheist friends, and then summon a priest and make a deathbed confession.

It didn't happen, when in 1983 Buñuel finally went to whatever heaven surrealists dream of.

CAMILLE CLAUDEL

The tragic life of Camille Claudel is inextricably linked to that of France's most famous sculptor, Auguste Rodin.

Rodin was born in November 1840, and studied at the Petite Ecole, a decorative arts school in Paris, from the age of 13. He was rejected three times by the Ecole des Beaux Arts (Fine Arts), and from 1858 made a living as a jobbing sculptor, turning out decorative stonework for the façades of new buildings, which he pursued on and off until 1882. As a sideline he also made decorative busts – the classic girl with the hat – which were the first works he signed.

The year 1864 was significant for Rodin – it was the year he took up with Rose Beuret, who was to be his lifelong companion (other mistresses notwithstanding), and it was the year he first submitted a sculpture (*Man with a Broken Nose*) to the Paris Salon. It was rejected. In December, Camille Claudel was born.

It wasn't until 1875 that Rodin finally had a work accepted by the Salon – a heavily reworked version of *Man with a Broken Nose*, re-titled *Portrait of a Roman*. Two years later, inspired in part by the Michelangelos he'd seen on a trip to Italy, Rodin leaped into the limelight with *The Age of Bronze*, an extraordinarily lifelike sculpture which prompted accusations that he'd simply made a cast from real life, and which brought him more fame than simple praise could ever have done.

In 1880, at the age of 39, Rodin finally achieved social and economic security with the commission from the government to provide the doors for the Museum of Decorative Arts. These were to become *The Gates of Hell* – and were still unfinished at his death, more than 30 years later.

Camille Claudel, for her part, had also shown promise at an early age, modelling clay with great dexterity, and was enrolled by her liberal parents (her younger brother Paul went on to become a famous poet, writer and diplomat) at the Académie Colarossi, one of the few art schools then open to girls. She was soon part of a group of young women being given weekly lessons by the well known sculptor Alfred Boucher.

When Boucher went to Italy in 1884, he handed off his pupils onto Rodin, and Camille and Auguste fell in love more or less at first sight. He was 43, she was 19. Over the next fifteen years – the most productive of Rodin's career – the pair worked together on some of the world's most famous sculptures (including *The Gates of Hell* and *The Burghers of Calais*), and Claudel was Rodin's muse, inspiration and lover.

Inevitably, her own work was put to one side, and it eventually became clear that she was never going to usurp Rose Beuret as Rodin's number one gal. Beuret had to do more than her own fair share of waiting, however. Rodin only wedded her after they'd spent more than 50 years together, and just 17 days before her death (probably from the shock of getting married) on Valentine's Day 1917. Rodin was only nine months behind her, dying in November 1917.

Claudel and Rodin broke up definitively in 1898, although things had been growing increasingly acrimonious between them for at least the past five years. Camille took a studio at 19 Quai Bourbon, on the Ile de la Cité, and worked there in solitude and increasing poverty on her own sculpture. She put on weight and neglected her health, and started showing signs of the persecution complex which would eventually destroy her.

' In 1906, to prevent Rodin from stealing her *oeuvre* and claiming it as his own (not so very far off the mark, given how much she'd put into Rodin's sculptures), she destroyed practically a decade's worth of her own work. Over the next seven years, Claudel continued to sculpt feverishly, and then smash up the results.

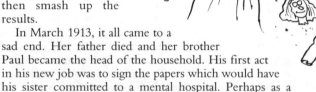

In March 1913, it all came to a sad end. Her father died and her brother Paul became the head of the household. His first act in his new job was to sign the papers which would have his sister committed to a mental hospital. Perhaps as a well-known poet and diplomat he wanted his mad sister out of the way – but it was a devastating thing to do. On Monday 10 March, just a week after her father's death, male nurses broke into Camille's studio and took her away.

She was incarcerated for 30 years. Staff at the hospital, near Avignon, later wanted to release Camille into the care of her family, but the family refused. She died as she had lived so much of her life, sad, lonely and unloved, on October 19 1943.

There's very little in the way of commemoration of Camille Claudel (notwithstanding the **Camille Claudel Sculpture Festival**, see page 15), though you'll occasionally find her sculpture in museums – the **Beaux-Arts** in Lille has a lovely bust, and the **Musée d'Orsay** in Paris has a couple of works. For the rest, you have to go via Rodin – who being Rodin has not just one but two important museums dedicated to him.

The **Musée Rodin** in Paris is housed in the lovely Hôtel Biron, which was bought by the French government in 1905, and used by Rodin himself from 1908. It's been open as a museum since 1919, and contains a comprehensive collection of his works, as well as those of Camille Claudel.

From 1893, Rodin lived with Rose Beuret at the **Villa des Brillants** in Meudon, in the southwestern suburbs of Paris. In an annex there's an interesting collection of assemblages and plaster casts showing the various stages of some of the bigger monuments, such as the *Gates of Hell* or the *Burghers of Calais*. Meudon is also where you'll find Rodin's tomb, adorned – of course – with a copy of the *Thinker*.

SALVADOR DALÍ

Although there's no denying he was a technical genius, the Spanish artist Salvador Dalí was nonetheless one of the most screwed-up individuals of the 20th century. His paintings, sculptures, films, photographs and ideas still have the power to shock, but you can't help feeling that was on occasion their only purpose – shock-value in art often translating into dollar-value.

Born and brought up in Spain, Salvador Dalí wanted to live in Paris after meeting Picasso there in 1926. Following a visit with Joan Miró in 1928, he joined the surrealists, and quickly became one of the best-known amongst them – especially after making the first surrealist film with Luis Buñuel in 1929, *Un Chien Andalou* (see page 97).

During the summer of 1929, on holiday in Spain, he was visited by the surrealist poet Paul Eluard (see page 158) and his Russian émigré wife, Gala. In no time at all, Gala and Dalí had eloped, and for the next 50 years she played the role of spouse, mother (she was ten years older than Dalí), muse and business manager to the increasingly famous artist. Whether she also played the role of lover has been the subject of furious debate – Dalí hated to be touched, and in any case had leanings towards men rather than women (though whether these were acted upon is itself debatable).

In 1931, Buñuel and Dalí collaborated again, on *L'Age d'Or* (see page 97), but ultimately, however, the surrealists and Dalí weren't made for one another – Dalí was too shocking even for them. He upset André Breton (see page 157) by saying his favourite train accidents were the ones in which the third-class passengers suffered the most, and he embraced the ideas of Hitler rather than the ideology of Lenin. His ludicrous moustaches can't have gone down well, either.

The surrealists censured Dalí in 1934 and threw him out in 1939 – not least for his turncoat behaviour over the Spanish Civil War. In spite of his sister's arrest and torture, and the killing of his friend Lorca (Dalí, Buñuel and Lorca had been at college together in Madrid), he supported Franco once he saw which side was going to win.

After a decade and a half in America, Gala and Dalí returned to Spain in 1955, and lived there until their deaths, in 1981 and 1989.

Dalí invented and reinvented himself so often we'll never know who he really was, but even if you can't love the man, many of his works still have the power to turn your head. My personal favourites are the lobster-handset telephone, and the sofa made in the shape of Mae West's lips.

Just off the teeming Place du Tertre in Montmartre, at the top of rue Poulbot, you'll find the **Espace Salvador Dalí**, which is not just the most comprehensive collection of Dalí works outside Spain but also rare amongst museums in selling off its exhibits.

PAUL GAUGUIN

Eugène-Henri Paul Gauguin was born in Paris in 1848 to Clovis, a left-wing journalist, and Aline-Marie, a part-Peruvian. When he was three years old, the family set sail for Lima – it seems his father had written something unpalatable in the French press – but Clovis died of a stroke on the journey. The rest of the family spent four years in Peru before returning to France.

In 1865, at the age of 17, Gauguin became a sailor, and discovered the south seas – but six years later gave up the wandering life to become a stockbroker. He was highly successful, and rapidly became a wealthy man. In 1873 he married Mette Sophie Gad, a Danish woman of means herself, and over the next ten years they had five children together.

At the same time, Gauguin got serious about painting. In 1874 he met Pissaro and other impressionists at their first major exhibition, and he bought paintings by Manet, Degas, Renoir and Pissaro, amongst others. He also took up the brush himself, and debuted in the Salon of 1876. By 1883, at the age of 35, he'd had enough, and decided to give up life in the commercial world.

For the family, it was a disastrous decision – by 1884 they were broke, and forced to move to Denmark, where Gauguin left them, returning alone to Paris.

Over the next four years he spent most of the time impoverished in Brittany, with a year off in 1887/88 in Panama and Martinique, before being persuaded by his dealer, Théo Van Gogh, to go and live with his brother Vincent, in Arles.

Gauguin arrived in Arles on October 23 1888, and thus began one of the most stormy nine weeks in art history. Each painter – whatever they subsequently said (Gauguin famously commenting 'I don't admire the painting but I admire the man') – learned a huge amount from the other, and each perfected the style that autumn which would set them apart from their contemporaries.

It all came to a messy end, of course. On December 22, according to Gauguin's

Intimate Journals, '(Van Gogh) took a light absinthe. Suddenly he flung the glass and its contents at my head. I avoided the blow and, taking him bodily in my arms, went out of the café … Not many minutes later Vincent found himself in his own bed … not to awaken till morning. When he awoke, he said to me very calmly, "My dear Gauguin, I have a vague memory that I offended you last evening."'

Later that day, Gauguin heard footsteps on the street, and spun round just in time to see Van Gogh coming at him with a razor. Gauguin stared him down, and Van Gogh ran off – going home to cut off a chunk of his ear and deliver it to the local brothel, washed and wrapped in cotton wool. Gauguin caught the next train to Paris.

He spent most of the next two years in Brittany, as part of the Pont-Aven school, and his relationship with one of his models and lovers in 1890 inevitably produced an illegitimate daughter in 1891 – just in time for Gauguin to scoot off to Tahiti (without the new family). Once there he fell ill, and started writing *Noa Noa*, which was eventually to be published in 1897.

In 1893 he returned to Paris, and in 1894 he made a last trip to Copenhagen to say goodbye to the family, before leaving Europe for the last time. Three years later, on hearing news of a daughter's death, he painted his most important work, *D'où venons-nous? Que sommes-nous? Où allons-nous* (Where do we come from? What are we? Where are we going?) and then – suffering from alcoholism, syphilis and depression – he attempted suicide, taking a massive dose of arsenic.

He survived, but increasingly suffered from the complications of syphilis – which didn't stop him siring another child in 1899, in Tahiti, and a final daughter in 1902, on the Marquesas islands. In 1903, blind and unable to walk, he died. The local bishop – no friend of Gauguin's, clearly – refused him a Christian burial, and had many of the painter's last paintings burned.

In 1923, with the papers having been returned to the family, Emile Gauguin published a limited edition of *The Intimate Journals of Paul Gauguin*, which was republished by Heinemann in 1952. It's a wild, rambling autobiography, written by Gauguin in the last months of his life, with little in the way of form or structure – but it's a great book, giving sometimes terrifying insights into Gauguin's tortured soul.

If you're in Paris you should also – of course – go and see his most famous paintings at the **Musée d'Orsay**.

ALBERTO GIACOMETTI

Alberto Giacometti was one of the greatest artists of the 20th century, though he himself wasn't satisfied with a single work. If his faithful brother Diego hadn't been on hand to cast his sculptures into permanence there's a good chance we wouldn't have anything at all to remember him by.

Giacometti was born in Stampa, in Italian-speaking Switzerland in 1901. His father, Giovanni, was a famous post-impressionist (and you'll find more of father than son in many Swiss galleries), and Alberto took to art from an early age, illustrating children's stories and drawing family portraits.

In 1922 he went to Paris to study sculpture, and in 1925 he and Diego set up their first studio, moving two years later to 46 rue Hippolyte-Maindron in Montparnasse – where they were to remain for the rest of Giacometti's life.

Early success – he was on show in Zurich in 1927, and Paris in 1928 – brought him into contact with the surrealists, and Giacometti's surrealist work is still amongst the best you'll find. But he committed the heresy of returning to the model – in this case, Diego – for inspiration, and left the movement, losing many friends in the process.

When his father died in 1933, Alberto, as the oldest son, should have been the chief mourner, but instead – with a complete absence of physical symptoms – he checked himself into the hospital his father had died in, and failed to attend the funeral altogether.

During the late 1930s, Giacometti's sculptures then began to grow smaller and smaller, leading to one of the 20th-century's finest art moments, in 1939. Invited to provide a sculpture for the central courtyard of one the pavilions at the Swiss National Exhibition in Zurich, Giacometti showed up at the venue a few days early. A truck was ordered to go and collect the sculpture from the station, but Giacometti – pulling a large matchbox from his jacket pocket – said 'There's no need, I have it with me'.

Inside the box was a two-inch plaster sculpture, intended for the huge plinth in the central courtyard. Even had the organisers not been Swiss, you can imagine the general sense-of-humour failure attending the scene – *reductio ad absurdum* had become a definite case of *reductio ad impossibile*.

Giacometti stayed in Geneva during the war, covering everything in white plaster in his efforts to create the perfect sculpture, but when he returned to Paris in 1945 – Diego had kept the studio in order – his entire output for the war years fitted comfortably into six matchboxes. While in Geneva, the 42- year-old Giacometti had met 20-year-old Annette Arm, and she apparently finally badgered him into letting her move in with him in 1946, and marrying her in 1949. For the last 20 years of his life, Annette was to be his most important model – though for his more basic needs Alberto continued his lifelong tradition of using prostitutes, unable to consummate a physical relationship with anyone close.

Life with Giacometti can't have been easy. He never took holidays or even weekends off, working every single day and most nights, year after year. After work, late into the night, he would be out walking the streets or sitting in bars – he was a close friend of Samuel Beckett's as well as of both Sartre and De Beauvoir – and he frequently ended up at his favourite brothel, the Sphinx. Even more infuriating, for Annette, was his insistence on wearing the same clothes day in, day out. On the rare occasions when she finally got him to the shops, he would come home with another identical outfit.

Even as his fame and wealth increased – from 1948 his work was on show in New York, at the Pierre Matisse Gallery – Giacometti continued to live on a shoestring, in the crumbling studio, and it's hardly surprising that his health began to fail, or that Annette took a separate and more comfortable apartment – though she came by every day to clean the studio and do the laundry.

Another regular visitor was the Romanian photographer and alcoholic dropout Elie Lotar (who had famously been given a camera by Cartier Bresson, only to pawn it). He was to become Giacometti's last great model, and it's the final bust of Lotar which adorns Giacometti's grave at Borgonovo, just up the road from Stampa, where he was born.

Giacometti was operated on successfully for stomach cancer in 1963, but continued to smoke over 80 cigarettes a day, drink endless cups of coffee and eat and sleep irregularly, haunted by his complete inability to finish his paintings or sculptures to his own satisfaction. In January 1966, he died of heart disease and chronic bronchitis, at the age of 64.

Giacometti's studio at 46 rue Hippolyte-Maindron in Paris no longer exists – in its place is a rather small, ordinary park – but the building on the corner of rue Chemin Vert gives you some idea of what it was like when Giacometti was working here from the late 1920s right through to the mid-1960s.

The best collection of Giacometti's works is in Zurich, but most of the world's major galleries have one or two examples of his sculpture and painting.

FERNAND LEGROS

If you can't make great art, you can always fake great art – and if you can't fake great art, you can at least fence great fakes. Such at least was the rationale of Fernand Legros, who sold many dozens of forged masterpieces, mainly to American collectors, during the 1960s and 1970s.

Born to French parents in Egypt in 1931, Legros started out as a ballet dancer, before turning up in France in the early 1950s – complete with a made-up distinguished service record in the resistance (his decorations, dated 1948, seemed to ignore the blinding reality that Legros was only 14 when the war ended).

Legros went on to become an art dealer, specialising in the likes of Derain, Dufy, Modigliani and Van Dongen, and always went to great lengths to provide certification of the authenticity of the paintings he sold – and it's said he was especially helped by an impoverished Van Dongen, who would rubber-stamp fakes of his own work at the end of his life.

But Legros' greatest scam was in getting the US Customs Service to do his job for him. Turning up with paintings in his luggage on arrival in America, he would declare them as cheap copies, and then look extremely shifty. Smelling a rat, the authorities would invariably call in art experts, who would pronounce the pictures genuine. Legros would then shrug his shoulders, pay the taxes due on original artworks, and walk off with the pictures, now able to sell them off as the real thing, as certified by the government.

In a later refinement of the same sting, he would have a modern picture painted on top of an expensive varnished forgery, and turn up at customs with a few chips in the paint, showing that there was indeed a picture underneath. The authorities would then feel they'd nailed their man, once again authenticating the 'older' painting as real.

Legros was eventually caught, of course, and jailed – otherwise we wouldn't be able to include him here. He died of throat cancer at the age of 52, in 1983. If you're in the market for fine art, of course, do your best to avoid anything which went through this fine-art dealer's hands.

VICTOR LUSTIG

The idea that someone actually got away with selling the Eiffel Tower (see page 229) sounds typically apocryphal – but it's true. What's more, the man who did it, Victor Lustig (or Count Victor Lustig, as he preferred to be called), successfully sold it not just once but twice.

Born in 1890 in Prague, he 'worked' the luxury transatlantic liner market before World War I, and then settled down in America as a full-time con-man. In 1925, on the run from the police, he found himself in Paris with another trickster, Dapper Dan Collins (a shabby dresser, no doubt). In the paper there was a snippet about how much the Eiffel Tower was costing to keep up, and a comment that it would probably be cheaper to scrap it than to maintain it.

Lustig promptly set himself up as a high-ranking government official (with Dapper Dan as his secretary) and sent invitations to five scrap merchants to come and meet him confidentially at the swanky Hotel Crillon. He explained to each the delicacy of the matter (there would be a public outcry), and asked them to tender their secret bid for the demolition work.

All five submitted bids, and Lustig selected the most gullible, a man called André Poisson (interestingly, the French for 'April Fool' is *poisson d'avril*), not only extracting from him the full amount for the Eiffel Tower itself but also a hefty bribe to secure the deal. Lustig and Dapper Dan ran off to Vienna with the money, where they waited for the scandal to break.

To their amazement, it didn't, Poisson having decided to swallow the loss. So back to Paris the tricksters came, and pulled off the sale a second time, with a new set of scrap dealers as marks. This time however the police were brought in, and Lustig and Dapper Dan beat a hasty retreat back to America.

Lustig continued conning his way through the next decade, before finally being jailed for 20 years in 1935 for his involvement in a counterfeiting scam. He died of pneumonia in Alcatraz, after serving twelve years of his sentence.

A simple lesson, then: however tempted you might be, resist strenuously any impulse you might have to buy the Eiffel Tower. Long after Lustig's demise, there are still plenty of sharks out there.

LEE MILLER

The American photographer Lee Miller lived an extraordinary life, shaped largely by her three years in Paris in her early twenties. Born in 1907 in Poughkeepsie, New York, she is said to have been raped by a family 'friend' at the age of seven, and persuaded by a well-meaning psychiatrist to separate sex and love. Whatever the truth of the story, Lee Miller certainly had plenty of affairs – usually brief.

She went to Paris for a year to study when she was 18, and met many artists there. Three years later, in 1928, she was back, working first as a model for Schiaparelli, and then meeting ace-photographer Man Ray and becoming his assistant and lover for three years. This was the period which allowed her to develop into a superb photographer herself, with an uncompromising eye for a wonderful shot, and the technical ability to make great prints.

In 1930 she suggested herself to the surrealist Jean Cocteau as the perfect person for the role of the female statue in the classic film *Le Sang d'un Poéte*, and she got the part – the only time she was ever really in front of the camera rather than behind it.

With her affair with Man Ray over, Lee Miller returned to New York and set up a successful portrait studio in 1933. A brief year later she married a wealthy Egyptian and went off to Cairo, living the life of a pampered spouse, though in the summer of 1937, in Paris, she met and fell in love with the English surrealist Roland Penrose. She returned to her husband in Egypt for two years, but in 1939 she returned to Penrose, who was waiting for her in England. They were to spend the rest of their lives together.

During the war, Miller found work at British *Vogue*, and took her most famous photographs, first of the blitz in London, then of the liberation of Paris on August 25 1944 – when she snapped old friends Jean Cocteau, Colette and Picasso on the same day. Finally, she was with the American troops when the concentration camps at Buchenwald and Dachau were liberated, and her pictures from the camps are some of the most direct and harrowing you'll ever see.

After the war she almost gave up as a photographer altogether, though she was nonetheless one of the first members of the Magnum Agency, and was still taking pictures of Picasso as late as 1970.

In 1947, finding she was pregnant, she married Roland Penrose, and became a mother that September, at the age of 40. Later on, as a doyenne of the arts, she co-founded the Institute of Contemporary Arts in London with her husband. She died of cancer in 1977.

You can buy newly printed Lee Miller photos from the original negatives at the Lee Miller Archives (www.leemiller.co.uk), as well as a number of books about her. Otherwise there are several collections of her pictures available in book form, though you may have to go through second-hand bookshops to find them.

AMEDEO MODIGLIANI

Born and brought up in Livorno, the Italian painter and sculptor Amedeo Modigliani was quick to show his enormous talent as an artist – in spite of never even remotely getting the hang of how to do hands or feet – but was hampered throughout his short life by weak lungs and a drink- and drug-dependent personality. It didn't stop him from becoming one of the greatest painters of the 20th century.

After studying art in Florence and Venice, Modigliani arrived in Paris at the age of 22, in 1906. Handsome already, he took up the Aristide Bruant look (see Toulouse-Lautrec, page 108), wearing a corduroy jacket, a bright scarf and a wide-brimmed hat. He also took to drink and drugs in a big way, falling not just for wine, rum and absinthe, but also dabbling with hashish, cocaine and even ether – none of which was to improve his already parlous health.

By 1909 he was in a sorry state, sick and destitute, and to be seen pushing his belongings along the streets in a wheelbarrow in the quest to escape angry unpaid landlords. He was constantly being arrested for drunkenness, and eventually returned home to Italy that summer for some much-needed rest and recuperation, starting off a trend which he would keep up for the rest of his life.

From 1910 to 1913 he turned to sculpture, having been influenced by the Romanian artist Constantin Brancusi, and he turned out some lovely primitive busts – but the dust was destroying his already enfeebled lungs, and as he couldn't afford to buy the materials, he was reduced to stealing stone from building sites.

From 1914 onwards, then, he focused exclusively on painting, bringing with him the sculptor's technique of elongating the neck and head. Unlike Van Gogh, he was irresistible to women and never short of models willing to pose (and more) for him, so he painted many portraits and more nudes, but few likenesses of himself.

In 1914 he had a short and stormy affair with the South African writer Beatrice Hastings, who was five years older than him. Their drunken fights were legendary, and Modigliani threw her through a window on one occasion.

During the middle years of the World War I, Modigliani was once again penniless – with the war on, his mother's monthly postal orders couldn't get through – and he was reduced to selling his drawings for the price of the next drink. But in July 1917 he met the 19-year-old Jeanne Hébuterne, his one true love, while out with his friend (and benefactor) Leopold Zborowski. Unfortunately he only had two and a half years left to live.

Hébuterne – herself a talented artist (she had studied at the Académie Colarossi, Camille Claudel's alma mater) – and Modigliani fell for each other and moved in together, and Zborowski put on Modigliani's first exhibition that October. None of the paintings and only a few of the drawings sold – hardly surprising, since the show was closed on the first day, for indecency.

With Modigliani sick and the weather worsening, Zborowski paid for the couple to spend the winter of 1917 in Nice, and by February the following year Jeanne was pregnant. After a brief separation (probably over Jeanne's mother also having come south with them) the couple reunited before their daughter was born – though the drunken father failed to register the child, who remained anonymous until she was adopted by Modigliani's family after his death.

Zborowski's tireless efforts to promote Modigliani's work finally began to pay off, and by June 1919 the couple – with Jeanne pregnant again – were able to move into a real home, on rue de la Grande Chaumière, in Montparnasse. That summer Modigliani's work started to fetch serious prices, but for the artist it was too late. Alcohol and drugs had ruined any chances he had for survival.

Modigliani took to his bed in the middle of January 1920, and it was only when a fellow painter dropped in to see him a few days later that a doctor was called. Jeanne, nine months pregnant, was hardly in a position to look after herself let alone Amedeo, and the flat was a mess, littered with bottles and half-eaten food. Modigliani died on January 24, and Jeanne, distraught, threw herself to her death from the fifth floor window of her parents' flat the following day. She was 21.

There isn't a Modigliani Museum – in France or anywhere else – but if you're in one of the world's top art galleries you're likely to come across one or more of his works. You can also visit Modigliani and Jeanne Hébuterne's grave, in **Père Lachaise cemetery**, in Paris. You'll find fresh flowers there at any time of the year, a testimony to his enduring popularity.

HENRI 'DOUANIER' ROUSSEAU

The world's most famous naïve artist was born in Laval in 1844. He had a relatively normal childhood, so the next we hear of him is in 1863, when he was caught with his fingers in the till at the local lawyer's office where he was working. After a month in prison, he joined the army for five years, only leaving when his father died, in 1869, to look after his mother.

In the same year he married the adorable 18-year-old Clémence Boitard, and in 1871 he found a job as a toll-collector at the Paris Customs Office, where he was to work for the next 22 years. Clémence bore him nine children, though seven died in infancy ('infantry' according to one potted online biography – but we'll assume that's a typo) and only one survived to adulthood. Clémence herself died of consumption in 1888.

Henri took to painting in his spare time, and in 1893 took early retirement to pursue it full-time, calling himself 'Douanier' Rousseau, even though he never rose anywhere near the full rank of Customs Officer. Supporting his modest pension by giving music, singing and drawing lessons, Rousseau studied hard, worked industriously and lived simply. His paintings were inspired, he said, by his time in the army in Mexico – though in truth he'd never left France, and the lush foliage, exotic animals and jungle scenes he painted came from zoos, botanical gardens and picture books.

It wasn't just in his painting, however, that he was naïve. Although (or perhaps because?) he was a kind, gentle man, he was forever the butt of other people's jokes or schemes – though he often seems to have been protected from the brunt of it by taking sarcasm and fake flattery at face value. It's even said he once agreed to vote in favour of expelling a painter who had become an embarrassment from the annual *Salon des Indépendants* – not realising the embarrassing painter was himself. It was only a joke, but a cruel one.

Rousseau, however, was indomitable, and absolutely convinced he was the greatest painter of his era. Prices for his works today don't prove him far wrong, but he was way ahead of his time – he would have been far better appreciated by the surrealists.

In 1899 he married again, but his second wife, Joséphine Nourri, also died young, in 1903. When he was 64, however, in 1908, his friend Picasso threw him a huge party which was to be the social event of his life. Originally intended in a somewhat lampoon-ish spirit, the party was attended by the whole gamut of the Paris art world. Buyers and dealers came in from America and Germany, and Georges Braque, Guillaume Apollinaire, Max Jacob and Gertrude Stein were all in evidence. Hung in pride of place was one of Rousseau's canvasses, *Portrait of a Woman* – bought by Picasso for a pittance from a second-hand shop especially for the occasion.

It was a huge success – even if dinner, which had been ordered from a nearby restaurant, never came (it had been ordered for the following night). People went out and returned with food and plenty of wine, and Douanier Rousseau loved it. He played his violin, and sang songs, and soon everyone was dancing. Towards the end of the party, with dawn breaking, he's said to have approached his host, paying him the highest possible compliment: 'Picasso, you and I are the two greatest painters of our time, you in the Egyptian style and I in the modern.'

Two years later, Douanier Rousseau died of gangrene, contracted from a cut on his leg which wouldn't heal. He was buried at Bagneux, in a pauper's grave.

Douanier Rousseau's studio in rue Perrel, in Paris (even the street itself no longer exists), has been faithfully recreated in the **Musée du Vieux-Château** in his home-town, Laval (between Rennes and Le Mans). There you'll find a collection of artefacts relating to his life, as well as two of the artist's paintings, along with an excellent collection of naïve art by other painters. The rest of his work is spread out across galleries worldwide – with several paintings in both the **Orangerie** and the **Musée d'Orsay** in Paris. My personal favourite, however, *Surprised! (Tropical Storm with a Tiger)* is in the National Gallery in London.

HENRI TOULOUSE-LAUTREC

Born into a noble family in Albi, at the end of 1864, Henri Toulouse-Lautrec was brought up in the family mansion, the 15th-century Château du Bosc. His father was a keen, if eccentric sportsman (he insisted on washing his socks in the river afterwards), with little time for the sickly Henri – who from the age of eight was spending far too much time bedridden with fevers and headaches for his father's tastes.

In 1878, aged 13, Henri's inherited brittle-bone syndrome (probably exacerbated by his parents being first cousins) manifested itself dramatically when he broke both femurs in separate accidents, first by falling off a chair, and then by slipping into a ditch, two months later.

He recovered, but his legs stopped growing, and although he was no dwarf (a common misapprehension), he was ill-proportioned, and certainly no looker. While recuperating, he took seriously to drawing and painting, and it became his one true passion. Against the objections of his father, Henri and his mother finally moved up to Paris in early 1882, so that he could study, and he was enrolled with the well-known portrait painter Léon Bonnat.

The two painters never hit it off, and it's suspected that Bonnat even went so far as to block Toulouse-Lautrec's works from becoming part of any national collection, right up to his death in 1922 ('You're good, Henri. Perhaps *too* good.'). Fortunately, Toulouse-Lautrec went on to study under the more sympathetic Ferdinand Cormon, where one of his fellow students was Vincent Van Gogh.

In 1884, Toulouse-Lautrec moved up to Montmartre. Being outside the city limits at the time, there were lower taxes on alcohol, and the area was a thriving hotbed of cabarets, dance-halls, night-clubs, brothels and bars – and popular with up-and-coming artists. Toulouse-Lautrec took to it like a duck to water, and was soon a familiar sight on the night streets. During the day, however, he worked prodigiously and prolifically, and in a brief, 16-year career produced more than 700 paintings, nearly 300 lithographs and over 5,000 drawings.

One of his models was Suzanne Valadon (see page 110), who would later go on to make a career of painting herself (no, not body-painting), though at the time she was also modelling for Degas and Renoir. In 1888, with Gauguin and Van Gogh about to raise hell down in Arles, Valadon and Toulouse-Lautrec had a fling, and the painter – like Erik Satie (see page 127), five years later – was completely smitten. But – as with Erik Satie – all the feeling was one-way, and Valadon and Toulouse-Lautrec soon parted company.

The following year the Moulin Rouge opened, and the next few years were Toulouse-Lautrec's heyday. He became friends with the famous Moulin Rouge dancers Jane Avril and La Goulue (see box, overleaf), and when the Moulin Rouge was re-launched in 1891 it was with Toulouse-Lautrec's posters – including most notably La Goulue herself. He also became friends with the singer Aristide Bruant, who commissioned Toulouse-Lautrec when he took over the Chat Noir for his new club, the Mirliton, leading to some of the artist's most famous posters, with Bruant wearing his distinctive red scarf and broad-brimmed black hat.

But the lifestyle was taking an awful toll on the artist, and by 1893 he was suffering terribly from alcoholism and syphilis, and had moved back in with his mother. His decline was pitiful, and he endured appalling alcoholic hallucinations. After a particularly bad attack of *delirium tremens* he was committed to a clinic in Neuilly in 1899. After producing a wonderful series of circus drawings from memory, he was released – but he went straight back to the bottle.

In the summer of 1901, down in Bordeaux for the sea air, he had a stroke, and died in September in his mother's arms at the family Château de Malromé, near

LA GOULUE

Louise-Josephine Weber was destined to become a laundress, but from the age of 16, in 1882, she would borrow freshly laundered clothes and go dancing every night in Montmartre.

She soon attracted a following, not just for her provocative behaviour, dancing on tables and tipping off men's hats with a well-practised kick, but for her sheer lust for life, and her phenomenal capacity for alcohol – hence the name, La Goulue, meaning 'glutton'.

It wasn't long before Renoir discovered her. She modelled for him, and he introduced her to more upmarket cabarets, leading to her being hired by the Moulin Rouge as its star attraction. She continued to be outrageous, and was the only dancer of the period to do her act hatless.

Her dance partner was a man called Jacques Renaudin, who led a double life as a respectable wine merchant by day and a cabaret dancer by night. Tall, thin and lithe, and dancing with extraordinary dexterity, he was known as Valentin le Désossé (the boneless), and was much in demand – but refused all forms of payment. Toulouse-Lautrec's most famous painting features La Goulue behind the sinewy silhouette of her partner.

In 1895, everything went pear-shaped, when La Goulue decided she wanted all the fame and money for herself. She left the Moulin Rouge and spent a small fortune on setting up her own club, but the punters stayed away in droves. In the same year – and who knows if it's related – Valentin le Désossé disappeared without trace.

La Goulue went on to work as an animal tamer, and one source claims she managed to shoot – albeit not fatally – both a man called Pézon, who taught her to tame animals, and a conjurer called Droxler, who she may or may not have married afterwards.

By the early 20th century, La Goulue herself was pear-shaped, and year by year she continued to put on weight and to suffer the increasing ravages of alcoholism. When she returned to Montmartre in the 1920s she was unrecognisable and destitute, selling flowers, peanuts and cigarettes on the streets to scrape a living. On her deathbed, in 1929, she asked the priest 'Father, will God forgive me? I am La Goulue.'

Langon. His father arrived unexpectedly in time for the deathbed scene, leading to confused reports about his last words, which were either addressed to his mother – *'Toi, maman, rien que toi'* – or to his father, who was flicking at flies with Henri's shoelaces – 'Old fool.' Toulouse-Lautrec was just 36 years old.

Long after his death, Toulouse-Lautrec's work stayed in his studio in Montmartre, as museums wouldn't take it (Bonnat at work?). But in 1922, the town of Albi welcomed back its most famous son, and hosted the collection you can still see there today.

The **Toulouse-Lautrec Museum** is housed in the Palais de la Berbie, an impressive brick-built 13th-century bishops' fortress next door to Albi's wonderful tall-naved cathedral. Inside is a collection of more than 1,000 works by Toulouse-Lautrec, and it's one of the best museums in France.

SUZANNE VALADON

Also born to a laundress, but a year older than La Goulue (see box, above), was Suzanne Valadon. The illegitimate girl supported herself from the age of nine as a circus acrobat, but gave up the profession in 1881, at the age of 16, when she fell off a trapeze, turning instead to the less risky *métier* of artist's model – and within a year she was immortalised in Renoir's *Bal à Bougival*, and again the following year in *Danse à la Ville*.

Like so many artist's models she was also soon pregnant, and after labouring through Christmas Day 1883 (anyone who's spent Christmas at home with my family will know the feeling), she delivered a baby boy called Maurice, on Boxing Day. The real father was never formally acknowledged, but when Maurice was seven, in January 1891, he was officially adopted by the Spanish art historian, Miguel Utrillo (and there's compelling evidence that Miguel was actually the father), and the boy became Maurice Utrillo (see box, overleaf).

Valadon continued modelling, and sat for many famous painters including Puvis de Chavannes, Degas and Toulouse-Lautrec (see page 108), having an affair with the latter in 1888. She was encouraged to take up painting herself, and spent years perfecting her skills before showing her works to anyone. By the end of the 1880s she had her own studio, where she kept a goat, feeding it on failed drawings and canvasses.

During Christmas 1892 she met Erik Satie, the composer (see page 127), at the noisy and cheerful Auberge du Clou, where he played piano for a living. The 26-year-old Satie proposed to the 27-year-old Valadon on their first date, on 14 January, and while she didn't accept, it nonetheless marked the beginning of a passionate six month affair at 6 rue Cortot. Valadon painted Satie's portrait and Satie drew hers.

Satie also made friends with the nine-year-old Utrillo, giving him, instead of his mother, flowers, and making him paper boats and teaching him to sail them on the lake in the Luxembourg gardens.

Satie himself gives two accounts of how the affair ended, in June, with the only common thread being the involvement of the police. In the first he says he went to complain that a woman was annoying him, and the police arrived to throw her out – while in the second he claims he went to the police to confess to throwing Valadon out of the window and killing her. When the police arrived on the scene they found Valadon gone – being an acrobat she'd survived the fall.

It was the end of Satie's only known relationship, and he continued to write her love letters for the rest of his life, though he never sent them. On Satie's death, in 1925, the whole bundle was given to Valadon – she burned all but one, which she showed people with her name and address at the top cut off.

In 1894, Suzanne Valadon became the first woman to be admitted into the Société Nationale des Beaux-Arts, and two years later, probably seeking security in order to be able to paint, she married the financier Paul Moussis. By 1906, after several moves, they were back at rue Cortot, this time at number 12, which is now the Musée de Montmartre, but had earlier been Renoir's first address in Montmartre. Utrillo, out of the sanatorium (see box, overleaf), lived and worked in a studio upstairs.

At the age of 44 she fell in love with André Utter, a 23-year-old electrician who had steered a drunken Utrillo home one night. She left Moussis in 1909, and married Utter in 1914. The following year she had her first solo exhibition, which was a great success – so much so that by 1923, she, Utter and Utrillo were installed in a château they had bought in Beaujolais, and Valadon was feeding her cats caviar on Fridays.

She painted prolifically, though was later abandoned by Utter. She moved back to Paris, with Utrillo, and they saw out her last days on Avenue Junot, just round the corner from rue Cortot. When she died, in 1938, Picasso, Derain and Braque came to the funeral.

MAURICE UTRILLO

Maurice Utrillo was a difficult child, and took to wine at an early age. Leaving school at 17, he was soon exhibiting signs of the alcoholism and madness which would torment him for the rest of his life, and he spent several periods incarcerated in asylums.

On the advice of a doctor friend, Valadon taught her son to paint, initially as a form of therapy, and he soon showed he had a real talent of his own. Under the watchful eye of his mother, his talent blossomed, and his fits of rage were mostly kept under control. His pictures are entirely urban, and usually unpeopled – largely because they were mostly painted using postcards rather than reality for inspiration.

From the mid-1920s onwards, Utrillo became famous in his own right, and his paintings sold well. At the age of 50, he was baptised, and two years later he married the energetic but enigmatic Lucie Pauwels (also known as Lucie Valore), who installed the couple in a nice house in Le Vésinet, a pleasant suburb west of Paris in a loop of the Seine.

For the next 20 years, until his death, Lucie looked after Utrillo, who painted and painted – some masterpieces, many fine works, and a surprising number of real duds. When he died, in 1955, 50,000 people followed the cortège to the Cimetière St Vincent, where Utrillo is buried with his mother.

Both Valadon's and Utrillo's works are spread widely in galleries around the world, though there's also the **Musée Utrillo-Valadon** in Sannois, in the northwestern suburbs of Paris. You can see pictures of Valadon by going to the **Musée d'Orsay**, where you'll find Renoir's *Danse à la Ville* – though the original of the *Bal à Bougival* is in the Museum of Fine Arts in Boston.

The **Musée de Montmartre** now occupies one of the houses Valadon and Utrillo shared, at 12 rue Cortot. Down the hill you'll find the Maison Rose which featured so often in Utrillo's paintings, just above the **Cimetière St Vincent**, where both painters are buried.

VINCENT VAN GOGH

The whole of Vincent Van Gogh's dramatic career as a painter was crammed into the last ten years of his short life, and it was only in the last five years that he painted anything approaching a masterpiece.

Born in 1853, he had an ordinary Dutch childhood, and was then taken on at the family's art-dealing firm at the age of 16. From 1872 onwards, until his death, he kept up an intense correspondence with his brother, Théo, and it's this more than anything which tells us what we know of his life and allows us a glimpse of the awful madness often raging in his head.

In 1873 the firm sent him to England, and for a while he lived at 87 Hackford Road, near the Oval, in London (your author used to live across the street, at number 44a – and you can add that to the growing list of 'things you didn't need to know'). He dropped out of art dealing, deciding first that he was better suited to teaching, and when that failed, to preaching.

By 1876 he was working as an evangelist amongst dirt-poor miners in Belgium, but he was soon taken off the job by the church, for being too intense and scaring off the parishioners. With a sense of failure which was to stay with him until his death, he took up art in 1880, and studied hard – financed by Théo – perfecting an unusual style which we now see as so distinctively Van Gogh. In April 1885 he painted his first original masterpiece, *The Potato Eaters*, and within a year was hammering on Théo's door at 54 rue Lepic, in Montmartre.

Théo reluctantly took his brother in, and they had a difficult two years together in Paris – about which we know little, as of course they then stopped corresponding. Van Gogh painted 28 out of his 43 self-portraits during this period, probably because he had trouble finding models wiling to sit for him – he was thoroughly anti-social and succeeded in alienating all who met him, refusing to greet people in the street, wearing filthy clothes, and being unkempt and unwashed. It was in Paris that he started drinking seriously, and absinthe may have further unhinged an already slackly hung mind.

In February 1888, Van Gogh moved to Arles (again sponsored by his brother), and once the weather had cheered up he had one of the most productive and happy few months of his life. Théo wanted Van Gogh to have company, however, and in July a small inheritance allowed him to sponsor Gauguin to go and live with Vincent at the so-called 'Studio of the South'.

Gauguin (see page 101) arrived in October, and if it was an artistically fruitful period for the pair of them, inevitably they got on each others nerves, especially after Van Gogh insisted on them both painting his way, out of doors, from nature – rather than indoors, from the imagination, which was what Gauguin wanted.

Things ended badly on December 23. After a spat the night before, Van Gogh came after Gauguin with a razor, and then later (in remorse?) hacked off part of his ear, delivering it personally to the local brothel before passing out in a blood-soaked bed.

The police were called, and Vincent was taken to hospital. Gauguin didn't visit, for fear of further disturbing the deranged Van Gogh, and caught the next train out. The two painters never saw each other again. Not long after recovering and being discharged from hospital, Van Gogh committed himself to the asylum in St Rémy de Provence, and spent nearly a year there, producing an astonishing 143 paintings in a fevered frenzy.

Van Gogh was quite right to be frightened of himself – when he was sick, he was very, very sick, suffering terrible seizures, extreme depression, nightmarish hallucinations and becoming ever more prone to appalling acts of violence. He would even poison himself by eating his oil paints and drinking his thinners.

In May 1890, Van Gogh moved to Auvers sur Oise, 30km northwest of Paris, under the supervision of the kindly Dr Gachet. Over the next few weeks he made a remarkable recovery and painted some of his finest works – but on 27 July he went out for a walk and shot himself in the chest with a pistol (you have to wonder: who the hell sold Van Gogh a gun?). It's quite possible he was feeling terrible about Théo's latest financial woes.

Van Gogh managed to get back to his room, but told nobody what was wrong – and when a doctor was finally called, it was only to discover that the bullet couldn't be removed. Vincent spent his last hours sitting in bed smoking a pipe, with Théo at his side. On July 29, the 37-year-old artist died, and was buried in a coffin covered with a huge array of yellow flowers, including his favourite, sunflowers.

In a tragic postscript, the event proved too much for Théo, who lost his mind, spent some time in an asylum himself, and died just six months after his brother, aged only 33. Théo's widow did everything she could to rescue the Van Goghs from oblivion, transcribing the letters and exhibiting the paintings.

She did an excellent job. While only one of Van Gogh's paintings sold in his lifetime (to a friend of Théo's), within a century after his death, the *Portrait of Dr Gachet* became, in May 1990, the world's priciest painting, when it sold at auction for US$ 82.5 million.

The best collection of Van Gogh's works is in the museum dedicated to him in Amsterdam, which has an excellent website (www.vangoghgallery.com) with all the paintings.

You can also go to **Auvers sur Oise**, where you'll find the **Auberge Ravoux**, which is now known as the **Maison de Van Gogh** – it's the only house he ever stayed in which has remained intact. You can visit Van Gogh's room, which was the cheapest in the establishment in 1890.

Not far away is the cemetery where Vincent and Théo Van Gogh are buried. The ivy running across the graves originally came from a sprig in Dr Gachet's garden.

FASHION VICTIMS

The world of fashion isn't anything as like as eccentric – or indeed fashionable – as it would like to think. But a few oddballs stand out from the crowd…

Coco Chanel

Gabrielle Bonheur 'Coco' Chanel did more than any other person to change the way women dress, and it's difficult now, nearly a century on, to realise how influential she really was.

Her early life is a confused mystery – she was always reinventing bits of her past – but most sources agree that she was born in some obscurity in August 1883 in the Auvergne. Her mother died young and her father abandoned the family, so she and her sister were brought up in a convent. By the time she was in her early twenties, however, she was working as a café-concert singer in Moulins and Vichy, and had taken the stage name Coco, which was to stay with her ever after.

Fortunately for her (she really wasn't a great singer) she was taken up by a wealthy cavalryman called Etienne Balsan, and went to live with him at his château outside Paris. As a keen horsewoman herself, she became the first woman to wear riding britches, and she started designing straw hats to wear to the races.

Encouraged (and indeed funded) by Balsan, she opened a small milliner's shop in Paris in 1909. In the same year she met the well-heeled, polo-playing Arthur 'Boy' Capel, who fronted her the money to move her shop to better premises at 21 rue de Cambon the next year.

The shop thrived, and Chanel had soon branched out into bespoke fashion – in spite of being a lousy seamstress herself – becoming the first designer to make practical clothes for women. Capel encouraged (and helped) her open up a second store, in Deauville, in 1914, and a third, in Biarritz, the following year, and with the war on and many shops closed for business, they thrived.

In Deauville she discovered the value of live models, promenading herself and her radical designs along the front, and she introduced trousers, striped sailor's shirts and collarless box jackets into women's wardrobes. In 1917 – apparently after a rather dramatic singeing incident – she cut off most of her hair and introduced the bob cut to the world.

By 1919, she had established herself as a couturier in Paris, and had moved to a bigger establishment at 31 rue de Cambon. Capel, however, wasn't so fortunate, being killed by driving too fast and losing control of his car on his way to Nice. But in spite of being married to someone else by then, he left a sizeable chunk of money to Chanel.

In 1920 Chanel was introduced to the perfume-maker Ernest Beaux in Grasse, and together they came up with Chanel Number 5, which became the first globally sold perfume, and made Chanel's fortune – her 2% royalty on gross sales in 1947 alone netted her more than a million dollars. Launched in perfume's first transparent bottle, Chanel Number 5 was also the first to carry a designer's name. The art-deco stopper was made in the shape of Chanel's favourite square in Paris, Place Vendôme.

Chanel's star was still on the ascendant. In the 1920s she launched the famous 'little black dress' and branched out into a hugely successful range of costume jewellery. She also dated the Duke of Westminster, claiming to turn down his marriage proposal with the immortal 'There are a plenty of duchesses, but only one Coco Chanel' – though most sources say it was he and not she who tired of the liaison.

As the most famous name in fashion, Chanel was hired for a million dollars by Samuel Goldwyn, in 1931, to come and dress his Hollywood stars (Katharine Hepburn and Gloria Swanson among them), but – unable to fit in with the studio system – she was soon back in France. Once there she moved into private quarters in the Ritz hotel, overlooking her beloved Place Vendôme. She would keep her rooms there for the rest of her life.

In 1939 it all started to go wrong. As war approached, she closed down her business, and revealed an unpleasant anti-semitic and homophobic side of her character (in spite of dallying in that direction herself on occasion). In 1941 she took up with Hans-Gunther von Dincklage, a Nazi officer, and lived openly with him at the Ritz.

The French never forgave her, and she lived in exile in Switzerland until she was able to make a fashion comeback in 1954, claiming to be upset with Christian Dior's latest corseted look for women. During the 1950s and 1960s she was a pariah in France but became increasingly popular in America, and designed beautiful clothes for Audrey Hepburn, Grace Kelly and Elizabeth Taylor.

She died at the Ritz in January 1971, aged 87. There were only three outfits in her wardrobe.

There's no obvious memorial to Coco Chanel, though her name lives on through the successful fashion house (www.chanel.com) – and there are plenty of books featuring photos and pictures of her designs.

Christian Dior

Christian Dior, the name behind one of fashion's most enduring brands, was born in 1905. The family's fertiliser fortune ('this business stinks') kept the Diors in some style, and with serious plans for Christian to become a diplomat, he was made to study political science. Having wanted to study art all along, Dior did the next best thing, hanging out in Paris with Jean Cocteau and his gay friends.

In a spirit of compromise (and aware, presumably, that Christian wasn't really ambassadorial material anyway) Dior's mother finally helped him open an art gallery, with his friend Jacques Bonjean – with the sole condition being that the Dior name be kept off the letterhead and shop front.

The stock market crash at the end of the 1920s ruined both his father and his partner, and his mother died after a routine operation in 1931, leaving Dior penniless. Fortunately, however, he started selling fashion sketches soon after this, and his hats, in particular, proved highly popular. In 1938 he was hired by Robert Piquet as a designer, moving to Lucien Lelong in 1941, where he became friends with the young Pierre Balmain.

At the end of the war, Dior was approached by the textile manufacturer Marcel Boussac to jump-start Philippe et Gaston, but said he would only work under his own name. In December 1946, he finally had his wishes granted, and Christian Dior opened its doors at 30 Avenue Montaigne – something which never would have happened if his mother had still been alive.

In February 1947, Dior launched 'The New Look' on the world, and it was a sensation. Years of war austerity were suddenly over, and big shoulders, narrow waists and flowing skirts were in.

Over the next decade Dior, the fashion house, went from strength to strength, introducing fabulously profitable licensing to the fashion industry in 1948, and designing successful variations on the clothes twice a year. But Dior the man was in failing health, having already had a heart attack in 1947, and was working himself (and his staff) to exhaustion.

Convinced he was ugly – not at all the case – Dior was forever going on keep-fit crash diets (not a brilliant strategy if you have a dicky ticker), and especially so when enamoured of the latest young thing. Exhausted and on holiday in Italy with his young Algerian lover after the September 1957 collection, a diet was the last thing Dior needed, and on October 23 he had a fatal heart attack. He was 52.

He was succeeded at Dior by the youngest-ever couturier, the 21-year-old Yves St Laurent.

The Dior holiday house. **Le Villa les Rhumbs** in Granville, on the Cherbourg peninsula, is now a museum, with Dior's early designs and dresses on display along with various perfume prototypes. There's an annual exhibition on a Dior theme, and you can wander round the gardens so beloved of Dior's mother.

Yves Saint Laurent

Yves Saint Laurent, the last true couturier, was born in Algeria in 1936, but grew up (like Dior!) in a wealthy household in Normandy. It didn't stop him being bullied at school – it still happens to gay boys, even if it shouldn't – or wanting to design theatre sets for a living. At the age of 17, however, he did well in a competition to design a 'little black dress' and turned his sights onto a career in fashion.

He went up to Paris the following year to study at fashion school, and was introduced to the editor of French *Vogue*, Michel de Brunhoff, who immediately published some of his drawings – bringing him to the attention of Christian Dior. Dior hired Yves Saint Laurent, and by 1957 there were already Saint Laurent designs in the Dior collection. When Christian Dior died on holiday that autumn, Yves Saint Laurent was nominated as his successor, and became the youngest couturier ever. From 1958 to 1960, his collections for Dior became increasingly radical, until (in a dirty trick) the company's conservative management finally lifted his immunity from national service.

Yves wasn't emotionally in tune with being in the army (*quelle surprise*), and after only three weeks had a mental collapse, and was sent to a psychiatric hospital.

Dior's management, sympathetic to the last, fired him. Fortunately, Pierre Bergé was on hand to come to the rescue. The two had met in 1958, when Bergé was the manager and lover of the painter Bernard Buffet, and had got together after Buffet had run off with the woman who was to become his wife. Bergé got Saint Laurent out of hospital and helped him file for damages with Dior, and they used the money to start up a new fashion house in 1961.

With Yves at the drawing board and Pierre at the business controls, the Yves Saint Laurent brand went from strength to strength, with the creation of the first dinner jacket for women in 1965, the launch of the first ready-to-wear boutique in 1966, and later the arrival of the first transparent fashion wear. Yves Saint Laurent himself however became increasingly reclusive as the years went on – in spite of having posed nude for his own perfume's advertising campaign in 1971 – and by the 1990s was only seen at the Paris fashion shows.

In January 2002, just two weeks before his 200th show was due to take place, the 65-year-old Yves Saint Laurent announced it would be his last, and that he was retiring from the business. In a moving speech, Yves Saint Laurent said 'I have nothing in common with this new world of fashion, which has been reduced to mere window-dressing. Elegance and beauty have been banished.'

In a spectacular bow-out, the show took place at the Pompidou Centre, and was beamed out on giant screens to the crowds outside. Over 90 minutes long, it featured 100 models and more than 250 outfits from the designer's 44-year career, and was closed by his long-time friend Catherine Deneuve singing '*Ma Plus Belle Histoire d'Amour*'. There wasn't a dry eye in the house.

For more than 40 years, Yves Saint Laurent kept the originals of his wonderful creations, and you can see them at the **Yves Saint Laurent Centre** in Paris. Altogether the collection comprises some 5,000 outfits, more than 10,000 pieces of jewellery, and over 2,000 pairs of shoes.

There's also a rather groovy website (www.ysl-hautecouture.com) though whether it will continue to be maintained now that the couturier himself has retired is open to question.

TRAVEL INFORMATION

Cimetière St Vincent 6 rue Lucien Gaulard, 75018, Paris; M̄ Lamarck-Caulaincourt, Abbesses; open every day; free.

Espace Salvador Dalí 11 rue Poulbot, 75018, Paris; tel: 01 42 64 40 10; M̄ Abbesses; open every day; €7.

Maison de Van Gogh 8, rue de la Sansonne, Auvers sur Oise; tel: 01 30 36 60 60; closed Mon and Feb; €5.

Musée des Beaux-Arts Place de la République, Lille; tel: 03 20 06 78 00; open Wed–Sun and Monday afternoons; €4.

Musée de Montmartre 12 rue Cortot, 75018, Paris; tel: 01 46 06 61 11; M̄ Lamarck-Caulaincourt, Abbesses; closed Mon; €4.

Musée de l'Orangerie 1 place de la Concorde, 75001, Paris; tel 01 42 61 30 82; M̄ Concorde; currently closed for renovation.

Musée d'Orsay Quai Anatole France, 75007, Paris; tel: 01 40 49 48 14; web: www.musee-orsay.fr; M̄ Musée d'Orsay (RER C), Solférino; open Tue–Sun; €7.

Musée Rodin Hôtel Biron, 77 rue de Varenne, 75007, Paris; tel: 01 44 18 61 10; web: www.musee-rodin.fr; M̄ Invalides (RER C), Varenne; open Tue–Sun; €5.

Musée Utrillo-Valadon Villa Rozée, Place du Général Leclerc, Sannois, in the northwestern suburbs of Paris; tel: 01 39 98 21 13; M̄ Sannois (RER C); closed Mon; ∈ 4.

Musée du Vieux-Château Place de la Trémoille, Laval; tel: 02 43 53 39 89; closed Mon and public holidays; ∈ 3.

Père Lachaise Cemetery 75020, Paris; M̄ Père Lachaise, Philippe-Auguste, Gambetta; open every day; free.

Toulouse-Lautrec Museum Palais de la Berbie, Albi; tel: 05 63 49 48 70; open every day except Tue in winter; ∈ 4.50.

Villa des Brillants 19 avenue Auguste Rodin, Meudon; tel: 01 41 14 35 00; web: www.musee-rodin.fr; open Fri–Sun, May–Oct; ∈ 2.

Le Villa les Rhumbs Granville; tel: 02 33 61 48 21; open every day May–Sep; ∈ 5.

Yves Saint Laurent Centre 11 rue de Cambrai, Paris; tel: 01 53 35 85 38; M̄ Corentin-Cariou; by appointment only.

Eccentrically Musical/
Eccentric Performers

There's something special about musicians, composers and performers which sets them apart from the rest of society – and that's true even of the ones who don't sleep in coffins, name everything they invent after themselves, or get killed by their own scarves.

ECCENTRICALLY MUSICAL

Composers and musicians are already a strange bunch ('I can hear noises in my head, doctor'), and France has had its fair share – from Jim Morrison falling out of Oscar Wilde's bedroom window in Paris and Erik Satie living in a cupboard in Montmartre, to the unlikely deaths of the composers Alkan, Chausson and Lully.

Charles-Valentin Alkan

Charles-Valentin Alkan was not only one of the most talented pianists of the 19th century, but also one of its most enigmatic composers.

He was born Charles-Valentin Morhange, in 1813 (the same year as Verdi and Wagner), though he, his elder sister, and his four younger brothers all took their father's first name, Alkan, as their last, a sign of respect in a good Jewish family.

All six children went on to become musicians, but Charles-Valentin was the most exceptionally gifted, entering the Paris Conservatoire at the age of six, and winning his first prizes from the age of seven. At 12 he gave his concert debut, and at 14 published his first composition. By the time he was 17 he was famous in salons across the capital, and during his twenties he was sharing pupils with his friend Chopin (see page 122). Other pals included Victor Hugo and Georges Sand (see page 144), and Franz Liszt was an admirer of his technique.

From the mid-1830s onwards he lived in two apartments, one above the other, on the fashionable Square d'Orléans, close to Chopin and to Zimmerman, the director of the Conservatoire. But in 1838, after publishing *Trois Grandes Etudes*, he disappeared from sight for six whole years.

He re-emerged (blinking into the daylight, no doubt) in 1844 with a big sheaf of compositions and a popular concert schedule – Liszt and Chopin both came to the first night – only to disappear again in a huff on finding out he'd been passed over for Zimmerman's job at the Conservatoire in favour of a far less talented musician.

In reclusive isolation – we know almost nothing of what went on in Alkan's life for the next 25 years – he continued to compose, turning out some extraordinary pieces. Writing, like Chopin, almost exclusively for the piano, Alkan's most significant compositions are his Grande Sonate (opus 33) and his 12 major key (opus 35) and minor key (opus 39) studies.

To say that these are hard to play would be a ludicrous understatement – they contain some of the toughest technical challenges a pianist can face. Alkan has even been accused of perversity, in making the performer's life a misery, though it's

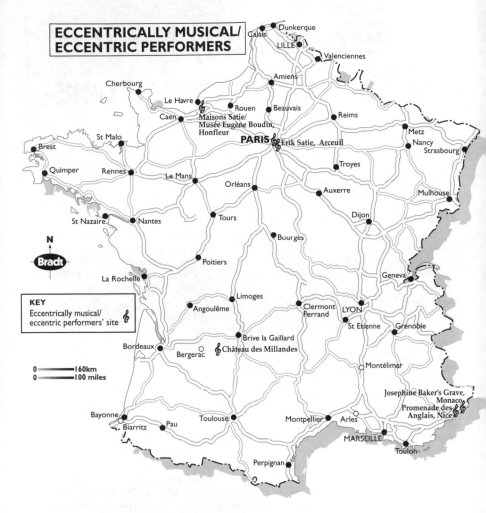

ECCENTRICALLY MUSICAL/ECCENTRIC PERFORMERS

Dunkerque
Calais
LILLE
Valenciennes
Amiens
Cherbourg
Le Havre
Rouen
Beauvais
Reims
Caen
Maisons Satie/
Musée Eugène Boudin,
Honfleur
St Malo
Metz
PARIS
Erik Satie, Arceuil
Nancy
Brest
Strasbourg
Quimper
Rennes
Le Mans
Troyes
Orléans
Auxerre
Mulhouse
St Nazaire
Nantes
Tours
Dijon
Bourges
N
Bradt
Poitiers
Geneva
La Rochelle

KEY
Eccentrically musical/
eccentric performers' site

Limoges
Angoulême
Clermont Ferrand
LYON
St Etienne
Grenoble
Brive la Gaillard
Bordeaux
Bergerac
Château des Millandes
Montélimar

0 ——— 160km
0 ——— 100 miles

Josephine Baker's Grave,
Monaco,
Promenade des
Anglais, Nice
Bayonne
Pau
Toulouse
Montpellier
Arles
Biarritz
MARSEILLE
Toulon
Perpignan

possible that being such a virtuoso player himself he didn't think the obstacles were so unfair.

Alkan also wrote more eclectic pieces, including *Le Chemin de Fer*, the first ever musical work dedicated to the railway, and *Marcia Funebre sulla Morte d'un Pappagallo*, a composition for a chamber quintet and singers, which translates literally into 'Funeral March for a Dead Parrot'. The nearest equivalent in English to the opening line, *'As-tu déjeuné, Jacot?'* would be 'Has Polly had his breakfast?'.

During his reclusive years Alkan also composed for the *pédalier*, a curious (and long gone) cross between a piano and organ, with the thirty bass strings connected to pedals instead of keys. As well as more conventional works, Alkan wrote at least two sets of *pédalier* Etudes for feet alone, and one bizarre – and rather intimate – duet for four feet. A clear case of 'you should get out more, Charles-Valentin'.

From 1873 onwards, at the age of 60, Alkan gave annual recitals, though he preferred to play arcane 18th-century works rather than his own compositions, helping his music into an obscurity which it only really emerged from in the 1970s.

In 1888, while reaching up for his beloved Talmud, Alkan was allegedly crushed to death by a large bookcase – though there are reports that Alkan's colourful demise may simply have been a fiction (invented no doubt by an imaginative piano student, sick of trying to overcome the difficulties in opus 39).

There's not much evidence of Alkan's life, but there are plenty of recordings of his works to choose from – with unquestionably the best being Ronald Smith's superb performances.

Ernest Chausson

Ernest Chausson had a short but interesting life. Born into a wealthy family in 1855 in Paris – his father was the aptly named and extremely prosperous Prosper Chausson, a public works contractor whose career neatly dovetailed with Baron Haussmann's rebuilding of the capital – Ernest had a privileged childhood and went on to study law, qualifying in 1876 and earning his doctorate in 1877.

Preferring the bars in music to being at the bar in a powdered wig, he dropped law, and went to study at the Conservatoire under Jules Massenet, who was then reaching the height of his fame. With 14 operas already under his belt (he went on to write a total of 44), he was a credible French alternative to – and indeed the antithesis of – the German heavyweight Richard Wagner.

Massenet and Chausson didn't get along – was Chausson the butt of endless jokes about being a *slippery* customer, or as bland as an apple *turnover* (chausson is the French word for both slipper and turnover), or was it just the old chestnut of 'musical differences'? (Actually, it was his failure to win the coveted Prix de Rome, but who's quibbling?)

Chausson went on instead to study under the celebrated César Franck, and visited Bayreuth in 1882 for the premier of Wagner's *Parsifal*, accompanied by the gifted young Vincent d'Indy (who went on to give lessons in later years to both Erik Satie and Cole Porter). They both became instant fans.

The following year Richard Wagner died, and Chausson (in an unrelated incident) married the pianist Jeanne Escudier. They honeymooned in Bayreuth, and went on to have five children. Chausson divided his time between composition, family, and friends – and his celebrated salon at 22 boulevard de Courcelles soon became *the* place to be seen. Degas, Monet, Puvis de Chavannes, Redon, Renoir, Mallarmé, Turgenev, Fauré and Debussy were amongst the regulars.

As an independently wealthy man, Chausson composed relatively little (he left behind only four orchestral works, for example, although his work often appears in compilations with other French Romantics). However, he was influential in French music, furthering the career in particular of the impoverished Claude Debussy. Sadly, on June 10 1899, on a short break at the family château at Limay, west of Paris, the 44-year-old composer set out for an evening cycle ride, but only made it as far as the front porch, cracking his head against the containing wall and dying instantly.

Frédéric Chopin

Fryderyk Franciszek Chopin was born in Poland in 1810, and was quickly recognised as a child prodigy, turning in his first *polonaises* at the age of seven. A week before his eighth birthday he gave his first major concert in Warsaw, and by the time he hit his teens he was a household name in musical circles across Europe.

In 1831 he set off for Paris, giving concerts along the way, and arrived in the autumn. His first major gig in the French capital – having transformed his first names to the more manageable Frédéric François – was a smash hit, and allowed Chopin to earn a handsome living giving piano lessons. In spite of being an extraordinarily gifted pianist, however, he himself performed only reluctantly and rarely.

After a failed engagement in 1835 to an émigré Polish girl (her family broke it off citing his ill-health and erratic lifestyle) he met Georges Sand (see page 144) in 1837, and the couple fell in love. She was six years older than Chopin, and provided him with the care and security he needed – though spending the winter of 1838 in Majorca with her nearly killed him. The former monastery they'd taken for winter digs was unheated, and the weather was unusually inclement. Chopin, never in the best of health, fell ill, and for weeks was too sick to leave the house. He nonetheless composed frantically, turning out some masterpieces.

The following summer, after a long convalescence, he moved in with Georges Sand at her country house in Nohant, near Bourges, in the centre of France, and he spent his summers here right up until 1846. They were the happiest times of Chopin's life – and the most productive, too, with most of his finest work composed at Nohant.

At first, Chopin and Sand were discreet about their relationship in Paris, where they lived in the winters, but they were soon being treated as a married couple by their friends, among them the painter Delacroix, and the composer Alkan (see page 119). They maintained separate addresses, but were rarely seen apart, except when Chopin was teaching.

Unfortunately his health was continuing to slide downhill, and it wasn't improved at all by breaking up with Georges Sand in the summer of 1847. Chopin had a minor breakdown and more or less stopped composing. The following spring, persuaded by a Scottish pupil to get out more, he set off on a tour of England and Scotland, where the damp climate pretty much put the last nail in his coffin.

On November 16, in a shocking state, he gave his last ever concert at the Guildhall, in London, for Polish émigrés, and returned forthwith to Paris. Too ill to give lessons, he was nursed through the summer by his sister, but succumbed in October to tuberculosis. He was 39 years old.

After a funeral service at La Madeleine, the cortège wound its way up to **Père Lachaise cemetery**, where Chopin is buried – all except his heart, that is, which was taken back to Warsaw by his sister, according to the composer's wishes, and enshrined in the Chapel of the Holy Cross there.

Unlike many composers, there are more memorials to Chopin than just the volume of work he produced. In the **Cité de la Musique** you'll find one of his pianos, while at the **Musée de la Vie Romantique** there's lots of Sand's stuff, and a cast of Chopin's left hand, with his long pianist's fingers.

There's also a statue of Chopin in the **Parc Monceau**, a bust in the **Luxembourg Gardens** and the famous Delacroix portrait from 1838 in the **Louvre**. The portrait only tells half the story, originally featuring Georges Sand as well, listening intently to Chopin's playing, but after Delacroix's death the painting was cut in half ('two for the price of one!'), and Georges Sand ended up in

Ordrupgaard, in Copenhagen. At an exhibition there at the end of the year 2000, Chopin and Sand were briefly reunited.

Detectives amongst you will also be pleased to hear that most of the nine different addresses Chopin lived at in Paris have their own commemorative plaques.

Jean-Baptiste Lully

The composer Giovanni Battista Lulli was born in Florence in 1632, and brought to Paris – complete with a French version of his name – when he was a child. Joining the court of Louis XIV (see page 86) as a dancer and violinist, he rose rapidly through the ranks, being appointed as a court composer in 1653, director of chamber music in 1661, and music teacher to the royal family in 1662.

Writing a series of theatrical ballets in collaboration with Molière, Lully was responsible for the first ever ballet in which a woman played the female role. In 1672 he managed to secure a monopoly on the production of operas, and over the next decade and a half he wrote a great many, mostly with Philippe Quinault as his librettist – Quinault who wisely said 'It is not wise to be wiser than necessary', a revealing remark about life at the court of the Sun King.

Lully had married in 1662, but was apparently overtly homosexual at court, and it's said that one of his most famous compositions, the popular song '*Au Clair de la Lune*', is a thinly disguised account of courtly promiscuity. 'Lend me your pen', says Harlequin to Pierrot, 'My candle's gone out. Open up your door, for the love of God.' Pierrot's not having any of it, 'I have no pen and I'm in bed. Go to the woman next door; her fire's well-stoked.'

With Louis XIV's marriage to Madame de Maintenon in 1683, Lully turned shrewdly to the composition of religious music. But during a performance of his *Te Deum* at the beginning of 1687, he unfortunately managed to stab himself in the foot with his baton (batons were longer then), and gangrene set in. Within two months, Lully was dead.

Beyond the music he left behind, nothing significant commemorates the life of Jean-Baptiste Lully, though you can allow yourself a wry smile the next time you hear children singing '*Au Clair de la Lune*'.

Jim Morrison

Jim Morrison, lead singer of The Doors, spent the last 16 weeks of his life in Paris, before being found famously dead in his bathtub at the age of 27, on July 3 1971. Rock and roll.

The Doors started up in 1965, and by the summer of 1967 they were celebrating their first hit, 'Light My Fire'. Jim Morrison, in particular was celebrating it to excess, over-indulging on drink and drugs, and showing a penchant for exhibitionism which would eventually get him arrested for indecency at a concert in Miami in 1969.

The singer grew a beard and grew withdrawn, and started writing poetry and distancing himself both from the band and from his fans. In 1970 he abandoned his common-law wife Pamela – they had been together since 1965 – and had a pagan wedding on the beach with Patricia Kennealy instead. But it was with Pamela he went to Paris the following year.

Pamela flew ahead to find the couple a flat, and checked into the smart Georges V hotel. She met a French model and her American boyfriend at the Café de Flore (where else) and they agreed to let the Morrisons stay at their place at 17 rue Beautreillis, since they wouldn't be using it themselves for a while. Jim arrived in Paris on March 11, and after a drunken week at the Georges V they moved to rue

Beautreillis. He shaved off his beard, and seemed set on a peaceable existence as a poet – until lunchtime at least, when he would start drinking heavily for the rest of the day.

In April he coughed up blood for the first time, and Pamela made him go to the doctor – who advised him to cut down on his drinking and smoking. The following month (with the model and friends back in town for a few days) they checked briefly into l'Hôtel on rue des Beaux-Arts. Jim insisted on the second-floor room in which Oscar Wilde had died in 1900 (it was the Hôtel d'Alsace back then). On May 7, he fell drunkenly from its window onto a parked car – but he was unhurt, and headed straight out to his favourite bar.

By June, he was a bloated wreck, and coughing up blood again, and his doctor warned him to quit drinking and smoking altogether. At the end of the month he visited the graves of Balzac, Chopin, Piaf and Wilde at **Père Lachaise cemetery** – though he can't have known that within two weeks he'd be joining them there.

The exact circumstances of Morrison's death will never be known – he was alone with Pamela in the apartment, and she was the one who found the body and called the police. It's suspected he may have snorted some of Pamela's heroin, mistaking it for cocaine – but given how weak he was by then, however, almost anything could have finished him off. In the police report, Pamela says he insisted on taking a bath after coughing up blood, but no autopsy was ever performed, and Jim Morrison was buried in Père Lachaise cemetery on July 7. Only five people came to the funeral. Within three years Pamela herself was dead in Hollywood of a heroin overdose.

Jim Morrison's grave is one of the most-visited sites in Paris, though the original graffiti-covered bust was stolen in 1990, and has been replaced by a more sober granite headstone. It's also one of the capital's most controversial monuments. On the tenth anniversary of Morrison's death, a near-riot broke out when the remaining Doors came to visit the grave, and fans got out of control.

Four years later, riot police had to disperse a noisy crowd with tear-gas, and on the 20th anniversary, in 1991, a crowd of thousands rioted at the grave, and again the police had to be called in. It didn't stop the fans from setting fire to the cemetery gates at midnight. The 30th anniversary, fortunately, went off a lot more peaceably.

All of the Doors' recordings are easily available, as are the two volumes of poetry published by Jim Morrison.

Edith Piaf

Edith Giovanna Gassion had a tough start in life by any measures. Born in 1915 in Belleville, then as now one of the rougher quarters of Paris, she was abandoned by her mother and brought up by relatives in extreme poverty. As a young girl she went on tour with her father, an acrobat, becoming part of his act at the age of eight and performing her own act from the age of nine.

As a teenager she was a street singer, going from building to building for a few pennies, and she never ended up with anything like a formal education – though she later loved to read and was an inveterate letter writer. In 1932 she fell in love with a man called Louis Dupont, and their daughter Marcelle was born in early 1933 – Edith was only just 17. Marcelle, often neglected while her mother was singing on the streets, died of meningitis two years later.

At the age of 19, Edith was 'discovered' by the impresario Louis Leplée, who put her on at his club as 'Le Môme Piaf' (The Kid Sparrow) – and at only 1.47m (4ft 10in) she really was petite. (She was following in good footsteps though: Jacques Tati – see page 135 – had been engaged at Leplée's cabaret two years earlier.)

Unfortunately Leplée was murdered in 1936, and Piaf, being close, was among the suspects. She was exonerated of all blame, but her reputation was tarnished, and she had to leave Paris for a year until the fuss died down. By this time she was with the composer Raymond Asso, who was her mentor and lover until 1939, when he was replaced in both capacities by the young singer Paul Meurisse.

Now simply Edith Piaf, she was commanding sell-out performances, doing radio shows and making an enormous number of recordings. The most famous composers of the era wrote for her, and she became hugely popular. During the war she made two films and performed in a play written for her by her friend Jean Cocteau (see page 149).

She also raised hackles by performing for the Germans in occupied Paris, and entertaining officers at her apartment above a brothel. But in fact she was doing good work for the resistance – she helped at least one Jewish musician escape, and at performances with POWs she would get her photograph taken with the prisoners, so they could then crop themselves out and use the portraits for false identity papers.

In 1944 her father died, and Piaf had him buried in Père Lachaise – at the same time she had Marcelle exhumed, and reburied with him, in the Gassion-Piaf tomb. Two years later she wrote *La Vie en Rose*, and set sail for America. After some initial confusion on the part of her American audiences ('who the heck's the little woman in black, and what's with the songs about heartbreak and tragedy all the time?'), they grew to love her, and Piaf shuttled back and forth across the Atlantic, dividing her time between France and the USA.

In 1948 she met Marcel Cerdan, the boxer, and they fell madly in love – but it wasn't to last. He was tragically killed when his plane crashed in October 1949, on his way to New York to see Piaf. Their brief correspondence, *Moi pour Toi*, is a beautiful thing. Three years later, Piaf herself was in a car crash which left her with a fractured arm and broken ribs. She was prescribed morphine, and with increasing pain already from rheumatism she gradually developed a dependence on the drug – as well as on alcohol.

In 1952 she married the songwriter Jacques Pills, and the couple installed themselves the following year in a luxurious apartment at 67 boulevard Lannes. Piaf continued to be as profligate off-stage as ever, spending vast sums on furs, jewellery and gifts, and managing to stay permanently in debt in spite of enormous earnings. But she also continued to work incredibly hard, rehearsing daily for hours on end and wearing out her friends with her extraordinary stamina.

In concert, she was devastating, and regularly brought her audiences to tears. People who saw her perform said you couldn't describe it – her arrival on stage prompted a collective wave of emotion which didn't subside until hours after the end of the show.

Throughout her career she also nurtured new talent, bringing both Yves Montand and Charles Aznavour to the fore, and recording songs which would instantly make their composers famous. By 1957, she and Jacques Pills were divorced, and Piaf's health was declining. When she gave her classic 1961 concerts at the Olympia in Paris, she could barely stand, yet the recordings are magnificent.

That winter Piaf met the 25-year-old Théo Sarapo, a Greek hairdresser who went on to become her co-performer in 1962. The couple were married in the autumn, but Piaf's cancer was now in its terminal stages. She was hospitalised in the spring, and spent the summer on the Riviera with Théo, before finally succumbing on October 11 1963. Théo drove her body up to Paris in secret, so she could be declared dead at boulevard Lannes.

In the process of composing her eulogy on the same day, Piaf's old friend Jean Cocteau himself dropped dead. She was 47, he was 74. Forbidden a mass by the archbishop of Paris for having lived publicly 'in sin', Piaf nonetheless had a huge funeral, with traffic brought to a standstill by the crowd of 40,000 which accompanied her coffin to **Père Lachaise cemetery**, where she was finally buried with her father and her daughter. The following day more than 300,000 Piaf records were sold in Paris alone.

Her husband, Théo, barely survived Piaf, dying in a car crash in 1970, at the age of 34.

Apart from the music she left behind – still wonderfully evocative – there's also the extraordinary **Musée Edith Piaf**. The museum is maintained by the Amis d'Edith Piaf association, whose Secretary-General, Bernard Marchois, will give you the access code for the apartment building where the collection's housed, in two rooms of his fourth-floor flat.

Through a family contact in the boxing business, Bernard Marchois met Edith Piaf in 1958, when he was 16, and knew her for the last five years of her life, not only becoming a visitor at boulevard Lannes, but also going to every single one of her performances from then onwards. The memories still make his eyes light up. 'You'd get gooseflesh just to see her come on stage,' he recalls. 'Nothing – nothing you can hear – can even begin to compare to the experience of seeing her perform live; ten times better than any of the recordings.'

In 1967, Marchois founded the association with various members of the family and friends, and the museum was opened in 1977. Since then, Marchois has spent 25 years unsuccessfully lobbying the French Ministry of Culture to integrate the Piaf collection into a future Musée National de la Chanson Française.

In the meantime, you can call ahead and make an appointment. The first thing you see when you come in is the life-size cut-out of Piaf in her classic black dress. Next to her, sat in a chair, is the enormous teddy bear bought for her by Théo – it's the same height as the singer.

The museum is a charming clutter of Piaf memorabilia, from gold records to concert dresses, and on the walls you'll see a huge range of drawings, paintings, photographs and letters, along with touching testimonials from old friends ('*Edith tu es et tu seras toujours ma préféré*', says a note from Jean Marais – 'Edith, you are and you always will be my favourite').

Piaf's porcelain collection adorns her inlaid furniture; the songwriter Moustaki's dressing gown lies draped across a sofa; and Marcel Cerdan's battered boxing gloves occupy another chair. And of course there's also the music – ask Monsieur Marchois for any song and he'll have it playing for you before you know it. It's faintly spooky to hear Piaf's voice pining through her songs when you're standing amongst her things.

You can buy recordings here, as well as books, including the beautifully designed volume put together by Marchois himself over a period of 28 years, which chronicles each and every single day of Piaf's life.

Cole Porter

Born and brought up in Peru, Indiana, Cole Porter came to Paris during World War I, and maintained an address there right up until 1937, when he was crippled in a riding accident on Long Island.

Volunteering to do his bit in 1917, Cole Porter's war career is a mystery – he himself gave many different versions of what he did, and it's been reported that he wore uniforms of varying ranks from both the French and American armies. He playfully insisted that he'd been in the French Foreign Legion, and it may even have been true.

After the war, Porter stayed on in Paris, funded by his indulgent multi-millionaire grandfather. At a wedding breakfast at the Ritz in 1918 he met Linda Lee Thomas, a wealthy, divorced, American socialite who was eight years older than him. They were made for each other – she coming from an abusive marriage, he being gay, and both having money and social status – and they married at the end of 1919. Their companiable marriage was to last until Linda's death in 1954, at the age of 71.

After an extended honeymoon in the south of France and in Italy, the couple moved to an enormous house at 13 rue Monsieur, and settled into a seemingly endless round of parties. One of their guests was the notorious Bricktop (see page 133) who went on to found her own club in Montmartre – and with Cole Porter a regular visitor it soon became the place to be seen. In the meantime Porter also made time to study composition at Vincent d'Indy's prestigious Schola Cantorum, and composed a stream of popular songs.

The rue Monsieur house was one of the most lavishly decorated in Paris, with the basement converted into a ballroom with floor to ceiling mirrors, and other rooms featuring platinum wallpaper, Chippendale furniture, exotic eastern furnishings and zebra skin upholstery. Cole Porter composed at a sleek, black, shiny, full-sized Steinway grand piano.

The parties they threw were legendary extravagances, with the wealthy and influential in attendance, and drink and drugs available in abundance. On occasion the entire party would be transported by a cavalcade of limousines down to the Riviera. Over the next decade and a half the Porters travelled the world, dipping into Paris for longer or shorter periods, but spending most of their time partying – in Venice, New York, on cruise ships and luxury liners, and across Europe. In France their constant to-ings and fro-ings led to them being referred to as 'Les colporteurs' (an amusing joke; a *colporteur* is a door-to-door salesman).

Cole Porter's musicals became the best known of the era, and the couple seemed to live a charmed life. But a riding accident in October 1937 left Porter's legs crushed and kept him in hospital for two years and in a wheelchair for another five. Over the next twenty years he would have more than 30 unsuccessful operations. After the 1958 amputation of his right leg, Porter lived as a recluse at the Waldorf Astoria in New York, until his sudden death at the age of 73 in 1964.

Cole Porter's songs still sound great in Paris, and they're the best – indeed only – commemoration of him you'll find in France today.

Erik Satie

The composer Erik Satie is way out in an eccentric league of his own.

The man often referred to as the 'Father of Modern Music' was born in London in 1866 to a Scottish mother and an English father. After his mother's premature death in 1872, the family moved to Honfleur, in Normandy, and his father remarried. With both father and stepmother being composers, Satie learned to play the piano at the age of seven, and was at the conservatoire in Paris from 1879 to 1886.

In 1887, with some money from his father, Satie moved to Montmartre, where he composed his three *Gymnopédies* in 1888 and his four *Ogives* in 1889 – spending most of the rest of his money on publishing the works. By the summer of 1889 he was sufficiently broke to be advertising for piano pupils, and he was working as the conductor of the orchestra at the Chat Noir. After this he became the resident pianist at the rowdy Auberge du Clou, and it was here he first met Debussy.

Increasingly hard up, he moved to a room at 6 rue Cortot in 1890, and the following year he joined the obscure Rosicrucian church, soon becoming the 'official composer' for the sect. He then became the sole member of his own church, the Metropolitan Church of the Art of Jesus the Conductor, having first excommunicated everyone else.

During the first half of 1893, Satie had his only known love affair, with the painter Suzanne Valadon, who he had met at the Auberge du Clou – and Satie proposed on their first date. By June, however, it was all over (see page 111 for more details of their relationship). In the summer of 1896, Satie was so poor he had to move to an even smaller room at 6 rue Cortot. It was so cramped you couldn't even open the door fully, and to enter the room you had to climb over the bed. It became known as Erik Satie's *placard* – or cupboard.

After two confined years, Satie moved to more spacious quarters, on the other side of Paris, in the suburb of Arcueil. For the next 27 years he lived here alone, never letting a soul cross the threshold. He covered up the windows, and somehow got hold of two grand pianos, which he stacked one on top of the other, the upper one becoming a repository for letters and postcards. Neither was in use – after his death one had its keyboard against the wall, while the other had its pedals tied together.

Satie lived in absolute poverty in Arcueil, with no running water, no gas and no electricity, but – in a mystery which has never been satisfactorily resolved – he was always immaculately turned out. Wanting to look good, but having no money to spend on clothes, he dressed classically – which was an irony as all his friends were bohemians. On the rare occasions when he had any money at all, he would spend the lot – and on receiving a small inheritance he blew it on a dozen identical grey velvet suits, which he used one at a time until they wore out. When he died, in 1925, he still had half a dozen brand new suits to go.

He would often walk up to Montmartre and back (over 10km each way!), as that was where all his friends and acquaintances would congregate, but he also spent long periods alone in Arcueil, writing letters, making thousands of delightful little drawings and composing. (After his death, a legend sprang up that Satie never opened his letters, but it's implausible, as he was punctilious in responding to correspondence. We can't know for sure, however, as although some unopened parcels and presents were found in his room, the letters were destroyed, leaving us only with the letters Satie himself sent.)

Satie was a gifted composer, but it didn't come naturally to him, and composition was always a terrible struggle. He would work entirely in his head, occasionally trying out odd sections at friends' houses, as there wasn't room for a piano at rue Cortot and the ones in Arcueil were unusable.

The critics of the day were scornful of Satie's music – and indeed even now he's vastly more popular abroad than in his home country, with the conservatoire not teaching his work, and the Satie repertoire never on the classical agenda. After being told his music was formless, he composed the wonderful *Trois Morceaux en Forme de Poire* – three pear-shaped pieces.

His manuscript instructions to pianists are also notoriously cryptic (surreal, even), with the most famous appearing on the *Vexations* – where there's a recommendation on how to prepare yourself before playing the short piece 840 times in a row (*'Pour se jouer 840 fois de suite ce motif, il sera bon de se préparer au préalable, et dans le plus grand silence, par des immobilités sérieuses'*). The *Vexations* has been successfully performed on several occasions (notably by John Cage), but what were Satie's real intentions for it? If any?

Approaching 40, Satie sent himself back to school, this time to the celebrated Schola Cantorum, where he studied orchestration and counterpoint with Vincent d'Indy and Albert Roussel. After three years he earned a certificate with the note *'très bien'*.

In 1915, he was commissioned by the Russian impresario Sergei Diaghilev, along with his friends Jean Cocteau (see page 149) and Pablo Picasso to write a ballet called *Parade*, and they included various revolutionary sound effects, including pistol shots, sirens and a typewriter in the score. A reviewer described the affect as 'surreal' – thus introducing the concept of surrealism to the world.

In 1920, at an art gallery opening, Satie then invented ambient music (*musique d'ameublement*), though it got off to a poor start – as soon as he started playing, people would pay attention, to his intense irritation. He'd be even more annoyed now, especially with the recordings, as the music was composed specifically not to be 'performed' or 'listened to'.

Satie continued to work, but in 1925 his health declined, and he was hospitalised with alcoholic cirrhosis complicated by double pneumonia. He lived on for several months, but never recovered, dying on July 1, at the age of 59.

When his studio in Arcueil was opened up, Satie's truly acquisitive streak was finally revealed. More than a hundred umbrellas, scores of clean handkerchiefs, and the remaining grey suits were found, along with heaps of newspapers, music scores, and books. His wardrobe, however, was quite empty – and it's been suggested that he may have used it as a place for meditation.

We're fortunate in having a great deal of Erik Satie memorabilia, largely thanks to the untiring efforts of Ornella Volta, who has been amassing and maintaining the Erik Satie Archives for the past thirty years – it's now an extraordinary collection of letters, manuscripts, drawings, paintings, posters, magazines, journals and of course recordings.

The Italian-born Volta became involved with Erik Satie almost by coincidence. In 1971 an orchestra leader she knew was preparing texts for the Venice Biennale, and asked her – since she was in Paris – to dig up some Satie material. She agreed, but failed to deliver, being struck down by an unexplained three-month sickness. By this time, however, she was hooked on Satie, and today she has practically all of his papers.

Over the decades, Volta has published an astonishing 12 books about Satie (most recently *Correspondance Presque Complète*), and built an impressive network of fellow Satie enthusiasts, which led to the creation of the Satie Foundation in 1981. For many years, Madame Volta would show you round a studio at 6 rue Cortot which was similar to the *placard* where he lived from 1896 to 1898. The room had been bought by Satie's great-nephew, and furnished with Satie's possessions by the foundation, but with the archive now being moved (see below) there's nothing left to see there – though there may be one day, as the mayor wants to buy it for the city.

Most of the Satie archives are in the process of being taken over by the **Institut Mémoire de l'Edition Contemporaine** (IMEC), but in Honfleur, Satie's home town, you'll be able to see some of the drawings and paintings which are going to be split between the **Maisons Satie** and the **Musée Eugène Boudin**. Valadon's portrait of Satie and vice-versa are there already, along with an excellent audio-visual walk through his life and works, and it'll be great when more of Volta's collection is integrated.

In Arcueil, on the south side of Paris, you'll find that the house Satie lived in, the **Maison des Quatre Cheminées**, at 34 rue Cauchy (it was 22, but they've renumbered), is pretty much unchanged. There are however plans to rehabilitate it as a walk-through museum, which should be wonderful when it's complete.

Satie's grave is at the **Arcueil cemetery** – in the first row on the left.

Adolphe Sax

Adolphe Sax was born in Belgium in 1814, and as a young man showed himself capable as an engineer with a bent for music. By the time he was 24, he already had patents out for his improvements to the bass clarinet, the first of many enhancements he would make on existing instruments.

But he's remembered today not for the bass clarinet upgrade, but for the instrument which bears his name – or to be more accurate one of the instruments which bears his name. For who, today, remembers the saxhorn, the saxtuba, or indeed the saxotromba, all of which he also invented? Nope, it's the saxophone family we know and love.

After a disappointment at the National Exhibition in Brussels in 1841 – it's said his precious saxophone was damaged by a rival before the show, and was unplayable – Sax moved to Paris in 1842. He gained more or less instant fame a few weeks later when the composer Hector Berlioz wrote a glowing review, predicting that within a few years all orchestras would feature the shiny new instrument.

That they didn't, is largely down to Sax's unfortunate habit of jumping into litigation at the slightest provocation, often tying himself and other inventors and practitioners into complicated and expensive lawsuits for years. He had his fair share of friends, but was also quick to make enemies, and was constantly involved in long and public quarrels. From 1858 to 1870, however, Sax taught saxophone at the conservatoire. Classes were then interrupted – the Prussian war? Another tedious lawsuit? – and sadly weren't reintroduced until 1942.

Sax died ruined in 1894, and no doubt teams of lawyers were on hand after the funeral to pursue his litigation beyond the grave. It wouldn't be until the 1920s that the saxophone would really take off, with the popularisation of jazz.

To see a fine collection of original saxophones, stop in at the **Cité de la Musique** at La Villette, in Paris.

ECCENTRIC PERFORMERS

It takes a lot to get up on stage, and most performers aren't entirely normal people – but even so it takes exceptional eccentricity to sleep in a coffin, keep a pet leopard on a leash or a jewel-encrusted turtle, or to go entirely the other way and dedicate your life to animal rights.

Josephine Baker

In her heyday, Josephine Baker wasn't so much a star as a phenomenon.

Born in St Louis in 1906, she was already working at the age of eight, and was onto her second husband, a railway porter, by the time she was 15. She was to marry three times more – in 1937 to Jean Lion, the French sugar magnate (whatever that is; though no doubt he was sweet enough); in 1947 to Jo Bouillon, the souped-up orchestra leader; and in 1973 to Robert Brady, an American artist – but she kept her second husband's name, Baker.

By 1921, she was performing in Broadway's first black musical, *Shuffle Along*. Having initially been rejected – too young, too thin, too dark – she learned the moves anyway, and when one of the cast dropped out she was taken on as the 'end girl', the comic character who can't quite keep up.

In 1925 she was given the chance of going to Paris with a new production, *La Revue Nègre*, and though the show itself wasn't a big hit, Josephine Baker was an instant sensation, dancing the Charleston finale wearing nothing but a feather-skirt. A year later she was at Les Folies Bergère, sporting a risqué outfit consisting of bananas sewn into an immodest girdle, and her fame was assured. By 1927 she was the best-paid performer on the continent, and in the 1930s she brought her family over from America and installed them in the Château des Milandes, in Périgord.

She loved pets, and not just your cats and dogs, either. Her favourite was a leopard called Chiquita, who she would promenade around Paris on a diamond-studded leash, but at various times she also had snakes, monkeys, goats, rabbits, parrots, fish, dogs and cats – and a pig called Albert.

In 1936, she returned to America to perform in the Ziegfeld Follies, but she was panned by critics and audiences alike, unready for black power of any kind, and she returned to France. By marrying Jean Lion she took on French nationality, and during the World War II she worked for the resistance, smuggling vital messages across the enemy lines in her underwear (the messages, not the enemy lines, were in her smalls). She was honoured afterwards by General de Gaulle, who awarded her the *Légion d'Honneur* in 1961.

After the war she adopted a dozen children with different racial and religious backgrounds – her 'Rainbow Tribe' – and installed herself with them at Milandes. She opened up her château and grounds to the public, to show how people of different cultures and nationalities could live in harmony together, and at its peak Milandes had more than half a million visitors a year.

She also returned periodically to the stage, both in France and in America, to keep the family in funds. In 1951, refused service at New York's famous Stork Club, she engaged in a battle of words with the influential columnist Walter Winchell, who did everything he could thereafter to run her down in print. Undeterred, Baker continued to refuse to perform in segregated venues or stay in segregated hotels. In 1963 she marched on Washington with Martin Luther King.

The upkeep of a huge estate and a big family proved in the end too much, and in 1969 she finally succumbed to her creditors, and lost the Château des Milandes – in spite of public appeals for help from such unlikely bedfellows as King Hassan II of Morocco, the Club Med, and Brigitte Bardot.

Fortunately, Grace Kelly gave her a villa in Monaco to live in, and Josephine Baker – now in her sixties – took to the boards once more. In 1973 she finally achieved the success she had always sought in America, and was given a standing ovation at the Carnegie Hall. In the spring of 1975 she took her show *Josephine* to Paris, and the 68-year-old performer received some of the best reviews of her life – but four days after the premiere she died of a cerebral haemorrhage in her sleep. Vast crowds attended her funeral, and she was given a 21-gun salute, the only woman in France ever to be so honoured. Her grave is in Monaco.

The 15th-century **Château des Milandes** is situated west of Sarlat, in Périgord, on the river Dordogne. You can visit the castle, which has a great collection of Baker memorabilia, and then be treated (in summer) to spectacular displays of falconry – though you can't swim in the J-shaped pool. Don't be confused by the rival Parc de Loisirs de Josephine Baker, a small theme park consisting of a bar-restaurant on the river Dordogne, along with mini-golf, a swimming pool, a tennis court, and a playground – which has nothing it seems to do with Josephine herself.

If you want to pay your respects to Josephine Baker, you can also do so at her sober grave in **Monaco's cemetery**. And you shouldn't miss the chance of seeing the 1991 film about her, *The Josephine Baker Story*.

Brigitte Bardot

Brigitte Bardot was born in Paris in 1934, and shot to fame as a young model when she made it onto the front cover of *Elle* in 1949, when she was still only 14. This brought her to the attention of the young Roger Vadim, and they were desperate to marry – though this was only allowed once she turned 18. Her career in cinema was already underway by then, and at the 1953 Cannes film festival she was a sensation.

Three years later she shot to international fame as the star of Vadim's film *Et Dieu… Créa la Femme* (And God Created Woman), and in spite of two more short, unhappy marriages, she went on to have a hugely successful career in the sixties as both a film and a pop star.

In 1974, having starred in more than 50 films by the age of 40, she retired from the screen, and ever since she's been a strong animal rights activist. Starting out with small-scale campaigns against cruelty to animals, she created the Brigitte Bardot Foundation in the 1980s, and is now the patron of an organization which works around the world fighting animal cruelty.

After you've watched Bardot's many film appearances you can't do better than supporting the Brigitte Bardot Foundation in Paris. There's an extensive website in English to help you on your way (www.fondationbrigittebardot.fr/en), and the French government officially recognised the foundation as a public service organisation in 1992.

Sarah Bernhardt

Sarah Bernhardt was certainly the greatest actress of her era and quite possibly the best actress of all time. She was born in Paris in 1844, the illegitimate daughter of a Dutch courtesan, and brought up in a convent. Turning to God at 16, she declared she wanted to take her religious vows, but her mother wouldn't have any of it, and she and her current paramour, the Duc de Morny, instead pushed Sarah into theatre school (which she hated).

When she turned 18, the Duc found her a job at the prestigious Comédie Française, but she was thrown out the following year for slapping one of the senior actresses. It didn't impede her career, however, and over the next decade she was given increasingly prestigious roles. During the 1870s she was welcomed back into the Comédie, and played the lead in many of the classic plays of the day.

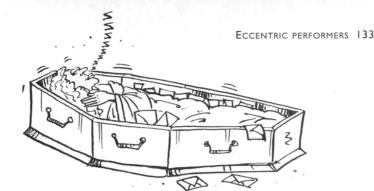

Like Josephine Baker, she loved pets, and her menagerie is said to have contained, at one time or another, pumas, lion cubs, alligators, monkeys, cats, dogs, chameleons and tropical birds, not to mention a boa constrictor and a jewelled turtle.

From 1880 onwards, Sarah Bernhardt was constantly on tour in both Europe and America. She made an extraordinary impression on audiences in more than a hundred different plays, not so much acting the part as personifying the characters – quite your 19th-century method actress. In 1892 Oscar Wilde wrote the play *Salomé* (in French!) for her, but it was banned during rehearsal in London, and only produced for the first time in Paris four years later.

Obsessed with death, she often took on roles which would allow her to die on stage, and both on tour and at home she frequently slept in a coffin lined with passionate letters from her countless lovers. It's said, too, that in her bedroom, in Paris, she kept a skeleton on display. All very neo-Gothic.

Sarah Bernhardt also starred in nearly a dozen films, starting with the 1900 classic *Le Duel d'Hamlet*, in which she played Hamlet himself, turning on its head the Shakespearean tradition of having boys playing the female leads.

But it was on stage that she swept people off their feet. In Nottingham, in 1906, she knocked out the 21-year-old DH Lawrence, while in London during World War I she bowled over John Gielgud as a boy. She must have been extraordinarily long on charisma, for by this time she was short of one leg. After having had knee trouble for years – supposedly ever since jumping off the ramparts in the last scene of *Tosca* on tour in 1905 – gangrene eventually set in, and her leg was amputated in 1915.

Indomitable to the last, Sarah Bernhardt insisted on being carried in a regal-style litter to visit the troops in the trenches, and she continued performing – in roles where she could sit – until her death in 1923, at the age of 78.

There's little concrete testament to the quality of Sarah Bernhardt's acting – the films are very hard to find – but you can see one of her dresses at the **Musée Galliera** (the fashion museum) in Paris, and you can visit her grave in **Père Lachaise cemetery**.

There are also any number of books about her, from her own 1907 autobiography, *My Double Life* (which should be taken with a whole pan of salt), to Ruth Brandon's 1999 *Being Divine*, which is the most interesting if not the most comprehensive of the modern biographies.

Bricktop

Ada Smith was born in West Virginia in 1894, and wanted to be a backroom entertainer from an early age. Of African-American and Scottish ancestry, she was witty and vivacious, and when she started working as a singer and dancer in Harlem and Chicago, her striking red hair soon earned her the name of Bricktop.

In 1924 she went to Paris, and a year later took the young Josephine Baker (see page 130) under her wing. In 1926 she bought the club Le Grand Duc, at 66 rue

Pigalle, and renamed it Bricktop's. It was soon the most fashionable cabaret in Paris, and over the next decade it attracted a chic clientele including the Windsors, John Steinbeck, Pablo Picasso, Evelyn Waugh, Ernest Hemingway and F Scott Fitzgerald – who famously said that his greatest claim to fame was that he'd discovered Bricktop before Cole Porter did.

Cole Porter (see page 126) did eventually catch up, and came to the club. Having seen Bricktop doing the Charleston (apparently calling out, in a rare heterosexual lapse 'What legs! What legs!'), he hired her to teach his guests the new dance, and even took her to Venice with him to sing and dance at his spectacular parties there.

Bricktop's wasn't just famous for its customers, however – great jazz was played there too, with typical attractions being the likes of Duke Ellington and Louis Armstrong. But in 1939, with the arrival of the war, Bricktop left town and returned to America.

Efforts to recreate the club in New York weren't successful, so in 1944 Bricktop opened up a café in Mexico City and ran the business there for five years, before moving on to Rome, where she opened up a café on the Via Veneto. She retired to Manhattan in 1961, though she still loved to sing and dance right into her early eighties, and she was a keen cigar smoker until she finally died in 1984, aged 89.

The scene around Pigalle is pretty tawdry these days, and it's difficult to imagine the area peopled by an immaculately elegant Cole Porter or F Scott Fitzgerald. Number 66, rue Pigalle, which was Bricktop's from 1926, is now a decaying place called the New Moon with a large scallop shell over the door. It looks like it went out of business decades ago.

Isadora Duncan

The woman famously known by Dorothy Parker as 'Duncan Disorderly' was born in San Francisco in 1878 to a poor but cultured family. As a teenager she was already a dancer, but it wasn't until the family moved to London and she was discovered by one of the leading actresses of the day that Isadora Duncan's career really took off.

Dancing barefoot in a Greek tunic and eschewing formal ballet was a sure way to attract attention in the heady early 1900s, and Isadora Duncan was soon taking Europe's stages by storm. Settling in Paris, she became one of the best paid performers of her era, and opened up dance schools to promulgate her distinctively swirly back-to-nature style.

In 1905 she took up with Gordon Craig, the son of Ellen Terry, who had made her name in the last twenty years of the 19th century as Britain's leading Shakespearean actress (Terry also partnered with the great Henry Irving at the Lyceum, and was the great-aunt of John Gielgud).

Isadora Duncan proceeded to scandalise society by having a daughter out of wedlock with Craig – Duncan was fiercely anti-marriage all her life – and then moved on to a passionate affair with the sewing-machine heir Paris Singer, which resulted in the birth of an illegitimate son. Far from stitching her up, Singer bought Duncan a lovely house in Neuilly, which she used as an atelier, and even after their affair went cold he continued to support her.

On April 19 1913, however, disaster struck. After a prolonged lunch with Singer and her children, Duncan was dropped off at the atelier in Neuilly from her chauffeur-driven Bentley, which went on towards Versailles to return the children and their governess back home. But when the Bentley stalled, and the chauffeur got out to crank-start the engine, the gears engaged, and the driverless car plunged into the Seine. An hour and a half later the drowned bodies of the governess and Duncan's two small children were fished out of the river.

Left Hearse at the world's only Museum of Horse-Drawn Hearses, Cazes Mondenard (RPL)

Below Watching over the coffin ready and waiting for Max Manent, at the Musée de l'Insolite, Loriol (PL)

Below right One of Fragonard's 200-year-old écorchés at the Musée Fragonard, Paris (PL)

Below left Yvan Quercy, curator of the Museum of Horse-Drawn Hearses (PL)

Above Heavenly grave at Léopold Truc's Paradis, Cabrières sur Avignon (PL)
Below left A pyramid fit for an Egyptologist, at Père Lachaise Cemetery, Paris (PL)
Below right Sartre and de Beauvoir, together at last, at the Montparnasse Cemetery, Paris (PL)

Paris society went into shock (the students at the Beaux-Arts decorated the entire garden and trees at the Neuilly house with white flowers) and the chauffeur was arrested for homicide – but Duncan insisted the charges be dropped, and he was released. For her part, she cut off her hair and flung it into the sea.

Singer bought her a château in Meudon, and within the year Duncan was pregnant again (but not with Singer's child). The baby boy, born in July 1914, on the eve of war, survived less than an hour. Duncan returned to America, and also returned to the stage, performing with six of her school pupils, whom she adopted and dubbed the 'Isadorables'. She danced well into her 40s, until in 1921, invited by Russia to open a dance school there, she met and fell in love with the 26-year-old poet Sergei Esenin.

Against all her principles, she married Esenin in 1922, in order to get him out of Russia, but the marriage was a stormy one – ending definitively on 27 December 1925, when the poet slashed his wrists in Russia in order to write his final elegy in his own blood.

Back in France, in 1926, Isadora Duncan wrote her autobiography, *My Life*, and moved to Nice. She took to drink and to cruising the bars and picking up rough trade. On September 14 1927, having persuaded the handsome young Bugatti concessionaire she might be interested in buying one of his cars, she went for a spin with him along the Promenade des Anglais. Tragically, the fringes of her long red shawl flew back in the wind, and were quickly caught in the rear-wheel spokes. Duncan was killed instantly, by her own scarf.

There are few if any souvenirs of Isadora Duncan's life in France. She's buried with her children at **Père Lachaise cemetery** in Paris, and – if, like me, you have a somewhat febrile imagination – it's hard to stroll along the **Promenade des Anglais** in Nice without thinking of the Bugatti and the long red shawl, and Isadora's tragic end, every time you hear a screech of brakes.

Jacques Tati

The life and works of Jacques Tati – born Tatischeff, to a Russian father, in Brittany, in 1908 – can be neatly summed up by the wonderful Robert Doisneau photograph used as a publicity still for the 1947 classic film *Jour de Fête*.

In the film, Tati plays the hapless country postman who attempts to speed up his mail round on a 1911 Peugeot bicycle. In the photo, Tati stands in the background, in his postman's uniform, looking bemused, with an inner tube over one shoulder and a bike pump in his hands. In the foreground lies the rest of the bicycle, entirely dismantled down to the last pedal, crank and mudguard.

As a young man, Tati was a keen boxer and an excellent football and rugby player, but in 1931 he took to the stage in cabarets and music halls with a series of comic sporting routines. He then worked in the French cinema, both as a scriptwriter and actor in short films, until the war put his career on hold.

After the war, Tati took an idea from a short he'd made called *l'Ecole des Facteurs*, and expanded it into his first feature-length film, *Jour de Fête*. Made in black and white at a time when colour was coming through, and shot in the manner of a silent film – most of the soundtrack consists of noises and sound effects rather than dialogue – *Jour de Fête* waited on the shelf for two years before anyone would release it. It's a delightful film.

For his next script, Tati created the character who was to take over the rest of his life, Monsieur Hulot. The trench-coated, shabby-trousered, pipe-smoking, mumbling Hulot, setting off comic visual and sound gags at every turn, starred in *Monsieur Hulot's Holiday* in 1952, *Mon Oncle* in 1958, *Playtime* in 1967 and *Trafic* in 1971.

From the start, Hulot was a huge hit, but Tati's originality and love of complexity and detail (the later films demand multiple viewings to catch all the gags) was to be his downfall. The public – and more importantly the industry – wanted more than one film every six or seven years. His production company went bust, and his classic films were sold off to his creditors for a song. Tati himself made one more film, the low-budget handheld movie, *Parade*, in 1974 – shot in Stockholm and presaging the Danish *Dogma* films by a good twenty years.

Fifty years on, Hulot remains one of the most lovable characters you'll ever see on screen. Unfailingly gentle, optimistic and innocent, he constantly gets into trouble, with society fatally at odds with his quiet non-conformism.

Jacques Tati will live on forever through his films, which are relatively easily available, and often show up in film festivals. Catch them where you can.

Théâtre Ver à Pieds

Catherine Pécheux and Christian Le Bras spend their working days in a high-security French government office building, in Reuil-Malmaison, west of Paris, at the opaque l'Institut Français du Pétrole (IFP). Catherine has been working there for more than 20 years – but her life changed in 1990, when she met Christian at amateur dramatics classes.

Now, with more than a decade of training behind them, the two find themselves at the heart of a unique theatre troupe called *Le Théâtre du Ver à Pieds*. What's unique about the group is that instead of you going to see them, they come to see you – and then perform in your house or apartment.

(The name *Ver à Pieds* is itself inspired. Literally, it's a nickname for a centipede or millipede [worm with legs], and therefore a nice name for a travelling troupe, but *vers* also means towards, meaning 'going there on foot'. *Vers* also means verse, and a *vers à pieds* is French for metered verse. As if that weren't enough, a *verre à pied* is a stemmed glass – one you'd only get out on special occasions.)

So invite your friends round, set up some extra chairs, and sit back while the troupe performs their latest offering for you. In 2002, when I saw them in Paris, the play on offer was *l'Aquarium*, by Louis Calaferte. The simple set (well, it has to be) consisted of a black backdrop, a pair of red gingham curtains denoting a window, a table and tablecloth, and three chairs. The performances were truly excellent – better than many professional shows I've seen – and the intimate atmosphere (few people are used to sitting this close to the spectacle) was electric.

The *Théâtre Ver à Pieds* is based in Orgeval, just west of Paris, and will travel anywhere in the capital or its suburbs to play for you – but they're not quite ready, just yet, for performances in English.

TRAVEL INFORMATION

Château des Milandes west of Sarlat, between St Cyprien and Beynac; tel: 05 53 59 31 21; web: www.milandes.com; open daily, Apr–Oct; € 7.50.

Cité de la Musique La Villette, 221 avenue Jean Jaurès, 75019, Paris; tel: 01 44 84 45 45; web: www.cite-musique.fr; M̄ Porte de Pantin; closed Mon; € 6.

Institut Mémoire de l'Edition Contemporaine (IMEC), 9 rue Bleue, 75009, Paris; tel 01 53 34 23 23; web: www. imec-archives.com; M̄ cadet; Mon–Fri afternoons; researchers wishing to consult the archives pay € 23 per year for access to the reading room, after proving the seriousness of their scholarship.

Luxembourg Gardens 75006, Paris, metro Luxembourg; free.

Maison des Quatre Cheminées 34 rue Cauchy, Arcueil; currently closed; tel: 01 46 15 08 80 (Arcueil town hall) for more information.

Maisons Satie 67 boulevard Charles V, Honfleur; tel: 02 31 89 11 11; closed Tue; €5.

Musée Edith Piaf 5 rue Crespin-du-Gast, 75011, Paris; tel: 01 43 55 52 72; M̄ Menilmontant, St Maur; open by appointment only; free (but it would be frankly churlish not to leave a donation).

Musée Eugène Boudin place Erik Satie, Honfleur; tel: 02 31 89 54 00; closed Tue, open afternoons only in winter; €5.

Musée Galliera (Musée de la Mode) 10 avenue Pierre 1er de Sibérie, 75008, Paris; tel: 01 56 52 80 00; M̄ Iéna; closed Mon and public holidays; €7.

Musée du Louvre 99 rue de Rivoli, 75001, Paris; tel: 01 40 20 50 50; web: www.louvre.fr; M̄ Louvre, Palais Royal; closed Tue; €7.50 (free on 1st Sun of month).

Musée de la Vie Romantique 16 rue Chaptal, 75009, Paris; tel: 01 48 74 95 38; M̄ Saint Georges, Blanche, Pigalle; closed Mon; permanent collection free (€5 for special exhibitions).

Parc Monceau 75008, Paris; M̄ Monceau; free.

Père Lachaise cemetery 75020, Paris; M̄ Père Lachaise, Philippe-Auguste, Gambetta; open every day; free.

Théâtre Ver à Pieds Orgeval (30km west of Paris); tel: 01 39 75 47 42 / 06 03 57 50 09; web: http://verapied.chez.tiscali.fr/; €230 (price includes performance and travel expenses).

Writerly Eccentric

Something about the process of writing seems to twist men's and women's brains, and most of them simply can't seem to be normal (whatever that is). In this chapter, though, we'll find some true French eccentrics – and a heap of eccentric expatriate writers who made France their home.

HISTORICALLY ECCENTRIC WRITERS

From cross-dressing novelists and nocturnal hypochondriacs to absinthe-soaked poets, sex-crazed noblemen and anti-clerical philosophers, France had more than its fair share of literary eccentrics.

Marie de Flavigny, Comtesse d'Agoult

Marie de Flavigny was born in Frankfurt on the last day of 1805 to a wealthy French émigré and the daughter of a German banker. With the restoration of the Bourbon kings, the family moved back to France, and Marie seems to have led an unexceptional life until, at the age of 21, she married a 37-year-old army colonel, Comte Charles d'Agoult, and moved in with him at his lovely family home at Arpaillargues, near Uzès, in Provence.

Two children later she was bored and running a salon in Paris, attracting the leading Romantics of the day. Hardly surprising then that in 1833 she was able to meet and fall hopelessly in love with Franz Liszt, the brilliant Hungarian composer and pianist. Marie then scandalised Paris by deserting her husband and children, and living openly with the lusty Liszt. Over the next ten years they divided their time between Italy, Switzerland and Paris, and she bore him three children. (The youngest, Cosima, later repeated history by leaving her first husband in order to marry the composer Richard Wagner.)

D'Agoult and Liszt finally went their separate ways in 1844, and the Comtesse started writing for the liberal press as a serious journalist, under the pen name Daniel Stern. Well ahead of her time in her liberal thinking, she was nonetheless not much of a feminist when seen from a 21st-century perspective – women should certainly be educated and have rights, she felt, but their place shouldn't be at the forefront of public life.

In 1846, she got Liszt out of her system by publishing her one novel, *Nélida*, a thinly disguised rendering of her life with the composer – except that in the novel, the Liszt character finds only limited success after the relationship ends, and is reunited, on his deathbed, with his lover.

Over the next decade she wrote her best works, most notably the excellent *Histoire de la Révolution de 1848* – a detailed and objective account of the revolution itself and the events surrounding it – though at three volumes it's a bit dense for most modern readers. After her death in 1876, her memoirs were published – although 50 years elapsed between the appearance of the first volume, *Mes Souvenirs* (her life to 1833, and her meeting with Liszt) and the second, *Mémoires* (her life up to 1854).

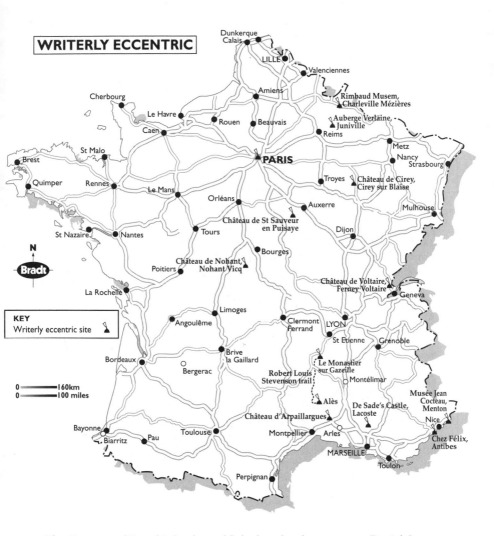

WRITERLY ECCENTRIC

Dunkerque
Calais
LILLE
Valenciennes
Cherbourg
Amiens
Rimbaud Musem,
Charleville Mézières
Le Havre
Rouen
Beauvais
Auberge Verlaine,
Juniville
Caen
Reims
St Malo
Metz
Brest
Nancy
Strasbourg
Quimper
Rennes
PARIS
Le Mans
Troyes
Château de Cirey,
Cirey sur Blaise
Orléans
Auxerre
Mulhouse
St Nazaire
Nantes
Tours
Château de St Sauveur
en Puisaye
Dijon
Bourges
N
Bradt
Château de Nohant,
Nohant/Vicq
Poitiers
La Rochelle
Limoges
Château de Voltaire,
Ferney Voltaire
Geneva

KEY
Writerly eccentric site

Angoulême
Clermont
Ferrand
LYON
St Etienne
Grenoble
Bordeaux
Brive
la Gaillard
Bergerac
Le Monastier
sur Gazeille
Robert Louis
Stevenson trail
Montélimar
0 ———160km
0 ———100 miles
Alès
Musée Jean
Cocteau,
Menton
Bayonne
Château d'Arpaillargues
De Sade's Castle,
Lacoste
Nice
Biarritz
Pau
Toulouse
Montpellier
Arles
Chez Félix,
Antibes
MARSEILLE
Perpignan
Toulon

The Comtesse d'Agoult's books, published under the pen name Daniel Stern, are fairly hard to find – and fairly heavy reading, too. But you can go and stay in the family home she abandoned to be with Liszt. The **Château d'Arpaillargues**, near Uzès, in Provence, is now a charming hotel, furnished throughout with antiques.

Charles Baudelaire

Charles Baudelaire was a contemporary of d'Agoult's, though a less genteel writer than the Comtesse would be hard to find. About the only thing they had in common, in fact, was that both supported the Republicans during the 1848 revolution – Baudelaire from the barricades and d'Agoult from her society salon.

Born in Paris in 1821, Baudelaire lived alone with his mother for a year after his father had died when he was only six, and the experience of having his mother to himself remained one of his happiest. His mother remarried, however, taking up with a man called Aupick, a career soldier who went on to rise to the rank of general and ended up in the French Senate.

Baudelaire had a good education, and showed early talent as a writer, but he was expelled from school at 17 for endless disruptive behaviour. He spent the next two years living a bohemian life in the *Quartier Latin*, whilst nominally enrolled in law school. In an effort to discipline the lad, his stern stepfather sent him off on a voyage to India when he was 21, but Baudelaire jumped ship in Mauritius, and was back in France eight months later. The exotic experiences of the voyage were to colour his poetry until his death.

Within months of his return from the South Seas, Baudelaire came into his inheritance from his father, and proceeded to blow more than half of it over the following two years, leading an extraordinarily profligate and dissipated lifestyle, and consuming enormous quantities of drink and drugs ('One must be drunk, always' was his maxim). By this time he had also contracted the syphilis which was eventually to kill him.

A combination of gullibility and inebriation soon led Baudelaire into indebtedness, and his situation was dramatically worsened when the family restricted his access to his inheritance – the annual allowance he received thereafter barely covered his debts, let alone any living expenses. Fits of depression, and violent outbursts – in both his life and his poems – were the predictable result. He was to remain financially straitened until his death.

After discovering the morbid works of Edgar Allan Poe (known to this day, amusingly, to French people as Ed Garpoe) in 1847, Baudelaire became his translator, and spent much of the next fifteen years in bringing out the American's short stories in French. Only in 1857, therefore, more than a decade after most of the poems had been written, was Baudelaire finally able to publish *Les Fleurs du Mal*, but it wasn't the success he'd been banking on. Indeed, Baudelaire was put on trial for blasphemy and obscenity for 13 of the 100 poems, and six were eventually banned – a bar not lifted until 1949. By today's standards, they're tame stuff, but they sealed his reputation as a dissolute pornographer rather than a major poet.

Between increasing fits of depression and despair, he continued to write, producing some of his finest works, and a second edition of *Les Fleurs du Mal* was published in 1861 – but his publisher's bankruptcy the following year led to further penury for Baudelaire, and his health, too, began to fail. He moved to Belgium in 1864, hoping to persuade a more sympathetic Belgian literary world to publish his works, and remained there until having a catastrophic seizure in the summer of 1866.

He spent his last year incapacitated in a Paris nursing home, and died at the age of 46, unrecognised and alone – though Manet was one of the few people who came to the funeral. At his death, the vast majority of his work was unpublished or out of print, but by the beginning of the 20th century Baudelaire was already being acknowledged as one of the greatest figures of French literature.

Marcel Proust

France's most famous hypochondriac was born in 1871 to an eminent doctor in the Paris suburbs, and was brought up in an affluent household. Asthmatic, Jewish and homosexual, he nevertheless looked back fondly on his year of military service at the age of 18, and had a lifelong weakness for being photographed in uniform.

He went on to study law at the Sorbonne and at the Ecole des Sciences Politiques, before settling down to a busy life as a dandy and a roaring snob. At the same time he was already busy writing articles and essays, and his first books were published while he was only in his early twenties. For the second half of the decade, Proust worked on an uncompleted autobiographical novel, before starting on translations of John Ruskin's works into French, with his mother, in 1899.

Proust was still living at home at the turn of the century, and after his father died, in 1903, his relationship with his mother became ever more neurotic. For two years she looked after her son, and catered for his every need, before expiring herself in 1905. For weeks after her death, Proust refused to leave the apartment, and was eventually treated for a month at a sanatorium.

From 1894 to 1896, Proust had had a passionate affair with the musician and composer Reynaldo Hahn, and even long after the relationship was over, Hahn remained Proust's confidante. The writer's other relationships tended to be with men within his employ, and he went to great pains to please them. One, a certain Alfred Agostinelli, was a married man. After the liaison ended, Proust enticed him back with the gift of an aeroplane – only to see Agostinelli killed in short order in an unfortunate plane crash.

To the outside world, however, Proust remained firmly in the closet. And indeed, from 1907 onwards, he lived in one, becoming increasingly reclusive, and spending his life in virtual seclusion. He sound-proofed his stuffy, over-heated apartment at 102 Boulevard Haussmann with cork tiles, and spent his days asleep and his nights writing in bed. He spent vast sums of money – of which he was lucky enough to have plenty – on medicine (including champagne, see page 189).

On the rare occasions he went out, Proust dressed in layer upon layer of overcoats and mufflers, and insisted on his hosts recreating the oppressively warm and airless atmosphere of his own room. Natalie Barney (see page 161) once wanted to meet the great writer, but after months of planning, and agreeing to his draconian terms, the eventual midnight rendezvous was a disappointment, with Proust nervous about draughts and conversation flagging.

The last 15 years of Proust's life were lived in almost total isolation, as he laboured nightly on his extraordinary 3,000 page, seven volume lifework, *A la Recherche du Temps Perdu* (Remembrance of Things Past – now translated as 'In Search of Lost Time'). In 1913 he self-published the first volume after André Gide famously rejected the manuscript on behalf of the publisher Gallimard. But when the second volume won the prestigious Prix Goncourt, Gide was quick in offering to publish the rest.

Proust was still making corrections to the manuscript on his deathbed in November 1922, and didn't live to see the complete work published – or his name elevated to the very highest ranks of literature.

Once you've finished the seven volumes of *A la Recherche du Temps Perdu*, it's well worth dropping into the **Musée Carnavalet** in Paris, which has a fine reconstruction of Proust's bedroom at 102 Boulevard Haussmann. The cork tiles are suitably oppressive, as are the thick covers, purple satin bedspread and heavy dressing gown on the iron bedstead. A nightstand beside the bed is full of notebooks, topped with a quill and an inkwell; and the room is completed with a battered chaise-longue and an over-used and misshapen horsehair-stuffed chair.

At **102 Boulevard Haussmann** itself, Proust's room is now a bank's boardroom – there's nothing to see, though there's a plaque outside attesting to Proust's having lived here from 1907 to 1919. These days it's an appallingly noisy street; you'd want cork tiles if you were trying to write in peace.

Arthur Rimbaud

Arthur Rimbaud, arguably the most brilliant of the symbolist poets, was the original tearaway. Born in Charleville, in the Ardennes, halfway between Paris and Brussels, he was a brilliant pupil at school, and was writing poems in Latin by the age of 14. The following year, however, he was graffiti-ing churches with '*Merde à Dieu*', and later running off to Paris for the first time on the train – only to be arrested for fare dodging. His former teacher kindly bailed him out.

In February 1871, Rimbaud went to Paris again (this time paying the fare by pawning his watch), but ended up starving on the streets and walking home – some 240km (it took him over a month). During the summer he sent some poems to Paul Verlaine (see page 145), who was already known as a symbolist writer, and in September the older poet invited the younger one up to Paris. Rimbaud was still only 16; Verlaine ten years his senior.

At first Rimbaud stayed with Verlaine's parents-in-law, but was soon thrown out for his rudeness, filthiness and boorishness. With Verlaine's son being born in the same month as Rimbaud's 17th birthday, the affair between the two poets predictably caused a huge scandal. The pair's drunkenness and public fights (absinthe clearly not making the heart grow any fonder in this case) led to Verlaine's wife Mathilde leaving with the baby.

In March the following year, Verlaine agreed to break up with Rimbaud, and Mathilde returned – but by July, Rimbaud and Verlaine were on the road again together, living as vagabonds. They travelled to Brussels and London, causing trouble wherever they went, but with Rimbaud nonetheless churning out marvellous verse – some of which, inevitably, was lost along the way.

In 1873, Rimbaud started *Un Saison d'Enfer* (A Season in Hell), largely inspired by his tempestuous relationship with Verlaine, and – life matching art – ended up being shot in the wrist by Verlaine after a scene in which the older poet threatened to kill himself if the younger one left. Later that day, with Rimbaud's wrist freshly bandaged, Verlaine reached into his pocket … and Rimbaud rushed to the nearest police officer, fearing he was going to be shot again.

Verlaine was arrested, and (on the basis of a deposition made by Rimbaud) sent to jail for two years. (Both the deposition and the ledger showing the charge are on display in the Police Museum in Paris, see page 199.) After finishing off *Un Saison d'Enfer* – still aged only 19 – Rimbaud gave up poetry for good. His mother paid for 500 copies to be printed in Brussels, but Rimbaud managed to burn 495 of them, before heading off into the rest of his life.

This turned out to be no less extraordinary than his time with Verlaine. During the rest of the decade he travelled widely, showing up in places as far apart as Norway and Java – where he was a mercenary in the Dutch army, until deserting in Sumatra. He worked as a docker in Marseilles, a teacher in Germany, and a thief in Vienna. He was an extraordinarily gifted linguist, and learned English, German, Italian, Spanish, Greek, Arabic and Russian.

In 1880, Rimbaud walked from the north of France over the Alps to the Italian port of Genoa, and set sail for Africa, where he was to spend his last ten years. He was the first white man to travel so widely through East Africa, where he worked as a successful trader and gun-runner, learning the local languages and living an ascetic existence. He stopped drinking, and was apparently straightforward and meticulous in his business dealings.

Back home in France, his fame was growing, and Verlaine published a book of his poems, *Illuminations*, in 1886 – but Rimbaud remained dismissive of his own work. At the beginning of 1891, a painful knee stopped him from walking, and he ceased trading before being carried on a stretcher across 300km of desert by bearers to the nearest sea-port. Back in Marseilles, in May, the cancerous leg was amputated, but it was too late for Rimbaud. After being nursed by his sister Isabelle (who only found out Rimbaud had been a poet after his death) he died in November.

Like Van Gogh (see page 112), who had shot himself the previous year, Rimbaud was just 37 years old.

In Charleville Mézières, on the appropriately named **quai Arthur Rimbaud**, you'll find the **Rimbaud Museum**, which has a good collection of artefacts relating to Rimbaud's life, and copies of the poet's manuscripts. There's also a fine memorial to him in the centre of town.

Rimbaud's poems themselves are much better in French than English, but if you do want a translation, try and buy one with the original French on the facing pages – it's notoriously difficult work (like most of the symbolists' poetry) to render into a foreign language.

Finally, there's a wonderfully bad film called *Total Eclipse* (1995), which traces the relationship between Rimbaud and Verlaine and features Leonardo DiCaprio in the role of Rimbaud. Worth renting on video, for all the wrong reasons.

Marquis de Sade

There's no question about it – Donatien Alphonse François de Sade was a complete pervert. As indeed you'd expect, for the man who gave the world the term for describing the infliction of pain as a means of sexual gratification.

Born into an aristocratic family in 1740 in Paris, the young Marquis de Sade made an early name for himself as a soldier during the Seven Years' War (1756–63), before marrying young and going on to live the reckless life of a libertine. Organising your standard orgy wasn't enough for de Sade's febrile imagination, however, and within months of getting married he was arrested for persuading a prostitute (at sword point) to perform various blasphemous and unsafe sexual acts (this being a family publication, I won't go on) with communion hosts, chalices and crucifixes.

For this, he was sent to prison for the first of many times in his life, spending a total of more than 30 years behind bars – mostly in asylums, labelled as criminally insane. In 1772, he was even sentenced to death, but reprieved at the last moment. As a terminal recidivist, he even found himself in the Bastille, in July 1789, just as the French Revolution was kicking off.

Unfortunately for de Sade – and presumably with a collective sigh of relief from armies of Paris prostitutes – the Marquis was transferred to the Charenton Asylum from the Bastille just ten days before it was stormed, and the remaining prisoners were let loose (creating yet another French public holiday). In the ongoing looting, de Sade's prison library was ransacked and his manuscripts destroyed.

When he was released, the following April, his wife – having sensibly sequestered herself away in a convent – refused to see him, and filed successfully for a legal separation. De Sade then spent the last decade of the 18th century remarkably trouble-free, and even had a play accepted by the Comédie Française – though his castle, at Lacoste, in Provence, was successfully pillaged in 1792 by a revolutionary mob while he was in Paris. (Even today, Provence has a higher than average number of break-ins.)

But a vice-free life was beyond de Sade, and in 1801 he was arrested for having written the violently pornographic *Justine*. In 1803 he was then confined for the last time to Charenton, where he languished until his death in 1814.

Most of his many works, although elegantly written, are still considered unpublishable in many parts of the world, even today. In spite of a certain amount of rehabilitation by radical thinkers in the second half of the 20th century, it seems most people still don't have much of a stomach for sadistic pornography and violence.

The Marquis de Sade's ruined castle in **Lacoste**, in Provence (just up the road from Ménerbes, the village in the Luberon put on the map by Peter Mayle's *A Year in Provence*) was bought by the fashion designer Pierre Cardin in 2001, and is now used as the site for a summer festival – Don Juan, that kind of thing. Cardin has also said he'll be organising 'evenings of debauchery' there – while stressing that there'll be no place for sadism. You can scramble round the ruins and explore the old town's pretty cobbled streets.

Many of de Sade's works are available in English, though they're pretty grim reading, whatever the revisionists say. A flick through *120 Days of Sodom* should be quite enough.

Georges Sand

Amantine-Aurore-Lucile Dudevant, née Dupin, and better known as Georges Sand (though her best friends called her Aurore), was one of the most unconventional women of the 19th century.

You'd never have suspected it from her early life, however. Born in 1804 and brought up in a wealthy family, she spent most of her childhood reading. She then married Baron Casimir Dudevant when she was just 18, and bore him a son and a daughter. By 1831, however, she was tired of married life in the country, and she moved up to Paris, becoming a journalist, a profession then totally dominated by men.

A year later she published her first novel, under the name Georges Sand, and word quickly got out that here was a young woman of enormous talent. Here, too, was a woman who was going to live life on her own terms. She started wearing a top hat and trousers (this, at a time when cross-dressing wasn't just unconventional, but illegal) in order to get decent seats at the theatre – and having discovered that men's boots were a good deal more comfortable than ladies' shoes, she wore them for the rest of her life, even under billowing skirts.

Sand loved to smoke, and did so in public, breaking a powerful taboo. She was soon notorious for puffing away at cigars, but also became an adept cigarette roller and greatly enjoyed using a hookah. Her only persistently nagging fear – evident from countless letters – was that she would run out of tobacco.

At the beginning of 1833, Sand caused a scandal by having a tempestuous affair with Marie Dorval, one of the most talented and attractive actresses on the Paris stage, but only months later, she was to meet and fall in love with the young poet Alfred de Musset. For the next year and a half they were inseparable, and both writers were to go on to make good use of the liaison, he in *Confessions d'un Enfant du Siècle*; she in *Elle et Lui*.

Over the next decade, Sand continued to write prolifically (and would continue to do so until her death, producing over 100 works in all), and became a major feature of the Salon scene, more than holding her own with the likes of Balzac, Baudelaire, Delacroix, Flaubert, Liszt and Zola.

In 1837 she met Frédéric Chopin (see page 122), like Musset, six years her junior, and their nine-year affair, from 1838 to 1847, was the happiest and most productive period of the composer's short life. When Chopin played for Sand she would lie underneath the piano on cushions – though when Delacroix stopped by to paint the happy couple he chose a somewhat more conventional composition for the portrait (see page 122).

After the 1848 revolution, Sand was briefly the French Minister for Propaganda, but she gradually retired from Paris life to her estate at Nohant, in the Berry, to concentrate on her writing. In her later years she had a long-lasting relationship with the engraver, Alexandre Manceau, until his death in 1865, and wrote pastoral novels which became huge bestsellers at the time and are still widely read in France today.

As a proto-feminist, insisting on women's rights to education and acting as a strong role-model for the era, Sand nonetheless loved the domestic life, and at Nohant would make vast quantities of jam during the fruit season. She continued to swim in the River Indre long after her doctors forbade it, and outlived many of her contemporaries, finally giving up the spirit in 1876.

As befits France's most famous woman writer of the 19th century, there's some good Sand-related stuff to see and do. Most obvious is a visit to the **Château de Nohant** at Nohant Vic, near Châteauroux, in the Berry, south of Paris. It was here that the author was brought up and where she spent most of her later life – and Chopin summered here from 1839 to 1846. Today you can visit the manor house and stroll in the lovely gardens.

In Paris it's well worth stopping in at the charming little **Musée de la Vie Romantique** in Montmartre, which has lots of Sand's letters and manuscripts, and various pictures of her and her set, as well as a fine family tree, demonstrating Sand's genuinely aristocratic roots. There's also a plaster cast of Sand's right arm next to one of Chopin's left hand.

There's also of course the huge body of Sand's work, including the 1,200 page *Story of My Life*, which should keep even the speediest of readers busy for a couple of hours.

Paul Verlaine

Paul Verlaine's father, like the father of Rimbaud, was a captain in the army, and the young Verlaine grew up in an ordinary household of the era. When he was 13, in 1857, however, he was profoundly influenced by reading *Les Fleurs du Mal*, which had just been published controversially by Baudelaire (see page 139).

Like Baudelaire, Verlaine determined to be a poet, and like Baudelaire he sought refuge in drink – notably the dreaded absinthe. Verlaine's first book, *Poèmes Saturniens*, was published in 1866, and followed three years later by *Fêtes Galantes*. In 1870, in spite (or because of?) his homosexuality, he married Mathilde Mauté de Fleurville, only to take up with the 16-year-old Arthur Rimbaud (see page 124) the following year.

Mathilde wasn't impressed, but she was persistent, and made constant attempts to win Verlaine back. Things came to an unpleasant head in the middle of 1872, when she and her mother confronted Verlaine and Rimbaud in a Brussels hotel, but when Verlaine left her stranded at the station, she returned to Paris and was soon granted a legal separation.

A year later, in a fit of desperation, Verlaine took a pot shot at Rimbaud with a pistol, and wounded him. He served time for his trouble, but in prison wrote perhaps his finest work, *Romances Sans Paroles*. After his release he went to England to teach French for a while, before returning to France to teach in the town of Rethel, in the Ardennes. By 1879, however, he had been expelled from the school, along with his favourite pupil, Lucien Létinois, for 'inappropriate behaviour'.

The couple decided to return to the land and attempted to run a smallholding together. They were hopeless farmers (no surprise there), however, and the farm soon went bankrupt. Worse, Létinois died of typhoid in 1883, and Verlaine's mother died in 1886. The poet relapsed into an absinthe-haze, dreaming nightly of Rimbaud. He was nonetheless becoming known as the most famous living French poet, and he continued to write an impressive range of works.

But his health was on the wane, and absinthe was killing him. In spite of his fame – at the age of 49 he was elected France's Prince of Poets – he lived in terrible poverty, and he finally succumbed just two years later, at the beginning of January 1896. Thousands followed his coffin to its final resting place in Batignolles cemetery.

There are various collections of Verlaine's poetry available in translation, but as with Rimbaud (see above) you should try and get hold of a bilingual edition, even if your French isn't great.

Up in the Ardennes, in the small town of **Juniville**, you'll find the **Auberge Verlaine**, which was – as the Auberge du Lion d'Or – Verlaine's favourite haunt from 1880 to 1882. It now puts on all kinds of Verlaine-related events and temporary exhibitions, and has the desk Verlaine wrote at, along with various portraits and photos of the poet.

Voltaire

François Marie Arouet, known to the world as Voltaire, was born in Paris in 1694. Brought up by Jesuits, he went on to study law, but soon turned his acid wit and enormous intellect to literature and philosophy.

He loved high society, and the good things in life, but he was also thoroughly non-conformist (particularly where church or government were concerned) and forever on the side of justice and the poor. His well-turned aphorisms – such as: 'To succeed in the world it is not enough to be stupid, you must also be well-mannered' – were a thorn in the side of the establishment, and he always had the last word. As an old man, he said: 'In my life, I have prayed but one prayer: Oh Lord, make my enemies ridiculous. And God granted it.'

Not surprisingly, he made many influential enemies and was frequently in trouble – he was twice jailed at La Bastille, and spent much of the rest of his life in exile. As he quipped on his way to prison, 'It is dangerous to be right when the government is wrong.' In exile, he also produced an enormous volume of work, from books and plays to (frequently anonymous) pamphlets and manifestos, as well as endless letters – more than 7,000 have survived.

In his early thirties, Voltaire spent three years in England (after having been given the choice of prison or exile, for insulting a powerful nobleman), and while there he took up the liberal philosophies of John Locke and Isaac Newton, and became an admirer of English customs and religious tolerance.

Back in France, he wrote his *Lettres Philosophiques*, which were highly influential in kicking off the French Revolution 50 years later, and he soon found himself in exile, yet again – this time for 15 years with the Marquise du Châtelet, at the Château de Cirey. The Marquise was one of the most impressive women of her day, being a talented mathematician, astronomer, and philosopher. She was also a married woman – but her army husband was often away.

Now in his 40s, Voltaire was determined to have the recognition in France which he already had abroad, and he lobbied hard to be accepted by the Académie Française. On being refused, he mounted a campaign of approval with the Pope, of all people, reading his works and flattering him, and finally persuading him, in a remarkable coup, to endorse his play *Mahomet* (even though it had previously been banned and burned as sacrilegious).

When the next vacancy came up at the Académie, in 1746, Voltaire couldn't be refused. He promptly used his maiden – indeed only – reading to demonstrate not just his extraordinary wit, but also to be highly confrontational. He was banished from court once again.

In 1749, following the death of the Marquise du Châtelet, Voltaire accepted the invitation of Frederick the Great to go to Potsdam, and he lived there until 1753. In 1759, after various unsatisfactory sojourns in Geneva, he bought the estate of Ferney, right on the Geneva border, and spent his last 19 years there.

One of the reasons Voltaire chose Ferney was precisely its proximity to Geneva. Being on the border allowed him to escape there whenever the French king bayed for his blood, but being in France allowed him to set up a theatre close enough to Geneva to tempt wayward Calvinists into pleasuring themselves. At the time (and it's not so very different now), Geneva's laws mandated everything from religious behaviour to how much you should eat and drink, and even what time you should get up and go to bed. Theatre-going sounded like far too much fun, and was therefore a strict no-no.

(If you don't believe me about Geneva, remember this is a place where you still can't flush your toilet after 10pm at night, and you can only do your laundry on one pre-designated day of the week. You also have to keep a regulated amount of food on standby – with occasional inspections by the 'pasta police'. All true.)

Under Voltaire, Ferney flourished, and became for a while the intellectual capital of Europe. Voltaire welcomed endless visitors, and took in anyone, rich or poor, who came to his door. He brought the great performers of the day to act in his theatre, and even went on stage himself – at a time when acting was very much a lowly profession.

When Edward Gibbon visited, in 1763 (taking time out from his *Decline and Fall of the Roman Empire*), the 69-year-old Voltaire performed both male and female roles in a three-and-a-half-hour play, followed by dinner and a ball for over 100 people, which ran until four in the morning.

James Boswell dropped in on Voltaire the following year, and the two played piano together and got along famously – until they started discussing religion (always a mistake). Voltaire poured ridicule and scorn on Boswell, who eventually retired hurt. (Voltaire, it should be remembered, once dedicated a book *'O Dieux'* – which means not only 'to the Gods' but also 'odious'.)

Voltaire took to preaching, which led to the local bishop refusing the writer communion, confession or absolution, in 1768. This was too much for the philosopher, who promptly feigned a mortal illness (a lifelong hypochondriac, he nonetheless trusted doctors no more than clerics, and once said 'The art of medicine consists in amusing the patient while nature cures the disease.'). A priest was called to deliver final absolution, but came well-prepared, with a profession of faith for Voltaire to sign. After a farcical scene, with Voltaire begging for absolution but refusing to sign, the priest finally caved in, and gave him the Holy Sacrament.

At the age of 83, Voltaire wrote his last play, and determined to see it performed in Paris. The five-day journey was too much for him, however, and he expired soon after arriving in the capital. In spite of the church's insistence that he couldn't go into hallowed ground, Voltaire was buried at an abbey in Champagne.

In 1791, with the revolution in full swing, Voltaire's remains were brought back to the capital to be housed in the Pantheon. More than half a million people came out to see the procession. His remains were stolen in 1814, however, and thrown away by religious fanatics, although the theft wasn't discovered for more than 50 years. That left just his brain (which passed from hand to hand for a century or so, before disappearing), and his heart, which is still in the Bibliothéque Nationale in Paris.

There's no shortage of works by Voltaire still in print, and on the whole the English translations are excellent.

You can also visit his two most important residences, the **Château de Cirey**, at Cirey sur Blaise, in the Haute Marne in Eastern France, which has a lovely, atmospheric recreation of Voltaire's time there, and the **Château de Voltaire**, in Ferney Voltaire, just outside Geneva, which has an excellent collection of Voltaire-related materials in their original setting.

(As a quaint historical aside, the Swiss still haven't forgiven Voltaire, more than 200 years after his death. You won't even find a mention of 'Voltaire' on any of the road signs across the Swiss border, which primly stick to 'Ferney' rather than Ferney Voltaire.)

ECCENTRICALLY MODERN FRENCH PENS

From Colette's ever-younger husbands to Roussel's travelling around the world but refusing to look out the window, and from Raspail's 1998 invasion of sovereign British soil to Perec's years of palindrome writing (not to mention the Surrealists and Existentialists), France has a choice collection of eccentric modern writers.

Albert Camus

Albert Camus was one of the most gifted French writers of the 20th century, and the foremost exponent of absurdist or existential literature – based on the very reasonable tenets that human life is meaningless in the face of death, and that individuals are powerless in making rational sense of their own experience. Perhaps, however, because by then he was a happily married man and a proud father of two, Camus tempered his later writings with humanism and moral responsibility, and fell out violently with Sartre and his followers as a result.

Camus was born into a poor working class family in Algeria in 1913, but proved talented at school, and worked at a variety of unskilled jobs to put himself through university in Algiers – although his studies were cut short by a bout of tuberculosis. He married and divorced while still in his early 20s, and also ran a theatre company, aimed at educating and entertaining the local working classes.

By 1938 he had already published his first two books, and was working as a journalist on *Alger Républicain*, an anti-colonialist newspaper. When war broke out, however, he went to France and became a prominent member of the resistance network. As a seasoned political hack he was the logical choice for the editorship of the underground Paris daily *Combat*, from 1943.

Meanwhile, the war also saw Camus remarry and become a father, and write his first, astonishing, novel, *L'Etranger* (The Stranger, or The Outsider), as well as a radical essay on the absurd, and two far-reaching plays. Unlike Sartre, however, Camus came to believe that absurdism didn't necessarily imply moral apathy, and his next novel, *La Peste* (The Plague), published in 1947, as well as being an allegory of the fight against fascism, made heroes of the few who fought against the plague, however futile their efforts.

In 1951, he inevitably fell out with Sartre, largely through having had the temerity to criticise the Soviet Union in an extended essay called *L'Homme Révolté* (The Rebel), and in 1956 he published what was to be his final novel, *La Chute* (The Fall), a brilliant dissection of deception and its consequences. The following year he won the Nobel Prize for Literature, and in 1958 he bought a house in Lourmarin, in Provence (just down the road from where Peter Mayle now lives, post-Ménerbes).

At the height of his fame and powers, having taken up the offer of his publisher, Michel Gallimard, to borrow his car instead of taking the train to return to Paris after the Christmas holidays, Camus spun off the road and was killed instantly. In the car was the manuscript of his unfinished novel *Le Premier Homme*, and in his pocket was the unused train ticket to Paris. Camus was only 46 years old.

The only way to reach Albert Camus is through his works, all of which are available in good translations in English. His essays and non fiction can be quite hard-going, but his three novels, *The Outsider*, *The Plague* and *The Fall*, are all excellent.

Jean Cocteau

Known today primarily for his films, Jean Cocteau was also a great avant-garde dramatist, poet, novelist and artist, with a firm belief that all art has its roots in poetry.

Clement Eugéne (later Jean) Cocteau was born into a comfortably bourgeois family in 1889, but all that was ruined when his father committed suicide nine years later. Cocteau became a rebel and was later expelled from school, but he clearly had charm as well as talent, as he was able to persuade many of the leading artistic figures of the day to give him a break.

Notable amongst them was the owner of the Russian Ballet, Sergei Diaghilev, who commissioned Cocteau to write the librettos for several of his productions. This led Cocteau to work with Erik Satie (see page 127) and Pablo Picasso on Diaghilev's ground-breaking ballet *Parade*, which was later described by a reviewer as 'surreal' – thus introducing the term 'Surrealism' to the world.

In 1919 the young writer Raymond Radiguet (see box overleaf) came to Paris and he and Cocteau, like Rimbaud and Verlaine half a century earlier, became lovers. It was doomed to be as short-lived as the earlier liaison – Radiguet died of typhoid in 1923, aged only 20.

Cocteau threw himself into his work, putting on plays, writing novels and poetry, and propping up the bar at *Le Boeuf sur le Toit* (so-called because there was indeed a statue of an ox on the roof), *the* place to be seen in 1920's Paris. Lee Miller (see page 105) took to dropping in between modelling assignments, and got herself cast as the essence of female beauty in Cocteau's first feature film, *Le Sang d'un Poéte*, in 1930.

By the late 1930s and early 1940s, however, Cocteau was slipping away into opium addiction – even as he was writing some of his best plays and film scripts. Fortunately the actor Jean Marais, 25 years his younger, turned up at the end of the war to console him, and to star in Cocteau's most famous films, *La Belle et la Bête* (Beauty and the Beast, 1946) and *Orphée* (Orpheus, 1949).

As he grew older, Cocteau treated himself to a facelift, and took to wearing dramatic matador's capes around town, as befitted one of France's greatest living artists – he was elected to the Académie Française in 1955. Cocteau died of heart failure on 11 October 1963, while writing the obituary of his great friend Edith Piaf (see page 124), who had died earlier the same day. He was 74, she was 47.

Many of Cocteau's published works are available in English, though some are

RAYMOND RADIGUET

The incredibly precocious poet and novelist Raymond Radiguet was born in 1903, but we know very little about him until he shows up in Paris for the first time in 1918, and again the following year, at the age of 16 (like Rimbaud, see page 142), when he takes up with Jean Cocteau, a decade or so his senior (like Verlaine, see page 145).

Radiguet wrote wonderful poetry, in the neo-classic style, shying well clear of the Dadaist and Cubist fashions of the day. At the age of 17 he started his first novel, *Le Diable au Corps* (*The Devil in the Flesh*) which was completed the following year and published in 1922, bringing him instant fame and wealth.

The novel is probably autobiographical, and recounts the story of a schoolboy taking up with a newly married woman whose husband is away at the war. It ends, bleakly, with the woman dying in childbirth, largely because in the freezing cold streets of Paris the youth doesn't have the nerve to get her checked into a hotel.

By 1923, Radiguet was completing his second novel, *Le Bal du Comte d'Orgel* (*Count Orgel Opens the Ball*), but was struck down fatally by typhoid before the year was out. He was not yet 21. Even without Cocteau's help on revising his manuscripts, it's clear that Radiguet had prodigious talent, nipped in the bud.

hard to find (*Opium: The Diary of a Cure* is particularly good, and particularly hard to get). It's also fairly easy to see his films, either as re-runs or on video.

There's also a cheerful **Musée Jean Cocteau** in Menton, on the Italian border, which features some of the artist's later mosaics and ceramics as well as various bits and pieces about his life – and the occasional temporary exhibition.

Colette

Sidonie Gabrielle Claudine Colette lived an extraordinary rich life spanning the last quarter of the 19th century and the first half of the 20th.

In 1893, at the age of 20, she married Henri Gauthier-Villars, who was 15 years older than her, and published under the pen name Willy (which was presumably less droll then than it would be today). Willy encouraged Colette to write – it's said he would lock her into her room until the requisite page-count was reached – and then published her work under his own name. The first four *Claudine* novels came out between 1900 and 1903, and were hugely successful, with the spin-offs including a stage musical and a range of perfumes and soaps (for washing with, not TV serials).

In 1905, sick of Willy, Colette left home, and a year later was divorced. She took to the stage, becoming a somewhat risqué music-hall performer (her main routine included outrageously baring her left breast) and embarked on a series of scandalous lesbian affairs – most notably with her co-performer, the Marquise de Belboeuf.

The Marquise, better known as 'Missy', was the estranged wife of the Marquis de Belboeuf, and the youngest daughter of the Duc de Morny (the man who pushed Sarah Bernhardt, see page 132, into a career in the theatre). Together, she and Colette performed nightly at the Moulin Rouge in an act considered saucy enough to be banned by the police. Colette also became friends (and probably lovers) with the American heiress Natalie Barney (see page 161), who was to remain her friend for the rest of her life.

By 1910, Colette was a famous author in her own right, and she had a column in the daily newspaper *Le Matin*. After accidentally conceiving what was to be her only child with the newspaper's editor, Henry de Jouvenal, Colette married him in 1912. During World War I she turned the de Jouvenal property into a hospital for the war wounded, and was given the *Légion d'Honneur* by a grateful nation.

Aged 47, Colette then lent her assistance in the summer of 1920 to Bertrand, her husband's 17-year-old son (by his first marriage), by helping him lose his virginity (paralleling the events in her novel *Chéri*). Bertrand repaid the compliment by taking Colette to Gstaad, when she was 50, where she proved that it's never too late to learn to ski.

Bertrand and Colette were lovers for six years, though when Bertrand's father found out about the affair he reacted predictably enough – by divorcing Colette. Bertrand, for his part, went on to marry Martha Gellhorn in 1933 – the writer who herself would later marry (and be the only person ever to leave) Ernest Hemingway (see page 167). Bertrand would still be telling journalists into his eighties that he'd wished he'd spent his life with Colette.

Colette herself continued to write enormously successful books (she wrote over 70, in all), and in 1935, at the age of 62, remarried for the last time, to a pearl dealer called Maurice Goudeket, who was 17 years her junior. They lived together at the Palais-Royal in Paris (Jean Cocteau, see page 149, was a neighbour and close friend), and she continued to publish, penning one of her most famous works, *Gigi*, in 1945.

In her sixties she was still attending five opening nights (and writing three reviews) a week, while in her seventies she wrote a further eight books. She became the first woman to be elected to the Goncourt Academy. She died aged 81, in 1954, and was given a state funeral.

Southeast of Paris, in the Yonne, the Château de Saint Sauveur en Puisaye (which overlooks the town of Colette's birth) has been converted into a **Musée Colette**. The old château houses a modern museum containing many photographs, reconstructions of Colette's Palais-Royal bedroom and living room, and lots of her stuff, including her prized collection of butterflies.

Georges Perec

Before his untimely death of cancer in 1982, Georges Perec produced some of the most eccentric literary works of the second half of the 20th century.

Born in 1936 to a family of Polish Jews who had emigrated to Paris in the 1920s, Perec had a rough start: his father died of wounds sustained in action in 1940, while his mother was deported in 1942 and died at Auschwitz. The orphaned boy was brought up by his uncle and aunt. After finishing school and completing his military service, Perec took a job in 1962 as an archivist at one of the Paris hospitals, and he stayed in the lowly paid job until 1979, when the fame and fortune accompanying the Prix Medici allowed him to quit.

In 1965, Perec won the Prix Renaudot for his first book *Les Choses* (*Things*), and in 1967 he joined the experimental writers' group OuLiPo (*Ouvroir de Littérature Potentielle*, or Workshop for Potential Literature), which became his intellectual home for the next 15 years.

Over a short career, Perec published more than 20 books, varying from collections of stories and essays, to novels and collections of crossword puzzles (from 1976 he invented puzzles for the magazine *Le Point*). Practically the only thing binding the *oeuvre* together is an intellectual delight in wordplay and games of logic. Perec loved playing with vowels, and once wrote an entire short story called 'What a Man!' where the only one used is 'a'. He was also keen on lipograms (pieces of writing where a particular letter is excluded), and in 1969 published what must be the world's longest – a novel of over 300 pages called *La Disparition*.

In the novel, the main character, Anton Voyl, finds himself in a world where the letter 'e' has mysteriously gone missing (in an amusing aside he comes across a piece of writing by the well known William Shakspar, which starts off: 'Living, or not living: that is what I ask: / If 'tis a stamp of honour to submit / To slings and arrows waft'd us by ill winds…'). Just imagine for a moment how hard it would be to write a whole book without being able to use words like *je, le, me, elle, une, être, madame* or *merci*; without being able to employ any adjective attached to a feminine subject (you have to add 'e'); or without being able to mention the seasons (*hiver, printemps, été, automne*). It beggars belief.

If that was hard enough, Georges Perec also takes credit for having written the world's longest palindrome. Not for him the elegant simplicity of 'Able was I ere I saw Elba' or 'A man, a plan, a canal: Panama'. No, Perec's reversible text is instead an entire short story, and runs to an incredible 1,273 words (5,566 characters, not counting punctuation).

Le Grand Palindrome therefore starts off: '*Trace l'inégal palindrome. Neige. Bagatelle, dira Hercule. Le brut repentir, cet écrit né Perec. L'arc lu pèse trop, lis à vice-versa…*' and ends several pages later with the same thing in reverse: '*…as rêvé: Ci va! S'il porte, sépulcral, ce repentir, cet écrit ne perturbe le lucre: Haridelle, ta gabegie ne mord ni la plage ni l'écart.*'

If you don't think that's remarkable, try composing one yourself…

Perec's career of word-games finally resulted in literary triumph, when *La Vie Mode d'Emploi* (Life: A User's Manual) was published in 1978 and won the Prix Medici. Within more than 100 stories, the book describes the interconnected lives of the inhabitants of a Paris apartment building, and it finally allowed Perec the financial freedom to write full-time.

In 1981, he went to Australia, to be writer-in-residence at Brisbane University, but he had to return to France early – diagnosed with the lung cancer which cut short his life just four days before his 46th birthday.

Jean Raspail

The French novelist Jean Raspail briefly made the news in the UK in 1998, when at the age of 73 he and a small army invaded and successfully captured Britain's Minquiers Islands, in the name of the Kingdom of Araucania-Patagonia – in belated revenge, apparently, for the prolonged British occupation of the Falklands (historically a Patagonian possession).

Raspail, claiming legitimacy as Patagonia's King Orelie-Antoine I, oversaw the

running-up of his kingdom's blue, white and green flag. His 'commandos' then left a few stickers and placards behind, and the entire party of seven set sail for home.

The following day, a passing British yachtsman noticed the strange flag and promptly replaced it with the Union Jack, thus ending one of the more eccentric recent episodes in Anglo-French affairs.

It was hardly a major diplomatic incident, however – the uninhabited Minquiers, in the English Channel, are not only diminutive, but also mostly underwater at high tide. At the British Embassy in Paris – after Jersey police had conducted a minor clean-up operation on the islands – Raspail handed over the Union Jack he'd pulled down in exchange for his Patagonian flag.

It wasn't Raspail's first brush with controversy. In the early 70s he published *Le Camp des Saints* (The Camp of the Saints), a novel which investigates the moral dilemma which would be raised if the millions of poor people in the developing world were to suddenly arrive at the doorstep of the rich west – letting them in would destroy the rich world; sending them back would destroy them. The book is the last word in political incorrectness, and yet even if you can't stomach its conclusions, it nonetheless raises plenty of interesting ethical questions.

From his mid-twenties onwards, Raspail travelled widely (through North and South America, the Caribbean, the Belgian Congo, Japan, Hong Kong and Macao) and since the 1950s has been writing novels and travel books about his experiences. He narrowly failed to be elected to the Académie Française in 1993.

Jean Raspail's works are mainly available in French, though *The Camp of The Saints* is easy enough to find in English, as is a novel called *Blue Island*, a powerful allegory of France's fall to the Nazis, and akin, in its way, to William Golding's *Lord of the Flies*.

There's also a suitably eclectic and opinionated website (http://jeanraspail.free.fr) – though it's unclear whether or not Monsieur Raspail himself knows about the site.

Raymond Roussel

Raymond Roussel was unquestionably the most unusual and eccentric writer of the early 20th century. Not only was he immensely arrogant ('My fame shall outshine that of Napoleon,' he once said) but – in spite of his undeniable originality and even talent – he was also spectacularly wrong, becoming one of the greatest failures the literary world has ever known.

Born outside Paris in 1877 to a mother who was a morphine addict and a father who was a singularly wealthy stockbroker, Roussel showed enormous early talent as a writer and musician. Like Proust (the Proust family lived nearby) the young Roussel was also withdrawn, obsessive, homosexual, and distinctly foppish. Always immaculately turned out, he wore his outfits only two or three times each – and collars only once – before throwing them out. One of the few surviving photographs shows him looking positively dandyish, sporting a natty tweed jacket, atop white flannels and shoes, and accessorised by a cane and a Panama hat.

His writing was no less eccentric. When he was 19, he sat down and wrote a poem called *La Doublure* which was over 5,000 lines long – and apparently tedious beyond belief. Later on he would write an unfinished poem called *Les Noces*, which even uncompleted ran to 20,000 lines, most of them interminably describing a child blowing soap bubbles.

His fiction, if anything, is even more opaque. Based on extraordinarily complex made-up rules, puns and other linguistic tricks, it's almost impossible to read, let alone understand.

In a book explaining his *modus operandi*, published after his death, Roussel described how he went about creating fiction. He would start with one word, and then change one letter to find a second word (in the example below, '*billard*' becomes '*pillard*'). He would then construct a sentence using each word, and use the two as the first and last of the story – the storyline itself simply attempting to lurch from one point to the other.

In the most famous example, a story starts with the phrase '*Les lettres du blanc sur les bandes du vieux billard*' and closes with '*Les lettres du blanc sur les bandes du vieux pillard*'.

The first can be roughly translated as 'The white letters along the edge of the old billiard table' while the second means 'The white man's letters about the old thief's gangs.' Getting from the beginning to the end of the story is a complete nightmare.

And it got worse. It took Roussel seven years to write the 40-page *Impressions d'Afrique* (a place he hadn't yet been to). With its multiple nested parentheses and incomprehensible footnotes, seven years is about how long it would take you to read it.

Roussel's works only made it into print at all because he spent a fortune on getting them published through vanity presses, and they only sold in handfuls – a short run of one of his poems was still in print over half a century after first publication. He also paid vast sums in putting on his unfathomable plays at major theatres, only to be ridiculed by the public.

His only admirers in his lifetime, inevitably, were the Surrealists ('The greatest mesmerist of modern times,' said Breton; 'The President of the Republic of Dreams,' added Aragon). But Roussel was above them all, and dismissively brushed off the comments of a group he considered far too obscure to be of any importance.

He travelled the world, without apparent purpose. In 1910 he went to India and Sri Lanka (then Ceylon) with his mother – who was pretty eccentric herself, insisting on travelling with a coffin, in case she were to die on the trip. Roussel never even looked out of the portholes of his cabin, writing furiously, day in, day out. He voyaged to China, Japan, Australia and New Zealand, and across America, but took no interest in his surroundings at all.

As he grew older he developed an irrational anxiety about suitcases and trunks. To get round the problem he had a huge mobile home built for himself (the precursor of the caravan) containing his office, bedroom and bathroom, and accommodation at the back for three servants. He travelled Europe in the contraption, with the curtains permanently firmly drawn, and in Rome was visited by an impressed Mussolini.

An obsessive worker, Roussel was also a compulsive eater, and put away enormous meals every day – eating up to 20 copious courses at a sitting. His extravagant lifestyle (and endless blackmail payouts to his homosexual partners) nearly bankrupted him.

Roussel died in a hotel room in Palermo, in Sicily, in 1933, but although many said it was suicide, the cause of death has never been clearly established.

Raymond Roussel's works are all available in French, but I can only imagine that even those which have been purchased are still widely unread. The English translations of his stories and poems are pretty hard to find, harder still to read, and practically impossible to make sense of.

Far more rewarding is Mark Ford's excellent biography, *Raymond Roussel and the Republic of Dreams* (see *Appendix: Further Reading/References*).

Jean-Paul Sartre and Simone de Beauvoir

The lives of Jean-Paul Sartre and Simone de Beauvoir are inextricably intertwined. For over half a century, from their meeting in 1929 to Sartre's death in 1980, they had an immensely strong but unconventional relationship. Neither ever professed fidelity to the other, they only shared the same living space very briefly (in World War II), and they neither had children nor common property. Yet they remained closer to each other than to anyone else, exchanging daily letters, and together they formed an intellectual powerhouse of mid-century philosophy and literature.

At first, they made a two-year pact which allowed them to have affairs, but in which they had to be completely honest and open with each other. This was then renewed annually, although Sartre made a number of propositions to *Castor* (literally 'Beaver', Sartre's pet name for de Beauvoir) over the years – which she routinely turned down.

The most unusual of their domestic arrangements was a sort of *ménage à trois*, which was described – only thinly disguised – by de Beauvoir in her first novel, *She Came to Stay* (1943). In real life, Olga Kosakiewicz had been one of de Beauvoir's students in 1933, and was seduced first by her, and then by Sartre. The novel was dedicated to Kosakiewicz – although in the book de Beauvoir actually kills off the Olga character.

In 1938, another of de Beauvoir's students, Bianca Bienenfeld, was also passed from de Beauvoir to Sartre. Although she had a deep friendship with de Beauvoir after the war (lasting right up to the writer's death, in 1986) Bienenfeld also wrote a dramatic exposé of the two philosophers, called *A Disgraceful Affair*, which was published in 1996.

Sartre and de Beauvoir only met through Sartre flunking his finals at the Sorbonne in 1928, coming last in a field of fifty. Retaking the year, he met the precocious de Beauvoir (she was two-and-a-half years younger than him) and they studied together. In the next exam, Sartre came first and de Beauvoir second – though she was only a 50th of a point behind, and it's widely thought that Sartre only pipped her to the post as he was retaking the exam, whereas it was de Beauvoir's first shot.

During the 1930s they both worked as teachers, though Sartre got off to an earlier start than de Beauvoir in being published. At the beginning of World War II, Sartre was conscripted, and spent his short military career launching weather balloons, until being captured in June 1940. As a prisoner of war he wrote frenetically, but earned a reputation as something of a soap dodger. Fortunately for his co-prisoners, he escaped in early 1941 and managed to return to Paris.

After the war, Sartre (now aged 41) and his mother took a flat together at 24 rue Bonaparte. Sartre had always been close to his mother – his father had died when he was only one – and he continued to live with her until 1962. What she thought of his comings and goings isn't recorded; but as a first cousin of the great missionary Albert Schweitzer, perhaps she was able to take a charitable view.

The new residence – Sartre was to live there for 16 years – was right across the square from Les Deux Magots, and the philosopher held regular court on the terrace as the consummate café man, and one of the most radical thinkers of his day. He was a true existentialist, believing that in a world without God, man must be responsible for his own actions, and he was a keen Marxist as well – nonetheless remaining firmly unaligned with any of the great political powers of the day.

He also continued to publish important works – though his more inspired ideas had sometimes seen earlier publication in de Beauvoir's books, and she spent a great deal of time editing and tidying Sartre's manuscripts. De Beauvoir, for her part, was increasingly famous in her own right – particularly after the publication of *The Second Sex*, a feminist masterpiece (shouldn't that be mistress-piece?) in 1949.

In 1952, de Beauvoir started a seven-year relationship with the filmmaker Claude Lanzmann, who was 17 years her younger, and he became the only person she ever lived with. After they broke up, she stayed on at the flat they had shared together at 11 bis, rue Schoelcher, until her death.

In 1962, Sartre took a studio on the 10th floor at 222 Boulevard Raspail. It was a short walk from La Coupole, just up the road, and Sartre and de Beauvoir met there every Sunday for lunch. In 1964, Sartre became only the second person to turn down the Nobel Prize for Literature (the other was Boris Pasternak), and although he continued to write after suffering a stroke in 1973, his health steadily declined. When he died in 1980, at the age of 74, a huge crowd followed the funeral procession to **Montparnasse cemetery**.

De Beauvoir spent her final years writing and editing works about her life with Sartre, with *Adieux* (A Farewell to Sartre) being published in 1981, and *Lettres au Castor* (Letters from Sartre – publishers shying predictably clear of the literal translation) in 1983. In April 1986, de Beauvoir followed Sartre to the cemetery, where they're joined in death in a way they never could be in life. Their grave is a simple one, and much visited, though it tends to attract more than its fair share of crappy tributes.

Most of the works of Sartre and de Beauvoir are easily available in English, and many are well worth reading. Particular recommendations are de Beauvoir's *The Second Sex*, which was one of the driving forces in getting post-war feminism off the ground, and *She Came to Stay*, her first novel.

As for Sartre, he's still widely taught, though I'm not a huge personal fan. That said, the trilogy *The Roads to Freedom* (*The Age of Reason*, *The Reprieve*, and *Iron in the Soul*), is magnificent. But don't lose your concentration in the last paragraph of *Iron in the Soul*, however, as it does run on for the best part of 100 pages.

You can visit **Les Deux Magots** on Boulevard Saint-Germain, and **La Coupole** on Boulevard Raspail, but the experience is almost certain to disappoint. All trace of whatever atmosphere Sartre and de Beauvoir brought to the cafés has long since disappeared, and the only philosophising you're likely to find yourself doing nowadays is to wonder how on earth they can justify charging you nearly € 4 for a coffee, € 5 for a mineral water and an eye-watering € 7.20 for a pastis.

The Surrealists

The Surrealists revolutionised the art world in the 1920s and 1930s. The group was founded by André Breton, Paul Eluard and Louis Aragon, and counted as its members eccentrics as diverse as Luis Buñuel (see page 97), Jean Cocteau (see page 149), Salvador Dalí (see page 100), Lee Miller (see page 105) and Alberto Giacometti (see page 103).

The term 'surrealist' itself was born out of the 1917 première of the radical ballet *Parade*, which was written by Erik Satie (see page 127) and Jean Cocteau for the Russian impresario Sergei Diaghilev. A reviewer described the production as 'surreal'.

Nearly a century on, the easiest way of getting in touch with the Surrealists is through photography, and particularly through the work of Man Ray and Lee

Miller (see page 105). There's also, however, a strong body of literature worth investigating, in particular the poems of Eluard and Aragon. Breton's writing, on the other hand, seems terribly dated now, and Apollinaire's plays don't make much sense in a 21st-century context (though the novel *Alcools* is still an excellent read).

Guillaume Apollinaire

Guillelmus Albert Vladimir Alexandre Apollinaire di Kostrowitzsky was born in Rome in 1880, the illegitimate son of the daughter of the Polish papal chamberlain. Mother and child then went to the French Riviera, she to gamble successfully and he to be brought up on the proceeds at expensive schools.

In the guise of a Russian Prince, Apollinaire, as he was now called (altogether less of a handful, really), travelled around Europe, falling for and being seduced by young things, until he finally settled in Paris at the turn of the century. After a (very) short career at a bank, he turned to journalism, and became an influential figure in the art world, more or less single-handedly establishing cubism as a respectable art form, with his 1913 essay *Peintres Cubistes*.

At the same time he got stuck into poetry (a famous poem about Bacchus is typeset in the shape of a bottle), playwriting (he was a champion of the theatre of the absurd), and satire. He also found time to write three novels (if you read only one, make it *Alcools*, from 1913), as well as a fair number of mildly pornographic texts, wrongly reckoning that 20th-century literature would be dominated by the works of de Sade (see page 143).

In 1914, he joined the army, and in 1918 was badly wounded. In hospital he wrote his last play *Les Mamelles de Tiresias*, just having time to be the first writer to describe one of his own works as 'surrealist' before his wounds proved mortal. He was 38.

Louis Aragon

Easily the least eccentric of the founding Surrealists, but arguably the most influential in terms of his writing, was Louis Aragon. Born in Paris in 1897, he served as an auxiliary doctor during World War I, was a staunch supporter of the Surrealists and the communists between the wars, and worked with the resistance against the Nazis in World War II. He was a prolific writer until a few years before his death in 1982, and his poems, essays and novels are still widely read and much loved in France.

André Breton

The poet, novelist and critic André Breton was one of the founders of the Surrealist movement, and was its self-styled leader during the 1920s and 1930s. Trained as a neurologist, he saw service during World War I as a surgeon, and met both Apollinaire and Aragon in the field.

After the war he went to meet Freud in Vienna, and came back with his head sufficiently full of ideas to write the Surrealist Manifesto in 1924, and to become the Surrealists' *de facto* leader. Even though the Surrealists had no formal membership list, Breton became an expert at co-opting artists who hadn't even thought about Surrealism into his fold, and equally adept at expelling anyone who swerved off the narrow path he defined – notably Salvador Dalí (a fair cop, really) and Alberto Giacometti (foul).

In 1937, Breton published the poetic novel *L'Amour Fou*, based on his relationship with Jacqueline Lamba (see below), but it wasn't enough to stop her leaving him once they reached America during World War II. First, however, they were to be the guests of Frida Kahlo and Diego Rivera in Mexico, in 1938, and whilst there Breton was quick to found *La Fédération de l'Art Revolutionnaire Independent*, with Leon Trotsky, who happened to be in town.

Breton returned (alone) to France in 1946, and set up court as the godfather of Surrealism, with a whole new generation of wacky students to occupy him. He died in 1966.

Paul Eluard

Paul Eluard remains my favourite among the Surrealist poets, combining warmth and humanity with the juxtapositions which are Surrealism's primary appeal (eg *'La terre est bleue comme une orange'* – 'the earth is blue like an orange'. It's a lovely image).

Eluard published his first volume of poems in 1913, at the age of 18. They had been written in a Swiss sanatorium, near Davos, where he was recovering from tuberculosis. While there, he met a glamorous young Russian émigré called Helena Ivanovna Diakonova, better known as Gala, and in 1917 the couple were married.

Horrified by World War I – and having been gassed during the fighting – Eluard became a militant pacifist and a radical nihilist, and joined the Dada movement, before becoming one of the founding Surrealists. With the publication of *La Capitale des Douleurs* (Capital of Pain), Eluard's finest Surrealist work, his reputation as a poet was assured.

In 1929, however, disaster struck. He and Gala went off to Spain for a summer break, and while there they dropped in on their old friend Salvador Dalí. Dalí and Gala promptly eloped together, and Eluard returned to Paris a crushed man. He subsequently disappeared off the map for seven months, and it was widely assumed he was dead – but in fact he'd only been voyaging in the East Indies.

On his return he met a young Alsatian (no, no, not a dog, in any sense) called Maria Benz, better known as Nusch, and she inspired some of Eluard's most charming poems. In 1934 they married.

By the closing years of the decade, Eluard was drifting away from Surrealism, unable to reconcile the movement with his political feelings about the Spanish Civil War, and in 1938 he and Breton finally parted ideological company. During World War II, Eluard and Nusch worked together in the resistance, and his poems from the period – notably *'Liberté'* and *'Rendez-vous Allemand'* – served as a rallying cry throughout France.

But with peace barely having broken out, Eluard was to experience his second marital tragedy. Nusch, aged only 40, had a fatal cerebral haemorrhage. Eluard threw himself into working for the support of international communism, and travelled widely as a cultural ambassador – unfortunately blinded to the reality of Stalinism. In 1950, however, he met his last love, Dominique, and his final volume of poetry, *Phénix*, published in 1951, is a triumph. Eluard died of a heart attack the following year.

Jacqueline Lamba

The painter Jacqueline Lamba is unfortunately primarily remembered not for her body of work but for having been married to André Breton (see above). Born in

1910, she was a huge disappointment to her parents, who had wanted a boy. Her father expired only four years later, and by the time she was 17 her mother had also shuffled of. She worked as an artist's model and soon became a painter herself.

Breton fell for her charms, and they married in 1935. Lamba was the darling of the Surrealist set, but inevitably, as a notable beauty, her work wasn't taken seriously – Breton, in particular, was a great deal more interested in her qualities as a housewife (*L'Amour Fou* or not). By 1941, as émigrés in New York, she had had enough.

Peggy Guggenheim was providing the couple with a small monthly income, and Lamba found that she and her work were at last being taken seriously. Adding spice to the explosive cocktail was Breton's refusal to learn English – Lamba was fluent. In 1942, she finally dumped Breton, and took up with the American sculptor David Hare.

Lamba and Hare lived and travelled together in the USA for nearly ten years, but in 1951 they broke up and Lamba returned to France. For the rest of her long life she devoted herself to her painting, becoming ever more reclusive. In summer she lived alone painting nature; in winter she returned to Paris to paint abstract cityscapes in isolation. After her death in 1993, more than 400 canvasses, from the 1930s onwards, were found in her studio.

Simone Weil

Doomed, unhappy, Simone Weil was one of the most formidable thinkers, writers and philosophers of the 20th century. Her death at the age of 34 was tragic, but almost certainly inevitable.

She was born in Paris in 1909 into a wealthy Jewish family, and she and her brother André were pushed on hard academically by a mother who'd been thwarted in her own desire to study medicine. Both André and Simone turned out to be brilliant – but also turned into compulsive hand-washers.

At the age of 12, André was already solving post-doctorate level equations, and would go on to be an eminent mathematician. For her part, Simone was destined to be a philosopher – and to have trouble with her food. At the age of five she is said to have refused to eat sugar because the French troops weren't getting it in their rations – the beginning of an ascetic rigorousness which would eventually kill her.

As a teenager, Weil became proficient in ancient Greek, learned several modern languages, and demonstrated enormous abilities as a writer and thinker. She also became increasingly political, abstaining on principle from the physical – she never had a lover, and routinely starved herself.

In 1928, at the age of 19, Weil came first in the entrance exam for the Ecole Normale Supérieure (arguably the best undergraduate establishment in France), just as Jean-Paul Sartre (see page 154) was coming last in his finals there.

After graduating in 1931, she taught philosophy for a number of years in various schools around the country, and was by all accounts an exceptional teacher. She avoided her colleagues, however, preferring to socialise with workers in local cafés, and sharing her salary with people out of work. She also refused to heat her flat, as a matter of principle, arguing that if the unemployed couldn't be warm, then nor should she.

In order to better understand the real needs of workers – and acting on her deeply held belief that writing could only be based on experience – Weil also did spells as a manual worker in factories, and as a labourer on farms, although she was hopelessly ill-equipped to do either. With uncommonly fine, weak hands, and poor eyesight, she was at best inept and at worst incompetent. It drove her to the depths of despair.

During the Spanish Civil War – despite her pacifism – Weil signed up with the International Brigades, and served briefly as a cook's assistant on the battlefield. (Her ever-protective mother came with her, encouraging her in a permanently uphill struggle to eat a full meal herself.) But the war only increased her disillusionment with ideology and even, for a while, with humanity.

Witnessing the failure of communism to improve workers' lives, she turned to anarchism and syndicalism, and went to work for the anarchist trade union movement. At the same time, she found herself turning towards Christianity, and in 1938 she formally renounced Judaism – after having had a mystical experience (quite possibly brought on by malnourishment) in Assisi the previous year.

When World War II broke out, Weil went to work on the vineyards in the Ardéche, and continued to write prolifically. Finally, however, she had no option but to flee France, so she went to England, and worked for De Gaulle's Free French movement instead.

Suffering from malnutrition and tuberculosis, she died in Ashford in Kent, in August 1943, refusing food and medicine to the end, in sympathy for the people of Occupied France. Only seven people came to her funeral.

In Weil's short, tragic, life only a handful of poems and a few essays were published. Some 16 volumes of her work were published posthumously, however, bringing her the fame and recognition in death which she had never sought in life.

Weil's works are easily available in both English and French, and she's widely taught at universities. Her ideas are still highly relevant today – she was the first to point out that wars are fought over economic materials, like oil, and not over essentials, like wheat, for example – and her writing is a great deal more accessible than that of many of her contemporaries.

EXPATRIATELY ECCENTRIC WRITERS

There's something about France – and especially Paris – which has always appealed to expatriately minded writers, from the salons of Natalie Barney or Gertrude Stein to the freedom of (profane) language offered to Henry Miller, James Joyce or Samuel Beckett. Other writers like Henry James or Robert Louis Stevenson travelled round France and created works far different from the rest of their *oeuvre*, while outcasts real or imagined – like James Baldwin, John Berger, Graham Greene or Somerset Maugham – made the provinces their home.

James Baldwin

Born in Harlem in 1924, James Baldwin became a preacher at the age of only 14, but by the time he finished school he had already given up on religion and moved on to writing. His work soon attracted attention, and he began winning prizes – and it was a literary fellowship which allowed him to escape what he saw as irremediably racist, homophobic America and move to Paris in 1948.

It was there – upstairs at the Café de Flore, on Boulevard Saint Germain, to be precise – that he completed his first novel, *Go Tell It on the Mountain*, in 1953. In Paris, he moved in on the existentialist set, but he also set up house in the south of France, at Saint Paul de Vence, with his partner, Bernard Hassell. He was to live there on and off, until his death, in 1987.

He would return to America through the 1950s to lecture and teach, and from 1957 onwards he spent part of each year in New York, but France had become his spiritual home, and it was there that he wrote his most important works. At Saint Paul de Vence you'd be as likely to find the jazz greats like Louis Armstrong or Miles Davis in evidence as artists from the French cinema or expatriate British writers.

James Baldwin wrote a number of novels (*Giovanni's Room*, from 1956, is a personal favourite) and collections of essays, including the staggering 1963 paean against racism, *The Fire Next Time*. It's essential reading, even 40 years on.

Natalie Barney

For more than half a century, Natalie Barney's house at 20 rue Jacob was *the* rallying point for the Paris literati – especially if you were an expatriate, and even more so if you were female.

Born into a wealthy American family in 1876, Barney was used to coming to Europe from an early age (her mother had studied painting under Whistler in Paris and at the Royal Academy in London), and learned to speak French, Italian and German. From her teens onwards, she became known as the Amazon, not just for being an expert horsewoman, but also for her habit of seducing beautiful women (a habit said to have been kicked off after she herself was seduced by Eva Palmer, the Huntley & Palmer biscuit heiress, during their summer holidays together).

In Paris in 1898, seeing Liane de Pougy, one of the most famous courtesans of the era, while out riding in the Bois de Boulogne, Barney made her move. The ensuing affair between the 41-year-old de Pougy and the 23-year-old Barney was both passionate and public. The liaison also delivered Barney's first published work, *Quelques Portraits-Sonnets de Femmes*. De Pougy for her part published a fictionalised account, *Idylle Sapphique*, which was an instant *succés de scandale*.

Barney's father was very much Not Amused. He had the plates and any copies of *Quelques Portraits* he could get his hands on destroyed, and recalled Barney to America in order to find a suitable husband. Before this could happen, however, the old man dropped dead (though not before his daughter had a bizarre three-week engagement to Bosie, better known as Lord Alfred Douglas, the man behind Oscar Wilde's downfall), and Barney inherited her father's millions.

She returned to Paris, and began a stormy relationship with the poet and novelist Pauline Tarn, who wrote under the pseudonym Renée Vivien. In the end, sick of her partner's infidelities, Vivien broke off the affair. In spite of Barney's best efforts to win her back – she even took her to the island of Lesbos, to celebrate Sappho – Vivien instead opted for a fatal spiral of anorexia and alcoholism, which killed her in 1909, aged only 32.

The same year was marked by Barney's move to rue Jacob, and the start of a regular Friday literary salon which would run almost continuously for the next six decades. The house was ideal, both for the salon and for Barney's continual promotion of her Sapphic ideals, hidden behind an anonymous wall, set back from the street by a courtyard, and featuring a garden with a small Greek temple.

All the great names in Paris passed through: Apollinaire (see page 157), Jean Cocteau (see page 149), André Gide, Ernest Hemingway (see page 167), Ezra Pound, James Joyce (see page 169), T S Eliot, Truman Capote and F Scott Fitzgerald – and on one occasion even Marcel Proust (see page 140). Not to mention the women, half of whom were lovers of Barney's at one time or another: Djuna Barnes, Marguerite Yourcenar, Isadora Duncan (see page 134), Sylvia Beach (see page 162), Gertrude Stein (see page 173), Alice B Toklas, Josephine Baker (see page 130) and Colette (see page 173) were all regulars.

On one occasion even Mata Hari (see page 150) was in evidence, riding naked through the garden on a bejewelled white horse; on another the entertainment consisted of a group of nude Javanese dancers. Food and drink was served by Barney's butler, who painted a new head of black hair onto his bald pate every day.

At the end of the 1920s, Barney (having been engaged to Bosie, briefly, remember) had a long-running affair with Dolly Wilde, Oscar's niece, and a brilliant letter-writer and wit in her own right. Unfortunately she also had an exceedingly addictive personality, and was a victim of drink and drugs, dying (like both her father and uncle) at the age of 46.

The greatest love of Barney's life (and she had many, many loves – her last liaison started when she was 85 years old), however, was the painter, Romaine Brooks. After Brooks's death, Barney's own health went rapidly downhill, and she only survived another two years before dying in 1972 herself, at the age of 96.

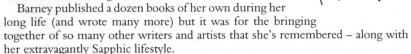

Barney published a dozen books of her own during her long life (and wrote many more) but it was for the bringing together of so many other writers and artists that she's remembered – along with her extravagantly Sapphic lifestyle.

Natalie Barney's books were published in small print-runs and are notoriously hard to find – and expensive when you do come across them. For its part, 20 rue Jacob is fronted by an upmarket shop called IF, selling homeware and clothes. The rest of the property has been developed and converted into apartments, though the garden and Greek temple are still there (if not actually visitable). It's all a stone's throw from **Les Deux Magots** and the **Café de Flore**.

Romaine Brooks' portrait *L'Amazone; Natalie Barney*, hangs in the **Musée Carnavalet**, right next to Proust's reconstructed bedroom.

Sylvia Beach and Shakespeare & Company

Unlike most of the people in this section, Sylvia Beach wasn't herself a writer – but she knew plenty of people who were.

In 1919, in her early thirties, she opened up a bookshop and lending library on rue Dupuytren, aimed at the large expatriate community of Americans in Paris. She called the shop Shakespeare & Company, and it was an instant hit. So much so, that two years later she moved to larger premises, at 12 rue de l'Odéon.

Her first task at the new shop was to follow up on a promise she'd made James Joyce (see page 169) at a party in 1920: that she would publish his new book, *Ulysses*. Given that parts of the massive work had already been labelled obscene in Britain and the USA, and that it had already been rejected by publishers large and small, this was no mean undertaking. The task was hardly made simpler by Joyce insisting on making voluminous corrections at the typesetting stage, and even on the final proofs, but *Ulysses* eventually appeared in 1922. Over the next decade, Beach sold some 29,000 copies of the work.

Shakespeare & Company, meanwhile, became the best known American address in Paris, and for twenty years it attracted the greatest ex-pat literary names of the era – from Gertrude Stein (see page 173) to F Scott Fitzgerald, from Ernest Hemingway (see page 167) to Ezra Pound, and from Samuel Beckett (see page 164) to Henry Miller (see page 171). The shop finally closed down in 1941, during the German occupation of Paris.

In 1951, a new American bookshop in Paris, called Le Mistral, was opened up at 37 rue de la Bûcherie, right across the river from Notre Dame cathedral. The prime piece of real estate had been bought with an inheritance by a man called George Whitman, and he proceeded to run a very similar establishment to Sylvia

ROMAINE BROOKS

Romaine Brooks was born in Rome, in 1874, to wealthy American parents, though her father doesn't seem to have played any useful part in her life beyond conception. Her mentally unstable mother wasn't much more helpful, spending most of her time and energy looking after Brooks's mad brother, and leaving Romaine alone to learn to draw.

In 1902, with both brother and mother departed, Brooks came into a decent inheritance, and devoted her time to art, studying in Paris and Rome and becoming part of an artists' and writers' community in Capri and on the Riviera. In 1903, she married a former lover of Somerset Maugham's (which was a disaster for all concerned), and she, like Barney before her, went on to have a fling with Lord Alfred Douglas.

She then moved to Paris, where she took up with Natalie Barney – and in spite of her partner's endless promiscuity, the couple's relationship endured for more than 50 years. In 1920, Brooks painted the famous (and marvellous) portrait *L'Amazone: Natalie Barney*, with Barney in furs, and a symbolic black horse in the foreground.

By 1925, Brooks was well established, and in that year she had exhibitions in London and New York as well as in Paris. But being independently wealthy and not overly sociable, we know very little about the rest of her life. Her autobiography, *No Pleasant Memories*, failed to find a publisher, as nobody would believe her.

In 1969, at the advanced age of 95, Romaine Brooks left Natalie Barney – apparently in an argument over another woman. Brooks died a year later.

Beach's pre-war shop, only with a post-war crowd. The Beat poets came to read here, and Lawrence Ferlinghetti (who went on to open up the excellent City Lights bookshop in San Francisco) wrote his thesis upstairs.

In 1962, on the death of Sylvia Beach, Whitman cannily renamed his shop Shakespeare & Company in her honour. In the four decades since, the vast majority of visitors haven't been made any the wiser that the current shop isn't the hallowed ground trod by Joyce and Hemingway. But it doesn't really matter – for nearly half a century, this *has* been Shakespeare & Company.

Upstairs, you'll find mattresses and beds amongst the creaking bookcases, and if you're a budding (or even aspiring) writer then you can stay over, in exchange for reading a book a day, putting in some time in the shop, and writing a short piece about yourself. If you do so, you'll be joining the company of an estimated 10,000 travellers who've spent at least one night in the shop.

On the top floor is the hallowed Writer's Room, where you'll find photos of the greats – and a further blurring between Beach's and Whitman's Shakespeares & Co. James Joyce and Henry Miller look out from photos alongside those of Lawrence Durrell and Allen Ginsberg. At the time of writing, in 2002, George Whitman himself, aged 90, was still running the shop.

The original **Shakespeare & Company** at 12 rue de l'Odéon is long gone, but there's a plaque high up on the wall saying that this is where *Ulysses* was published. The new shop (George Whitman's) is at 37 rue de la Bûcherie, opposite Notre Dame, and still has the largest secondhand collection of English language books in Paris – though they're not cheap. It's a place for browsers, not searchers, as there's no apparent order to the mammoth collection which spreads across numerous rooms and several floors, interrupted by mattresses and beds for the next big names in modern literature. Maybe.

Samuel Beckett

Samuel Beckett, the eccentric existentialist most famous for his often bleak plays, supposedly once said 'There's nothing so bad it can't grow worse. There's no limit to how bad things can be.' Asked what he'd found most worthwhile, at the end of a long, interesting and rewarding life, he answered 'Precious little' – and yet in reality he enjoyed a drink and the company of his friends more than most people.

Born in 1906, near Dublin, Beckett studied French and Italian at Trinity College, and went to Paris in 1928 to take up a teaching job at the Ecole Normale Supérieure. He was soon to meet James Joyce (see page 169), and was inspired by the older Irishman to take up the pen himself, quickly showing the calibre of his writing with his first poem 'Whoroscope', which won a competition and earned him a valuable ten pound prize from Nancy Cunard.

Beckett returned to Dublin to study for his Masters, but soon dropped out and led a rootless existence for several years until settling permanently in Paris in 1937. The following year, he was attacked in a street brawl and stabbed with a knife. A student called Suzanne Deschevaux-Dusmesnil was cycling past, and stopped to call an ambulance and help Beckett to hospital – and she and Beckett went on to become lifelong companions. They married secretly in 1961, and were to die less than six months apart from each other, in 1989.

During the war, the couple worked in the Resistance, and were very nearly caught by the Gestapo after one of their cell members was tortured into betraying them. But they escaped to Roussillon, in the south of France, and worked as peasants there for the rest of the war.

Back in Paris, after the Liberation, Beckett started writing primarily in French (famously saying it allowed him to write without style), and went on to produce some of the 20th-century's finest plays and most original fiction. His best-known work, *En Attendant Godot* (*Waiting for Godot*), was written at this time, though not performed until the beginning of 1953. It was a huge success, right from the start, and brought Beckett his first fiscal rewards after 25 years of financial hardship. The play was inspired, it's said, by the endless conversations Beckett and Suzanne would have out in the fields during the war.

Beckett went on to write further iconoclastic masterpieces, such as *Fin de Partie* (*Endgame*), where the main character's parents spend the entire play trapped in dustbins, and *Oh Les Beaux Jours* (*Happy Days*), where the principal character, Winnie, starts off buried in sand up to her waist, and by the second act is in up to her neck. Through it all she remains unfailingly positive and optimistic, though we, as the audience, fear it cannot end so happily.

In 1969, Samuel Beckett won the Nobel Prize for Literature, but typically went into hiding and sent a friend to receive it on his behalf. The increased fame and public acclaim sat ill on Beckett's shoulders, and during the 1970s he increasingly shied away from company, even while continuing to write and publish new works. In 1986 he wrote his last work of prose, *Stirrings Still*, a wonderful close to a great career, and three years later he died, just five months after Suzanne. They are buried together in **Montparnasse cemetery** with a characteristically unadorned granite gravestone engraved only with their names and dates.

Arguably the best way to appreciate Samuel Beckett is by going to see one of his plays – *Waiting for Godot*, *Endgame* and *Happy Days* are perhaps the most representative – but failing that the scripts are well worth reading, as is his fiction.

John Berger

John Berger is so much more than just a writer – over the past half century he's been an art critic, poet, essayist, short-story writer, TV presenter, playwright, painter and Booker prize-winning novelist. He's also one of the most politically engaged people I've ever met. Labelled as a Marxist, he's nonetheless firmly against 'global solutions', and ultimately more of a humanist than anything else. He's been living in France now for nearly 40 years, and for most of the past 30 his home has been a rented barn in a French Alpine village.

Berger was born in London in 1926, and dropped out of public school as a teenager to study art. At 18, with the war on, he joined the army, but, unwilling to take up a commission, he sat out his military service at a training camp as a lance corporal. The army was his first real contact with the working class, and some of the new recruits were functionally illiterate – something which wouldn't be the case today. Berger wrote letters to their families and sweethearts for them, in exchange for them doing jobs they were better at than him.

After the war, Berger painted and taught drawing, and from 1952 onwards became an influential art critic, writing for the *New Statesman*. He finally stopped painting altogether in 1956, to concentrate on his writing (though he has returned to drawing in the past decade), and emigrated to France in 1963. He lived first in Bonnieux, in Provence (just over the hill from Lourmarin, where Camus had bought a house in 1958, and along the valley from Ménerbes, where Peter Mayle was to write *A Year in Provence*, 20 years later).

In 1972, he became a household name in the literary and art worlds, first with the insightful BBC series *Ways of Seeing* (the follow-up book is still a must-have), about the way art is looked at (and why), and then by winning the Booker prize, with his novel G.

G, a tale of migrant workers and a latter-day Don Juan in pre-World War I Europe, remains the only book to have won the *Guardian* Fiction Prize and the James Tait Black Memorial Prize at the same time as taking the Booker. It's a pity (though inevitable, perhaps) that G itself has therefore been somewhat overshadowed by the 1972 Booker prize-winning ceremony, at London's Café Royal.

Berger, having discovered that Booker McConnell's wealth was based on Caribbean sugar plantations (where slavery continued into the late 19th century, in spite of having been formally outlawed in 1833), gave half his prize money to the Black Panthers. It caused an outcry. Senator Joseph McCarthy's propaganda (and to some extent the Black Panthers' own gun-toting imagery) had made people frightened of an organisation whose main function was in fact to seek better education, housing and health for African Americans, along with protection from police brutality – at a time when these things were far from taken for granted.

Thirty years on, Berger stands by his decision. 'I have no regrets, and if I was in the same position again I would do it again. I saw it, like the book itself, as an act of political engagement.'

It wasn't, and isn't, an isolated act. Berger's more recent work includes a trilogy about modern peasant life, *Into Their Labours*, completed in 1991, and *King*, a novel covering 24 hours in the life of a homeless community alongside a motorway – a book extraordinary for not even featuring the author's name on the cover (yet another political statement by Berger). Between the two, he wrote *To the Wedding*, a novel about the separated parents of an HIV-positive French girl coming together across Europe for their daughter's wedding in Italy. All the author's royalties were given to The London Lighthouse, an Aids charity.

Berger meanwhile, now in his late 70s, lives a simple life in the mountains, helping to make hay with the local farmers in the *alpages* at the beginning of summer, and enjoying home-grown food and a glass of wine of an evening. If he has one vice, it's his motorcycle, a gleaming 1100cc machine which is his pride and joy. Donning leathers, he fires up the engine and is off down the winding road towards the valley, banking into the first corner with a grin.

John Berger's books are easily available – and well worth the effort. The Booker prize-winning *G* and *Ways of Seeing* are as fresh now as they were when they were published in 1972, and the more recent works demonstrate a lovely visual writing style which keeps them fresh and original.

Graham Greene

Graham Greene was born in 1904, the son of the headmaster of the local public school. Already a shy child, he ended up suffering a minor nervous breakdown after being victimised by his fellow pupils – it was bad enough to be the head's son, but worse still to be crap at games. His father sent him to an analyst, which resulted (predictably enough) in Greene playing Russian roulette with his elder brother's revolver.

The gun accompanied him up to Oxford University, where he read modern history, drank too much, and ran up debts between spins of the chamber and pulls at the trigger. He found a job as a sub-editor in Nottingham, and while there met his future wife, Vivien, who was also instrumental in his 1926 conversion to Catholicism. They married in 1928, and Greene moved on to *The Times*, in London, editing the famous letters page.

After several failed novels, he delivered the blatantly commercial *Stamboul Train* in 1932, and from then onwards wrote full time, alternating between popular and more serious works. Greene continued through his life to pursue risk, ostensibly in search of good material for his books, and ended up in many of the world's most dangerous spots. He caught malaria in Liberia, and travelled to Kenya, Malaysia and Vietnam during various wars. He was in Duval's Haiti, Castro's Cuba and the Panama of Messrs Noriega and Torrijos – the latter being the inspiration for *Getting to Know the General*.

How much of the travelling coincided with his work for the British foreign intelligence agency, MI6, has never been clear, but Greene always did avow his lifelong friendship to the defector Kim Philby (the third man to defect, in 1963, after Burgess and Maclean; as opposed to Greene's 1949 screenplay *The Third Man*).

Greene had many liaisons outside of his marriage, and separated from Vivien in 1948, although the couple were never divorced. In 1959, in Cameroon, he met Yvonne Cloetta, the French wife of a Swiss Unilever employee, and the two started an affair which lasted until Greene's death, 32 years later – though she, like him, never divorced.

As a result of meeting Cloetta, Greene installed himself in Antibes, on the Côte d'Azur, to be closer to her – at first in the Royal Hotel, and then from 1966 in a small apartment overlooking the port. Here (in spite of the persistent traffic noise) he would write his daily quota of words, and then lunch with Cloetta and her dog at Chez Félix au Port. For two months a year, from 1967 to 1989, Greene and Cloetta would go and live at Greene's house on the island of Capri.

Cloetta was clearly the one true love of Greene's life, and he once said (in a remark you'd want to take seriously after the Russian roulette incidents) he would put a bullet through his head if she wasn't there. He referred to her privately as his 'happy, healthy kitten', and teased his readers of *Travels with my Aunt* in 1969 with a dedication to HHK.

In 1982, Greene wrote a 25-page pamphlet entitled *J'accuse* (*à la* Zola), denouncing corruption on the Côte d'Azur, which was promptly banned in France. Greene returned his *Légion d'Honneur* in protest. He lived the last two years of his life in Vevey, in Switzerland, with Cloetta, and died in 1991, aged 86. Cloetta died 10 years later, at the end of 2001 – so you can expect a rash of new biographies any moment now.

Graham Greene's books have been translated into more than 25 languages and over 30 million copies have been sold – so you shouldn't have any problem finding something to read, either new or secondhand.

If you're in Antibes, treat yourself to lunch at **Chez Félix au Port**, where Greene and Cloetta had lunch together nearly every day for decades.

Ernest Hemingway

Ernest Hemingway lived most of his life outside France (and far preferred Spain anyway) but his sojourns in Paris between 1921 and 1926 were to be formative for the young writer, and produced the works which first brought him fame.

Born in Illinois in 1898, Hemingway graduated from high school in 1917 and went on to work as a reporter in Kansas City. His poor eyesight prevented him from signing up for active service during World War I, so he drove an ambulance instead, and was wounded on the Italian border in 1918.

Back in America, he wooed and married Hadley Richardson in 1921, and the couple went off to live in Paris, on the advice of the influential writer Sherwood Anderson. Far from the struggling writer himself, Hemingway had plenty of resources in Paris – not only was he working as a stringer for the *Toronto Star*, but the young couple also had Hadley's inheritance to spend.

Hemingway lost no time in doing the rounds of the salons and meeting the great and the good, and was soon a familiar figure to the likes of Ezra Pound and Gertrude Stein (see page 173). The Hemingways travelled frequently in Europe, skiing in winter and running with the bulls in Pamplona in summer. Hemingway meanwhile honed his style, and in 1925 his first book of stories, *In Our Time*, was published.

The year 1925 also saw Hemingway meet F Scott Fitzgerald, who gave him a copy of his recently published *Great Gatsby* – Hemingway read it at La Closerie des Lilas, his favourite café. The two men got on well, as drinking pals, but Zelda, Fitzgerald's wife, wasn't impressed with Hemingway at all – memorably describing him as 'bullfighting, bull-slinging, and bullshitting'.

Hemingway spent the summer of 1925 at the terrace of La Closerie, writing the first draft of *The Sun Also Rises* in under eight weeks. The novel was the first one to really describe the 'Lost Generation' (Gertrude Stein coined the phrase) – the men and women who had survived World War I, and now only wanted to bar-hop, or run with the bulls.

The Hemingways left Paris the following year, which was to see not only the publication (to great acclaim) of *The Sun Also Rises*, but also the foundering of their marriage – following Hemingway's meeting Pauline Pfeiffer, whom he went on to marry in 1927.

In 1936, Hemingway met Martha Gellhorn (the greater writer, in this author's opinion) in Florida, and the couple went to Spain together to cover the Spanish Civil War. They married in 1940, setting the scene for yet another divorce – only this time Hemingway was the one being dumped, for the first and only time. But by 1944, having hijacked Gellhorn's press credentials, Hemingway was back in Paris, at Harry's Bar, for the liberation.

Years later, in 1961, after yet another marriage, and electro-shock therapy for depression, Hemingway shot himself with his favourite gun – choosing the same quick method for suicide his father had perfected in 1928.

There are two books of Hemingway's which specifically deal with Paris, *The Sun Also Rises* (called *Fiesta*, in the American editions), and *A Moveable Feast* (published posthumously), which has some fine first-hand (but not necessarily accurate) impressions of Paris in the 1920s.

There's less of Hemingway's Paris around in the 21st century than locals would have you believe, and **Les Deux Magots**, the **Café de Flore** and the ilk are pretty efficient clip-joints these days. But you can still get a decent (and authentic) feed at **La Closerie des Lilas**, Hemingway's favourite café. Expect, nonetheless, to pay around ∈ 80 a head.

Hemingway's principal residences in Paris were at **74 rue du Cardinal Lemoine**, just off the Place du Contrescarpe, where you'll find a big plaque affirming his presence there on the third floor from January 1922 to August 1923, and at **113 rue Notre Dame des Champs**, where he lived intermittently from February 1924 to January 1926 – although there's no memorial of any kind.

Henry James

If Hemingway preferred Spain to France, Henry James, author of some of the finest novels in the English language, preferred Italy. But France left its mark on him, too, and his 1884 travelogue, *A Little Tour in France*, is absolutely marvellous.

James was born in 1843, into a well-off family. His father lived on a fat inheritance, and provided the best education possible for his children, largely by shipping the family around Europe in search of top tuition. So James was schooled in Paris from 1856 to 1858, and in Geneva from 1859 to 1860, as well as studying in Bologna and Bonn, before going briefly to the Harvard Law School – where he soon discovered the advantages of literature over litigation.

In his twenties, James travelled widely in Europe, before settling in Paris in 1875, where he was a contributor to the *New York Tribune* (he eventually resigned from the paper because the editor wanted more gossipy pieces). In 1876, he moved to England, which was to become his permanent home, but he continued to visit the continent regularly. In the autumn of 1882, with half a dozen books already under his belt, he took a little tour of France.

Travelling alone, mostly by train, he visited many of the places which have since become tourist meccas – the Châteaux of the Loire, Carcassonne, Nîmes, Arles and the Pont du Gard – as well as many lesser-known attractions. He returned to the capital confident that 'France may be Paris, but Paris is not France'.

The resulting prose was first published in the *Atlantic Monthly* during 1883 and 1884, and then revised extensively for book publication – which includes the following delightful preface:

> We good Americans I say it without presumption are too apt to think that
> France is Paris, just as we are accused of being too apt to think that Paris is
> the celestial city. ... It had already been intimated to the author of these light

pages that there are many good things in the *doux pays de France* of which you get no hint in a walk between the ornaments of the capital; but the truth had been revealed only in quick-flashing glimpses, and he was conscious of a desire to look it well in the face. To this end he started, one rainy morning in mid-September, for the charming little city of Tours, from which point it seemed possible to make a variety of fruitful excursions. …

I must not speak, however, as if I had discovered the provinces. They were discovered, or at least revealed by Balzac, if by any one, and are now easily accessible to visitors. It is true, I met no visitors, or only one or two, whom it was pleasant to meet. Throughout my little tour I was almost the only tourist. That is perhaps one reason why it was so successful.

Notwithstanding James' bizarre transition from first to third person and back again, these days the provinces are even more 'easily accessible to visitors', but you won't be 'almost the only tourist'. Nonetheless the book unveils a great deal about France which is still true, including the autumn weather:

George Sand has somewhere a charming passage about the mildness, the convenient quality, of the physical conditions of central France, *'son climat souple et chaud, ses pluies abondantes et courtes.'* In the autumn of 1882 the rains perhaps were less short than abundant; but when the days were fine it was impossible that anything in the way of weather could be more charming.

James went on to write dozens of other books, before finally dying in Rye in early 1916, after suffering a series of strokes.

James Joyce

James Augustine Aloysius Joyce was the firstborn of 15 children, in a Dublin household which slipped further into poverty with every new arrival. He was educated at Jesuit schools, and then at University College, Dublin, before sent to Paris to study medicine. Instead he boozed and whored away the scant family savings, and was back home within a few short months.

In 1904, at the age of 22, Joyce met Nora Barnacle, a chambermaid, and the two eloped to Europe, where they were to live together until Joyce's death in 1941 (though they didn't marry until 1931). At first they lived in Pula (in what's now Croatia), before moving on to Trieste in 1905. Joyce scraped together a poor living as a language teacher, while Nora brought up their two children.

Over the years, their circumstances improved gradually, as Joyce's writings began to be recognised (due in no small part to the championing of Ezra Pound), and their income was supplemented by gifts from patrons.

In 1920, the family moved to Paris, and within weeks of arrival Joyce had met Sylvia Beach (see page 162) and she had agreed to publish his most radical work yet, *Ulysses*. For four months in 1921 the family lived at 71 rue du Cardinal Lemoine – and if they had stayed on another three months they would have witnessed the arrival of the young Hemingways, across the street at number 74.

Before the book came out, Beach must frequently have had cause to regret agreeing to publish *Ulysses*. The instalments printed earlier by small presses in America and Britain had already been branded obscene on both sides of the Atlantic, and Joyce was a terrible author to work with, making endless corrections not only at the typesetting stage, but also on the final proofs.

The publication – and effective banning – of *Ulysses* in 1922 brought Joyce instant international fame and recognition, if not wealth. But with a generous monthly stipend from Harriet Weaver, an English benefactor, the family was able to dine out every night, and Joyce could sit down and write the almost incomprehensible *Finnegans Wake*, without having to worry about money.

He had other problems, however. Since 1907, his eyesight had been failing, and repeated operations didn't do much to improve matters. By 1928 he could no longer read print, and could only see his own words if he wrote with a blunt black pencil. He was also dreadfully thin, and barely ate. At the age of 45, he weighed only 51kg, even though he was a tall man.

As if this weren't enough, his daughter Lucia was descending into madness in her early twenties. In 1931, Joyce's friend Samuel Beckett (see page 164) had to be banned from the house for a year after he'd made it clear that Lucia's advances were unwelcome. Two years later, after increasing schizophrenic bouts, Lucia cut the family's phone line to stop people calling Joyce, and from 1934 until her death 48 years later, at the age of 75, she was institutionalised.

Finnegans Wake was finally published in 1939. Like *Ulysses* before it, it came out on February 2, Joyce's birthday, which he enjoyed coinciding with Groundhog Day. For all the years of work, it was simply too difficult for readers (then or now), and *Finnegans Wake* failed to bring Joyce commercial success.

In 1940, with the German invasion of France, he moved to Zurich, where he died unexpectedly of a stomach ulcer at the beginning of 1941, aged 58.

Few people have ever read more of Joyce than a couple of stories from the *Dubliners* – and when you start reading *Ulysses* (hard work) or *Finnegans Wake* (nearly impossible) you can see why. *Finnegans Wake* even ends in the middle of a sentence which is only completed by the opening of the book, making it truly circular. Filling the 600-odd pages in between you'll find a lyrical, drifting stream-of-consciousness written in a language of word-plays and invention which can take years to understand. Most people don't bother.

There's an excellent Joyce resource on the web (www.robotwisdom.com/jaj/), which is owned and maintained by the astonishingly erudite Jorn Barger, if you want to know (a great deal) more, or just dip into the texts.

Somerset Maugham

All that most people remember now of Somerset Maugham is a dry, acerbic wit and some vaguely recollected book titles, but during the 1930s he was the highest-earning author in the world. He himself never felt he was a top-ranking writer, however, classing himself (in his autobiography, *The Summing Up*) as being 'in the very first row of the second-raters'.

Maugham was born in 1874 in Paris – his father was at the British Embassy there – and his first language was French. But his mother died of tuberculosis when he was eight, and his father of cancer two years later, leaving the orphaned Maugham to be brought up in England by an uncle.

After school, Maugham read literature and philosophy at university in Heidelberg, and then trained in London to be a doctor, qualifying in 1897. After a year in practice, however, he took up his pen and moved to Paris, where he struggled at first as a budding writer, and then shot to success as a playwright – by 1908 he had four plays on concurrently in London's west end.

When war broke out, the 40-year-old writer volunteered as an ambulance driver (as Hemingway would, three years later), and while in Flanders fell in love with a 22-year-old American called Gerald Haxton (as Hemingway wouldn't). He was to be Maugham's 'secretary' for the next 30 years, and they travelled extensively together, across the world.

During 1915, Maugham was also continuing an affair back in England, with a married woman, Syrie Wellcome, daughter of the famous charity-founder Dr

Barnardo, and Syrie was now pregnant with Maugham's child. Her husband, Sir Henry Wellcome, agreed to a divorce (indeed, he Wellcomed it), the child was born, and Maugham and Syrie were married in 1917. They spent very little time together, however, and were themselves to divorce in 1927 – with Syrie and their daughter Liza receiving a handsome settlement including a house in London, £3,000 a year, and a Rolls Royce.

Meanwhile, 1915 also saw *Of Human Bondage* published, which boosted Maugham's reputation as a writer. He was then recruited as a British spy, and sent to Russia in 1917 to gather intelligence about the Revolution – but he was badly hampered in his espionage activities by his shyness and stammering.

In 1919, Maugham published *The Moon and Sixpence*, about Paul Gauguin's self-imposed exile to Tahiti (see page 101), and it was a huge success. He spent the proceeds on a vast property at Cap Ferrat, called the Villa Mauresque, and he and Haxton lived a sumptuous life there from the end of the 1920s onwards. The guest list included royalty, politicians, artists and prominent (and not so prominent) homosexuals – although Maugham himself stayed quietly in the closet all his life. He continued to write (no, not in the closet) for four hours every morning, and became the wealthiest writer of his era.

On the outbreak of World War II, Maugham went to America, and it was there, in 1944, that Haxton died, of tuberculosis. Maugham returned to Cap Ferrat after the war, and spent the last 20 years of his life with Alan Searle, his final 'secretary' (who was 30 years younger than him), before dying in Nice, at the age of 91, in 1965. On his deathbed Maugham is said to have asked for reassurance that there was indeed no life after death.

Maugham's most famous novels – *Of Human Bondage*, *The Moon and Sixpence*, *Cakes and Ale*, and *Up at the Villa* (not, surprisingly, anything to do with the Birmingham football club) – are easily available, as are various collections of his finely turned short stories.

The Villa Mauresque, at Cap Ferrat, is very much private property, of the fenced-off, video-surveillanced, guard-dogged variety.

Henry Miller

Henry Valentine Miller was born in New York in 1891. After graduating from high school, he took a variety of jobs to support his first wife, Beatrice, before finding more stable employment with the Western Union from 1920.

In 1923, Miller met June Mansfield, who was working as a taxi dancer (one hilarious potted biography refers to her as a 'taxi driver'; not the same thing at all in 1920s New York), and who went on to become his second wife the following year. She agreed to support Miller while he was finding his feet as a writer, and in 1928 paid for them to cross the Atlantic and spend nine months travelling around Europe by bicycle and train (something Miller strangely never really wrote about).

The following year they were back in New York, broke again, but by February 1930 Mansfield had raised enough money for Miller to return to Paris alone, to write, and Miller began work on what would become *Tropic of Cancer*. Mansfield finally joined him in September, but returned to New York in November; Miller nearly starved to death that winter, and had to resort to begging on the street and sleeping at a different place every night.

In 1931, Miller was offered a job as a proof-reader on the *Tribune*, where his friend Alfred Perlès was working, and finally dragged himself up out of the gutter. Later in the year he met Anaïs Nin (see below), and the two became fast friends, critics of each others work, and lovers. Nin was married, so the last part was kept secret until Nin's husband, Hugo Guiler, a banker, had himself died, in 1985 – and her published diaries were carefully self-censored to remove references to her ardent trysts with Miller.

When Mansfield returned to Paris at the end of 1931, Miller introduced her to Nin, and the two women became fascinated with one another. By the time Mansfield went back to New York, early in 1932, the jealous triangle was complete, and when Mansfield came back to Paris that October the scenes between the three were passionate and violent: it ended with Mansfield asking for a divorce, and leaving. Nin and Miller were both to write about Mansfield for the rest of their lives, but Mansfield herself sank into history without trace.

With Hugo's help, Miller went to Dijon, where he taught English, and loathed it beyond belief; after only one term he returned to Paris. He had by now completed *Tropic of Cancer*, but couldn't find a publisher, so in the end, Nin fronted the money (earned by writing pornography at a dollar a page for an anonymous client), and the book was finally issued by Obelisk in 1934.

It wasn't a commercial success on its first release, and was banned in America for 30 years, but the book was reviewed positively by George Orwell in England. When Orwell came through Paris in 1936, on his way to the Spanish Civil War, he paid Miller a visit, and Miller gave him his warm corduroy jacket against the harsh winter weather in Spain.

Tropic of Cancer was followed by *Black Spring* in 1936 and *Tropic of Capricorn* in 1939, but Miller remained destitute, as his books were the subject of endless court cases in America. When they were finally openly published, in the 1960s, they sold in huge quantities – but by this time Miller himself was in his sixties.

After *Tropic of Capricorn* was published, Miller went to stay in Greece with his friend Lawrence Durrell, and his six months there were some of the happiest of his life. When war broke out, however, he returned to America, where he was to live (in Big Sur, on the Californian coast) until his death in 1980.

Henry Miller's books seem fairly tame to a 21st-century sensibility, and it's hard now to see what all the fuss was about. *Tropic of Cancer* and *Tropic of Capricorn* both cover Miller's life and loves in Paris, while the three volumes of *The Rosy Crucifixion* (*Sexus*, *Nexus* and *Plexus*) deal with the author's life and preoccupations before leaving America in 1930. My favourite works, however, are *The Colossus of Maroussi*, about his time in Greece, and *The Air-Conditioned Nightmare*, about his travels through the United States at the end of World War II, which still stands up as an indictment of all the things that are wrong not just with America but with the modern world.

Miller's main address in Paris was **18 Villa Seurat**, which is a lovely private house at the bottom end of Montparnasse, with curved white plaster frontages on a cul-de-sac full of artists' studios (the street was originally the home of the pointillist Georges Seurat, hence the name).

Anaïs Nin

As compulsive diarists go, Anaïs Nin was as obsessive as they get. From the age of 11, when she sailed off to New York, until shortly before her death in Los Angeles in 1977, she wrote screeds every day – a total of 35,000 pages in all. Even in the published version, massively cut down, it runs to seven dense volumes.

Nin was born in Paris in 1903. Her father was a famous Spanish pianist, while her mother was a well-known Danish-French singer – and both were Cuban-born. As a girl she was abused by her father, and in 1914 her mother took her to New York to continue her schooling away from Daddy. At the age of 16, however, she left school, preferring to work her way alphabetically through the literary greats at the public library, rather than continue academic studies.

As a shy girl, Nin had little to do with men (her father notwithstanding), and preferred moon-bathing and diary-writing to boy-dating. In 1923, as an act of conservative rebellion against her mother's desire to find her a wealthy Cuban husband, she married the neighbours' son, a young banker called Hugo Guiler. He was to remain her husband until her death more than 50 years later.

The couple were relocated to Paris by Guiler's bank at the end of the 1920s, and it was there in 1931 that Nin met Henry Miller (see above). They quickly became involved on every level, and Hugo seems to have turned a blind eye. During 1932, Nin also developed a desperate fascination for Miller's wife, June Mansfield, though there's still a debate over whether the relationship was physically consummated. Whatever – by the end of the year Mansfield was filing for divorce, and had returned alone to New York.

Nin published her book-length study of DH Lawrence in 1932, gaining some critical if not commercial credibility, and in 1934 met her father again for the first time in two decades. It's said that she then spent three months having an affair with him, to purge herself of her childhood trauma, before dumping him, in revenge. Meanwhile she was writing pornography for an anonymous man at a dollar a page, and spending the proceeds on publishing Henry Miller's *Tropic of Cancer*. She also had an affair with her psychiatrist, Otto Rank (one of Freud's favourite pupils) and wrote her first novel, *The House of Incest*, which was published in 1936.

When war broke out, Nin and Guiler moved to New York, but in 1947 she met the 28-year-old failed actor Rupert Pole, and the two fell madly in love. Rather than divorce her beloved Hugo, Nin set off across America with Rupert to California, and for the next thirty years she lived an extraordinary double life, spending half her time with Guiler in New York, and the other half with Pole in Los Angeles. For a decade, she even lived as a bigamist with him, having married Pole in 1955. If she hadn't confessed to the taxman, the truth may never have come out.

When she died in 1977, her diaries had won her a strong feminist following, but it was only the publication of her erotica, *Delta of Venus* and *Little Birds*, after her death, which provided a small fortune for her east- and west-coast husbands.

Gertrude Stein

Gertrude Stein was born into a prosperous family of Jewish immigrants in Pennsylvania in 1874. She then spent her first years in Vienna and Paris, before her parents moved to California when she was five. After studying psychology and medicine, she moved to Paris in 1902, and was to live in France for the rest of her life.

In 1903, she and her brother Leo moved into an apartment at 27 rue Fleurus, and the pair started collecting art – including works not just by the well-known artists of the day such as Cézanne, Gauguin and Renoir, but also by the Johnny-come-lately Fauvists and Cubists like Derain, Matisse and Picasso.

At a party in 1907, Leo was introduced to Alice B Toklas, who became Gertrude's companion, cook, housekeeper and muse for the rest of her life (in spite of being called 'Pussy', by Gertrude, apparently). Alice moved into the flat in 1910 – and by 1912, Leo was feeling the strain. He moved out the following year.

During World War I, Stein and Toklas drove a Ford truck around Paris delivering hospital supplies, and narrowly avoided putting dozens of pedestrians into hospital themselves – Stein was an atrocious driver. They were awarded medals by a grateful French government after the war, all the same.

While Natalie Barney (see page 161) held her salon up on rue Jacob on Fridays, Stein and Toklas made rue Fleurus *the* place to be on Saturday nights, and by the 1920s their salon was an essential stopover if you were a budding American writer – like the young Hemingway (see page 167), for example. Stein herself was a terrific self-publicist, reminding newcomers to the salon that she was the fourth great name in American letters, after Edgar Allan Poe, Walt Whitman and Henry James (see page 168).

In truth, Stein was developing an *oeuvre* which was influenced by Cubism and emphasised the sound and rhythm of words – mostly to such an extent that it's unreadable. Her least inaccessible work is *The Autobiography of Alice B Toklas*, actually mostly an autobiography of Stein herself, which was published in 1933. Following its success, Stein and Toklas travelled to New York in 1934 for a lecture tour, and were welcomed back by a newspaper headline proclaiming 'Gerty Gerty Stein is Back Home Home Back'.

From 1923 onwards, Stein and Toklas spent their summers near Belley, in the southern Jura, and from 1929 they rented a house in the village of Bilignin, just west of town, for six months of each year. Here, Toklas would concoct the recipes that eventually became the source material for *The Alice B Toklas Cook Book*, which was published in 1954, and contains an unusual recipe for 'Haschich Fudge' (though she always claimed never to have tried it herself).

The couple spent the war at Bilignin, and – both being of Jewish descent – were lucky to avoid being sent to a concentration camp. It would have been easy enough for them to go to Switzerland, but they chose instead an impoverished existence in France. After the liberation in 1944, they returned to Paris, and found their paintings undamaged.

Gertrude Stein died in 1946, aged 72, and left most of her estate to Alice B Toklas. After Stein's death, Natalie Barney took great pains to look after Toklas, and Toklas herself published her *Cook Book* at the age of 76, and followed it with her memoirs, *What is Remembered*, at the age of 87. She died in 1967, aged 90.

Although there's a plaque at 27 rue Fleurus, where Stein and Toklas lived from 1903 to 1938, two blocks up from the Luxembourg gardens, you certainly can't visit what's now a very classy, very private building. The house they rented in Bilignin from 1929 to 1944 is also very much keep-off-private-property.

Robert Louis Stevenson

The author of such popular works as *Treasure Island*, *Kidnapped*, and *The Strange Case of Dr Jekyll and Mr Hyde* was born in Scotland in 1850, and it seemed likely he would follow in his father's footsteps and become an engineer. Instead he pursued his studies as a lawyer, though after qualifying he dropped out altogether to become a writer.

At the age of 25, having completed a canoe journey through Belgium and France (which would become *An Inland Voyage*, his first book), he met Fanny Osborne at an artists' colony at Grez sur Loing, south of Paris. She was in France with her two children, having left her husband, and studying painting. The independent American woman, a decade his elder, was irresistible to Stevenson.

Two years later, Fanny returned to America to seek a divorce, leaving behind a lovesick Stevenson. As a distraction, while waiting for her return, Stevenson headed south, and undertook the journey which was to make him famous as a writer – a 230km walk across country, with a donkey for company.

He set off with Modestine, a particularly stubborn animal, from the village of Le Monastier sur Gazeille (near Le Puy en Velay) on September 22 1878, and walked into St Jean de Gard (near Alès) on October 3, 12 days later. He immediately sold Modestine and her saddle for a paltry – even then – 35 francs before catching the stagecoach on to Alès, impatient to collect his mail. Only then, and in spite of all the frustration and irritation Modestine had caused him, did Stevenson allow himself the luxury of a quiet weep for his four-legged companion.

The resulting book – *Travels with a Donkey in the Cevennes* – was published the following year and was an immediate success, allowing Stevenson to pursue his career as a remarkably prolific writer, and to travel all around the world with Fanny, who was now Mrs Stevenson, and her children.

In 1886, reeling from an opium-induced nightmare in Bournemouth (believe me, Bournemouth can have that effect), Stevenson sat down and feverishly scribbled the first draft of *Dr Jekyll and Mr Hyde* in just three days. A harsh word from Fanny made him throw the 30,000 word manuscript into the fire – but he rewrote it, delivering a new 34,000 word draft three days later. Stevenson had effectively written a short novel in six days – and ten weeks later it was published, to great acclaim.

With a constant eye on Stevenson's health, the family moved to the South Seas in 1889, and settled on Upolu, in what's now Western Samoa, in Polynesia. He continued to write prolifically until a brain haemorrhage (almost certainly caused by overwork) struck him down at the age of 44. His last words were positively Jekyllish: 'What's that? Do I look strange?'

There's a small but thriving industry celebrating Stevenson's journey through the Cevennes in 1878, and you can even hire your own donkey and repeat the journey yourself. The route is designated as a *Grande Randonnée* and marked as GR70 on large scale French maps. Easily the best resource available if you're interested is Freddy Stiévenart's website (http://users.skynet.be/sky42224/) which gives you all the practical information you'll need – including the places where you can hire donkeys.

In Scotland you'll find a company called CNDo (www.cndoscotland.com/walking/donkey.html) which offers a two-week walking holiday covering most of the route – though it's a sadly donkey-free experience. And of course Stevenson's books continue (rightly) to be popular today and as widely read as ever.

Oscar Wilde

Oscar Fingal O'Flahertie Wills Wilde was born in Dublin in 1854, and was a brilliant pupil at school. He won prizes for Greek at Trinity College, Dublin, before going up on a scholarship to Magdalen College, Oxford, in 1874, where he earned two first class degrees in succession. At Oxford, Wilde cultivated aestheticism, and became renowned as both a dandy and a wit.

In 1879 he moved to London, and started writing for a living, publishing poems and essays, and even going on a lecture tour of the USA in 1882. On his return he married Constance Lloyd and rapidly produced two sons, Cyril and Vyvyan, along with a string of plays which were to seal his reputation as the foremost dramatist of the era.

Life changed, however, when he met Lord Alfred Douglas ('Bosie') in 1891, and fell madly in love with him. The period was Wilde's most productive – in spite of the banning of *Salomé* in 1892, which he had written in French for Sarah Bernhardt (see page 132) – but the relationship between the two men was simply too much for Bosie's father, the Marquis of Queensberry.

Before everything went pear-shaped, Bosie and Wilde went off on holiday to Algeria at the beginning of 1895, and while there are said to have introduced the

26-year-old André Gide to the delights of the local boys – while indulging in a bit of sex-tourism themselves.

It was a brief vacation, however, and the famous court case ensued. After Wilde unwisely sued the Marquis of Queensberry for libel, and lost, he was arrested, charged, tried and found guilty, and sentenced to two years of hard labour. He spent six months at Wandsworth prison, and the rest of the sentence at Reading Gaol. Prison broke both his health and his spirit, and on his release in 1897 he emigrated to France.

In exile in Paris, Wilde took the name Sebastian Melmoth, though it didn't stop him from being shunned on the street by his former friends. Aubrey Beardsley, who had provided the illustrations for *Salomé*, famously crossed the street to avoid him (though it didn't do him much good, as he was dead of consumption by 1898, aged only 25).

Meanwhile, Wilde's persistent ear infection – he had complained about it even before going into prison, and while there had had repeated syringings – got worse. During the early autumn of 1900, he had more than 50 doctor's visits, and in October he had an ear operation. It was too late – the infection had spread to the brain and he died in his hotel room at the end of November, aged only 46. (Would his father, a famous ear surgeon, have been able to help?)

Oscar Wilde died as he lived, terminally witty. A month before he gave up the ghost, he said: 'I am in a duel to the death with this wallpaper, one of us has got to go,' and in his last days, sipping champagne on what was soon to be his deathbed, he muttered: 'Alas, I am dying beyond my means'.

The hotel in Paris where Oscar Wilde died is still there, though it's now l'Hôtel rather than the Hôtel d'Alsace. If you do opt for room 16, where Wilde expired, try not to do a Jim Morrison (see page 123), who fell drunkenly out of the window here onto a parked car in 1971, a few months before his own untimely death.

You can also visit Wilde's grave, in **Père Lachaise Cemetery**, in Paris. Originally buried in Bagneux Cemetery, Wilde was transferred here in 1909, and the **Epstein memorial** to him was erected in 1914 – erected being the right word, as the cemetery management insisted on a fig-leaf being added before the monument was complete. The fig leaf (and some) was removed by vandals / restorers in 1922.

And of course there are Wilde's works, which still sparkle with wit and poignancy more than a century on.

TRAVEL INFORMATION
Auberge Verlaine (formerly the Auberge du Lion d'Or) 1 rue Pont Pâquis, Juniville; tel: 03 24 39 68 00; web: www.chez.com/museeverlaine; by appointment only.

Café de Flore 172 boulevard Saint Germain, 75006, Paris; M Saint Germain des Prés; tel 01 45 48 55 26.

Château d'Arpaillargues Arpaillargues, 5km west of Uzès, Provence; tel: 04 66 22 14 48; fax: 04 66 22 56 10; web: www.leshotelsparticuliers.com/arpaillargues.htm; double rooms around ∈ 230.

Château de Cirey Cirey sur Blaise, between Saint Dizier and Chaumont; tel: 03 25 55 43 04; open afternoons in summer only – call ahead to check.

Château de Nohant Nohant Vic, 10km north of La Châtre, southeast of Châteauroux; tel: 02 54 31 06 04; open every day; ∈ 4.

Château de Voltaire, Ferney Voltaire, near Geneva; tel: 04 50 40 53 21; open Jun–Sep; closed Mon; free.

Chez Félix au Port 50 boulevard Aguillon, Antibes; tel: 04 93 34 01 64.

La Closerie des Lilas 171 boulevard Montparnasse, 75006, Paris; M̅ Port Royal; tel: 01 40 51 34 50.

La Coupole 102 boulevard Montparnasse, 75014, Paris; M̅ Vavin; tel 01 44 20 14 20.

Les Deux Magots 6 Place Saint Germain des Prés, 75006, Paris; M̅ Saint Germain des Prés; tel: 01 45 48 55 25.

l'Hôtel (formerly Hôtel d'Alsace) 13 rue des Beaux Arts, 75006, Paris; M̅ Saint Germain des Prés, Louvre; tel: 01 44 41 99 00; fax 01 43 25 64 31. See also page 253.

Montparnasse cemetery 75014, Paris; M̅ Gaïté, Raspail, Denfert-Rochereau; open every day; free.

Musée Carnavalet 23 rue de Sévigné, 75003, Paris; M̅ Saint Paul, Chemin Vert; tel: 01 44 59 58 58; closed Mon; free.

Musée Colette Saint Sauveur en Puisaye, 40km southwest of Auxerre; tel: 03 86 45 61 95; open daily in summer, except Tue; off season open on weekend afternoons only (call ahead to check); ∈ 5.

Musée Jean Cocteau quai Monléon, Menton; tel: 04 93 57 72 30; closed Tue; ∈ 4.

Musée de la Vie Romantique 16 rue Chaptal, 75009, Paris; tel: 01 48 74 95 38; M̅ Saint Georges, Blanche, Pigalle; closed Mon; permanent collection free (∈ 5 for special exhibitions).

Lacoste between Ménerbes and Bonnieux, 50km east of Avignon; tel: 04 90 75 84 97 (town hall).

Père Lachaise cemetery 75020, Paris; M̅ Père Lachaise, Philippe-Auguste, Gambetta; open every day; free.

Rimbaud Museum Quai Arthur Rimbaud, Charleville Mézières (on the north side of town); tel: 03 24 32 44 64; closed Mon; ∈ 4.

Shakespeare & Company 37 rue de la Bûcherie, 75005, Paris; tel: 01 43 26 96 50; M̄ Saint Michel.

Eccentric Food and Drink

It's an old cliché, but the French really do take their food and drink seriously. There are more restaurants per capita country-wide than anywhere else in the world, thousands of festivals and fairs with a food- or drink-related theme (see Chapter 1), and even food and drink museums – a concept which doesn't seem the least bit strange to the average French person. Whilst researching this book I constantly ran up against people who couldn't believe I was going to include them – just because they ran a prune museum, or a museum dedicated to a single type of biscuit.

ECCENTRIC FOOD

Regional delicacies and extravagances are celebrated on feast days (both religious and culinary) and often also have their own museum dedicated to them – and in some cases multiple museums. So there are two for chocolate, four for *foie gras* and at least seven for snails – though curiously none I could find at all for frogs' legs or pigs' trotters. The hundreds of millions of oysters shucked and guzzled every year go practically unremarked upon, while the billions of garlic cloves eaten may do a great deal for the nation's health (if not its breath) but don't appear to warrant a shrine.

Saddest of all, however, has been the recent closure of the Musée du Cochon at Villard de Lans, 35km southwest of Grenoble, following the death of the owner. You used to be able to see a full history of the pig there (including its religious and symbolic significance through the ages), along with an all-too detailed description of the uses a skilful butcher can make of the humble porker.

Biscuits

The village of Sare, 15km inland from Saint Jean de Luz, tucked into a loop of the French-Spanish border, and just south of the disarmingly named Saint Pée sur Nivelle, is home to the **Musée du Gâteau Basque**, arguably France's tastiest biscuit.

The *Gâteau Basque* first made its appearance in the 17th century, when it was often baked in the shape of a small pig. A hundred years later, visitors were already praising the local *Biskotxak*, but it was only the addition of delicious *crème patissière* (a sort of custard) in the 19th century which really led to the biscuit's wider popularity.

Today, you can see all the steps leading up to the mouth-watering end-result at the museum in Sare, which has an authentically re-created Basque kitchen (a *sukalde*), along with 19th-century cooking implements. You won't be disappointed if you're hoping to find a boutique at the end of the visit, selling fancily wrapped biscuits.

Cheese

It's a fact: France is easily the cheesiest nation on earth. They simply love the stuff, and consume around a million tonnes of it every year. It's a separate course in every meal, and there are huge cheese stalls in every market. My local shop has two entire cheese aisles.

It's impossible to say just how many varieties there are in France, but the answer is certainly well over 500. That said, a few pasteurised, mass-produced cheeses, which you'll see weighing down supermarket shelves, inevitably account for around half of all sales. But go into any French home and you'll find the makings of a decent cheese board – the chances are you'll have a choice of unpasteurised delights, made from cows' milk, goats' milk and ewes' milk, and something pungent, something soft, something hard and something blue on offer.

Two of the most famous French cheeses, Camembert and Roquefort, and dozens of smaller ones, even have their own museums. If you're in Ambert, in the Auvergne, halfway between Clermont Ferrand and Saint Etienne, for example, drop in at the **Maison de la Fourme d'Ambert et des Fromages**, where you can find out all about the history of the tasty local blue cheese, as well as other varieties from the Auvergne, complete with tastings in a cheese cellar. Equally, if you're near Troyes, make the detour to Chaource, where you'll find a small **Musée du**

Fromage dedicated entirely to the Chaource cheese, which looks like a short fat Camembert, but tastes more like a chalky goat's cheese. It's excellent with white wine.

Camembert

Camembert-like cheeses are made all over France (all over the world, in fact), but only in Normandy will you find the real thing. So it's hardly surprising that the town of Vimoutiers, in the heart of Normandy, is home to the **Musée du Camembert**. Here you can visit a reconstituted cheese dairy and see the world's most impressive collection of Camembert labels. You'll be shown the history of the cheese and be able to find out just how it's made today. Allow a good hour if you're going to do the Camembert-tasting as well.

Vimoutiers was 90% destroyed in World War II, so there's little of the ancient history of the town left to see – but there is an excellent statue of a cow in front of the town hall. If you're here over Easter, you can also take part in the cider and Camembert fair, and watch the finish of the Paris–Camembert spring-classic cycle race.

Just 5km southwest of Vimoutiers is the tiny village of Camembert itself, which has both a Camembert House and a Camembert Monument. The **Maison du Camembert**, built in the shape of a Camembert box in 1992, has a small exhibition on the cheese, and a boutique. At the bottom of the village you'll find the Camembert Monument, dedicated to Marie Harel, the woman thought to have invented the cheese several centuries ago. The monument was inaugurated in 1927, after a New York doctor started up a subscription for a stele, claiming the cheese had cured him of a nasty stomach complaint.

Roquefort

The village of Roquefort sur Soulzon, just south of Millau, has been capitalising on its unique system of caves – where expensive blue cheese just happens to mature perfectly, ventilated by cracks and fissures called *fleurines* – for well over a thousand years. Today more than 2,000 people (and over 100,000 sheep) are kept gainfully employed in producing thousands of tonnes of the cheese every year, and you can visit both of the biggest producers, **Roquefort Société** and **Roquefort Papillon**.

The visits take you deep into the caves where the big cheeses (the actual cheeses, not the company management) are laid down to mature for up to six months before going to market. You'll find out just how the cheese is made and matured, and the vital role of the *Penicillum Roqueforti* in the whole process. The Papillon visit is free, but the Société version includes free cheese sampling at the end.

You can also climb up to the top of the rocks for a great view out over the Larzac Plateau, where José Bové (see page 66) farms and makes Roquefort himself – when he's not raising hell or doing time, that is.

Chestnuts and mushrooms

Deep in the woods between Bergerac and Cahors, is the old *bastide* (fortified village) of Villefranche du Périgord, and it's here that you'll find a charming little chestnut and mushroom museum.

La Maison du Châtaignier, des Marrons et des Champignons will tell you everything you need to know about the fruits of the sweet chestnut tree, though doesn't entirely explain why the *Châtaignier* produces edible *Marrons* (sweet chestnuts) but the *Marronnier* (horse chestnut tree) produces inedible *Marrons* (conkers). You'll also find out the difference between a frightening variety of edible and poisonous mushrooms, but if you're out mushrooming yourself you'd be wise to check that what you've collected is tasty but harmless – you can do this, charmingly, at any pharmacy in France.

Don't leave without a box of delicious *marrons glacés*.

Chocolate

Chocoholics will be pleased to know that there are two establishments dedicated to the obsession in France, the Chocolate Museum in Biarritz, and the Chocolate Palace in La Côte Saint André, between Lyon and Grenoble.

Le Musée du Chocolat

Created by Serge Couzigou, the famous *Maître Chocolatier*, Biarritz's chocolate museum is marvellous. You can follow chocolate's history from its introduction into Europe from the new world in the 16th century (Columbus brought cocoa beans back with him in 1492, but nobody worked out what they were for until Cortez arrived at the court of Montezuma in Mexico in 1519).

There are old documents, machines and moulds, along with 19th-century ads extolling chocolate's virtues, but it's the fifty-odd chocolate sculptures here which really catch your eye. There's a roaring lion, a bird with outstretched wings, a famous nude or two, and various abstracts – all edible. To save the sculptures from greedy fingers, however, the guided tour includes plenty of tastings along the way.

Le Palais du Chocolat

Third-generation chocolate maker Pierre Jouvenal opened up the **Palais du Chocolat** at La Côte Saint André in 1994, and it now attracts more than 10,000 visitors a year. The setting certainly helps – the establishment's housed in the Château Louis XI, an extravagant building in a great position.

The tour takes in the history, geography and botany of chocolate, and you'll find plenty of choco-memorabilia, along with an excellent chocolate fountain which spreads the delicious odour through every room. There are chocolate tastings, of course, and the visit ends where you'd expect, at the museum shop. Here you can buy the exquisite chocs made by the Patisserie Jouvenal in town, which was started in 1912 by Pierre's grandfather Emil.

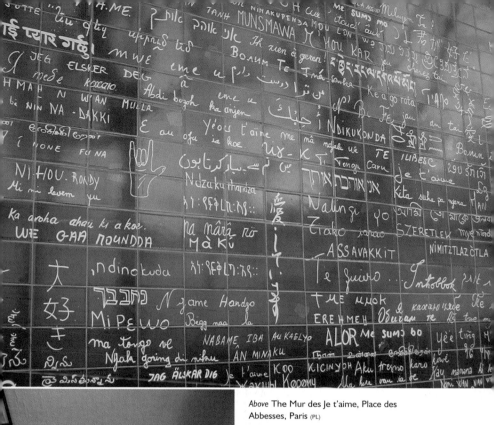

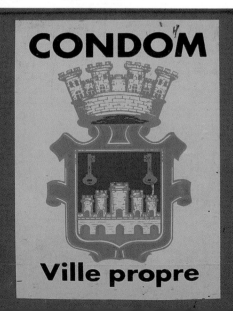

Above The Mur des Je t'aime, Place des Abbesses, Paris (PL)

Left Rare two-seater bidet, at the Musée de l'Insolite, Loriol (PL)

Below left 'Best before 1948': a British condom at the Condom Museum (PL)

Below 'Keep Condom clean' – the signs on the municipal rubbish bins (PL)

Right One of several Statues of Liberty in Paris; this one is at the CNAM (PL)

Below The Stars and Stripes continue to fly over Lafayette's grave at the Picpus Cemetery, Paris (PL)

Below Stylish signage for the Hotel Félix, Castelsarrasin, with its pistol-packing entrance

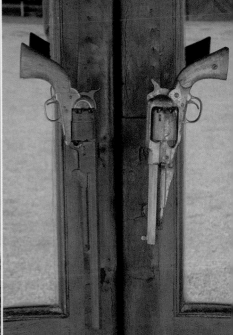

Foie gras

The French love their *foie gras*, and that's why you'll find no less than *four* museums in France dedicated solely to its production.

Incredibly, making a duck's or goose's liver extra fat, by force-feeding it during the last few weeks of its life, doesn't even turn out to be as barbaric as you think. According to connoisseurs, in fact, it's only natural – since it's only what migratory ducks and geese would ordinarily do to themselves, before setting off on the long haul to far-away climes, the liver being the most efficient place in the body to store extra fuel. So that's OK, then, is it?

Running from north to south, you can visit the **Maison de l'Oie et du Canard** at Thiviers, the **Musée du Foie Gras** at Frespech, the **Musée du Foie Gras et des Traditions Populaires** at Samatan, and the **Musée du Foie Gras** at Roquettes.

The first of the four, which co-locates with the tourist office, is the broadest in interest. It's the personal initiative of local goose- and duck-mad Robert Cruège, and tells you everything you need to know about ducks and geese, how and when to force-feed them, and what they can be used for (everything from continental quilts to toothpicks, apparently, quite apart from all the ducky dishes you can eat).

The **Musée du Foie Gras** in Frespech claims to be the unique and only museum of its kind in France, which manifestly isn't true, but shouldn't stop you going. Opened in 1994, by local producer Yves Boissière, in the family barn, the museum was created to preserve the heart (not to mention the liver) of the *foie gras* tradition. Here, you can learn how to force-feed a duck in the Occitan language, which is still used by the Boissière family, and see how the Egyptians had already cottoned on to the idea more than 4,500 years ago.

The **Musée du Foie Gras et des Traditions Populaires** in Samatan is by contrast less exotic, consisting essentially of a rather twee display in the tourist office. But Samatan nonetheless boasts one of the most important poultry markets in the country, and regularly shifts one and a half tonnes of *foie gras* every Monday morning, rising to over four tonnes a week in the peak season running up to Christmas, so it's a business to take seriously. The Monday *foie gras* market is followed by a cacophonous live poultry sale.

Finally, the **Musée du Foie Gras** in Roquettes, just outside Toulouse, traces the history of *foie gras* from antiquity to our times, and follows up with tastings of all the duck products made on-site – of which there are plenty.

Honey

There are places all over France where you can go and see bees do it (with apologies to Cole Porter, see page 126), but two places are of special note, the **Cité des Abeilles**, near Pau, and the **Musée de l'Abeille**, at Valcebollère, in the Pyrenees near Andorra.

The **Cité des Abeilles** (Bee City) doubles as a serious research centre and a place where you can buy an excellent range of first-rate honey and candles. You can visit the hives (of several varieties) and learn everything you need to know about bees (including how they do it), and the guides are a positive mine of information.

At the **Musée de l'Abeille**, further along the Pyrenees, you can also see working hives and the production of honey and royal jelly. You can taste a dozen flavours of honey, from rhododendron to heather to chestnut, along with honey-related products such as nougat, sweets and gingerbread. There's a separate exhibition which details the local wildlife (with an endearingly naff chamois tableau) and mushrooms, both edible and poisonous.

Pigeons

If you fancy pigeons, then the **Ecomusée du Pigeon** near the village of Lombers, 20km south of Albi, is just for you. If you also fancy pigeon-pie, then you're really in luck.

The Ecomusée was created in 1984, and today nurtures over 3,000 breeding pairs, which produce around 900 pigeons a week for domestic consumption. Being an eco-museum, you can also find out about the history of the pigeon, and learn something of the 309 different species known to man (10 are extinct; another 58 endangered). They have racing pigeons, messenger pigeons, pet pigeons and doves, all housed in an enormous traditional wooden dove-cote.

The two-hour visit, accompanied by a pigeon-professional, shows not just the history and the practice of raising pigeons, but takes you right into the dove-cote itself (mind the droppings), and closes with a video showing pigeons around the world and through the ages.

This being France, you can then buy home-produced pigeon-pâté, pre-prepared dishes such as baby pigeon with peas, and freshly plucked, drawn and oven-ready birds. Even if you can't make it to Ecomusée yourself, you can still order up pigeon delicacies online through the website, at www.pigeons-du-mont-royal.com. Finally, the Ecomusée collects old postcards of pigeons and puts them on display, so if you have anything interesting drop it in the post (or send it by carrier pigeon!) to Les Pigeons du Mont Royal, 81120, Lombers, France.

Prunes

They've been making prunes in the Lot et Garonne for the best part of a thousand years, and even today the *département* produces the lion's share of France's prunes and prune products. It's logical, therefore that it's here, at Granges sur Lot, between Clairac and Castelmoron, that the prune-producing Bérino-Martinet family have created the **Musée du Pruneau Gourmand** (the Greedy Prune Museum). You can visit either by car or by pleasure boat, as they have a small dock on the river Lot where you can tie-up.

The museum traces the history of prune production right up to the present day (the small factory is an integral part of the visit), and features an exceptional collection of prune ovens, alembics, prune sorters, old labels and packaging, and the farm implements used in cultivating plums (which is not the plum job you'd expect it to be at all). It ends in the boutique, with tastings of some of the excellent prune products they make right here on the spot, including stuffed prunes, prunes coated with chocolate and exquisite prunes in Armagnac. It's also one of the very few places left where you can still buy *eau de vie de pruneau* (as opposed to the more commonplace *eau de vie de prune*).

In summer, they create an amusing labyrinth, by mowing paths through a huge field of maize, with the theme being suitably Proust-like (see page 140): 'A la Recherche du Pruneau Perdu'. If you're in the area on the last Saturday in July, be sure not to miss the **Prune-Stone Spitting World Championships** which are held in Sainte Livrade sur Lot, a (prune) stone's throw away, 12km upriver.

Sardines

Who went with Napoleon to Russia and accompanied Maurice Herzog up Annapurna? The humble, tinned sardine in oil, of course – as Philippe Anginot, self-styled *sardinologue* and sardine sociologist would be the first to tell you. For the past 20 years or so, Anginot has lived, breathed and probably even eaten sardines, building up a collection of over 1,000 different sardine cans, and performing important ethnological research into how the sardine fits into the human psyche.

As the curator of the **Musée Imaginaire de la Sardine**, Anginot had a semi-permanent exhibition space in Sête (France's number one sardine port) until the end of 1999. On show here was his spectacular collection of cans, along with a dozen shop-window sized sardine tins, highlighting themes such as '*La relation entre la sardine, le zodiaque et la symbolique judéo-chrétienne*' (the relationship between sardines, the zodiac and Judaeo-Christian symbolism).

These days, however, the *Musée* is more of a travelling sardine side-show, which appears at various festivals around the country, particularly in Brittany and along the Mediterranean coast. At the show you can pick up and exchange favourite sardine recipes with other sardine-mad enthusiasts, and enjoy musical extravaganzas ancient and modern, on the sardine theme – although even Anginot confesses he doesn't know when and where it's going to appear next (and he's a pretty slippery customer himself; it took me ages to track him down in Montpellier in 2002).

Snails

While there's no doubting that for some the snail is a pure delicacy, for most of us it's just an excuse to get familiar with the unbeatable combination of garlic, parsley and melted butter. Snails are farmed all over France (by *héliciculteurs*), and at least seven of the farms welcome visitors. So why not go along and witness the mysteries of these extraordinary hermaphrodites, which take up to ten hours to perform the sexual act (albeit only once or twice a year), before ordering up a dozen of the finest at your local restaurant?

Working from north to south, there are farms you can visit at Olizy (near Reims), Bernon (between Troyes and Auxerre), Montigny (near Bourges), Jau (on the point of the Médoc), Lorignac (between Saintes and Bordeaux), Vaunac (near Périgueux) and Auxillac La Canourgue (deep in the Lozère, near Mende).

The **Musée de l'Escargot**, at Olizy Violaine, is run by Marie-Françoise Moreau (presumably an *hélicicultrice* rather than an *héliciculteur*), who will show you round the hatchery and nursery of the farm on an excellent hour-long visit.

La Fontaine de Bernn, at Bernon, also offers visits, and rather endearingly elects a 'Miss Snail' on the first of May every year – an enviable tribute. The establishment also holds the record for having prepared the world's largest snail *cassolette*. If you want to beat the record yourself you'll need at least 8,100 snails, 120 litres of stock, 25 litres of white wine, 20kg of mushrooms, 5kg of hazelnuts, 5kg of raisins and 3kg of capers – and a very big saucepan.

The **Boiteau Luma**, at Montigny, for its part, recommends March to May as the most interesting time to visit, as that's when all the biological states of the grey snail can be seen at the same time – though you can come and taste their snail products all year round. The farm also provides stunt snails for the local film studio, apparently.

Between the vineyards and the sea, **L'Escargot du Médoc** has a lovely situation and friendly owners and is part of the 'farm welcome' network. Both large and small grey snails are farmed here, way up in the point of the Médoc, and fed on a delicious diet of clover. You can see the whole snail cycle here, from their being bred, hatched and fattened, all the way to the cooking pot. You can buy snails, too – dead or alive.

Just across the Gironde, at Lorignac, the **Domaine de Charentes Escargots** also gives an especially welcoming tour of its snail farm, ending up with a plateful of snails and a glass of the very palatable local wine.

In the Périgord, between Thiviers (where there's a *foie gras* museum, see page 183) and Sorges (home to the truffle museum, see opposite) there's a fine snail farm at Vaunac, called **La Ferme des Guézoux**. Restored a dozen years ago by Béatrice and Pierre Fouquet, the farm makes for an interesting visit – just follow the snail signs – and the snails themselves are particularly tasty.

Finally, easily the remotest of the farms listed here is **La Ferme Hélicicole du Moulinet**, in the Lozère, France's least populous département. Established by Chantal Jacovetti in 1992, the farm is at 650m above sea level, and Jacovetti welcomes visitors to come and see the breeding rooms, nurseries and fattening fields, where around 150,000 snails are produced annually.

Strawberries

Small, native strawberries have been popular in Europe for a very long time – the Romans were particularly fond of them – but it wasn't until the beginning of the 18th century that the larger strawberries we mostly eat today arrived on the continent. They were brought back from Chile by a naval officer called – in a completely implausible coincidence, given that strawberry plants had already been called *fraisiers* for centuries by then – Amédée François *Frézier*.

Frézier turned up in Plougastel, in Brittany, in 1713, with five plants, and the town quickly became (and indeed still is) the strawberry capital of France. How fitting, then, that there should be a **Musée de la Fraise et du Patrimoine de Plougastel** in the Breton town. Downstairs there's a permanent exhibition spread across five rooms entitled '*La Fraise dans tous ses états... de Frézier à nos jours*' which traces the history of the strawberry and its development in France, while upstairs there are more closely focused documentation and exhibition areas aimed specifically at the strawberry specialist.

Sugar

It's good stuff, sugar, and there's a lot more to it than just a couple of spoonfuls in your morning tea, too. As you'll quickly find out, if you visit the **Musée de l'Art du Sucre** in Cordes sur Ciel, 25km northwest of Albi.

The museum – and indeed everything in it – is the creation of the hugely talented Yves Thuriès, who opened up a patisserie workshop at the top of the old town of Cordes in 1988. The following year he expanded it to include the sugar museum, which shows off his astonishing range of sugar sculptures, many of which have won national and international prizes.

The range and dexterity is breathtaking, with multicoloured and enormously detailed sculptures including subjects as diverse as a busty winged-victory attended by prancing unicorns; a gecko clinging to a branch; baskets and bouquets of flowers; Poseidon charging out of the surf in a horse-drawn chariot; entwined herons; spread-winged eagles and writhing snakes; Mercury triumphant; and a pouting beauty with rampant dolphins. It's all made from sugar, and it's extremely sweet, if not always totally tasteful.

The medieval town of Cordes sur Ciel is also fascinating, so take time to enjoy it – but be warned that it can get pretty crowded in high season.

Truffles

There's a lot of mystique surrounding the humble truffle, but you have to get beyond the dull exterior and experience the unique smell and pungent flavour inside before you could begin to agree that all the fuss might just be worthwhile, and that the breathtaking prices could almost be justified.

Most of the best truffle markets are in Provence (see page 5), but it's in Sorges, just north of Périgueux, that you'll find the **Maison de la Truffe**, and an excellent Truffle Trail you can follow. Opened in 1982, it's a tribute to the work of one man, Jean-Claude Savignac, the mayor of Sorges, and is dedicated to the *tuber melanosporum*, the black truffle of Périgord.

The museum explains how, why and where truffles grow, how they're found, and why they're so expensive, as well as detailing the many different varieties. If you're with a group, you can then go out with the local truffle-hound along the 4km-long truffle trail, and experience the delight of truffling for yourself.

Old vegetables

Bernard Lafon was lucky enough to grow up in a small but fine château outside Bordeaux in the 1950s. His grandmother would tour the family farm looking for ingredients for the day's meals, and would cook up soups and dishes based on the local produce, with as much emphasis on nettles, dandelions and elderflowers as more prosaic ingredients.

As a young adult, Lafon realised that the increasing industrialisation and homogenisation of agriculture was ruining the diversity he had enjoyed as a child – high-yield disease-resistant strains of everything from wheat to tomatoes were wiping out local species altogether. So at the age of 25, in 1977, he decided to make a stand, and produce 'old vegetables' at the family property.

It was hardly a runaway success. In his first year, he managed to sell just 45 jars of nettle preserve – barely enough to take the sting out of the bottling bill. But today the processing plant turns out 350,000 jars of old vegetables and fruit a year, and the property attracts over 20,000 visitors annually.

In the 1990s, Lafon launched a *musée gourmand*, called **Oh! Legumes Oubliés** which features an open-air museum where you can see old-time fruits, vegetables and edible flowers being grown in different areas (for the record, begonias taste a lot like sorrel, with a fine, lemony tang), and a boutique selling a variety of local produce and excellent recipe books.

You can sign up for tastings, too, where you'll get to try up to 20 different local specialities, made on the premises, starting with an exquisite cocktail made from Périgord verjuice, elderberry wine and lemonade, and followed by nettle quiche, crêpes with Jerusalem artichokes (*topinambours* in French), and dwarf gooseberries dipped in bitter chocolate. Tastings and documentation are available in French, English and German – but you need to call ahead to make advance arrangements.

In the spring, there's also a festival of forgotten vegetables (see page 14), and in the autumn you shouldn't miss the festival of forgotten fruits (see page 30).

ECCENTRIC DRINK

In spite of falling wine consumption by the French (but then even soldiers used to have a standard ration of a litre and a half per man per day) France remains the world's largest wine producer, and easily its biggest consumer. More than a fifth of the world's wine is produced here, and average per capita wine consumption is over three times that in Australia and four times that in the UK. So you'll find every wine-growing region (and that effectively means every region except

Brittany) in France celebrating the grape harvest, and wine playing an integral part in every festivity. But there's nothing especially eccentric about that.

Equally, you can visit many of the breweries and distilleries large and small across the country, with Alsace being the place to go if you want to see large amounts of beer being made (try **Kronenbourg**, for example). For spirits, there's everything from the slick professionalism of **Cointreau** at Angers, to charming family-run businesses in the Dauphiné, such as the **Distillerie Charles Meunier et Successeurs**, at Saint Quentin sur Isère, just across the river from Voiron (where you'll find the vast Chartreuse cellars, see page 190).

What there isn't a museum of, curiously, is **absinthe**, the near-mythological drink which was blamed for the madness of any number of turn-of-the-century artists, and which was banned in Europe and America in the early decades of the 20th century. Absinthe simply means wormwood, but that was only one of the many ingredients in the potent drink, which was established in France in the 19th century by the French distiller Henri-Louis Pernod, based on a recipe gleaned from a Swiss physician (improbably called Dr Ordinaire).

In real absinthe (which makes the heart grow profoundly misanthropic, rather than fonder), the key ingredients seem to be not the wormwood extract but a mixture of herbs which pull you up as they drag you down – though since the intoxicating effect wears off before the alcohol, there's an unfortunate tendency to overdo it. So perhaps it's no wonder that *La Fée Verte* (The Green Fairy) was the ruin of so many artistic temperaments, from Verlaine and Rimbaud (see page 145) to Toulouse-Lautrec, Van Gogh and Oscar Wilde (see page 108, 112, and 175). Then again, the number of cheap (and highly toxic) absinthe copies on the market – there were more than 200 producers at its peak – could be equally to blame. Just so you know, however much you may like the stuff marketed as absinthe today (Spain and the UK are both producers), people who've experienced the real thing assure me that they are alike only in name.

Pastis, the aniseed-based drink most commonly associated with absinthe (largely because of the similar *louche*, the clouding effect created when you add water, but also because of the Pernod brand-name) also has nothing to do with the 'green fairy' at all. But that doesn't stop it being France's favourite aperitif – although like wine, there's nothing eccentric about that either.

For a more unusual drink, you need to head north, to Normandy, where there are still buried barrels of **Calvados** to be found, if you know where to dig. Calvados, the name of the *département* (supposedly because a ship called the *San Salvador* was wrecked there after the Spanish Armada) is also the name of the local spirit distilled from cider. It's been around for centuries, and is much-revered. So it was no surprise, when the Germans occupied France in the early 1940s, that many local producers buried their favourite barrels out in the fields. When the allies arrived, most were dug up, and shared out in a festive spirit. But some were lost – and still await lucky treasure-hunters.

Armagnac

Armagnac, France's oldest spirit, reflects the meeting of three different cultures – the vines were introduced by the Romans, the stills were brought over by the Moors, and the barrels were imported by the Celts. The spirit still drives a good part of the economy of the Gers, in southwestern France, and is the mainstay of the town of Condom (see page 237), so it's only right and proper that there should be an **Armagnac Museum** there.

Created in 1954, the museum has been housed since 1981 in a lovely building right in the middle of town, and features an interesting collection of tools and historical artefacts relating to the making of Armagnac. The most extraordinary of these is the 1885 *Taissons Pressoir*, from Bas Armagnac, which is the world's largest wooden wine press, weighing in at 18 tonnes. It's impossible to work out how on earth they got it into the room.

There are also a couple of anti-hail devices – one's a canon, the other's a bell – which can't ever have been remotely effective, but demonstrate the real danger of losing a whole year's worth of grapes in just a few minutes during a violent summer storm. Upstairs, inside the mansarded loft, you'll find out how to make a barrel and how to distil Armagnac, but it seems incredible that the one thing you can't do at the Armagnac Museum is to actually buy the stuff. The Condom municipality is really missing a trick.

On the other hand there are ample tasting opportunities during the annual *Flamme d'Armagnac* festivities (see page 31) which celebrate the lighting of the flame under the Armagnac stills, usually in November.

Champagne

Few people can resist a glass of bubbly, and even fewer would argue that the best bubbly is the real thing: French champagne from the French Champagne region. It's not just that nothing else can legitimately be called champagne, but that the experts' best-rated sparkling wines consistently come from the area around Reims and Epernay.

About 250 million bottles of champers are produced every year, and used to launch ships, celebrate victories, anniversaries, birthdays, engagements, births, christenings, and marriages (and occasionally even divorces and deaths), and even to bathe in. It's a hugely popular drink, considering its price, so it's good news to find out that it's not just an indulgence, but a medicine, too. At least, anyway, according to the detailed nine-page flyer from the Champagne region's tourist board.

After a long list of historical and medical citations, the document catalogues the list of ailments for which champagne is unquestionably beneficial. These include abdominal wind (it worked for Proust, see page 140, anyway); food allergies (the high magnesium and sulphur content of champagne is said to help); distension, flatulence and indigestion (it happily solved Bismarck's notorious problems in that department); constipation; *'crise de foie'* (which fortunately doesn't exist medically outside France – it's essentially just feeling somewhat the worse for wear following over-indulgence); obesity and cellulite (though it won't make you thinner); depression and anxiety (yes, well); insomnia (ditto); migraine ('I drink to forget'); and of course loss of libido.

In short, quaff a glass of champagne with every meal, and you'll soon be fit as a fiddle. But no more than one glass, please.

You can visit practically every champagne producer in the Champagne region (there are hundreds), and the largest and most famous houses offer free tours of their cellars. Contact the tourist offices in **Reims** and **Epernay** for further information.

Chartreuse

Northwest of Grenoble, at Voiron, is the world's largest liquor cellar (164m long), and it's well stocked, full of **Green and Yellow Chartreuse**, the sticky *digestif* which is still made according to the old monastic recipe first committed to parchment in 1605. Even today, only three monks know the names of the 130 different plants used, how they're mixed and distilled, and when the Chartreuse is ready to drink.

Both the green and the yellow are made from the same 130 plants, but in a different mix, and with a dramatically different alcohol content. Green Chartreuse, at 55%, is the stronger, more complex drink (and supposedly the only green liquor with all natural ingredients in the world), while Yellow Chartreuse, at 40%, is considerably softer and smoother.

Popular with a broad range of drinkers – Charles de Gaulle had a glass every night, and it's one of Hunter S Thompson's favourite pick-me-ups – Chartreuse is today used more often as a base for cocktails than as an after-dinner tipple.

You can visit the cellars and the distillery, where you'll find innumerable barrels (oak, from Russia and Hungary), and a short history of the famous liqueur, along with a rather more dramatic 3D film. There are tastings afterwards, and it's all free. Tours are available in English, German, Italian and Spanish as well as French, but you should book well ahead for these.

Cherry Rocher

The Rocher family have been making sticky alcoholic drinks in La Côte Saint André (where you'll also find the Palais du Chocolat, see page 182) for eight generations, ever since 1705, when the young Barthélémy Rocher set up in business here.

Today, the distiller is known after its trademark liqueur, *Cherry Rocher*, a powerful potion made from seven different sorts of cherry, and you can visit the **Musée des Liqueurs** at the factory, where you'll find 15th-century cellars and the distillery itself. There's an interesting range of historical distillers' materials on display, along with a unique collection of old posters, eulogizing alcoholic beverages and demonstrating just how they might have improved your life a century or more ago.

You can also get to see the whole Cherry Rocher range. As the company says, add *'du punch et de la couleur à vos cocktails'* with its *Curaçao Bleu*, *Crème de Banane*, *Liqueur d'Abricot Bergeron* or *Liqueur de Poire Williams* – though ideally not all at once in the same glass. There are also a number of variants on the *Crème de Cassis* theme, if you're looking for something to liven up a *Kir*; various fruits bottled in alcohol; and four different types of *marc*, the potent brew distilled from what's left over after grape pressing (ie grape skins and pips).

Finally, for the connoisseur, there's Cherry Whisky, an unbeatable blend of best oak-aged scotch whisky infused with the unforgettable taste of three different sorts of cherry. It's an aperitif with a difference.

French tasters of world whiskies

Since 1998, two good friends, Arnaud and Laurent (a rum merchant and a programmer; they met at a Scottish distillery), have been on a personal mission to taste the world's whiskies, and file reports on their website. Done in only a semi-serious spirit – they're hedonists rather than proselytes – the pair hold irregular tastings of the most obscure whiskies they can find.

So you'll find reviews of *Old Arrack* coconut-whisky from Sri Lanka, cask-strength ten-year-old *Lammerlaw* from New Zealand, *Singharaj* from Thailand, corn-whisky from Kentucky, *Great Outback* single-malt from Australia and *Mount Everest* whisky from Nepal. There's Czech *Printer's*, Tanzanian *Regency*, Maltese *John Brown*, whiskies from Japan, South Africa, Spain and Turkey, and more French whiskies than you'd think plausible.

To get a whisky onto the site (strictly non-commercial, of course), you'd need to ship it to Arnaud and Laurent first, who will then taste it in a spirit of enormous self-sacrifice and decide if it's web-worthy. And of course it does need to be from somewhere particularly unusual or unexpected, and taste unusually good (or indeed bad). Arnaud and Laurent live in Paris in the real world, but they're only accepting visitors in the virtual one, at their *Whiskies Insolites* website.

TRAVEL INFORMATION

Armagnac Museum Condom; tel 05 62 28 31 41; closed Tue, open afternoons only off-season; € 4.50.

Boiteau Luma Montigny, between Sancerre and Bourges; tel: 02 48 69 57 93; best visited between March and May; by appointment only.

Chartreuse cellars and distillery Voiron, 25km north of Grenoble; tel: 04 76 05 81 77; web: www.chartreuse.fr; open daily Apr–Oct, Mon–Fri Nov–Mar; free.

Cité des Abeilles Saint Faust, near Jurançon, just west of Pau; tel: 05 59 83 04 60; web: http://citedesabeilles.com; open weekend afternoons year-round and every afternoon except Monday in summer, but it's good to call ahead; € 5.50.

Cointreau Angers; tel: 02 41 31 50 50; web: www.cointreau.com; guided tours Mon–Sat at 3.30pm, also at 10am in summer; € 5.50.

Distillerie Charles Meunier et Successeurs Saint Quentin sur Isère, just across the river from Voiron, near Grenoble; tel: 04 76 93 66 70; daily, Apr–Dec, Jan–Mar by appointment only; € 4.

Domaine de Charentes Escargots Lorignac, between Saintes and Bordeaux; tel: 05 46 49 03 86; web: www.charentes-escargots.com; open Tue and Thu afternoons, from 4.30pm; € 7 (includes a glass of wine and a dozen snails).

Ecomusée du Pigeon just outside the village of Lombers, 20km south of Albi and 5km west of Réalmont; tel: 05 63 45 52 33; web: www.pigeons-du-mont-royal.com; open every afternoon; € 4.

Epernay tel: 03 26 53 33 00 (tourist office); web: www.Epernay.net.

L'Escargot du Médoc Jau, at the tip of the Médoc; tel: 05 56 09 55 40; web: http://membres.lycos.fr/escargotdumedoc/; open every afternoon mid-Jun to mid-Sep, also other times, by appointment.

La Ferme des Guézoux Vaunac, just off the N21, north of Périgueux; tel: 05 53 62 06 39; web: http://pro.wanadoo.fr/escargot.perigord/; open every day Jul–Aug, and the rest of the year by appointment only; € 3.

La Ferme Hélicicole du Moulinet Auxillac La Canourgue, near Mende, just east of the A75 autoroute, between junctions 39 and 40; tel: 04 66 32 65 32; web: http://perso.wanadoo.fr/escargot.lozere/; recommended May–Sep, but open by appointment all year round; € 3.

La Fontaine de Bernn Bernon, between Troyes and Auxerre; tel: 03 25 70 08 34; by appointment only.

Kronenbourg 68 route d'Oberhausbergen, in the Cronenbourg district of Strasbourg; tel 03 88 27 41 59; open Mon–Fri, by appointment; free (with free beer!).

Maison du Camembert Camembert; tel 02 33 39 43 35; open Easter to end Oct; free.

Maison du Châtaignier, des Marrons et des Champignons Villefranche du Périgord (at the tourist office); tel 05 53 29 98 37; closed Mon afternoons and Sun; free.

Maison de la Fourme d'Ambert et des Fromages Ambert, halfway between Clermont Ferrand and Saint Etienne; tel: 04 73 82 49 23; open every day in summer, by appointment the rest of the year; ∈ 4.

Maison de l'Oie et du Canard Thiviers, 15km north of Sorges (see Truffles, page 187), between Limoges and Périgueux; tel: 05 53 55 12 50; open year-round, but times vary, so call ahead to check; free.

Maison de la Truffe Sorges, 20km north of Périgueux; tel: 05 53 05 90 11; open every day, free.

Musée de l'Abeille Valcebollère, up a dead-end valley 10km southeast of Bourg-Madame (and not far from the Spanish enclave of Llívia, see page 239); tel: 04 68 04 58 26; by appointment only.

Musée de l'Art du Sucre Cordes sur Ciel, 25km northwest of Albi; tel: 05 63 56 02 40; web: http://thuries.fr/musee_du_sucre; open every day, closed Jan; ∈ 3.

Musée du Camembert Vimoutiers (in the tourist office); tel 02 33 39 30 29; closed Mon mornings and Sun; ∈ 3.

Musée du Chocolat 14 avenue Beau Rivage, Biarritz; tel: 05 59 41 54 64; open every day; ∈ 5.

Musée de l'Escargot Olizy Violaine, 30km west of Reims, just by junction 21 on the A4 to Paris; tel: 03 26 58 10 77; by appointment only.

Musée du Foie Gras Souleilles, near Frespech, 12km southeast of Villeneuve sur Lot; tel 05 53 41 23 24; open every day, closed Jan; ∈ 4.

Musée du Foie Gras Ferme du Beaucru, Roquettes, 20km southwest of Toulouse, across the river from the main road to Muret; tel: 05 61 76 38 98; open mid-Mar to Dec, on weekends and public holidays; ∈ 4.

Musée du Foie Gras et des Traditions Populaires Samatan, 50km west of Toulouse; tel: 05 62 62 55 40; closed Tue and Sun; free.

Musée de la Fraise et du Patrimoine de Plougastel Centre Culturel Louis-Marie Bodénès, Plougastel, across the river from Brest; tel: 02 98 40 21 18; www.musee-fraise.infini.fr; open Mon–Fri; free.

Musée du Fromage Chaource, 30km south of Troyes; tel: 03 25 40 10 67; closed Tue; ∈ 3.

Musée du Gâteau Basque Sare; tel: 05 59 54 22 09; web: http://perso.wanadoo.fr/musee.gateaubasque/; open mid-Jun to mid-Sep, Mon–Fri afternoons, also sometimes in Apr and May (but call ahead to check, as times vary); ∈ 5.

Musée des Liqueurs Cherry Rocher La Côte Saint André, between Lyon and Grenoble; tel: 04 74 93 38 10; web: www.cherry-rocher.fr; open afternoons Jun–Sep, Sunday afternoons only in Apr and May, and from Oct–Dec; closed Mon and Jan–Mar; free.

Musée du Pruneau Gourmand Domaine du Gabach, Granges sur Lot, between Marmande and Agen; tel 05 53 84 00 69; open every day; ∈4.

Oh! Légumes Oubliés Château de Belloc, just outside Sadirac, close to Créon, 10km east of Bordeaux; tel: 05 56 30 62 00; web: www.ohlegumesoublies.com; open afternoons daily from mid-Apr to Oct; ∈6.

Palais du Chocolat 25 rue de la République, La Côte Saint André (between Lyon and Grenoble); tel: 04 74 20 35 89; open every day; ∈3.

Reims tel: 03 26 77 45 25 (tourist office); web: www.tourisme.fr/reims/.

Roquefort Papillon Roquefort sur Soulzon, 25km south of Millau; tel: 05 65 58 50 08; open every day; free.

Roquefort Société Roquefort sur Soulzon, 25km south of Millau; tel 05 65 59 93 30; open every day; ∈3.

World Whiskies (*Whiskies Insolites*) www.thelin.net/whisky/; email: whisky@thelin.net.

Eccentric Collections

There are nearly 10,000 museums and collections you can visit in France, and each one has its merits, no doubt. But there are some which really stand head and shoulders above the rest for true eccentricity. They've been separated here, for convenience, into those in Paris, and those in the provinces.

ECCENTRIC PARISIAN

'Paris is worth a Mass' said Henry IV, famously (see page 81), and if he'd been a cheesy advertising copywriter he might have gone on to say 'because there are simply masses of things to do and see!' Amongst them, any number of world-famous art galleries, specialist collections, museums, monuments and festivals are there to tempt you – but instead why not visit the police museum, where you'll find lots of murder weapons, the museum of fakes, where most things simply aren't the genuine article, or head under the city into the sewers or the catacombs?

Catacombs

Up until 1780, there were big communal cemeteries in the heart of Paris, and most notably the Cimitière des Innocents, roughly where Les Halles stands now. Huge pits were dug for the dead, covered over when they were full, and the stench was appalling. Even in unsanitary 18th-century France, it soon became clear this was something of a health risk.

The in-town charnel-houses and cemeteries were closed, and new ones (including Père Lachaise, Montmartre and Montparnasse) were established outside what were then the city limits. The existing cemeteries were cleared for development, and the bones within were transported from 1785 onwards into a special part of the quarries underneath Paris. An area of 11,000m² comprising a kilometre-and-a-half of tunnels was set aside as a vast ossuary, and the bones were stacked artfully there in recesses up to 30m deep. It took the best part of 50 years to move the skeletons of the six million or so corpses to the quarries – and that was only those in the upper layers of the original cemeteries.

You can visit, and it's a deeply spooky place, as you'd expect. Bones are stacked floor to ceiling, and occasionally decorated with classic skull and crossbone motifs. It's a constant cool 10°C, winter and summer, so take a sweater, and although it's well lit, a torch is always a good idea when you're underground in a place like this.

Quite apart from the bones of millions of dead French people, the curiosities you can see here include a small fountain built in 1813 (the carp which used to swim here went blind), and a place called La Crypte de la Passion, which was named in memory of the concert given clandestinely here in 1897 by nearly 50 members of the Paris Opera.

The catacombs only take up a tiny proportion of the estimated 300km warren of

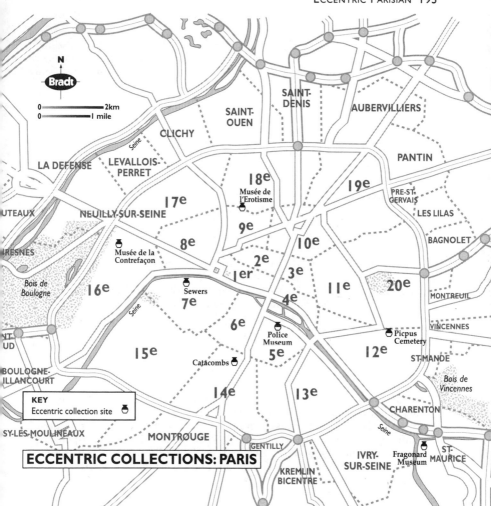

ECCENTRIC COLLECTIONS: PARIS

quarry tunnels which still run under the city. The most spectacular ones – including the 12m-tall gypsum galleries under Montmartre – were blocked up definitively after quarrying stopped in 1813, but many of the tunnels under the left bank still exist.

Visiting, however, is not just strictly illegal, but highly undesirable, as all manner of weirdos populate the underworld. If you must go, however – because you *have* to see the places where the resistance hung out during the war, or you want to visit the famous 'beach' or 'sauna' – take with you an experienced guide, and wear fishing waders and a miner's helmet, complete with a decent lamp. And don't say I didn't warn you.

The bits of the **Paris Catacombs** open to the public are accessed from Place Denfert-Rochereau, which was formerly (and rather appropriately) called Place de l'Enfer, until Denfert-Rochereau made a hero of himself defending Belfort against the Prussians (see page 233).

Erotisme

On Boulevard de Clichy, right in the heart of seedy old Pigalle, and a mere garter's-throw from the Moulin Rouge (where else?) you'll find the extraordinary **Musée de l'Erotisme**. And once you've worked your way past the predictably tittering teenagers and the occasional dirty old man, it's a fascinating experience.

Over seven floors, there's a truly comprehensive range of erotica through the ages, proving Cole Porter right: everyone does it. You'll find pre-Columbian, Greek, Roman, Etruscan, Egyptian, African, Chinese, Japanese, Javanese, Indian, Mexican and Peruvian artefacts – all in use long before the 20th century, too. (Though of course much of the material wasn't considered erotic *per se*, back then and was more to do with talismans relating to fertility, religion and death. But still.)

Put together by the director, Alain Plumy, and his partner over a 30-year period, the collection is comprehensive, and ever-growing, taking in not just ancient icons but latter-day pornography, too. In the middle, on the third floor, there's a truly marvellous bilingual display concerning prostitution in the first half of the 20th century, when Paris was *the* place to come if a *bordel* was what you were looking for.

Postcards from the era show how luxurious some of the establishments were, without hiding the hard truth that prostitution's always been a rough (even if occasionally lucrative) way of making a living. There are great pictures and descriptions of 'One Two Two' (122 rue de Provence), one of the swankiest joints of the day, and popular with everyone from the future King Edward VII to Cary Grant and Humphrey Bogart. Piaf even sang here during the occupation, and there are poignant pages from the working girls' notebooks, tallying up their dues by day for the clients serviced, and detailing the house cut. You can even see a photo of Edward's curious two-seater sexual contraption (whose use remains unexplained), and Le Sphinx, in Montparnasse (favourite haunt of Alberto Giacometti, see page 103), with its vast Egyptian entrance hall.

Finally, there's a rare shot of the famed Liane de Pougy taken at around the time of her notorious affair with Natalie Barney (see page 161), and an even rarer picture of Amélie Hélie, better known as the Casque d'Or (and wonderfully played by Simone Signoret in the eponymous 1951 film), who had a much-publicised fling with Toulouse-Lautrec's favourite model and *danseuse-extraordinaire* La Goulue (see page 110), before becoming one of the most idolised courtesans of the early 1900s.

It's all a remarkable testament to change. Fifty years ago most of the things on show here would have been illegal (even in France), and even now you'd still have a hard time explaining much of what's in the street-front window to your kids. But before you know it, they'll be the ones pondering over how to explain it all to you.

Fakes

Behind a perfectly ordinary bourgeois door in the upmarket 16th arrondissement (the real thing, no fake this) is the splendid **Musée de la Contrefaçon** – Paris's museum of counterfeits. Created by the Union des Fabricants, the small museum presents various commercially available products, together with examples of roundly condemned fakes, so you can be sure that what you're buying next time is the genuine article.

You can therefore admire fake cigars (considerably larger than the real thing), fake and real Biros (totally indistinguishable from one another), fake David Bowie cassettes and Reebok trainers (both better-looking than the real thing, to this untrained observer), and early over-sized (ridiculous, really) Lacoste crocodiles.

Hermès scarves are presented with their imitations, and a long list of differences (but I still couldn't tell which was which), and the fake Hermès ashtray is rather nice, even if the packaging's undeniably naff. Both the real and the fake plastic toys, however, look crap.

Then there are the imitators, particularly of drinks. Dom Perignon is faked as Dom Popignon. Suze has some 180 copycats around the world, the most amusing of which is Buze (pronounced *booze*, presumably), while Pernod becomes Perrenod and Byrrh becomes Pire. Moulinex is copied as Minolux, Barbie as Babie, and the Game Boy as a Game Child. There are false watches, football kit, car parts, cigarettes, sunglasses and banknotes (the Italian one is especially good). There are even Roman fakes, in the form of counterfeit amphorae stoppers.

Police are said to be on the lookout for criminals planning on opening a *counterfeit* counterfeit museum nearby.

Femme

The **Musée de la Femme et de l'Automate** in Neuilly sur Seine was one of Paris's most unlikely museums – so that's probably why it's closed down now and being restored, with the intention that some day it re-opens as a plain old collection of 19th-century mechanical puppets. Which is all very well for parents with children (or even for the child within), but it was the *Femme* part that was so unusual.

The Musée de la Femme was apparently the lifetime collection of a rich (and strange, it has to be said) benefactor, and consisted of all kinds of artefacts unified only by the fact that they were all to do with women. So there were models of Joan of Arc, photos of famous French stars like Brigitte Bardot (see page 132) and Mireille Mathieu, letters from celebrated women responding to requests for autographs (Margaret Thatcher sent a photo; how charming), a corset once belonging to Marie-Antoinette (see page 87), and shawls, shoes and gloves belonging to the famous of yesteryear.

It's all gone, now, sadly – and nobody at the Neuilly town hall is saying why, or what's happened to the erstwhile collection.

Hot water bottles

Another now sadly gone museum is the **Musée de la Bouillotte** (the hot water bottle museum), which was on rue Polonceau, in the downmarket Barbès quarter of Montmartre.

It was opened in the middle of 1997 by Albert Weinberg, a genial hot water bottle fan, who managed to collect nearly 150 rare and unusual specimens over a career of browsing antique markets and bric-à-brac shops, and then put them on show in the main room of his flat. Amongst his prizes were all manner of bed warmers, from coal-filled copper pans on sticks, to stone and earthenware jars, to rubber bottles in hand-knitted carry-sacs. One was made from an exploded brass shell from World War I.

Weinberg also had some real curiosities, like the red velvet-covered pan used to warm up the seat of your car. He even had a *moine*, a complex contraption made of wood which suspended a brazier full of coals underneath the elders' bedcovers in a monastery. Named after the young monks who originally performed the bed-warming task (I should coco!), it's one of only three I've ever seen – the other two are in the Hearse Museum (see page 208) and the Musée de l'Insolite (see page 209). Nuns had it easier, with a hot water pillow used to keep their knees warm during long prayers.

Weinberg died at the end of 1999, alas, and the collection disappeared with him.

Picpus Cemetery

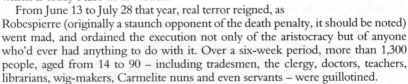

During the French revolution, the guillotine (see page 68) was originally set up in the centre of town, for maximum spectator potential. But in the early summer of 1794, with residents by now sick of the stench of blood, it was moved outside the city limits, to the Place de la Trône Renversée (the upturned throne), which is today Place de la Nation.

From June 13 to July 28 that year, real terror reigned, as Robespierre (originally a staunch opponent of the death penalty, it should be noted) went mad, and ordained the execution not only of the aristocracy but of anyone who'd ever had anything to do with it. Over a six-week period, more than 1,300 people, aged from 14 to 90 – including tradesmen, the clergy, doctors, teachers, librarians, wig-makers, Carmelite nuns and even servants – were guillotined.

Their headless corpses were taken by wagon to a confiscated garden off what's now boulevard Picpus, and thrown into open pits, after being stripped of their clothing. With the guillotining of Robespierre himself, on 28 July, however, the reign of terror came to an end, and the open graves were sealed. Two years later the land was bought by the Princesse de Hohenzollern Sigmaringen, whose brother was one of the victims buried there, and she had the property walled up as a private memorial.

A few years later, the influential de Noailles family – who had lost several members to the guillotine's blade – had the same idea, and it was agreed that it should become a permanent holy place. A church was built, and a religious order brought in to offer up continual prayer – and indeed on the day I visited there was a nun in residence, busy praying.

From the early 19th century onwards, relatives of the guillotined could buy a plot in the cemetery, which is why you'll find Lafayette, a hero of the American revolution, buried there – he was married to one of the de Noailles family. The Marquis is actually buried in American soil, as he thoughtfully brought a load of earth over with him when he returned to France a decade before his death – and the American flag still flies over his grave. During the occupation, in World War II, it was the only place in the whole of Paris where the stars and stripes flew continuously, and every fourth of July Americans in Paris are invited to participate in a memorial ceremony at the graveside.

At most times of year the Picpus cemetery is deserted, and an oasis in Paris. In spring, birds trill, butterflies flutter, and a couple of beehives buzz gently. All that's left of the chapel which was here at the eastern end, where the gruesome inventory of clothes and possessions was once performed, is a free-standing stone doorway. Behind a closed gate are the two infamous grave ditches, which were only identified in 1929 – a third ditch was ready and waiting but never used. Beside this is the cemetery where only the descendants of the guillotined (and Lafayette) are buried.

Inside the church is a complete list of the victims, on tablets, and their names, ages and professions bring home to you the awful reality of the terror. Curiously, the plaques at the graves claim 1,306 victims, but there are 1,307 names in the church, a mystery the curator couldn't (or wouldn't) explain to me.

The entrance to the **Picpus cemetery** is at 35 rue de Picpus, even though the actual graveyard itself is much closer to boulevard Picpus, over to the east.

Police

Unlike the so-called Black Museum (actually the Crime Museum), at London's Metropolitan Police Headquarters, the **Musée des Collections Historiques de la Préfecture de Police de Paris** is open to the public. It's situated in the main nick for the 5th arrondissement, and to enter you simply need to cross the courtyard, walk up the steps to the main reception desk (where you'll see lots of ordinary police activity going on), and then head up two floors in the lift (which you'll notice also gives you the alarming option of going down four floors, where presumably they have dungeons).

It's an informative but scary place – the first thing you see when you come in is a rather too well-used firing-squad post, dating from World War II. After that the visit takes a chronological look at French police history, starting with lots of royal death warrants (all signed by a bloke called Roy), and then moving rapidly on to the French revolution.

There's a formidable guillotine blade on display, rust (or is it blood?) stained but still razor-sharp, across from the July 13 1793 police log noting the arrest of Charlotte Corday, after she had assassinated the police administrator Jean-Paul Marat in his bathtub with a kitchen knife. She was guillotined herself four days later.

As you work your way through the 19th century, you come across various waxworks of policemen in uniform (look out for the one with the wicked sideburns, and a couple sporting comic little goatees and handlebar moustaches), and drawings and engravings of various 'infernal machines', as used by terrorists of the era. Nearby is the *Machine de Fieschi*, an extraordinary contraption featuring 25 gun barrels in a line, which left 19 dead on July 28 1835, while across the hall are a series of all-too-graphic models showing just how the guillotine worked, and how the heads and bodies were disposed of (body into a box, head into a basin). There's a nasty model of a *baiser de vierge* (an iron maiden), too, and a collection of real irons for chaining prisoners up.

In a heavy ledger you can see the entries and papers relating to Verlaine and Rimbaud (see page 145 and page 142) in 1873, after the older poet had shot the younger in the wrist, while on the opposite wall are charts showing the evolution of finger-printing and how to distinguish irises (eyes, not flowers) apart. There are also propaganda posters from the 1930s, including one appearing to show an avuncular police officer stealing a gold watch from two small children.

On a more sobering note, there are German weapons from World War II, and a collection of yellow Jewish stars, all personalised. And then there are the instruments of violence and murder, with a huge range of weapons from knuckle dusters to knives to guns to rolling pins. You can even see the train ticket which led to the conviction of Henri Landru, one of France's most infamous mass murderers, who was guillotined in 1922 after having killed nine wealthy women during World War I. Landru's mistake? Repeatedly buying return tickets to his country house for himself, but only singles for his victims…

Finally, you can examine the rope used by Dr Marcel Petiot to drop his murder victims down into his home-installed furnace during World War II. He was only

caught because the smell coming from the chimney was causing a fuss. When police entered the house they found the remains of 27 people, and more than 40 suitcases full of clothes. Petiot confessed to killing as many as 63 victims, in total, claiming they were all Nazi collaborators, but it was widely suspected he'd lured in rich Jewish clients, promising to smuggle them out of France, instead. Petiot was guillotined in 1946.

Sewers

The **Musée des Egouts** (the Sewer Museum) is a great deal less interesting than it used to be. A century ago there were real guided tours through the extraordinary network of tunnels which were built in the 1860s, and even up until the early 1970s you could still take a boat ride underground along the open sewers.

For now, you'll have to content yourself with being able to walk down into the sewers and several hundred metres into the system, where you'll find an interesting exhibition tracing the history of water supply and drainage in Paris since ancient times. The smell isn't anything like as bad as you'd expect. At one point, however, there's a truly revolting lookout, where you can reel at the sight of raw sewage (and the rest) shooting underneath. You're protected from falling in by a gratifyingly sturdy waist-high metal fence.

You'll also be glad to hear that the museum has its own separate toilet facilities.

Spectacles

Pierre Marly obtained his optician's diploma in 1948 and opened up his first shop in Paris in 1951. The following year, he made a big splash by designing radical new specs for Audrey Hepburn, and the Pierre Marly brand hasn't looked back since – they're still the spectacles of choice among plenty of the rich and famous.

Over the decades, Marly collected all sorts of unusual eyewear, and put it on display above the shop, in a semi-formal museum setting known as the **Musée des Lunettes et Lorgnettes Pierre Marly**. You could pop in and goggle at nearly 3,000 sets of specs, monocles, lorgnettes, pince-nez, binoculars, eyeglasses, spyglasses and even contact lenses.

The earliest item dated from the 14th century (and looked pretty painful, as the frame-pieces were nailed together), but most of the collection (like optical history itself) was a great deal more recent. So you could see the glasses which Elton John and Jackie Kennedy made famous (or which made them famous?), along with Sarah Bernhardt's monocle, wooden frames for the Inuit, hilarious frames from the seventies, and specs for pets.

The collection has now been passed on to the town of Morez, in the Jura (which is logical, as it's the eyeglass capital of France), and is due to go back on display during 2003 at the at the **Espace Lamartine**. In the meantime you can still have your glasses made for you at **Pierre Marly**'s shop, in Paris.

Veterinary science

The **Musée Fragonard**, which is part of France's national veterinary school, is one of the weirdest museums I've ever been to. It's also one of France's oldest, having been launched in the year of the school's inauguration outside Paris in 1766 – though only opened to the public in 1991.

Walk up the sweeping staircase and through the grand French doors into the museum itself and it's like stepping back 100 years or more. The museum is a single, vast room, with dusty shelves and glass-fronted cabinets from floor to ceiling, filled with specimen jars large and small, minutely hand-labelled, and containing everything you'd expect from a museum of veterinary anatomy – and quite a few things you wouldn't expect at all.

It's broken down essentially into three sections – animal skeletons and body parts; monsters and deformities; and Fragonard's terrifying *écorchés* (see below).

In the first section there's a wide range of animal skeletons, from a whole elephant, rhino and human being, to the heads of hippo, buffalo and jaguar. Further into the museum there's a whole corral of other skeletons, but before you get there, you can check out the old jars and dried specimens, including a badger's lungs, a dog's tongue, a dromedary's intestines, a horse's stomach, and a seal's liver, dated 1902. There's half a dromedary's liver in a jar (a gift, apparently – 'Why! Just what I wanted! However did you guess?'), a mummified cat, and a mule foetus. So far, so good.

As you move on, however, you'll start seeing the stuff of nightmares, monstrous abnormalities which should never have been born (and often weren't). Animals with no head, or two heads. Single-headed animals with two bodies. Limbs welded together. Brains too big for the skulls to hold them. Organs deformed beyond recognition. Fortunately, before you get as far as Fragonard, there's a cabinet on the left dedicated to 'things found in cows' – scissors, part of a hat, cutlery, a woollen bonnet, stockings, chicken wire, pins and nails, wood, a lizard, a length of rope, that kind of thing – which provides a little levity.

But then you enter real horror-land, the domain of the Fragonard *écorchés*.

Honoré Fragonard was a cousin of the famous painter Jean-Honoré Fragonard, and both were born in 1732, in Grasse (where you'll find the Fragonard perfume empire today). He was an enormously gifted anatomist, and was appointed as the nation's first Professor of Anatomy in 1766, when the veterinary college was opened. Fragonard's specialist subject, however, was the skinning and preserving of specimens, using a technique which has since (mercifully, frankly) been lost to science.

He is thought to have created around 700 *écorchés* (flayings, literally) in total, of which about 20 survive, here at the Musée Fragonard. They fall somewhere deeply unsettling, between extraordinary anatomical science and macabre, gruesome artistry. There's a llama, a goat, an antelope, three monkeys, and the entire nervous system of a horse, strung out from its eyeballs to its tail. There are also two human heads (looking like nothing more than Giacometti's last sculptures of Lotar, see page 104), and three small children, diabolical gnomes staring hideously out at you.

Most strikingly of all, however, there are two dreadful tableaux. In the first, a brutish-looking flayed man is clearly meant to be Samson, as he's wielding an ass's jawbone. While in the second, and most famous *écorché* of all, there's a man riding a horse – both horse and rider are fully flayed – presumably intended to be something out of Albrecht Dürer's Riders of the Apocalypse.

It's not a place to go to alone.

When you're done, it's worth walking down towards the river, where you'll find **La Barcarola**, a cheerful pizzeria which is doing its best to rival the museum's taxidermy department – there's a rampant fox on the dessert cabinet, and another above the bar.

ECCENTRIC PROVINCIAL

Once you're out into the provinces, it's hardly surprising that most of the eccentric collections are held by private individuals. Especially when those collections are things like horse-drawn hearses, for which we have to thank the genius of Yvan Quercy in the Tarn et Garonne, or vast amounts of old machinery, collected over decades of scrap-merchanting by Maurice Dufresne near Tours. You can also visit Max Manent's astonishing collection of the unusual in the Rhône valley, Maurice Renard's weather vanes near Troyes, Alain Bardo's many, many Father Christmases near Grenoble, and at least five different collections of bicycles around the country, from Brittany to Provence.

Bicycles

As a country that's bike mad (see page 5), you'd expect France to have a bicycle museum, and indeed it does – in fact it has several. There's the **Vélo-Parc**, just inland from Lorient, in Brittany; the **Musée du Vélo**, at Cormatin, between Dijon and Lyon; the **Musée du Vélocipède** at Cadouin, in the Dordogne; and the **Musée du Vélo et de la Moto**, in Provence. There's also a bicycle museum attached to the Sewing Machine Museum in Amplepuis, between Lyon and Vichy (see page 212)

The **Vélo-Parc** is more of a holiday centre than a museum, and caters primarily to school groups and the like, but it docs have a fine collection of bikes, and it's one of the few places where you can get to sit on a penny farthing or a hobby horse. There's a rather earnest exhibition area which explores not just the history of the bicycle, but also its sociological and technological impact.

The **Musée du Vélo** on the other hand has a superb collection of bikes and bike trivia spread over two floors of a great big barn of a building. The earliest model is an 1818 Draisienne, a sort of two-wheeled hobby horse, with wooden wheels and primitive steering, but no drive mechanism. You can then follow the history of the bicycle, through the invention of pedals, the increase in size of the front wheel (the penny farthing), and the arrival of chains and gears. There are also some extraordinary turn of the century tricycles, as well as a butcher's bike, a Thai cycle taxi and an ice-cream seller's tricycle. The bikes themselves are complemented by an amazing collection of cycle memorabilia, from commemorative plates and wine labels to stamps, board games, cycle jerseys, lights, bells and whistles. It being France, there's also a shop selling local produce and wine.

The **Musée du Vélocipède** in the Dordogne, for its part, has the most comprehensive collection of cycles I've ever seen. It's the work of Gérard Buisset, who got switched on to historical bikes while working as a window dresser in Paris in the 1960s, when he had to find a dozen models to complete an important commission. He's been hunting old cycles ever since, and now has more than 300 – of which around a quarter are on display at any one time. Here, in the lovely Cistercian Abbey in Cadouin, you can see not just bicycles and tricycles but also totally implausible quatricycles and quinticycles, from 1817 to the present day.

ECCENTRIC COLLECTIONS: PROVINCES

Dunkerque
Calais
LILLE
Valenciennes
Cherbourg
Amiens
Le Havre
Rouen Beauvais
Caen Reims
St Malo Metz
Brest **PARIS** Tiles, Pargny Nancy
(see map 195) sur Saulx Strasbourg
Velocipedes, Troyes Weather Vanes, Creney
Plouay Rennes Witches,
Quimper Le Mans Bergheim
Orléans Mulhouse
Auxerre
N Witches, Concressault
St Nazaire Nantes Tours Dijon
Maurice Dufresne, Bourges
Marnay Velocipedes,
Poitiers Le Bois Dernier
La Rochelle Pipes, St Claude Geneva
KEY Sewing Machines,
Eccentric collection site Clermont Amplepuis
Ferrand Teddy Bears
Angoulême Limoges Hats, Chazelles sur Lyon LYON
Boules, St Bonnet St Etienne Grenoble
le Château
Brive Le Petit Musée du Father Christmas,
0 160km Bordeaux Tobacco, la Gaillard Bizarre, Lavilledieu Lans en Vercours
0 100 miles Bergerac Velocipedes, Insolite, Loriol
Matches, Clairac Cadouin Montélimar
Hearses, Cazes Mondenard Matches, Insects, St Léons Insects, Sérignan
Najac du Comtat
Bayonne Velocipedes, Corkscrews,
Biarritz Tiles, Château de Bosc Ménerbes
Pau Blajan Toulouse Montpellier Arles Insects, Nice
Rizla+, Fuveau Escoffier,
Mazères sur Salat MARSEILLE Villeneuve
Loubet
Crops & Whips, Sorède Toulon
Perpignan

Bradt

The **Musée du Vélo et de la Moto** is the most recent of France's bike museums, opening in 1998, and in its current location, at the Château du Bosc, near Avignon, only since 2001. It's the result of 35 years of work and research by Claude Reynaud, who also makes Côtes du Rhône for a living. He's a truly serious bike nut, having not only pieced together this excellent collection, but also written eight books on the subject. There are 135 machines on display, including some wild motorbikes – notably the 1920 four-cylinder bike designed by Louis Blériot (see page 42) which ran with the clever ad 'it doesn't drive, it flies!', and the 1922 Mégola, which intriguingly had it's five-cylinder engine built into the spokes of the front wheel.

Petit Musée du Bizarre

Tucked away in the hills of the Ardèche is the hamlet of Bayssac, and it's here that Serge Tekielski, better known as Candide, created his **Petit Musée du Bizarre**, in the early 1970s. Spread through the ground floor and cellars of his fine house, the museum was dedicated to the works of the self-taught, and focused in particular on sculpture in the rural tradition.

Many of the more than 200 works are tributes to the ingenuity of shepherds, woodcutters, cowherds and *paysans* over the ages, with pipe-bowls, olive branches, vine roots and soft stone carved into marvellous forms. There's an extraordinary pair of wooden clogs in the shape of naked feet (positively surreal – they wouldn't look out of place in a Magritte painting), a delicately engraved bed made of walnut wood to celebrate the birth of a son in 1904, and a wooden watch-fob which tells the story of Joan of Arc.

Tekielski also collected and held temporary exhibitions of naïve art, which fitted in well with the theme of the museum. Sadly, however, he died in the summer of 2002, and at the time of writing the fate of the museum itself was still uncertain. Call his widow for the latest update.

Cigarette papers

Cigarette papers – which effectively means Rizla+, since it has a 75% market share of the three billion papers sold annually – have nothing whatsoever to do with hashish, marijuana, weed, dope or draw (call it what you will). Nothing at all. And nor is the continued decline in the use of rolling tobacco, and the concomitant rise in Rizla+ sales, any indication to the contrary, either.

Not, anyway, according to (Rizla+ owner) Imperial Tobacco's ever-friendly press office, who insist that almost all their cigarette papers are used for making hand-rolled cigarettes. That's true, the company says, even for the extra-large sizes, claiming they're popular with truck drivers – though in all my years of loitering around service stations and transport caffs across Europe, I've yet to see any truck driver toking away on anything which could remotely be confused with a large spliff.

Anyway, never mind all that – it looks as if cigarette papers are here to stay. But few people realise how long they've already been with us. They were actually invented in France as soon as tobacco itself arrived in Europe, in the early 16th century, by Christian Lacroix, the first of seven generations of paper men. But it wasn't until the introduction of Indian rice paper, in 1865, that the business really took off, and in 1867 the Rizla+ trademark was born ('Riz' plus 'La' plus a cross). In 1874, Léonide Lacroix built a paper-making factory at Mazères sur Salat, in the foothills of the Pyrenees, which continued to be one of the world's main sources of cigarette papers (and the small town's principal employer), until it was closed down by Imperial Tobacco in the spring of 2002.

Fortunately, Imperial Tobacco didn't nobble the **Musée Rizla+** in Mazères, which is really well worth visiting, even though the factory is now closed. You can find out everything there is to know about the making and selling of cigarette papers, straight from the horse's mouth. There's a reconstruction of Léonide Lacroix's office, a demonstration of the production line, and a great series of old posters advertising the Rizla+ (cigarette-rolling) experience.

For more on the Rizla+ lifestyle (as promulgated by Imperial Tobacco), go to www.rizla.com – as long as you're over 18, of course.

Corkscrews

At the bottom of Ménerbes, the village in the Luberon made famous by Peter Mayle's *A Year in Provence*, you'll find the **Musée du Tire-Bouchon**, with over 1,000 different types of corkscrew. There's every variation imaginable, from the end of the 17th century, when the corkscrew was invented, to the latest in 21st-century technology. There are gold and silver models, porcelain, ivory and wooden handles, and any number of different cork-drawing mechanisms on display. Most fit into the decorative rather than functional category, as you'd expect.

The museum was opened by Yves Rousset-Rouard in 1993. According to local lore, he needed something to keep him gainfully employed while waiting for his replanted vines to mature sufficiently to make decent wine. Whatever the truth, the museum makes for an interesting diversion, and the bottles of Côtes de Luberon on sale are perfectly palatable.

The question you leave with, of course, is why did it take so long to invent the corkscrew, given that wine's been around for at least 2,000 years? The answer's simple: until recently, wine wasn't stored much at all, as narrow-necked bottles couldn't be produced in the quantities necessary, and a narrow neck is essential to creating an air-tight seal.

So wine was kept in amphorae, and later in barrels and jars, and drunk as soon as it was ready. It was only improved glass-production techniques which brought bottles into common circulation in the 17th century, and therefore called for an easy way of pulling out a firmly pushed-in stopper.

Crops and whips

There's nothing like the call for riding crops and whips as there used to be (with the possible exception of the apparently burgeoning fringes of the sex industry), but there's still a place where you can see them being made, at **Sorède**, just inland from Argelès sur Mer, in the foothills of the eastern Pyrenees, right on the Spanish border.

The village depended for centuries on the propitious conditions here for growing hackberry trees (*Micocoulier* in French), which make the best crops, whips and indeed pitchforks. Around a hundred years ago, when horses were still the main form of transport, the industry in this valley alone supported dozens of workshops and small factories, and close to 600 people.

By 1981, however, there was only one establishment left, and it was on its knees. It was fortunately taken over at that point by a rehabilitation centre and whipped into shape. Today, it employs some 60 people, working the old-fashioned way, and turning out everything from the simplest pitchfork to the most extravagant circus whips used in dressage. You can go and visit, and find out just how a simple bit of tree ends up as an Hermès riding crop.

Maurice Dufresne

Maurice Dufresne has been interested in machines and machinery all his life. Born in 1930, he trained as a blacksmith from the age of 14, and worked for 20 different employers before founding his own scrap and salvage business in his late twenties. The business, at Villeperdue, 20km or so south of Tours, is still going strong today, and for more than forty years has been the main provider of materials to the extraordinary **Musée Maurice Dufresne**, at Marnay, near Azay le Rideau, on the Indre river.

The museum was opened in 1992, and features an incredible collection of more than 3,000 objects, the vast majority of which have been salvaged and restored by Dufresne himself. There are three themes across the 40 rooms: vehicles, machinery, and weapons. In the first category there's a vast collection including cars, motorbikes, trucks, fire engines, tractors, traction engines, steam engines, carts, a Russian sledge, a road roller, a penny farthing, a hearse, a Blériot monoplane, a glider, and a Peugeot electric car dating from 1941.

As far as machinery is concerned, it's mostly old agricultural machines, but there's also an impressive turbine, a fine linotype machine, and an original mobile guillotine, used in the region during the terror of 1794. Next door, a unique and macabre collection of 18 wax heads dating back to 1924 keeps up the lively atmosphere.

Finally, there are three rooms of weapons, starting with a full 15th-century samurai uniform and moving through a big collection of swords and sabres, to pistols and rifles – including some 350 of them artistically displayed around the walls.

With the scrap business just down the road, and Dufresne as energetic as ever, the collection just keeps on growing, and attracts more than 50,000 visitors a year. If you visit the scrap business itself, at Villeperdue, 25km east of Marnay, you never know what you'll find on offer.

Escoffier

Long, long before Nigella Lawson and Jamie Oliver, celebrity chef-dom was invented single-handedly by Auguste Escoffier, in the 1880s. Born into a poor family in 1846, Escoffier started work at the age of 13 at his uncle's restaurant in Nice, and cooked his way up over a period of over 20 years into the finest kitchens in Europe. He was instrumental in the 1880s and 1890s in revolutionising the sumptuous menus at the Grand Hotels in Monte Carlo and Rome, the Ritz in Paris, and the Savoy and the Carlton in London.

Escoffier became a living legend. Hugely popular and admired, he was the first chef to branch out into his own line of products, and he wrote best-selling books which are still in use today amongst professionals. His endless list of recipes included such favourites as *Pêche Melba*, which Escoffier created in 1892 at the Savoy, to celebrate a triumphant performance of *Lohengrin* in Covent Garden by the Australian opera singer Dame Nellie Melba.

Escoffier had a long and fruitful partnership with the Swiss businessman César Ritz, opening up the eponymous Ritz hotel in Paris in 1898, and the Carlton in London the following year – where Escoffier stayed until his retirement in 1920, at the age of 74. He lived his last years in Monaco, and died there in 1935, succeeding his wife by just two weeks. To his dying day he believed that good cooking was the one true path to human happiness – and who would I be to gainsay such an authoritative source?

The house he was born in, in the hilltop village of Villeneuve Loubet, is now the **Escoffier Foundation**, and contains an abundance of cooking memorabilia, along with photographs and letters, and a whole roomful of extravagant menus on the top floor. There's an exhibition space showing the simplicity of Provençal living a century and a half ago, in sharp contrast with the luxuriousness of life in the grand hotels and on the majestic ocean liners, where you could expect to be served up a tiger made with rice, a railway train made of sugar, or a dish of peaches in an ice-carved swan. Depending, of course, in which class you happened to be travelling.

Father Christmas

Up in the hills above Grenoble, just as you come to the village of Lans en Vercours, there's a most unusual private museum. There's the **Magie des Automates** itself (which happens to be the best collection of mechanical puppets I've ever seen), and the garden area behind it (where you'll find little chalets with animated teddy bears demonstrating local arts and crafts) – a veritable teddy bears' picnic. Here, in a series of little mountain chalets, regional arts and crafts are performed by these animated teddies, so you'll see cheese being matured, walnuts being collected, mushrooms being gathered, and wine being made. There's even a chalet where you can see *fart* being applied to skis in a process known in French as *fartage* (I'm not making this up – *fart* is the French for ski-wax, and *fartage* is the French for ski-waxing.)

But the exhibition at the museum's heart is the **Hameau de Père Noël**. It's the creation of Alain Bardo, who was born in Marseille in 1946, studied art, and then took up a career as a window dresser. After a decade in the business, he started specialising in mechanical puppets, which he then rented out for seasonal window displays. With the *automates* staying at home for most of the year, Bardo decided to open up a museum in 1982 on the premises, but it soon became far too small for the number of visitors and puppets alike – and more importantly, there was nowhere to display his increasingly large Father Christmas collection.

At the beginning of the 1990s, therefore, Bardo moved to the current establishment, and was finally able to house his Father Christmases in the style they deserve. Today, there are more than 1,500 Father Christmas-related artefacts on display, and the effect is overwhelming. The earliest, a three-foot tall Father Christmas on a trolley, pushing himself along with ski sticks, dates from around 1910, while the latest is always as new as the current year.

There are Father Christmas scissors, toothbrushes, pencils, pens, mugs, tins, soft drink cans, glass bottles, books, toys, lapel pins, watches, candles, sweets, dinky cars, boxes, posters and chocolates – and figurines beyond number. You'll find Father Christmas stained glass, Father Christmas mobiles, a Father Christmas sewing machine, a Father Christmas slot ball game (all the way from Australia), lead-metal Father Christmas figures from America, rice-paper Father Christmases from the Philippines, and a Father Christmas Camembert box (a gift from the Camembert Museum in Vimoutiers, see page 181). There's an elves' workshop, sleighs, cotton-wool snow, and even a letter box for posting off your Christmas wish list.

The jewel in the crown is an unnervingly life-like (and life-sized) animated Father Christmas sitting in a chair, who will explain the story to you if you're patient.

The Hameau de Père Noël is deep within the Magie des Automates, where you can see over 300 mechanical puppets in action, in a variety of creative tableaux. In the circus scene there's a pink panther being trained, while in the skating rink you can't help feeling sorry for the girl who's fallen off the ice. Alligators in sombreros strum guitars, drunks reel around lampposts, medieval characters serenade, elves frolic and an orchestra from the Tyrol does its stuff.

Hats

'If you want to get ahead, get a hat,' runs the old slogan, although these days hat manufacture is but a shadow of its former self. And it's obvious why. Look at any picture from the early 20th century and you'll see few hatless people in the crowd; look around today, and hats are distinctly rare (Ascot and American baseball caps notwithstanding). It's a shame.

France's millinery capital was the town of Chazelles sur Lyon, north of Saint Etienne, which had nearly 30 hat factories employing over 2,500 hatters as recently as the 1930s. Today, there's just one factory left, and it's the last in France to make genuine felt hats (from felt made with the hair of rabbits and hares).

One of the disused hat factories in Chazelles, however, was enterprisingly turned into the **Musée du Chapeau** in 1983, with the aim not just of preserving hatting history, but also of making people more hat-conscious. The museum covers the whole gamut of hats in fashion, trade and politics, and has an excellent collection of unusual headgear from the 18th century onwards, with bishops' mitres, chefs' toques, military headwear, police képis and outrageous fashions all on display. You can see the hats of the famous, too, from Cousteau's cap to Mitterand's trilby to Grace Kelly's gorgeous haute couture models.

There are also comprehensive displays about the industry, and the manufacturing process which turns rabbit fur into high fashion, with reconstructed workshops and millinery machinery. There's even a jukebox full of – you guessed it – hot hat hits.

Hearses

Up above the village of Cazes Mondenard, deep in the Tarn et Garonne, lives a man called Yvan Quercy, and his speciality is collecting ... horse-drawn hearses. I rang him up one summer's day to ask if I could visit his museum, and his response was typical. 'Museum? I have more than one museum. I have four! See you on Tuesday! Eat with us!' And indeed, it's true. As well as the hearses (at the **Musée du Corbillard**), there's a separate museum of other horse-drawn vehicles, a museum of old tractors, threshers and other farm machinery, and a museum of old farm implements. Fortunately Quercy has plenty of warehousing space.

Quercy cuts a splendid figure, from his broad-brimmed black hat, to his extravagant jet-black handlebar moustache, to his taste in flamboyant neckwear (he was sporting a spotless white shirt and a bootlace tie on the day we visited), resembling nothing more than an actor-manager of the 1870s, complete with the appropriately rich voice.

Seventy now, Quercy started his career as a wine merchant in Bordeaux, before moving on to become a casino manager. Serving up to a thousand meals a day eventually lost its appeal, however, so Quercy sold up, bought his estate in the country, and turned to making wine and local produce. Meanwhile he also took up collecting. Twenty years later he had more than enough to open a museum, and he now passes his time in giving wonderful conducted tours.

Starting at the bottom of the expansive property, the first thing you come to is a shed full of horse-drawn vehicles of all descriptions, from gigs, dog carts, phaetons, coaches and charabancs, to a *vigneron's* dray, and a fire wagon. There are two old cars, looking somewhat out of place, but it turns out they're cinema props.

Moving on, there's an enormous collection of rustic farm implements, in various states of restoration, including a nasty hook which you can use to remove a pig's toenails (if that's your thing). There are some true oddities, too, like the *moine* used for heating the elders' beds in a monastery (see page 197), and lots of old radio sets.

Next up is a barn full of hearses and wagons awaiting restoration, but across the yard is the real prize, a shed full of horse-drawn hearses which have already been done up. A red carpet leads between the black hearses, embellished with formal designs and often capped with black material and heavy velvet. At the end of the room is a pulpit, from which Quercy delivers a theatrical address if there's a sufficient crowd, and there are two wax acolytes in the absence of ordinary small boys.

Altogether, Quercy now has more than 110 hearses, with another 20 or so awaiting collection around the country. But that's not all. Back up at the *auberge*, there's a collection of old threshers, other farm machinery, and tractors, some dating back to pre-World War I. There's a Massey Harris and even a Porsche ('my other tractor's a Porsche'), along with an ancient caterpillar-tracked engine.

Back indoors, you'll have worked up a decent appetite, and that's what you'll need if you're eating *chez Quercy*. His wife, Mary-France, served up a remarkable lunch consisting of heavy home-baked bread, and home-made *foie gras*, *saucisson sec*, *magret de canard* (smoked duck breast) and black pudding, washed down with the local Vin de Pays de Sardes, a hearty red wine.

And that, I kid you not, was just the starter. We went on to a sumptuous plate of *écrevisses* (freshwater crayfish) on a bed of salad, followed by *confit de canard* (fatty duck cooked in duck fat) with shredded and pounded garlic in olive oil, a plate of cheeses, and a *croustillon au miel* (honey tart). I very nearly had to give in to the temptation of trying out the dining room's most unusual feature, a rather homely looking period double bed by the fireplace.

Insects

After the 1996 film *Microcosmos* came out, detailing the amazing world of insects, French people went entomology-mad, and there's now a superb centre at Saint Léons, deep in the heart of the Aveyron, northwest of Millau, called **Micropolis, la Cité des Insectes**. The choice of Saint Léons is no accident, as it's the birthplace of the famous 19th-century entomologist Jean-Henri Fabre. At Micropolis, there are a dozen different themes spread out over a large site, which encourage you to see life from the insect's point of view, and it's a crazy multimedia experience – but also a truly enlightening one.

Fabre crops up a second time at Sérignan du Comtat, just outside Orange, where you'll find **l'Harmas de JH Fabre**, the house he lived in for the last 36 years of his life. It's now a museum, centred on Fabre's laboratory, which has been maintained exactly as it was when he died in 1915. More than 60 years' worth of the great entomologist's work is on display, along with his collections of fossils, minerals and seashells, and a good number of his watercolours.

An hour or so southeast from Sérignan brings you to yet another entomological collection, this time at Fuveau, 10km southeast of Aix en Provence. Here, at the **Mas des Papillons**, you'll find the thousands of butterflies and beetles which the owner, Daniel Dubois, has collected from the four corners of the globe. It's a colourful presentation, by a colourful character, and not to be missed.

Insolite

Naming your collection the **Musée de l'Insolite** (Museum of the Unusual) could be called arrogant – but that's not the case in the small town of Loriol, where Max Manent's museum is unusual beyond your wildest imaginings.

Manent was born in 1925 in Montélimar and studied at the Beaux Arts in Lyon. As a young artist with independent means, he was free to experiment in many directions, and so he did, painting and sculpting, but also travelling widely and collecting unusual objects wherever he went.

His paintings are divided broadly into three periods, green (up to 1949), blue (up to 1960) and brown (since 1960), but Manent has also tried new techniques, such as oil on glass. The widest range of his own paintings in the museum is from the highly original brown period (though some of the models could be considered overly made-up – as if they've been down a kohl-mine, in fact), and Manent has exhibited widely, winning prizes around Europe for his work.

These days, however, in his late seventies, Manent mostly looks after his museum, which is housed in the vast building he acquired here in 1979. Although there are some 26 rooms, 31 doors and 48 windows, 'only' 11 rooms are given over to the museum itself, where you can see the estimated 35,000 objects Manent has collected over the years. The tour (you need to allow a good two hours) is given by Manent himself, and laced with extraordinary anecdotes. It starts with a room full of clippings about the artist, and moves quickly on to a selection of medals, and letters to Manent from various French presidents, Grace Kelly, and the Pope.

Under the stairs there's a life-size religious crèche, sculpted by Manent, which is unique in featuring the birth, crucifixion and resurrection of Christ. You then head upstairs, under some unusual Manent gargoyles, past a collection of brass and copper bed-warmers, to a bare room wall-papered in old film posters. In the same room there are cameras and projectors, thousands of old postcards and photos, and some prosthetic limbs from World War I. Next door, in the African room, is a huge array of old masks, hides, trophies, weapons, butterflies and postcards of African natives.

Across the hallway you'll find moustache-irons, ear-trumpets, rare musical instruments, képis, typewriters, china (including a teacup with a protective flap for keeping your moustache dry), and a guillotine blade. Next door again, there's a collection of 15,000 cigar bands (including ones with Adolf Hitler and Joseph Stalin on them) and around 200 old pipes. Rare furniture includes a smoking chair (with an ashtray under one arm, and a space for your kit under the other) and a Louis XIII musical chair – when you sit on it, the music starts to play from the music box inside.

The tour leads from here (for adults only) into the erotica and pornography room, where more than 2,000 dirty pictures (depicting every vice known to man and some which were brand new to me) compete for space with 80-odd gynaecological instruments, a collection of chastity belts and ancient sex toys, and a smattering of bidets, including a rare double bidet (the only one in France). There's a Bible inside the commode, if you're feeling faint at this point, and a decorated wax shop-window model from 1900 or so, dubbed the 'Venus de Manent' to top things off.

A short walk along the corridor brings you to the last room upstairs, which is Manent's funeral parlour. Decorated with all kinds of frescos and religious icons (there are five Joan of Arcs), the main feature of the room is Manent's own coffin, ready to receive him. Lying atop it is a sculpted nude, while kneeling behind is a female bewigged death figure, with a scythe in one hand and a cigarette-holder in the other. It's more than a little spooky.

So it's good to end the tour in the humour room, downstairs – although you'll need seriously good French to understand most of the puns, which are the essence of the artworks on display here.

Matches

Give a chap – and it always *is* a chap – a lot of time and a lot of matches, and you'll be amazed at what he comes up with.

At the ancient abbey in Clairac, in the southwest of France, there's a famous bevy of around 100 mechanical puppet monks to guide you around, but upstairs there's an amazing collection of edifices built in matches, dubbed the **Forêt des Allumettes**. They're the works of the enigmatic Monsieur Blanc, who spent the last years of his life (he died in 1998) building scale reproductions of famous buildings, with an incredible eye for accuracy.

There's the Mont Saint Michel (at a scale of 1/400th, using 66,800 matches and taking 1,200 hours to build), Chartres cathedral (1/125th, 65,000 matches, 1,300 hours), the Sacré Coeur (1/250th, 83,000 matches, 1,200 hours), and the Eiffel Tower (1/450th, 3,370 matches, 230 hours) along with many more, including several of the châteaux in the Loire valley, the Pont du Gard, and more cathedrals than you could shake a (match)stick at.

At Najac, also in the southwest of France, you'll find the **Musée de l'Art de l'Allumette**, which is more transport-based, and is the work of several authors rather than just one. There are battleships, steam trains, cars and motorbikes – including a quarter-size Harley-Davidson which is simply breathtaking. Don't ask why, just admire. Najac is also well worth visiting in its own right, as it has a stunningly situated medieval castle dating from the mid-13th century.

Pétanques and boules

The **Musée International de Pétanque et Boules** is situated in Saint Bonnet le Château, 30km west of Saint Etienne, which calls itself the *Capitale Mondiale de la Boule* with some justification – more than 70% of the boules sold worldwide are made here. Not only that, it was in Saint Bonnet that the game was revolutionised by the invention of the steel boule in 1928 by a young locksmith called Jean Blanc – and Jean Blanc boules (better known as JB) are still in use today.

Variants on the game of boules date back a good 10,000 years, and it was popular in France from the middle ages onwards, with wooden balls being used. These wore out quickly, however, so people took to studding the balls with nails. It wasn't until the mid-19th century, though, when factory-made nails first appeared, that boules started to become standardised.

Nail-studded wooden balls were largely abandoned following the invention of cast bronze boules in 1923 by Vincent Mille and Paul Courtieu in Lyon, though they themselves were soon supplanted forever by Jean Blanc's balls of steel. Since 1930, the vast majority of boules worldwide have been made of two steel hemispheres welded together, and most of them are now made by Obut (web: www.obut.com), in Saint Bonnet, which churns out more than four million boules a year.

The boules museum has a great collection of boules ancient and modern, lets you in on the secrets of the manufacturing process, and shows the different versions of the game which are played around the world. There are wooden boules, nail-studded boules, and even the latest carbon-fibre boules, and plenty of different jacks (*cochonnets*), which are the small wooden balls thrown out as the target for all the rest. Naturally, there's also a handful of 'Fannys' on display.

Throughout southern France, in particular, there's a tradition that if you score no points at all (ie: you lose 13–0), you have to kiss the 'Fanny'. How this tradition started is a mystery, and many versions of the story exist. The most endearing (and therefore the most improbable), however, is that a Savoyard waitress (called Fanny) used to let the losers kiss her on the cheeks – but when the local mayor was the loser she stood on a chair and lifted up her skirt, making him kiss the cheeks of her buttocks instead.

These days, what with the nationwide shortage of willing Savoyard waitresses and all, the Fanny you'll find at most boulodromes is a pair of more or less lifelike sculpted or painted buttocks. (If you simply must own a Fanny of your own you can buy a 28cm model for a mere €19 at web: www.laboulebleue.fr/en/Catalogue/Boutique.htm. La Boule Bleu, based in Marseille, also sells a full range of absolutely first-rate boules for the serious player.)

Pipes

Saint Claude, in the Jura, is the world capital of briar pipe-making and the French capital of diamond cutting, so it's no surprise to find the **Musée de la Pipe et du Diamant** there. Pipes have been made in Saint Claude since the beginning of the 17th century, but it was the fortuitous discovery of briar (some say from Corsica; some say from North Africa) in the middle of the 19th century by a Saint Claude pipe-maker which saw the industry really take off, and Saint Claude corner the briar industry in the process (put that in your pipe and smoke it).

Pipe-making still provides direct employment for around 200 people in Saint Claude, and there's even a brotherhood, called the *Confrérie des Maîtres Pipiers*, which elects an annual *Premier Fumeur de France*, who wins a briar pipe sculpted in his own image by the master pipe carver Paul Lanier.

The museum, across the street from Saint Claude's fortified cathedral, gives you the full history of pipe-making, and shows the whole process from briar root to finished product. There's a big range of pipes on display, including some of Paul Lanier's more exotic creations (you can actually order pretty much anything you want in the form of a pipe-bowl from Lanier). Look out for horses, elephants (you smoke through the trunk), lions, monkeys, dogs (including one with a duck in its mouth), and Aesop's fables (the fox and the crow, the hare and the tortoise, etc).

There's also an exhibition of the English Crown Jewels (and you thought they were in the Tower of London), along with diamonds, precious and semi-precious stones, and even synthetic gems, along with the tools and machines used in gem-cutting.

(It's worth noting that *la pipe* is also unfortunately French slang for fellatio, particularly among the gay community, so expect a certain amount of sniggering around the entrance to the museum – and be careful which of your French friends you send the souvenir Musée de la Pipe postcards to.)

Sewing machines

Think 'sewing machines' and the chances are you'll think 'Singer sewing machines' (or if you know your industrial history, then Walter Hunt and/or Elias Howe sewing machines) but the first practical sewing machine was actually invented in France, 20 years before Singer sang, so to speak.

The inventor was Barthélémy Thimonnier, from the town of Amplepuis, halfway between Lyon and Vichy. As an apprentice tailor he was interested in being able to work more quickly, and in 1829 he produced a machine called the *couseuse* which could sew chain-stitch six times faster than the best seamstress. He patented it in 1830, and started up the first sweatshop, in Paris, with 80 machines in operation – only to see the factory attacked and the machines destroyed by a mob of incensed tailors in January 1831. He was lucky to escape with his life.

Thimonnier retired hurt to Amplepuis, but continued refining the *couseuse*, patenting a backstitch machine in 1832 – only to see Walter Hunt reinvent his work in 1834, producing the first American sewing machine. Hunt (later the inventor of the safety-pin, in 1849) abandoned the machine, however, and never filed a patent, as he believed it would lead to massive unemployment. The shuttle was taken up instead by Elias Howe, who filed the first US patent in 1846.

Four years later, Howe was somewhat stitched up by Isaac Merritt Singer, who not only designed and perfected a practical sewing machine based on Howe's work, but made millions out of it. Howe later received compensation and royalties from Singer, but it all came rather too late, as he was to expire in 1867, at the age of only 48. Thimonnier, for his part, had eked out the rest of his life in disillusioned poverty, only receiving recognition for his achievement long after his death in 1857.

The **Musée de la Machine à Coudre** in Amplepuis has a collection of close to 150 rare sewing machines from 1830 onwards, as well as several tableaux including a scene of Thimonnier at work and another of a typical fashion workshop of the 1920s. There's also a rather good (if unlikely) collection of old velocipedes, including one of (five times winner of the Tour de France) Bernard Hinault's, along with evocative early cycling-related posters. Quite why there's also a collection of old irons, and another of butterflies, isn't explained.

Spectacles

For more information on the former **Musée des Lunettes et Lorgnettes Pierre Marly**, and its more than 3,000 sets of wacky and interesting spectacles, monocles, lorgnettes, eyeglasses, binoculars and spyglasses, which should be opening up in Morez in the Jura in 2003, see page 200.

Teddy bears

There's a fine teddy bear museum (**Musée de l'Ours en Peluche**) right in the heart of the old town in Lyon, but sadly it's currently closed, and at the time of writing nobody was giving anything away about when (or even if) it was due to reopen.

Which is a pity, as when I last went, there were more than 5,000 teddy bears to be seen – making the visit no picnic, believe me. Apart from the rare and old bears on display, dozens of teddies had been dressed up as craftspeople and workers in amusing tableaux, and there was also a teddy mountain, with uncountable quantities of the little lovelies stacked up.

In the absence of a real museum, check out France's premier teddy bear site online, at www.oursement-votre.com.

Tiles

There's a whole lot of tiling going on, so it's only natural to have a couple of tile museums, one on the eastern border of the Champagne region, in Pargny sur Saulx, and the other way down at the other end of the country, between Pau and Toulouse, at Blajan.

Pargny sur Saulx, near Bar le Duc, is the world clay tile capital (exporting as far away as Singapore), so it's naturally proud of its **Musée de la Tuile**, where you can see not only all manner of tiles of various shapes, forms and sizes, but also find out how clay tiles are actually made – along with all the bits and pieces which make a roof entirely weatherproof.

Blajan, down near the Pyrenees, is also a tile-making centre, mainly for the distinctive roman tiles which grace roofs all across southern France. The **Musée de la Tuile** here is mainly dedicated to showing you through the whole tile-making process, from moulding through to baking – though there are some unusual 18th-century frescos on the walls which you shouldn't miss.

Tobacco

France produces a sizeable quantity of tobacco (7,000 farmers still grow it, generating some 26,000 tonnes a year), the vast majority of which inevitably goes up in smoke. So if you want to know everything there is to know about pipe tobacco, rolling tobacco, chewing tobacco and snuff, not to mention the difference between Gauloises and Gitanes, then go no further than France's national tobacco museum (**Musée d'Intérêt National du Tabac**) in Bergerac, on the northern edge of big tobacco-growing country.

The museum, situated in a fine 17th-century *hôtel particulier* on the amusingly named Place du Feu (*'Vous avez du feu?'* is French for 'have you got a light?') was established in 1950 and underwent a complete overhaul in 1982. It focuses on the history – and particularly cultural history – of tobacco, and is spread over four rooms.

In the first you can find out about the history of pre-Colombian tobacco and its importance in Amerindian societies, as well as its spread to Africa at the end of the 16th century, via the slave trade.

In the next room, there's a detailed explanation of tobacco's first cultivation in Europe (from 1560, at Clairac, in fact, where you can also find fabulous matchstick constructions, see page 210), and its use first as a medicinal product (right up there with arsenic and leeches in the health-giving department) before catching on as a social habit – especially in the form of snuff.

The third and fourth rooms specialise on the explosion of tobacco use in the 19th century, and all the accoutrements that go with it, from snuff boxes and cigarette holders to cigar cases, tobacco pouches and ashtrays. There's a surprising dearth of government health warnings.

Weather vanes

Weather vanes have existed since antiquity, with the earliest one recorded being manufactured in 48BC and placed on top of the Tower of the Winds in Athens. As indicators of wind direction, they've always been placed as high as possible, so it's only natural that vanes would adorn churches. Since the 10th century, however, apparently because of a papal bull saying so, church vanes have invariably been in the shape of a cockerel. This ostensibly refers to Saint Peter denying Jesus three times before the cock crowed – but handily taps into the important role of cockerels in a whole range of ancient superstitions.

(The oldest reference in France to a weather cock is actually to one in England. It's in the 11th-century Bayeux Tapestry, where you can see a bloke up on the roof of Westminster Cathedral installing a weather vane, while on the right of the same scene the dead King Edward is being carried in on his bier.)

During the 18th and 19th centuries, weather vanes began to appear on public buildings and ordinary houses, and this marked the departure from the traditional cockerel, with pennants being used at first and later more creative scenes appearing. Today, they're increasingly popular, and there's even a small museum, just outside Troyes.

The **Musée des Girouettes** is the creation of Maurice Renard and his son Olivier. The family has been repairing church roofs and restoring weather vanes from father to son since 1885, and the collection comprises rare weather cocks from 1650 onwards, and all manner of weather vanes ancient and modern. Every vane which comes out of the workshop, which you can also visit, is hand-made to order, and the establishment turns out more than a hundred of the copper beauties every year. And let's face it: there's nothing quite like a vane for your vanity.

Witchcraft

There are two museums in France dedicated to witchcraft, with very different focuses – the **Musée de la Sorcellerie**, in Concressault, in the heart of the Berry, north of Bourges, which plays very much to the double-double-toil-and-trouble crowd, and the **Maison de la Sorcière**, in Bergheim, on the German border, which details the history of the 40 women burned at the stake here as witches in the 16th and 17th centuries.

The **Musée de la Sorcellerie** has everything you could hope for in the line of cauldrons, broomsticks, potions, powders, cobwebs, mannequins etc, and general satanic nastiness done in a tongue-in-cheek fashion. Dig a little deeper, however, and you'll find out a lot about the historical and legendary witches in the region, which is particularly witch, err rich, in local lore. When you've had your fill, don't miss the unique opportunity of having yourself photographed as a witch on a broomstick.

Altogether more serious is the **Maison de la Sorcière** at Bergheim. Employing the striking use of life-sized portraits of today's Bergheim women as you enter, the museum details the fate of some 40 local women who were burned at the stake as witches between 1582 and 1683. The museum, housed in a former school building dating back to 1550, has the original trial documents (in old German, as this was part of the Habsburg empire at the time) detailing the individual cases, and showing that clemency in those days simply meant being beheaded before you were burned. It's a pretty sobering place.

TRAVEL INFORMATION

La Barcarola 5 avenue Général de Gaulle, Maisons Alfort; tel: 01 43 76 71 00; M̲ Maisons Alfort.

Escoffier Foundation (also known as the Musée de l'Art Culinaire) Villeneuve Loubet, 10km west of Nice; tel: 04 93 20 80 51; web: www.fondation-escoffier.org; open Tue–Sun afternoons, closed Nov; €4.

Espace Lamartine Morez; tel 03 84 33 39 30; web: www.lunetiers-du-jura.com.

Forêt des Allumettes (part of the **Abbaye des Automates**) Clairac Abbey, on the river Lot, about half way between Marmande and Agen; tel: 05 53 79 34 81; open daily Apr–Oct, Wed and weekends Nov–Mar; €10.

L'Harmas de JH Fabre Sérignan du Comtat, 7km north of Orange; tel: 04 90 70 00 44; usually open daily except Tue, but call ahead to check; €4.

Hameau du Père Noël (part of the **Magie des Automates**), Lans en Vercours, about 15km southwest of Grenoble; tel: 04 76 95 40 14; web: www.magiedesautomates.com; open daily, closed Oct (and absolutely best, of course, around Christmas); ∈ 6.

Maison de la Sorcière Bergheim, 20km north of Colmar; tel: 03 89 73 63 01; open Wed–Sun afternoons Jul–Aug, Wed and Sun afternoons only May, Jun, Sep, Oct.

Mas des Papillons (sometimes known as the Musée des Insectes) about two kilometres east of Fuveau, on the small road leading to Les Michels (Fuveau itself is 10km southeast of Aix en Provence); tel: 04 42 68 15 88; closed Tue; ∈ 3.

Micropolis, la Cité des Insectes Saint Léons, 20km northwest of Millau; tel: 05 65 58 50 50; web: www.micropolis-cite-des-insectes.tm.fr; open Mar–Nov, Tue–Sat; ∈ 10.

Musée de l'Art de l'Allumette Najac, about 50km north of Albi; tel: 05 65 29 75 29; open daily Apr–Sep, by appointment Oct–Mar; ∈ 4.

Musée du Chapeau Chazelles sur Lyon, north of Saint Etienne; tel: 04 77 94 23 29; web: www.museeduchapeau.com; open Wed–Mon afternoons; ∈ 4.

Musée des Collections Historiques de la Préfecture de Police de Paris (Police Museum); 1 bis, rue des Carmes, 75005, Paris; tel: 01 44 41 52 50; M̄ Maubert-Mutualité; open Mon–Sat; free.

Musée de la Contrefaçon 16 rue de la Faisanderie, 75016, Paris; tel: 01 56 26 14 00; M̄ Porte Dauphiné; open Tue–Sun afternoons, closed weekends in Aug; ∈ 2.50.

Musée du Corbillard (and three other museums) Minguet, on the hill rising to the east of Cazes Mondenard, itself about 20km west of the main road running from Cahors to Montauban (follow hand-painted signs out of the village); tel 05 63 95 84 02; call ahead to reserve your visit and a table for lunch; ∈ 30 covers guided tour plus the full blow-out.

Musée des Egouts (Sewer Museum) opposite #93 on the Quai d'Orsay, 75007, Paris; tel: 01 47 05 10 29; M̄ Pont d'Alma (RER C), Alma Marceau; open daily; ∈ 3.

Musée de l'Erotisme 72 boulevard de Clichy, 75009, Paris; tel: 01 42 58 28 73; M̄ Blanche; open daily 10am–2am; ∈ 7.

Musée Fragonard Ecole Nationale Vétérinaire d'Alfort, Maisons Alfort, southeast of Paris; tel: 01 43 96 71 72; M̄ Maisons Alfort; odd opening hours, so call ahead – in theory open most weekends and some weekday afternoons; ∈ 3.

Musée des Girouettes Creney, on the northeastern outskirts of Troyes; tel: 03 25 81 17 18; by appointment only; free.

Musée de l'Insolite 28 Grande Rue, Loriol, on the Rhône, between Valence and Montélimar; tel 04 75 61 63 88; by appointment only; free.

Musée d'Intérêt National du Tabac Maison Peyrarède, Place du Feu, Bergerac; tel: 05 53 63 04 13; web: www.france-tabac.com/musee.htm; Tue–Fri, and Sunday afternoons; ∈ 3.

Musée International de Pétanque et Boules Saint Bonnet le Château, 30km west of Saint Etienne; tel: 04 77 50 16 23; open afternoons Apr–Oct, mornings by appointment; ∈ 2.

Musée des Lunettes et Lorgnettes Pierre Marly in Paris has now been moved on, and is due to re-open in 2003 at the Espace Lamartine in Morez, in the Jura; tel: 03 84 33 39 30; web: www.lunetiers-du-jura.com.

Musée de la Machine à Coudre (the **Musée Barthélémy Thimonnier de la Machine à Coudre et du Cycle** – to give it its full name), Amplepuis, about 70km northwest of Lyon; tel: 04 74 89 08 90; open afternoons mid-Jun to mid-Sep, and on Wed, Fri–Sun afternoons the rest of the year; ∈ 4.

Musée Maurice Dufresne Marnay, about 6km from Azay le Rideau, and 20km southwest of Tours; tel: 02 47 45 36 18; web: www.musee-dufresne.com; open daily Feb–Nov; ∈ 10.

Musée de l'Ours en Peluche Lyon; tel: 04 72 77 69 69 (tourist office); web: www.lyon-france.com; currently closed.

Musée de la Pipe et du Diamant Saint Claude, in the heart of the Jura, 60km north of Geneva; tel: 03 84 45 17 00; closed Sun, open afternoons only Oct–Apr; ∈ 4.

Musée Rizla+ Mazères sur Salat, just off the A64 autoroute from Pau to Toulouse, in the foothills of the Pyrenees; tel: 05 61 97 48 22; generally open, but call ahead to confirm your visit; ∈ 3.

Musée de la Sorcellerie Concressault, about 60km north of Bourges; tel: 02 48 73 86 11; web: www.musee-sorcellerie.fr; open daily from Easter to Halloween; ∈ 5.50.

Musée du Tire-Bouchon Domaine de la Citadelle, below Ménerbes, off the main road from Avignon to Apt; tel: 04 90 72 41 58; open daily in summer, Mon–Fri in winter; ∈ 5.

Musée de la Tuile Blajan, about 25km north of Saint Gaudens, between Pau and Toulouse; tel: 05 61 88 22 05; open most afternoons in summer, but call ahead, free.

Musée de la Tuile Pargny sur Saulx, between Vitry le François and Bar le Duc; tel: 03 29 75 10 64; generally open summer Sundays, but call ahead; free.

Musée du Vélo Le Bois Dernier, near Cormatin, about 20km west of Tournus and 10km north of Cluny; tel: 03 85 50 16 00; web: http://museeduvelo.free.fr; open daily, closed Jan to mid-Mar; ∈ 4.

Musée du Vélo et de la Moto Château du Bosc, near Domazan, between Nîmes and Avignon, and close to the Pont du Gard; tel: 04 66 37 30 64; web: http://perso.wanadoo.fr/musee.velo-moto; call ahead to check opening times, as they vary; ∈ 5.

Musée du Vélocipède Cadouin, in the Dordogne, between Bergerac and Sarlat; tel: 05 53 63 46 60; open daily; ∈ 4.

Paris Catacombs Place Denfert-Rochereau, 75014, Paris; tel 01 43 22 47 63; M̄ Denfert-Rochereau; open Tue–Sun; ∈ 5.

Picpus Cemetery 35 rue de Picpus, 75012, Paris; tel: 01 43 44 18 54; M̄ Nation, Daumesnil, Picpus, Belair; open Tue–Sun afternoons, closed Aug; ∈ 4.

Pierre Marly 2 Avenue Mozart, 75016, Paris; tel: 01 45 27 21 05; M̄ Ranelagh, Jasmin.

Petit Musée du Bizarre Bayssac, just outside Lavilledieu, which is on the main road from Montélimar to Aubenas; tel: 04 75 94 83 28; uncertain whether it will re-open following Tekielski's death.

Sorède just inland from Argelès sur Mer, in the foothills of the Pyrenees; Centre d'Aide par le Travail (CAT); tel: 04 68 89 04 50; open every day in summer, and in winter by appointment; free – but contributions accepted.

Vélo-Parc Domaine de Menehouarne, Plouay, just north of Lorient, in Brittany; tel: 02 97 33 15 15; web: www.veloparc.com; open Apr–Sep, Tue–Sat, daily in Jul and Aug; ∈ 4.

Eccentric Edifices

Buildings, from shotgun shacks to flamboyant Gothic cathedrals, do something to fire the imagination. They also have a tendency, in the best hands, to become works of art in their own right.

ART BECOMING LIFE

Through the ages there have always been the occasional people who make art their life and life their art. There are those, too, who do the same thing with their homes, and that's what you'll find here – places which after 20 or 30 years of work take on a life of their own. You'll find Normandy's Sistine Chapel, a 19th-century postman's ideal palace or a priest's retelling of pirate legends in granite rocks, the wonderful properties of Robert Tatin and Jacques Lucas, and houses covered with mosaics made from shards of broken crockery.

What you'll only rarely find, and this seems endemic of our times, is anyone young engaged in such a lengthy enterprise. Five centuries ago, sculptors were willing to spend decades on a cathedral façade, knowing it was anonymous work and wouldn't be finished in their lifetimes. Half a century ago, people were still willing to start out on a project which could take 30 years to achieve, and might yield little or nothing. But today – can we blame television? the culture of instant gratification? – the best you can hope for is the minimum effort and five minutes of fame.

The Broken Crockery House

Robert Vasseur was in his mid-forties when he had the idea that his house in the pretty Normandy town of Louviers, halfway between Rouen and Evreux, would look a whole lot more interesting if it were decorated with mosaics. Not just slightly decorated, either. By the time of his death, at the age of 93, in 2001, he had spent half a century on the job, and his house was almost entirely covered, inside and out – as indeed was most of the garden.

The mosaics which make up **La Maison à Vaisselle Cassée** are mostly made from broken crockery and pottery, with seashells used as embellishments. They're immensely precise, set in abstract, geometric patterns – but the whole is practically impossible to deal with. There's far too much visual information for one brain to take in at one time.

Since Vasseur's death, the town has been trying to buy the house so it can be opened as a museum, though so far (at the time of writing) with no success. The **Louviers Municipal Museum**, however, has been known to exhibit Vasseur's work.

If you happen to be in Louviers, don't miss Europe's only set of cloisters suspended above water. Supported by bridges over the river, the Penitent's Cloisters were built in the 17th century, and are a fine place for prayers – and indeed penitence.

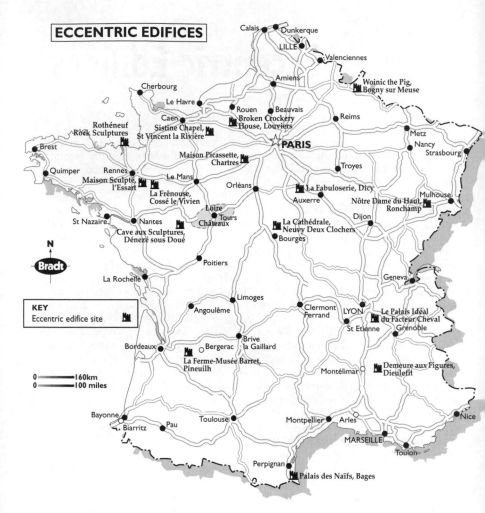

ECCENTRIC EDIFICES

Calais
Dunkerque
LILLE
Valenciennes
Amiens
Woinic the Pig, Bogny sur Meuse
Cherbourg
Le Havre
Rouen
Beauvais
Reims
Metz
Caen
Sistine Chapel, St Vincent la Rivière
Broken Crockery House, Louviers
Nancy
Strasbourg
Rothéneuf Rock Sculptures
Brest
PARIS
Maison Picassette, Chartres
Troyes
Quimper
Rennes
Le Mans
Maison Sculpté, l'Essart
Orléans
La Fabuloserie, Dicy
La Frênouse, Cossé le Vivien
Auxerre
Nôtre Dame du Haut, Ronchamp
Mulhouse
St Nazaire
Nantes
Loire
Châteaux
Tours
Dijon
Cave aux Sculptures, Dénezé sous Doué
La Cathédrale, Neuvy Deux Clochers
Bourges
Geneva
Poitiers
La Rochelle
Limoges
KEY
Eccentric edifice site
Angoulême
Clermont Ferrand
LYON
Le Palais Idéal du Facteur Cheval
St Etienne
Grenoble
Brive la Gaillard
Bordeaux
Bergerac
La Ferme-Musée Barret, Pineuilh
Montélimar
Demeure aux Figures, Dieulefit
0 ——— 160km
0 ——— 100 miles
Bayonne
Biarritz
Pau
Toulouse
Montpellier
Arles
Nice
MARSEILLE
Toulon
Perpignan
Palais des Naïfs, Bages

La Cathédrale

Thirty kilometres northeast of Bourges you'll find what must be France's most unusual – and most recent – cathedral, simply known as La Cathédrale. Started in 1961, by the then 30-year-old ceramicist Jean Linard, it was built alongside his lovely house and studio, set in pretty woods near Sancerre.

The house itself was also built by Linard, and features some excellent ceramic gargoyles with plants growing out of them, the shrubbery looking comically like hair. The most unusual feature of the 'cathedral' itself, however, is its roof – the sky – making it (as Linard only half jokes) the tallest in the world.

Otherwise the monument to Linard's devotion consists of a pyramidal baptistery, covered in brightly coloured glazed-tile shards and topped off with an asymmetric cross, leading via a series of angular arches to a nave supported by blue-tiled buttresses, and the open-air choir, bordered by vivid mosaics. It's not to everyone's taste, but it's certainly impressive. You'll also see Linard's sculptures which fit somewhere in between Gaudi and Calder, while in the trees are hung mirrors and mobiles, and there's an unusual mosaic-tiled waterfall. Everything, in fact, you could hope for.

To visit, you'll need to call Jean Linard at home. Be warned, however, that arrangements can be marred by his somewhat mercurial temper.

La Cave aux Sculptures

The hamlet of Dénezé sous Doué (literally: 'Dénezé the under-achiever', *doué* meaning 'clever', and *sous* meaning 'under'), just west of Saumur, is home to an extraordinary treasure, La Cave aux Sculptures.

The underground chambers here were dug out of the sandstone by hand, in the second half of the 16th century, and into the walls and ceilings were carved several hundred unusual sculptures – but the use and purpose of either the cave or the sculptures remains obscure.

Some of the figures, such as a caricature of Catherine de Medici (see page 82) have led people to believe it was a Protestant hideout, at a time when they were being hounded by Catholics, while others feel the sculptures must be the works of a mysterious sect. Angels and grotesques abound, along with the occasional medieval obscenity, but there are no inscriptions which might shed light, and the period was an extremely turbulent one in French history, with religious wars raging through the century.

Whatever the truth about their function (if, indeed, any), the sculptures are certainly the result of an over-heated medieval imagination, and well worth going to see.

La Demeure aux Figures

In contradiction with pretty much everyone else in this chapter (mostly dead or at least very old), is the painter and sculptor Roland Dutel, who was only born in 1955, and has been decorating his house and garden with 'found' materials only since 1989.

La Demeure aux Figures can be found up in the Drôme, in the small town of Dieulefit. The house and courtyard are covered with charming sculpted figures made from ceramics, old building materials, discarded junk and cement, and backed with mosaic patterns. In the middle of the courtyard there's a fabulous imaginative fountain, while under the house the cellar's been turned into a series of sculpted grottoes. Work on the property continues.

La Fabuloserie

South of Paris, between Auxerre and Montargis, you'll find La Fabuloserie, an extraordinary collection of more than a thousand works of *art brut*, which was put together by Alain Bourbonnais during the last thirty years of his life. As a child, Bourbonnais had wanted to be an artist himself, but was instead pushed into a prosperous career as a public works architect – which ironically enough gave him not just the means to become a collector, but also to buy the lovely property in the countryside at Dicy, which is today La Fabuloserie.

Wherever Bourbonnais travelled for his work, he would seek out untrained and unknown artists who were creating naïve art and *art brut*, and return home to Paris with new works – by postmen, miners, stonemasons, factory workers or farm labourers, all created using 'found' materials, like bits of string, old tins, *papier maché*, wire, or plastic.

In 1970, watching the evening news one night, he happened to hear that Jean Dubuffet was giving his entire collection of works away to Lausanne, in

Switzerland, as nobody in France wanted it. It was only then that he realised that what he had been collecting for more than ten years was *art brut*. He went to meet Dubuffet, and as a result of their cooperation opened up a gallery in Paris, dedicated to art out of the ordinary (*l'art hors-les-normes*).

After ten years, however, Bourbonnais and his wife Caroline realised that they weren't shopkeepers but collectors, so they moved to the house in the country, and fixed up the outbuildings as a permanent exhibition. In 1983, after being pressured by friends, they opened it up to the public, as a museum, and Bourbonnais' widow has continued to manage the collection (and an exhibition of Alain Bourbonnais' own paintings and drawings) since her husband's death, in 1988. It receives thousands of visitors a year, and is truly remarkable. Fabuloserie, even.

La Ferme-Musée Barret

The farmer Franck Barret, who lived outside Pineuilh, in the western Dordogne, was a bit of a visionary. So from 1948 onwards it was only natural that he should fill his house with painted sculptures of the apparitions which came to him at night. These included various religious figures, singly or in groups, as well as animals and monsters, and even a caveman and a Martian. Decorated with feathers and fur, they're more than just a little spooky.

La Frênouse

Robert Tatin worked most of his life in the building trade, but he had another side to his character, as one of the most interesting French painters and sculptors of the 20th century. Fortunately for us, he spent the last twenty years of his life creating La Frênouse, a superb museum attached to his house in Normandy, which shelters a lifetime's worth of paintings, watercolours, drawings and ceramics, and features an extraordinary sculpture garden.

Tatin was born into a modest family in 1902, and although he did well at school – and was noted by his teachers as an excellent draughtsman – he trained as a decorator, and worked first as a painter and then as a carpenter. In the late 1940s, his unusual works were 'discovered' by a major newspaper, which resulted in Jean Dubuffet coming to see him. Their collaboration was to be short lived, however.

Needing a change of air, Tatin went to South America for five years, travelling through Brazil, Argentina, Uruguay, Paraguay and Chile, and winning the first prize for sculpture in the 1951 biennale in São Paulo. Back in France, in 1955, he lived for a while in Vence, in the south, while continuing to work as a building contractor in Normandy.

It wasn't until 1962, having won the Paris Critics' Prize the year before, that he settled at La Frênouse, an ancient house (parts date back to the 6th century) near Laval. He then spent the next 20 years creating the installations which make up the museum today, completing it only shortly before his death in 1983.

The way to the museum is up a 100m footpath, adorned with 19 of Tatin's best and most distinctive sculptures, each representing one of his preoccupations. The series starts with French classics Vercingetorix and Joan of Arc (see page 83), and then proceeds to the verbs *'être'* and *'avoir'*, before moving on to a terrific series of artists, including André Breton (see page 157), Le Douanier Rousseau (see page 107), Toulouse Lautrec (see page 108), Valadon and Utrillo (see page 110) and Paul Gauguin (see page 101).

You then come to the *Porte des Géants*, which represents Tatin's five favourite painters, Rembrandt, Van-Gogh (see page 112), Leonardo de Vinci, Goya and Delacroix. Near here, in the garden, you'll also find Tatin's tomb. The museum itself, containing Tatin's other artworks, is spread around a cross-shaped pool, and you should look out for the two magnificent gateways, the *Porte du Soleil* and the *Porte de la Lune*, each measuring 5.50m tall.

Lovers' Wall

It's only to be expected that if there were to be a lovers' wall it would be in Paris, and that if it were in Paris, it would be in Montmartre. And so it is. Climb up the steps out of the Abbesses metro station, and there it is, on one side of a tiny public garden – a wall containing the phrase 'I love you' a thousand times, in 311 different languages.

The idea of building the wall came to a young Parisian called Frédéric Baron, who started a world tour of 'I love yous' in 1992, without ever leaving the capital. Carrying round a precious notebook, he knocked on doors (frequently embassy doors) trying to find as many different ways of saying the phrase as possible. When he had a thousand 'I love yous', he asked the calligraphic artist Claire Kito to create a single image containing the whole lot, and the mural painter Daniel Boulogne to translate it onto a wall. The result is the 40m^2 **Mur des Je t'aime**, which was inaugurated in October 2000. It's not a great place to go and wail, however.

Maison Picassiette

There seems to have been nothing unusual about Raymond Isidore's early life – and certainly nothing that would point towards him becoming one of the greatest practitioners of *art brut* in the 20th century.

Isidore was born in Chartres in 1900, and lived there all his life until his death in 1964. In 1929 he bought a piece of land on the eastern side of the town, and built a small house there for himself, his wife, and her three children from her first marriage. He worked at a number of odd jobs, and spent the last years of his life as a sweeper at the local cemetery.

But in 1938 he seems to have decided it might be an idea to brighten the place up, and he started covering the inside of the house with mosaics made of broken crockery and glass, which he would find at the municipal dump. As fortune would have it, he had enormous talent, and the work he did is fabulous.

Isidore eventually covered not just the inside of the house (and the furniture) with his mosaics, but also the outside of the house too, as well as building a chapel, a courtyard and a Jerusalem wall outside. How his family survived living in a three-roomed house, with wet cement and tens of thousands of shards of glass and pottery everywhere, doesn't bear thinking about.

He soon earned the name Picassiette, a play on the words *'pique-assiette'* (sponger) and the inevitable Picasso, who was still considered controversial during the 1950s. It wasn't particularly flattering, but Isidore didn't seem to mind, and the house was soon universally known as La Maison Picassiette.

The house itself is a marvel. Even the flowerpots and troughs are covered with bright mosaics. Once inside, you'll find the three small rooms a mass of decorative work, with motifs ranging from the secular to the religious, and including all manner of animals, flowers, monuments, people, boats, plants and geometric patterns. The stove, the table, the chairs, the footstools, the bedside table and even the bed itself have all been decorated with mosaics too.

Outside, there's a chapel and a summer house, every square inch of which is covered with mosaics, and a courtyard decorated with dark glass, featuring a large tomb, with a model of Chartres cathedral on top. Finally, there's the Jerusalem wall, with a big mosaic picture of the old city of Jerusalem above images of famous buildings from around the world, including St Basil's cathedral in Moscow, the Coliseum in Rome, Mont Saint Michel, and the Leaning Tower of Pisa.

The house was bought by the city of Chartres in 1981, and is now open to the public as a museum – but see it soon, as it's fragile and it's uncertain how long it will last with 30,000 people a year visiting. It's situated down a footpath at 22 rue du Repos, a ten-minute walk east from the centre of Chartres.

La Maison Sculptée

Near Rennes stands one of the most extraordinary works of late 20th-century art, La Maison Sculptée. Created by Jacques Lucas over a 30-year period, it's a huge warren of a place, with the boundaries blurred between what's indoors and what's outside. Artistic and architectural nods are made in the direction of Facteur Cheval (see below), Gaudi, Robert Tatin (see page 222) and Amerindian art, but the whole is all Jacques Lucas.

Born in 1944, Lucas loved to build hideaways and play-houses as a child, and frequently made his own toys. After studying art and archaeology he spent a decade at France's Ministry of Cultural Affairs, which gave him the opportunity of seeing a huge range of Breton sculpture, and, crucially, of meeting Robert Tatin in 1967.

The meeting was decisive in Lucas' purchase of l'Essart, a series of old and abandoned buildings near Rennes – and only 60km or so from Tatin's property, la Frênouse. During the winter of 1969, Lucas constructed his first out-sized sculptures, which are today incorporated into a large ensemble some 50m long.

Over the next 15 years, Lucas turned the property into the Maison Sculptée, working from the beginning of the spring until the end of the autumn each year, and using untold quantities of cement, lime and sand. Each morning he would build foundations and structures in reinforced concrete, and each evening he would use the previous day's now-dried work as the basis for new sculptures.

By 1983 he was ready to put the finishing touches to the ensemble, and over the next three years created most of what's actually visible today. At first sight it all looks extraordinarily organic and abstract, but look closely and amidst the curving lines of what could almost be bark, roots and leaves you'll find the shapes of curious animal and bird figures, trapped in the stone. There's a labyrinth, a crypt, and gardens and sculpted ponds to visit, and the whole is a stunning piece of work.

With everything pretty much complete, Lucas moved to Nice, where he still lives today, in a painter's studio. He spends the summers at l'Essart, however, maintaining the property and making repairs where necessary. In the winter months he paints in Nice.

After concerns during the late 1990s that the whole place might be torn down, following financial troubles, the future of the Maison Sculptée is now thankfully secure, as a specially created trust now owns the property and is already planning new activities to take place there, including sculpture workshops, from the summer of 2003.

Le Palais Idéal du Facteur Cheval

The little village of Hauterives in the Drôme is home to one of France's – and indeed the world's – strangest works of art, Le Palais Idéal du Facteur Cheval. Built single-handedly by the local postman, Ferdinand Cheval, between 1879 and 1912, it's a unique example of naïve art.

Facteur Cheval (as he's now universally known) was born in 1836. Of humble origins and poorly educated (he left school at 13), he appears to have done nothing of any interest whatsoever before stubbing his toe on a twisted four-inch chunk of local tufa in 1879 – ten years into a dreary postal round which dragged 32km around the local hills. Picking up the offending rock seems to have kick-started the idea of a strange and fantastical castle, a palace that united all of the primitive and ancient cultures – not to mention a wealth of random images plundered from the penny magazines and junk mail of the day.

You can imagine what the neighbours thought when he started building it.

Facteur Cheval was the first to admit he wasn't the ideal candidate for the job. After the Palais Idéal was completed, 33 years later, he confessed 'I was not a builder, I had never handled a mason's trowel, I was not a sculptor. The chisel was unknown to me; not to mention architecture, a field in which I remained totally ignorant.' Sounds suspiciously like the man who built my extension.

Fortunately for the feisty Facteur, however, his lack of skills was matched only by his astonishing determination, and from the day after the 1879 toe-stubbing incident, he started collecting the crazy materials for the Palais Idéal – a task which he reckoned took 10,000 days, working an average (on top of the postal round) of over nine hours per day.

At first he simply carried stones in his pockets, but later he started using baskets, hauling up to 50kg of rocks at a time, along with the mailbag. When this all got too much, he turned to a faithful wheelbarrow, stockpiling rocks during the day and returning for them with the barrow at night. (The rock-filled barrow can still be seen at the Palais Idéal.)

As the Facteur walked the hills and worked day and night, he experienced extraordinary visions of what needed to be done next – probably brought on by severe loneliness, exhaustion and hunger. Sleeping only two or three hours a day, it nonetheless took him 20 years just to build the outer walls.

In his own words, 'I would be the first to agree with those who call me insane. The tongues started to wag in my hometown and surrounding district. I was laughed at, disapproved of and criticized but, as this kind of mental alienation was neither contagious nor dangerous, they didn't see much point in fetching the doctor.'

And that was before he started in on the embellishments. Now retired, Cheval spent the next 13 years adding heroic statues, carved floral motifs, grottoes, geese, angels, gnarled roots, temples, leaves, fountains with sculpted water, tropical fruit, spires, the Bethlehem manger, turrets and crenellations – not to mention Egyptian mummies, primeval giants and stone palm trees.

It's not to everyone's taste. Indeed, among the inscriptions by the Facteur himself which clutter every facet, the most apposite is probably the phrase 'It has to be seen to be believed.' Measuring 26m by 14m, and up to 10m tall, the palace's enormity and complexity can only be truly appreciated by visiting.

With the Palais finally complete in 1912 (though looking at it you'd have to ask yourself how on earth he knew when to stop), the Facteur, now 78, still had one task ahead of him: building his own mausoleum. He'd hoped to be inhumed inside his life's work – but seems to have been unaware of the French law against it. Undiscouraged, the irrepressible handyman spent another eight years building an elaborate vault for himself in the local cemetery, completing it just 20 months before his death in August 1924.

The first outsider to fall for the Palais Idéal's charms was the French surrealist, André Breton. He and his surrealist pals quickly made a shrine out of the place, no doubt appreciating the irony of having an intentionally uninhabitable palace. Since then it's gained a big following amongst artists worldwide, and has been classified as a historic monument. It attracts around 140,000 visitors a year, so don't expect to have it to yourself.

Palais des Naïfs

It's only a matter of chance that the Palais des Naïfs exists at all. Started in 1954, without planning permission, by François Carrère, a Catalan wine-producer and self-taught artist, it took ten years to build, and another 15 years of court cases before it was finally decided to let it stand – on artistic merit. It then became a squat for ten years before catching the eye of the artist Françoise Caux, who bought the place, renovated it, and turned it into a museum, which finally opened in 1991.

It's a charming building, closer to a ship than a house, and well worth the visit. Inside, there's a unique collection of naïve art, dating back as far as the 16th century, along with more modern works for sale. Unfortunately, however, the Palais des Naïfs was 'provisionally' closed on the death of its founder at the end of the summer of 2002 – hopefully it will be re-opened by the time you read this. In the meantime there's a moderately wacky website with naïve art for sale – but it's probably worth checking the museum is functioning again before spending up big on paintings.

The privacy of a pyramid

As in life, as in death. Walk up to the 23rd section of the world's most famous cemetery, Père Lachaise, in Paris, and you'll find a spanking-new pyramid. Built by its future incumbent, Mr Sacchet, a keen Egyptologist, it was still being decorated by him when I passed by in 2002. He wouldn't be drawn about when he was planning to take up residence, or whether he was going for the full mummification when he did, but he seemed in excellent health, so don't expect the pyramid to be occupied any time soon.

It's hardly your Great Pyramid at Giza. In fact it's under 3m tall – but then Mr Sacchet didn't have 100,000 Egyptian slaves on hand to help him out with the building work. Inside it's positively spacious, however, and (like the pyramids in Egypt), the interior is richly decorated with beautiful hieroglyphs and ornate funerary scrolls. It looks like the perfect place for that final rest.

Rothéneuf rock sculptures

Just up the coast from St Malo, overlooking the Plage du Val, at Rothéneuf, on the Normandy coast, you'll find what's left of a set of extraordinary rocks which were sculpted here over a century ago – by the local vicar.

Adolphe-Julien Fouré was born in 1839, and took up a living as a priest in Paimpol (home today to the sea-shanty festival, see page 24), until in 1870, as the result of a bout of illness – probably a minor stroke – he found himself deaf and dumb at the age of 31. He retired from the world, to the small parish of Rothéneuf, and being a big, solid man, decided that the best thing to do with his abundant spare time and energy would be to create one of the world's largest sculptures attributable to a single artist.

Working only with a hammer and a cold chisel, and no plans at all, l'Abbé Fouré set out to tell the legend of the Rothéneufs, a notorious family of 16th-century pirates, in the local granite cliffs. (The choice of the pirate family was an interesting one, as they were all reputed to have exceptional hearing – something Fouré would probably have given his left ear for.)

He came to the cliffs every day, year after year, and over more than a quarter of a century he created some 300 characters in the rock, including pirates, sea monsters, demons and even a crocodile. The sculpture covers an astonishing area of 500m², with each rock carrying the name of a different pirate – Bennetin, Eugène, la Goule, la Haie, Job and Rochefort.

The only tragedy is that the whole thing is being slowly eroded away by the wind and the waves. Look at a postcard from Fouré's time (you can track these down in Saint Malo), and you'll see that at least half the detail, and probably more, has already been worn away by erosion.

Sistine Chapel

Hate the crowds at the Vatican? Can't get to Rome? Don't speak Italian? Why not head across to Normandy, instead? For here, tucked away in the hamlet of Saint Vincent la Rivière, there's a remarkable replica of the Sistine Chapel's famous ceiling.

It all started in 1968, when the then 60-year-old painter and restorer Irial Vets saw a small ad offering a dilapidated church for sale. He went and had a look, and bought it right away, reckoning it was the perfect candidate for his Sistine Chapel scheme. Starting off using a feature in Paris Match as his model, he soon realised that he would have to make the trip to the Vatican himself, and ended up visiting the real Sistine Chapel several times.

By 1972, the ceiling was finished, and frankly it's a marvel. There are some necessary approximations, largely because the proportions of the two buildings are somewhat different, but it's a masterful piece of work. Vets used to say, with a dash of humour, that he was the reincarnation of Michelangelo – and it's not so very far from the truth.

With the ceiling sorted, Vets' next project was the building of a fitting tomb for himself, and he spent years creating the chapel's centrepiece, which is decorated with six coffers celebrating his life as a dandy and a lover of the arts. As Vets said, if he already had a pope's chapel, there was no reason why he shouldn't also have a king's tomb.

The funeral wreath on the tomb is adorned with the inscription '*A moi-même*' (to myself), and while the birth date is inscribed, the date of death remains a question mark. For sadly, when he died in 2001, Vets' wish to be buried in his own church wasn't respected.

It used to be that Irial Vets and his long-time companion (she wishes to remain anonymous) would open up the church for visitors on Sundays, driving down from the coast where they lived. Since Vets' death at the age of 93, in 2001, however, the chapel has remained firmly closed, and it's not being maintained at all. One can only hope that Vets' grandson, who inherited the wonderful work, re-opens it to the public – or that it's bought by the state and opened as a museum.

Woinic, the world's biggest pig

You're an unemployed 21-year-old metal worker, and you have a few drinks on New Year's Eve with your mates, so you decide the best thing to do with your free time … is to build the world's biggest pig (wild sow, actually). So began an astonishing 11 years and 12,000 hours of work for Eric Sleziak, who started welding on January 1 1983 and completed Woinic, the world's biggest boar, on December 15 1993.

The result is truly magnificent. Weighing in at 56.5 tonnes (including 6.5 tonnes of solder), Woinic is over 8m high, 14m long and 5m wide (that's one fat pig).

Woinic lives at Bogny sur Meuse, up in the Ardennes, and there are signs in the area pointing your snout in the direction of the huge metal worker's hanger where Woinic hangs out, dwarfing everything around it. If you ask Sleziak nicely he'll take you right inside…

ECCENTRIC ARCHITECTURE

Very little architecture is genuinely eccentric, but buildings often have a good tale to tell. So you might find yourself getting the finger from the Statue of Liberty, or discerning François Rude's rudeness on the Arc de Triomphe, or just wondering if it might be you that next cycles up or bungee-jumps off the Eiffel Tower.

Arc de Triomphe

The Arc de Triomphe is one of France's most famous monuments, perfectly situated at the top of the Champs Elysées, and a typically over-stated tribute to military glory. What few people today realise, however, is how different it might have been.

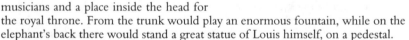

The first proposal for a monument here came from an engineer called Ribart, who suggested in 1758 that Louis XV might care to have a giant elephant built on the spot. And we're talking *giant*. Stairs would lead up to a banquet hall inside the elephant itself, with room in the ears for musicians and a place inside the head for the royal throne. From the trunk would play an enormous fountain, while on the elephant's back there would stand a great statue of Louis himself, on a pedestal.

Sadly, the elephant never happened (think what a tourist attraction that would be!). Instead, it took Napoleon to get things off the ground. Ordering the building of two triumphal arches, a small one at the Tuileries and a larger one at the top of what's now the Champs Elysées, was the easy part. The tricky bit was actually building the larger one. The site chosen was chalky and unstable, and costs soared. More worryingly, it began to look as if the arch wouldn't be ready in time for Napoleon's wedding to Marie Louise of Austria, scheduled for 1810.

As it happened, it wasn't – as the wedding day approached, in fact, the triumphal arch was only a few feet high. Chalgrin, the architect, solved the problem brilliantly, by building a full-scale model using scaffolding and painted canvas, and incredibly it was this which dominated the Paris skyline for the next 22 years. Only in 1832 did work recommence, and the Arc de Triomphe wasn't finally completed until 1836. Napoleon himself had just one brief chance to see the finished work, as he rolled through the arch on his return to Paris, having been exhumed in Saint Helena in 1840.

The Arc de Triomphe is a magnificent monument, twice the height and just over twice the breadth of the Arch of Constantine on which it's modelled. On its completion, the sculptors Jean-Pierre Cortot, Antoine Etex and François Rude were commissioned to add monumental bas-reliefs to the arch, and it's Rude's (La Marseillaise, on the right, looking down the Champs Elysées) which is easily the finest.

It's also Rude's work which is the rudest. Having fallen out with the mayor of Paris (as one does), Rude sculpted his enemy's head onto one of the many soldiers way up at the top, and had the fellow rudely playing with himself. It's extremely difficult to spot – but it's there. (Rude, for his part, is buried in the Montparnasse cemetery, under a statue of himself sporting a truly extravagant beard.)

Underneath the arch you'll find the eternal flame marking the tomb of the unknown soldier. On no account should this be used for frying eggs or other party tricks. You *will* go straight to jail without passing go.

To get to the Arc de Triomphe you'd be mad not to use the underpass, but keep an eye out for pickpockets. Inside, there's an interesting museum which is mostly bypassed by people on their way to the roof, 52m above the 12 avenues radiating out from the arch like the spokes of a wheel. The view from here is terrific, with the Louvre to the east and the Grande Arche de la Défense to the west. The avenues you look down, incidentally, were only built that way by Baron Haussmann so as to be wide enough to march an army down in times of trouble. Now that's revolutionary.

La Défense

West of the Arc de Triomphe a few kilometres, you can hardly miss La Défense, a big clutch of office skyscrapers centred on La Grande Arche, in dramatic contrast to anything else in Paris.

La Défense was originally just a small memorial to the capital's refusal to surrender to the Prussians in 1871, during the siege of Paris, but in the 1970s the area was cleared and developed into what you see today, one of the largest shopping and office complexes in Europe. All the infrastructure (public transport, roads, parking etc) is underneath a huge open square surrounded by futuristic office buildings, and faced on one side by the truly monumental Grande Arche.

Built to commemorate the 200th anniversary of the French Revolution in 1789, La Grande Arche is nothing more than a vast, hollowed-out 110m-sided cube. It was the winning design from nearly 500 submitted in an architecture competition for the building to complete the axis running all the way from the Louvre to the Obelisk to the Arc de Triomphe and out to La Défense. Faced with glass, grey granite and Carrara marble, it weighs in at 300,000 tonnes, and it's so big that the cathedral of Notre Dame would quite comfortably fit inside the archway. Speed up to the top in the terrifying external lifts for a great view from the roof terrace – though not so great when the pollution's heavy.

La Défense is under ten minutes from the Arc de Triomphe by metro or RER suburban trains and you'll find the area thriving during the daytime but absolutely moribund at night. The Grande Arche de la Défense attracts an impressive half a million visitors a year.

Eiffel Tower

Arguably the most famous building in the world, the Eiffel Tower is a puny featherweight compared to La Grande Arche (see above), weighing in at a mere 10,000 tonnes to the arch's 300,000, in spite of being nearly three times the height. So light is it, in fact, that a one-metre scale-replica made of pig-iron would weigh just 294g (not much more than half a pound), and a 30cm (one foot) version would weigh under eight grams (about a third of an ounce). About the heaviest thing on the tower is the paint, which comes in at 60 tonnes alone.

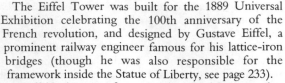

The Eiffel Tower was built for the 1889 Universal Exhibition celebrating the 100th anniversary of the French revolution, and designed by Gustave Eiffel, a prominent railway engineer famous for his lattice-iron bridges (though he was also responsible for the framework inside the Statue of Liberty, see page 233).

Eiffel had a suite of rooms at the top of the tower (bet he was fit) which served as office space and gave him the best imaginable address in Paris: Gustave Eiffel, Tour Eiffel, Paris. He entertained guests there, including famously Thomas Edison once, until 4am, complete with piano accompaniment (you'd want a decent tip for carrying a piano up 1,710 stairs, wouldn't you?).

For 41 years, the Eiffel Tower was the tallest building in the world – it was only overtaken in 1930 by the Chrysler building in New York, and in 1931 by the Empire State (which itself reigned tallest for 41 years, curiously). But even though it's currently 324m tall, including the antennae, it never sways more than 12cm in the highest wind – a testimony to Eiffel's engineering genius.

From the start, people wanted to get to the top of the tower, and it was climbed in its opening year by the future Edward VII, Sarah Bernhardt (see page 132) and Buffalo Bill. It wasn't popular with everyone though, and a petition was drawn up and signed by 300 Paris notables (including both Maupassant and Zola) demanding that the eyesore be torn down. In 1909, at the end of its 20-year lease, it nearly was – only saved by its new importance as a telegraphic relay station.

More than 200 million people have now been up the Eiffel Tower, and the vast majority have come back down again safely. But it inevitably attracts its fair share of suicides, and around 400 people have jumped off over the years, most of them coming to a sticky end further down the tower, as it flares out substantially on the way down.

The Eiffel Tower acts as a magnet for publicity seekers and sports nuts, too. In 1905, 227 candidates raced their way up to the second level, with the winner managing the feat in an implausible time of only three minutes and 12 seconds. In 1912, Franz Reichfelt fatally tested an early version of the parachute here, while in 1923, Pierre Labric cycled down the stairs to win a bet. In 1925 the Eiffel Tower was sold not once but twice by Victor Lustig (see page 105) to gullible scrap dealers.

Above Chestnut-bursting overshoes: next year's obligatory fashion accessory for the well-heeled (JMD)

Right George Sand's arm and Frédéric Chopin's hand at rest in the Musée de la Vie Romantique, Paris (PL)

Below The life-sized finger from the Statue of Liberty at the CNAM, Paris (PL)

Above In search of the lost prune, at the Prune Museum, Granges sur Lot (PL)

Right The annual snow-golfing tournament in Megève (NS)

Below right English teacup with moustache-protector, at the Musée de l'Insolite, Loriol (PL)

Below Edith Piaf and her life-sized teddy at the Edith Piaf Museum, Paris (PL)

The tower was climbed on the outside by mountaineers in 1954, flown under by an American pilot in 1984 ('Just for fun', he said afterwards), and parachuted off by an English couple the same year. A New Zealander bungee-jumped off the second level in 1987, and the authorities let him hang there upside-down for quite a bit longer than was strictly necessary, as a warning to others.

For the centenary celebrations, in 1989, a tightrope walker made the horrifying 700m journey from the second level of the Eiffel Tower to the Trocadéro, across the Seine, and in 2002, a man called Hugues Richard beat his own 1998 record by cycling up to the second level in under 20 minutes on a mountain bike. It really does take all sorts.

The tower is hugely popular, with more than six million visitors a year, so expect to queue to go up. You can walk up to the second level, but it's lifts only from here on up to the top. On a clear day the views are fabulous, as it's still far and away the tallest building in Paris, at one and a half times the height of the nearest contender, the Tour de Montparnasse.

If you're feeling flush, there's a fine restaurant, the **Jules Verne**, on the second level, reached by its own private lift. Book way, way ahead, and ask for a window table for dinner, for a fabulous view of the Paris city lights. Don't expect to get away for less than € 150 a head, however, unless you're going for the cheapo € 50 lunch menu.

Loire Châteaux

The Châteaux of the Loire valley are lovely, but frankly pretty uneccentric for the most part – just a question of royalty doing its thing from the 14th to the 16th centuries, which was mostly building big showy châteaux along the Loire and Cher rivers for a bit of country peace in the summer. But if you're in the area…

Amboise

Five kings of France, from Charles VII to François I, spent time at the Château d'Amboise, and it was also the place where Leonardo da Vinci passed his closing years, up to his death in 1519. He's buried in the St Hubert chapel in the château, a marvellous flamboyant-Gothic building. Check out the ramps leading to the upper floors, for fat noblemen who were too unfit to make it up the stairs without being carried on mules.

Blois

The Château de Blois isn't eccentric at all, but it's still easily the best example of renaissance architecture in the area, and sports a very fine staircase in the main courtyard.

Chambord

Château Chambord really is the last word in *folie de grandeur*. Built by François I between 1518 and 1545, it has a staggering 440 rooms, 365 bedrooms and 84 staircases. The housework's a nightmare, but there's a great double-helix staircase with two flights of stairs intertwined but never meeting.

Chenonceau

The Château de Chenonceau is the great icon of the Loire valley, with its double-storeyed arches stretching out across the river. It was originally the property of Diane de Poitiers, but after Henry II died of his jousting wounds, in 1559, it was taken over by his widow, Catherine de Medici, who built the lovely extension – which was then used as a hospital ward for the wounded during World War II.

Parc des Mini-Châteaux

Best of all, of course – at least as far as this book's concerned – is the Parc des Mini-Châteaux, at Amboise, where you'll find faithful scale reproductions (quite big ones, in fact) of 44 of the Loire's châteaux, peopled with over 2,000 figurines, water wheels and windmills, and toy trains running through the countryside.

Ville Souterraine

When you've had your fill of castles (and the mini-châteaux, above, should see your appetite well-sated), head underground to the Ville Souterraine, at Bourré, just along the river Cher from Chenonceau.

The underground tunnels here provided most of the white stone used to build the châteaux you see above ground, and for the last few years some of the old quarry façades have been in the process of being sculpted to make it look like an underground town. Already there's around 1,500m² of sculpted surface area, featuring a stone umbrella left outside a front door, a dog nosing its way into a house, a swallow's nest, a woman leaning out of an opened window and many more details from everyday life – except that it's all 50m below the surface of the earth.

The complex also includes a mushroom farm in the abandoned quarries, where you can see various species being grown, and indeed pick your own.

Notre Dame du Haut

Near Belfort, above the village of Ronchamp, stands one of France's most interesting churches, Notre Dame du Haut. Designed by the Swiss architect, Le Corbusier, in the early 1950s, after war damage had destroyed the chapel already there, the church is one of the most original in the world, and unique architecturally.

The commission was a difficult one. The hill had been an important pilgrimage site since the 13th century, and drew big crowds at certain times of year (notably on 15 August, the Feast of the Assumption of the Virgin Mary), yet the local population was tiny, and didn't need a big building. Le Corbusier, at the height of his powers, dreamed up a perfect solution, which is what you can see at Ronchamp today.

The result is a structure which still looks strikingly modern half a century after its completion, and which defies most of the normal expectations about what churches should look like. There isn't a straight line in sight, and the roof appears to be ark-like, suspended above whitewashed walls by three pillars on the inside corners of the building. Walls curve away to angular corners, and it's not clear where the door is until you get up close.

Inside, the chapel is lit by a multitude of small stained-glass windows on the south wall, with extra light filtering in from the gap between the walls and the roof, while high up, the venerated 17th-century Virgin and Child can be seen from both inside and out, where the outdoor chapel welcomes the larger pilgrimages.

The church is visited by around 100,000 people a year, though unless you happen to be there during a major religious festival you'd never know it – especially in winter, when it takes on a rather run-down look (it could use a fresh coat of whitewash, to be frank).

Pompidou Centre

The Pompidou Centre (properly the Centre National d'Art et de Culture Georges Pompidou, but better known simply as the 'Beaubourg' after the adjoining street) in the heart of Paris, staggeringly, receives even more visitors than the Eiffel Tower (see page 229), with nine million people passing through it every year, and more than 150 million having visited since it opened in 1977.

Although it's enormously popular now, the centre caused a huge scandal when it was first built, partly for the radical content (it houses modern art as well as a huge library) but mainly because of the building itself. Designed by Richard Rogers and Renzo Piano, the centre is famous for being architecturally inside-out, with most of the infrastructure colour-coded and adorning the outside of the building – blue for air, red for lifts, yellow for electrics, green for water, grey for walkways and white for the building itself. The array of external ducts, pipes and escalators still has the power to surprise.

More than 50% of the visitors come to use the fabulous library, with its half a million books, more than 2,600 magazine and newspaper subscriptions, and 1,800 reading desks, but thousands come daily too to see the **Musée National d'Art Moderne** (MNAM), an encyclopaedic collection comprising everything from compacted cars to Andy Warhol screen prints. It'll be interesting to see what happens to the MNAM when the new contemporary art gallery – twice the size of the Bilbão Guggenheim apparently – opens in 2006 at the former Renault factory in Boulogne-Billancourt.

Statue of Liberty, Paris

France has a bit of a thing about the Statue of Liberty, but then it is French, after all. It was built in Paris and took the best part of a decade to complete, from 1875 to 1884. The structural engineer behind the statue (or more to the point inside it) was Gustave Eiffel (see page 230), who was already famous as a railway engineer. The design, on the other hand, was by the French sculptor Auguste Bartholdi. (Bartholdi was also responsible for the 22m-long red sandstone Lion of Belfort, which celebrates the resistance of a certain Denfert-Rochereau against the Prussians in 1871. A smaller bronze copy can be seen in Paris on the appropriately named Place Denfert-Rochereau, where you'll also find the entrance to the Catacombs – see page 194 – perhaps explaining why the earlier name for the square was Place d'Enfer.)

Entitled *Liberty Enlightening the World*, the monumental statue – at 47m, it's only fractionally shorter than the Arc de Triomphe (see page 228) – was intended to be a gift from the people of France to the United States to commemorate the centennial of its independence in 1876.

Unfortunately the 'people of France' wouldn't dig very deep into their pockets, and although there was enough money to start work in 1875, Bartholdi was only able to take a finished arm with him to America for the centennial celebrations. Appealing to greed rather than charity, a lottery was launched, which successfully raised the rest of the cash needed, though the statue wasn't inaugurated until 4 July 1884, eight years late. The following year it was dismantled and shipped in 350 pieces to New York, where it was reassembled, and where you can see it today, on Liberty Island.

There are, however, four places in Paris where you can see copies. The largest is on the western end of the Allée des Cygnes, a narrow island on the Seine just downstream from the Eiffel Tower. Here, there's a 14-tonne copy of the original which was given to Paris in 1885 by American ex-pats – although you only really get a decent view of it from the river itself. An even smaller copy, also dating back to 1885, can be found on the western side of the Luxembourg Gardens.

You can also see an excellent series of exhibits, including models of the work in progress (and a full-size finger), at the **CNAM** (Conservatoire Nationale des Arts et Métiers), in the deconsecrated church which also hold's Blériot's Channel-crossing monoplane (see page 42).

Finally, there's a full-sized copy of the flame from Liberty's torch on the Pont de l'Alma, which was given to Paris by the *Herald Tribune* to celebrate the statue's 100th anniversary. A little over ten years later, in 1997, Princess Diana was killed in a car crash in the tunnel just underneath, so the flame became something of a memorial to her.

If you're a Bartholdi fan, there's also a **Bartholdi Museum** in the middle of Colmar, in the house the sculptor was born in. There are studies here for all his famous works, and many original busts and statues, as well as drawings and watercolours, left to the town by his widow.

TRAVEL INFORMATION

Arc de Triomphe Place Charles de Gaulle, 75008, Paris; tel: 01 55 37 73 77; web: www.monum.fr/m_arc/; M̲ Charles-de-Gaulle-Etoile; open daily except public holidays; ∈ 7.

Bartholdi Museum 30 rue des Marchands, Colmar; tel 03 89 41 90 60 / 03 89 20 68 92 (Colmar tourist office); open Mar–Dec, closed Tue; ∈ 4.

La Cathédrale Les Poteries, on the edge of Neuvy Deux Clochers, 30km out of Bourges, on the way towards Sancerre; tel: 02 48 26 73 87; by appointment only; free.

La Cave aux Sculptures just outside the hamlet of Dénezé sous Doué, a few kilometres west of Saumur, on the Loire; tel: 02 41 59 15 40 or the Dénezè tourist office: 02 41 59 21 62; open daily Jun–Sep, and some afternoons Apr–May, closed Mon; ∈ 5.

Château d' Amboise Amboise, 35km west of Blois; tel: 02 47 57 00 98; web: www.chateau-amboise.tm.fr; open daily except 25/12 and 01/01; ∈ 6.50.

Château de Blois Blois; tel: 02 54 90 33 33; open daily except 25/12 and 01/01; ∈ 7.50.

Château Chambord Chambord, 20km east of Blois; tel: 02 54 50 40 00; web: www.chambord.org; open daily except 25/12 and 01/01; ∈ 7.

Château de Chenonceau Chenonceaux, 10km south of Amboise; tel: 02 47 23 90 07; web: www.chenonceau.com; open daily except 25/12 and 01/01; ∈ 8.

CNAM (Conservatoire Nationale des Arts et Métiers), 60 rue Réamur, Paris, 75003; M̲ Arts et Métiers, Réaumur-Sébastopol; tel: 01 53 01 82 00; web: www.arts-et-metiers.net; closed Mon; ∈ 5.50.

La Demeure aux Figures Dieulefit, 30km due east of Montélimar; tel: 04 75 46 86 84; open by appointment, on summer afternoons only; free.

Eiffel Tower Champ de Mars, 75007, Paris; tel: 01 44 11 23 45; web: www.tour-eiffel.fr; M̄ Champs de Mars (RER C), Bir Hakeim; open daily; ∈ 10.20.

La Fabuloserie Dicy, 12km from J18 off A6 from Paris, towards Montargis; tel 03 86 63 64 21; web: http://fabuloserie.chez.tiscali.fr/; open weekend afternoons Apr–Nov, every afternoon Jul, Aug; ∈ 5.50.

Ferme-Musée Barret La Goubière, just outside Pineuilh, 2km south of Sainte Foy la Grande, on the river Dordogne, between Bergerac and Bordeaux; tel: 05 57 46 43 55 (Franck Barret's son and daughter-in-law); by appointment only; free.

La Frênouse (also known as the Musée Robert Tatin) just outside the village of Cossé le Vivien, 20km southwest of Laval, in Normandy; tel: 02 43 98 80 89; web: http://pointcomlaval.free.fr/musee; usually open daily Apr–Sep, afternoons Mar and Oct, weekend afternoons in Feb, Nov and Dec, closed Jan; ∈ 6.

La Grande Arche de la Défense La Défense, under ten minutes from the Arc de Triomphe by metro or RER; tel: 01 49 07 27 57; web: www.grandearche.com; M̄ La Défense; open daily; ∈ 7.

Jules Verne restaurant Eiffel Tower, Champs de Mars, 75007, Paris; tel: 01 45 55 61 44; M̄ Champs de Mars (RER C), Bir Hakeim; reserve way ahead.

Maison Picassiette 22 rue du Repos, a ten-minute walk east from the centre of Chartres; tel: 02 37 34 10 78 / 02 37 36 41 39; open daily Apr–Oct, closed Tue and Sun mornings; ∈ 4.

La Maison Sculptée on the D92, between Châteaugiron and Janzé, 30km southeast of Rennes; tel: 02 99 47 07 59 (summer), 04 93 83 11 96 (rest of the year); web: www.rom.fr/lucas; open in summer, by appointment only.

La Maison a Vaisselle Cassée 80 rue du Bal Champêtre, five minutes northwest of the centre of Louviers, in Normandy; currently closed; tel: Mme Marie, on 02 32 09 58 57, for an update.

Mur des Je t'aime Place des Abbesses, 75018, Paris; M̄ Abbesses; always open; free.

Notre Dame du Haut just above Ronchamp, on the main road from Belfort to Vesoul; tel 03 84 20 65 13; usually open, though may be closed on Tue. A working church, so no obligatory entry fee – but you are asked to contribute ∈ 2 when you visit.

Palais Idéal du Facteur Cheval Hauterives, 60km east / southeast of Lyon and 47km northeast of Valence; tel 04 75 68 81 19; web: www.aricie.fr/facteur-cheval/; open daily except 25/12 and 01/01; ∈ 5.

Palais des Naïfs 9 avenue de la Méditerranée, Bages, 12km south of Perpignan; tel: 04 68 21 71 33; web: www.palais-des-naifs.com; provisionally closed.

Parc des Mini-Chateaux Amboise, 35km west of Blois; tel: 08 25 08 25 22; web: www.mini-chateaux.com; open daily Apr–11 Nov; ∈ 12.

Pompidou Centre Place Georges Pompidou, 75004, Paris; tel: 01 44 78 12 33; web: www.cnac-gp.fr; M̄ Rambuteau, Hôtel de Ville, Châtelet; closed Tue; ∈ 10 (day pass for whole centre); ∈ 5.50 (MNAM only).

Pyramid (Père Lachaise cemetery) 23rd section, 75020, Paris; M̄ Père Lachaise, Philippe-Auguste, Gambetta; open every day; free.

Rothéneuf Rock Sculptures Plage du Val, Rothéneuf, along the coast from Saint Malo, on the road to Cancale; opening times vary – call the brasserie Le Benetin, tel: 02 99 56 97 64 for details (it's a good place to eat, too, with fine sea views); €4.

Sistine Chapel Saint Vincent la Rivière, just south of the small town of Broglie, 20km southeast of Lisieux, in Normandy; currently closed.

Ville Souterraine Bourré, 30km south of Blois, 3km east of Montrichard; tel: 02 54 32 95 33; web: http://perso.wanadoo.fr/delalande/sommaire.html; open daily Apr–Nov; €5.

Woinic Bogny sur Meuse, in the Ardennes, 15km north of Charleville Mézières; Contact Eric Sleziak (tel 03 24 32 03 54), Woinic's creator, or the Bogny sur Meuse tourist office (tel 03 24 32 11 99) to arrange a visit; free.

Eccentric Towns, Parks and Gardens

There's something marvellously idiosyncratic about certain towns. Llívia refuses to be French in spite of being in France; the staff at one of Eze's restaurants are almost as prickly as the famous cactus garden there; and Condom simply won't face up to having an amusing name (and being situated on an even more amusingly named river).

The same is true of some of the parks in France, whether they're unusually themed (crocodiles, anyone?), or just plain unusual (the Désert de Retz). Finally, there's simply nothing you can do to stop people taking over their own gardens and turning them into works of art – and France has more than its fair share.

ECCENTRIC TOWNS
Bitche
There's nothing remotely eccentric about the small town of Bitche, up in France's northeastern corner – other than its name, of course, and it's curious self-branding as 'The Green Pearl!' (or, given its proximity to Germany, *'Die Grüne Perle!'*). There's an excellent example of a late 17th-century Vauban fortress which you can visit, a crystal museum, a place you can see clogs being made, and plenty of opportunities to taste the fresh and fruity local Moselle wines. It's all very pleasant, and bitchiness is in short supply. So no bitching about the drippy weather, please.

Condom en Armagnac
The pretty town of Condom, in the heart of the Armagnac region, 40km southwest of Agen, remains, incredibly, irony-free. Drop into the tourist office and there's not the slightest hint there might be anything even mildly amusing about the town's name.

Instead you'll be directed to the cathedral (very fine, as it happens), or the Armagnac Museum (see page 188), or encouraged to see the Flamme d'Armagnac (see page 31), and then sent on your way with a 40-page brochure – which doesn't even acknowledge condom vs Condom, and fails to mention the Musée du Préservatif (the Condom Museum), even though it's clearly marked on the map. It's as if the town hall naïvely hopes that if nobody says anything about it, the jokes will simply die away.

It doesn't help, of course, that the attractive river flowing through town is called the Baïse – the umlaut being desperately important in preventing you from pronouncing it as a very rude word. Neither does the town do itself any favours with its numerous slogans, all of which are moderately hilarious to the English speaker. *'Condom, tous vos plaisirs'*, reads one; *'Condom, porte de bonheur'*, boasts another'; *'Condom, au bord de la Baïse'* risks a third, *'Condom, au fil de la Baïse vagabonde'* encourages a fourth.

As it happens, the origin of the word condom itself is obscure. Some claim there was a Dr Condom in the 17th century, while others prefer the derivation from the

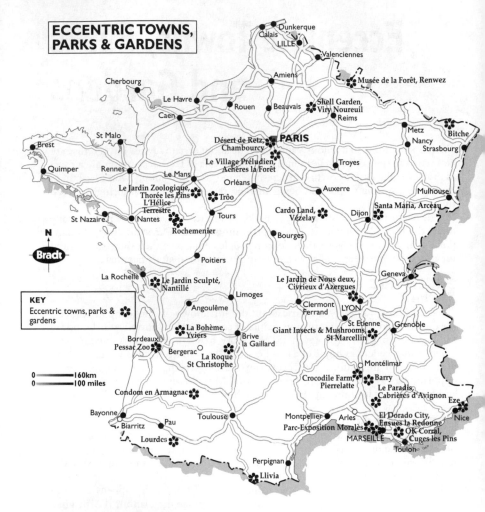

ECCENTRIC TOWNS, PARKS & GARDENS

KEY
Eccentric towns, parks & gardens

0 ▬▬ 160km
0 ▬▬ 100 miles

Latin *condus*, a preservative (and the French word *préservatif* might add weight to that argument). But the town name Condom is simply a contraction of the Gallo-Roman Condatómagus.

It doesn't stop there being a **Musée du Préservatif**, of course, which does its bit to celebrate the *redingote anglaise* ('English riding coat' being French for 'French letter'), and increase awareness about HIV/Aids and how to prevent the transmission of sexual diseases. There's a history of the condom, with an engraving of Casanova blowing up 'balloons', some old packaging (including a British condom which should have been used by the end of 1948), and good multimedia displays showing how condoms are made. During 2002 there was also an excellent temporary exhibition on how the condom is being used in Africa to stem the tide of HIV infection.

For more information about the delights of Condom and the Baïse, you can contact the tourist office or log on to www.condom.org – although at the time of writing they'd only got as far as the home page, which has a tantalising but inactive button advertising 'Rockin' Condom'. You should also contact them to check the **Musée du Préservatif** opening times – usually every day, but in summer only.

Eze

The tiny medieval fortress-village of Eze, poised above the Côte d'Azur, and just west of Monaco, is self-consciously perfect, but no less appealing for that – though it can get seriously over-run in summer. The reason it's here in this book, however, is for the absolutely fabulous **Cactus Garden**, which spills over several levels and features hundreds of succulents and cacti, large and small, with breathtaking views down to the sea, 400m below.

The garden was created in 1949 by the agronomist Jean Gastaud, and planted with species mainly coming from Latin America. There's often something extremely exotic in flower, and it makes for a heady experience. It's right at the top of the village, however, and a bit of a hike up from the car park, so bring sensible shoes.

You can then eat at **Le Cactus**, a nearby restaurant, if you're not up to shelling out for the extremely swanky nosh at the **Château de la Chévre d'Or**. The local tourist office rather shamelessly points out that all the members of the Irish rock group U2 either own homes or holiday in Eze, so if you see blokes wearing sunglasses and leather jackets and looking self-important, you know what's up.

After eating, you can make the lovely walk all the way down to the coast along the **Sentier Frédéric Nietzsche**, which was where the great philosopher worked out some of his bleakest thoughts, when he was here in the 1880s. It takes about an hour to get to Eze Bord de Mer, and rather longer to climb back up.

Llívia

There may be a corner of a foreign field that is forever England, but there's an enclave in southern France, called Llívia, which is forever Spain. Situated a few kilometres into France, in the Pyrenees, it's an anomaly of history dating back to the 1659 treaty ceding several formerly Spanish territories north of the Pyrenees to France.

The treaty seems to have been pretty shoddily drafted, as it didn't actually specify where the border was to run, but only that 33 Spanish villages should become French. The intention was fairly logical – that the boundary should follow the watershed along the Pyrenees – but it was subverted by the people of Llívia, who weren't a bit interested in becoming French.

As Llívia was actually the capital of the region known as the Cerdagne, it was able to use the legitimate loophole that it wasn't a village at all, but a town, and therefore couldn't be counted amongst the 33 communes to become French. Even more strongly in its favour was the fact that the river flowing through it, the Ségre, may start in the French Pyrenees, but it then loops round and flows back into Spain.

After much wrangling, the French agreed it could be granted an exception, and temporarily remain Spanish. More than three centuries later, Llívia is as Spanish as ever, although the language mostly used is an odd dialect closer to Catalan than pure Spanish. A good example is the welcome page from the Llívia website:

> *Des del fascinant món d'Internet, us volem donar la benvinguda a aquest petit i meravellós enclavament dels Pirineus. … Sigueu doncs benvinguts a Llívia, on esperem que gaudiu de tot allò que tenim al vostre abast.*

Llívia is between Bourg Madame and Font Romeu, just a few kilometres inside France. There aren't usually any border formalities to go through, and I once cycled right across the enclave without even realising I'd gone to Spain – the Spanish shop signs and the inflated peseta prices should have given me a clue, however. There's not a great deal to do or see, though there is a small and rather charming apothecary museum.

Lourdes

There's nowhere else in France quite like Lourdes, a small town in the foothills of the Pyrenees which attracts around five million people a year from around the world, making it second only to Paris in terms of the number of bed-nights spent in hotels, and Christendom's most visited shrine.

The vast majority of visitors come in search of a cure, and after taking the miraculous waters from the shrine here, a surprising number certifiably find one. How much of a miracle is being worked, how large a part faith plays, and how much is down to pure statistics (a reasonable number out of five million sick people a year should get better anyway – as Voltaire (see page 146) famously said, 'The art of medicine consists in amusing the patient while nature cures the disease.') is hotly debated, but it doesn't stop the flow of hopefuls.

They come because Our Lady of Lourdes appeared here 18 times in 1858 to a 14-year-old girl called Bernadette. On the first occasion, on 11 February, the sickly, undernourished girl was out collecting firewood when she saw an apparition dressed in white, wearing a blue sash, and with a yellow rose on each foot. It made the sign of the cross, and disappeared.

The third time the apparition appeared, she spoke, and told Bernadette to make sure a chapel was built on the site. She also instructed her to drink at the spring she was pointing at – which was only a muddy puddle until Bernadette scratched at the surface. After repeated appearances, and badgering from Bernadette, the apparition confessed *'Que soy era Immaculada Conceptiou'* – patois for 'I am the Immaculate Conception', and the church did indeed build a shrine on the site.

Bernadette herself left the area, retiring to a convent in Nevers, in the centre of France, but the shrine attracted more and more of the faithful, especially after 1873, when the first reports of miraculous healings appeared. A basilica was built in 1876, but was replaced by the huge concrete church you see today in 1958, as its capacity was far too small for the crowds then coming to Lourdes.

The ailing Bernadette finally gave up the ghost in 1879, at the age of 35, and was buried at the convent, but in 1909 she was exhumed, and found to be perfectly preserved, in spite of the damp tomb she'd been buried in. She was exhumed again in 1919 and 1925, and found still to be uncorrupted – though as her skin was now discoloured in parts, wax coverings were made for her face and hands. She was then placed in a reliquary in a special shrine, and beatified by Pope Pius XI, before being sanctified in 1933.

If you're going to Lourdes, it's well worth planning your visit, especially if you're going in the main pilgrimage season, from April to October, and most definitely if you want to take part in the year's biggest event, the Feast of the Assumption, on 15 August, when the town tends to be full to capacity.

If you want to see Bernadette herself, she's in Nevers, in the middle of France, at the **Chapel of the Espace Bernadette**. Around half a million people a year come to pay their respects to the perfectly preserved saint.

Troglodyte villages

A combination of the right geography and geology, and a moderately turbulent history, have left France with a whole clutch of troglodyte villages, several of which you can visit.

Rochemenier

One of the most unusual sites is at Rochemenier, just west of Saumur, and only a couple of kilometres from La Cave aux Sculptures (see page 221). Most of the complex here was built into existing quarries from the 13th century onwards, though the underground chapel is considerably older, dating from the Carolingian period (AD750–960).

In all, there are some 20 buildings you can visit, including two troglodyte farms with outbuildings (in-buildings, really), several very old houses (with recreated furnishings), and a modern cave house, showing how it might be to be a latter-day troglodyte yourself.

Endearingly, the Rochemenier site also doubles up as a conservation centre for old breeds of poultry, which have largely been replaced in modern farming by faster-growing species, so don't be surprised to see troglodyte ducks, geese, chickens and turkeys wandering around. And if you come any time in spring or summer you'll probably think Louresse-Rochemenier has a rosy future – it's a major rose-producing area, after all, with more than a million rose-bushes from here being sold a year.

If you don't manage to get to Rochemenier, at least check out the website, which has a great page in Esperanto!

L'Hélice Terrestre de l'Orbière

Not far from Rochemenier, about 20km northwest of Saumur, is the extraordinary Hélice Terrestre de l'Orbière. Over a twelve year period, from 1981 to 1993, the artist Jacques Warminski converted the former troglodyte village into a major artwork, based on a spiral both above ground and below it.

On the surface you can see his Amphi-Sculpture, full of swirling concrete shapes, reflecting what's inside, where you'll find a series of underground galleries centred on a remarkable spherical room. The whole thing intends to present the contrasts between inside/outside; above/below; convex/concave; and seen/unseen, and is truly remarkable.

Jacques Warminski himself, sadly, died suddenly in 1996, at the age of only 50, but his companion, Bernadette, keeps the place going, and in summer there are all sorts of cultural activities which take place in and around the complex, from theatre and dance performances to jazz concerts. It's well worth the visit.

Trôo

On the Loir (not to be confused with the Loire), 50km north of Tours, you'll find the little village of Trôo (which is almost too good to be Trôo, and allegedly named after the English mispronunciation of the word 'trou', meaning 'hole'). Here, there's a whole community of 'neo-troglodytes', who've taken over and refurbished the cave houses which were built into the cliffs here from the 11th century on. You can also visit some of the caves which haven't yet been gentrified, which run deep into the cliffs.

La Roque Saint Christophe

Some of France's oldest and most extensive troglodyte dwellings can be found at La Roque Saint Christophe, a small village on the Vézère, between Les Eyzies and Montignac (where you'll find the Lascaux II cave paintings). Around 50,000 years ago, Palaeolithic cave dwellers lived here, but the caves were done up substantially in the Middle Ages, and fortified from the 11th century onwards.

La Roque was captured by the English during the Hundred Years War in 1401, but they only hung onto it for five years before being defeated themselves. There's a legend that they hid their treasures in a goat's hide in one of the many rooms in the complex before leaving, but if anyone's ever found it, they're not fessing up.

In 1588, in an attempt to prevent its continued use as a Protestant hideaway, it was largely destroyed, and remained abandoned until the 20th century, when tourism was invented. The complex runs across five levels, and offers a fascinating glimpse of what life more than 500 years ago might have been like (dark and dirty, mainly).

Given the situation, high up above the Vézère, you'll be glad to know that there's a reassuring railing to stop visitors plunging off the cliff into the river below.

Barry

The troglodyte dwellings at Barry, overlooking the Rhône valley, just outside Bollène, were inhabited continuously from prehistoric times until the beginning of the 20th century. The area isn't fenced off or anything, so you can wander round the caves and stone houses built into the hillside here at your leisure. Back in the 18th century, there were still around 500 people living up here, but after a series of cave-ins, the population dwindled to 50 in the 19th century, and the last resident, a widow, died before World War I. There are fabulous views from the top of the hill, up near the ruins of the Château de Bollène.

ECCENTRIC PARKS
Cardo Land

A few kilometres west of Vézelay, at Chamoux, in the Morvan, is one of France's most curious parks, Cardo Land, created by the artist Cardo, and open to the public since 1985.

Born in Spain, in 1924, to talented and creative parents, Cardo was on the silver screen by the age of five, and at 15 was a professional dancer. His father, an anarchist, was killed during the Spanish Civil War, so the family moved to France, where Cardo became renowned as a tap dancer, performing with the likes of Fernandel, Bourvil and Edith Piaf (see page 124). He even taught Brigitte Bardot (see page 132) how to dance flamenco.

A dancer's career is not forever, however, so Cardo turned his hand to painting and sculpture, and started making etchings. With a wife and child, and a new baby on the way (ever the artist, Cardo fathered a total of eight children, with four different mothers) he moved out of Paris in the 1960s, selling up and buying a ten-hectare property in the Morvan.

Here, he finally had the time and space to give his imagination a free rein, and he started building full-scale dinosaur sculptures. It was only a matter of time before he had enough of them to open up the property as a theme park, Cardo Land. Today, there are more than 50 sculptures you can see, including an 11m-long stegosaurus, a sabre-toothed tiger and a woolly mammoth. The sound effects are excellent.

There's also a small palaeontological museum, a re-creation of the cave at Lascaux (called Lascaux III, natch), and an exhibition of Cardo's other works, which include paintings and sculptures. Keep an eye out for Cardo himself, who's looking increasingly like Fidel Castro.

Crocodile farm

Halfway between Montélimar and Orange, in the Rhône valley, and right next door to an enormous nuclear power station, you'll find Europe's only major crocodile farm, **La Ferme aux Crocodiles**. Inside a vast tropical greenhouse, you

can go and look at more than 500 crocs doing their thing – which mainly, it must be said, is lying around.

The farm is the brainchild of Luc Fougeirol, who's been something of a reptile fan since his youth, and has seen every species of crocodile in the wild on three continents. In 1990 he was given a certificate pronouncing him competent to breed and exhibit crocodiles (bet there isn't much call for those), and the following year he imported 335 baby crocs into France.

The originals are now fully grown and have bred successfully, and the farm today is part scientific study centre and part tourist attraction. It's a major force in global crocodile conservation, and publishes a good deal of original research. As far as visitors are concerned, there's a fine guided tour, which works its way over the gangways crossing the crocodile ponds, and down into the new tunnel which allows you to see the crocodiles' bellies. It's quite an experience.

Désert de Retz

The Désert de Retz was the handiwork of François Racine de Monville, who between 1774 and 1789 created a huge Anglo-Chinese garden (complete with 17 follies), near Chambourcy, 20km west of Paris.

De Monville was born in 1734, and as a wealthy aristocrat didn't have to worry about earning a living – the nearest he ever came to it was in 1771, when he won a bet with the Duke of Chartres that he couldn't shoot down a flying pheasant with a bow and arrow. He could.

From 1774 onwards he dedicated his time to the creation of the Désert de Retz (only called a desert because it was isolated), which was to comprise not just exotic trees and plants from around the world, but also a series of follies ('*fabriques*'). These included Europe's first Chinese House, a temple dedicated to Pan, a pyramid-shaped ice-house, and an obelisk.

Most original of all, however, was the Column House, which became de Monville's summer residence. A magnificent oval-shaped fake ruin, over 15m tall, it looks like a broken section of a giant Roman column, but actually contains four usable storeys inside. De Monville opened the gardens up to the public, and famous visitors included the ubiquitous Benjamin Franklin as well as the much-maligned Marie Antoinette (see page 87).

With the revolution in full flow in 1792, de Monville somehow managed to flog off all his property, including the Désert de Retz, to Lewis Disney-Ffytche, an English aristocrat, whose remarkable gullibility in the circumstances could be explained by possible inbreeding – his daughter, Sophia, went on to marry her first cousin ('Keep the money in the family, dear. Don't worry about the chin.').

In 1793, not surprisingly, the property was confiscated by the government, and the following year de Monville was arrested and condemned to death by the Revolutionary Tribunal. Having plenty of money, he bought his freedom daily by the old ruse of having himself hospitalised, and used the time sensibly in improving his badminton game. After Robespierre's execution, de Monville was released, though ended up being killed three years later by a gangrenous gum.

The Désert gradually declined over the next 250 years, and even though it was appreciated by André Breton and Co (see page 156), nothing was done to maintain it. Most of the trees and plants went to rot, and many of the follies disappeared forever. It was only saved in the 1970s by direct action from the government – though unfortunately restoration work has been brought to a halt by a series of legal cases, and you can't currently visit. Nonetheless, in spite of so much of it having been lost over the centuries, the Désert de Retz is still the best remaining 18th-century folly-garden in France – and quite possibly anywhere.

Giant insects and mushrooms

Not to be missed on any account, between Grenoble and Valence, near Saint Marcellin, is the **Forêt aux Champignons et Insectes Géants**, an unusual collection of sculptures of giant insects and mushrooms. No longer will you mix up your beetles or be confused by which mushrooms are edible and which are poisonous. You'll be able to see the world through a snail's or fly's eyes and find out how high fleas could jump if they were our size – about 50m, or up onto the top of the Arc de Triomphe (see page 228), or over the Statue of Liberty (see page 233), is the answer. There's also a collection of the world's biggest insects, preserved under glass, plenty of picnic spots, and donkey and pony-trap rides for the children.

Komir, the jealous hippo

As anyone who's ever been on safari knows, hippos cause more deaths in Africa than any other animal. But that didn't stop Jean Ducuing, a former biscuit salesman, from making his baby hippo, Komir, the star attraction of his new zoo when it opened at Pessac, near Bordeaux, in the late 1970s.

Over the next 23 years, Ducuing and Komir were inseparable, and played together almost every day. Posters for the zoo showed Ducuing with his head inside Komir's enormous mouth. Hippos aren't normally especially friendly, but Komir was. Until, apparently, Ducuing bought himself a shiny new tractor, and spent far too much time on it for the hippo's tastes. Komir started sulking.

On 1 November 1999, he appeared to have had enough. Seeing Ducuing cycling past his enclosure, Komir ploughed through the electric fence, and it was all over in a matter of moments. Ducuing didn't stand a chance, with four tonnes of jealous hippo charging him at 40km/h.

The **Pessac Zoo** was taken over by Ducuing's widow, but the question remained about what to do with Komir. Nobody really wanted him put down, but then again, his continued presence only brought back bad memories. The problem was solved six months later, when Komir ingested a large rubber ball, which killed him. The circumstances were said not to be suspicious.

At the zoo today you'll find a wide variety of animals, especially from Africa and Asia, and the establishment has a fine record of births in captivity – two tigers were born there in 2000, and another three in 2001, along with a rare lemur from Madagascar. After Komir's death, the zoo has now acquired a new baby hippo, a female called Pupchon.

Musée de la Forêt

In the woods of the Ardennes, up near the Belgian border, you'll find the excellent Musée de la Forêt, an open-air museum dedicated to the life and art of woodcutters.

The museum, opened in 1988, was the brainchild of Henri Vastine, who has created dozens of forestry scenes in clearings in the woods, peopled by 130 life-sized wooden men. You'll see them splitting wood with an adze, using two-handled saws, building fires and felling trees. More than 3,000 woodcutting tools are on display, along with ancient machinery, including a couple of old steam engines which were used to power band-saws in the past.

For 2003, the great news is that Mr Vastine has finally found the time to give his wooden men language lessons, so when you next visit you can expect them to be speaking not just French, but English and German too. *'Ich bin ein holzarbeiter'*, indeed.

If you do visit, make sure which side of the Belgian border you're on, as the commune of Botassart, 20km away from Renwez, but over in Belgium, has nicked Henri Vastine's idea and installed copies of his wooden men, causing some friction between the two communities. Don't be fooled – the Renwez men are the originals.

Parc-Exposition de Raymond Moralès

Raymond Moralès, born in 1926, is one of France's greatest living metal-sculptors, and his work is on display at his property between Fos and Martigues, just west of Marseille – it's an easy place to find as it's surrounded by a high wall crowned with dramatic metal sculpted faces.

After a career as a blacksmith, the artist created his own museum in 1982, the Parc-Exposition de Raymond Moralès, which comprises hundreds of distinctive works made of forged and welded metal. Some of the sculptures are reminiscent of the early surrealists' anguished and tormented works, with human features melding into insect or animal forms. It's truly powerful stuff, though frankly I found it all pretty disturbing.

Wild West attractions ... in Provence

If you're near Marseille and in the mood for donning leather *chaparajos* and a Stetson, then you're in luck (pardner!), as there are not one but two wild west theme parks in the area.

The first, inevitably, is the **OK Corral**, about 20km east of Marseille, near Cuges les Pins. Here you'll find 26 exciting rides, including the frankly terrifying Lasso Loop, and a recreated Wild West village. During the afternoons there are various shows put on, including the 'Indian Attack' (shouldn't that be 'Native American Attack'?), and of course the proverbial 'Gunfight at the OK Corral'. You can even camp out in surprisingly well-appointed tepees on the site. As the prices are fair, you can't even complain about being scalped.

The other park is **El Dorado City**, at Ensues la Redonne, just west of Marseille. It's divided up by theme (Western, Mexican, Native American and Canadian), and actors and stuntmen in each area will perform traditional shoot-outs etc for you. There are 14 rides including the Grand Canyon free-fall experience; El Sombrero, a vertiginous carousel; and a bucking bronco machine. You can see the French cancan performed and a Wild West train attacked, and listen to any amount of country music. Yee ha!

ECCENTRIC GARDENS
La Bohème

Deep in the Charente, in the triangle formed by Angoulême, Bordeaux and Périgueux, you'll find La Bohème, the house and garden created by Lucien

Favreau, a local plasterer, over a period of decades, up to his death in 1990, at the age of 78.

The house is decorated with big naïve-art frescos, while in the garden (and in the field across the road) there are sculptures large and small of some of the public figures of Favreau's day, from Charles de Gaulle to the French singers George Brassens and Mireille Mathieu. You'll also find sculptures of animals and symbolic subjects such as a hand and heart representing the comedian Coluche. Fortunately, it's all lovingly maintained by his descendants.

Le Jardin de Nous Deux

If you're a bored, retired, corset-maker living 20km northwest of Lyon, it's only natural that you'd decide to spend the rest of your days building permanent souvenirs of the great architecture you'd seen on holiday with your wife.

So, at least, reasoned Charles Billy, in 1975, before spending the next 18 years, until his death in 1993, creating the quite extraordinary Jardin de Nous Deux (garden for the two of us). With his wife ferrying the stone and Billy sculpting, the couple constructed copies of the Tower of Pisa, the Arc de Triomphe (see page 228), the Villa Adriana at Tivoli, church cloisters, mosques, palazzi from Venice, and even a Roman arena.

Billy and his wife have sadly now passed on, and the Jardin de Nous Deux can't currently be visited – though there are plans for the state to buy it, and turn it into a museum and a fitting memorial to the indomitable couple. Meanwhile it's becoming seriously overgrown. You can still see a handful of Billy's sculptures in the local church gardens, however.

Le Jardin Sculpté

Just south of Saint Jean d'Angély, in the heart of the Cognac region, there's an amazing sculpture garden (Le Jardin Sculpté). It's the work of Albert Gabriel, who only started sculpting full-time on his retirement in 1967, at the age of 63, having been a manual worker all his life.

Gabriel died in 1999, but fortunately the garden was taken over by the commune of Nantillé, so you can still see his wonderful collection of several hundred works. Made of painted cement over wire scaffolding, they depict all sorts of famous and less well-known personalities, as well as religious figures, natives of different countries around the world, and a troupe of half-naked dancing girls. It's probably not exactly the sort of thing you'd want at home, but it's great to visit.

If you want to see the garden and house you first need to go to the town hall in Nantillé – and it's advisable to call ahead to warn them you're coming.

Le Jardin Zoologique

When his duck died in 1974, Emile Tougourdeau decided the only fitting memorial would be a sculpture of the bird, which he painted while it was still damp (the sculpture, not the duck), so the cement could properly absorb the colour.

It was the start of a 15-year obsession which led to his garden, just outside Thorée les Pins, 40km south of Le Mans, becoming truly zoological. The duck was soon joined by flamingos, peacocks, bears, deer, buffalo and a tree full of parrots. Tougourdeau then moved on to people, adding St Francis of Assisi and a Mexican with a big sombrero feeding a mule together, a group of drinkers toasting passersby, a bride and groom, an Indian goddess, and a couple of *gendarmes* to keep the place in order.

In its heyday it was absolutely fantastic, but unfortunately the garden hasn't been maintained at all since Tougourdeau's death in 1989. The sculptures, surrounded by trees, have gone green and mouldy, and badly need restoring. I spoke to the mayor of Thorée les Pins, who said the commune was keen to buy the property, but negotiations with Tougourdeau's widow, Denise, didn't seem to be going anywhere.

As a result, you can't visit the garden, though hopefully it will be bought, restored and re-opened, as it would be a tragedy to lose the place.

Le Paradis

Up in the hills facing the north side of the Luberon, in Provence, above the little town of Cabrières d'Avignon, is an absolutely charming sculpted garden called Le Paradis. It was the lifework of a local farmer called Léopold Truc, who came here every day for lunch and spent most of his evenings and every weekend building his paradise amongst the pine trees.

He started off soon after World War II, with a *Borie* (one of the ancient dry-stone huts you see all over Provence), adding a couple of rooms to each side of it for storing his tools, and then decorating the whole thing with a mosaic made of broken terracotta, pebbles, seashells and snail shells. He then laid out cobbled mosaic pathways, decorated with scallop and clam shells, and lined them with totem-pole like sculptures made from old flowerpots and decorated with shells and chips of broken tiles and crockery.

In all, he spent more than 40 years on the project, adding new sculptures and even whole buildings with no obvious function – though there are any number of seats and benches from which you can admire the place. Every surface of every building or sculpture is covered with geometric designs and patterns, made using coloured tile-fragments, seashells, the undersides of crabs, lobster carapaces and snails. Faces, birds, flowers and animals peer out from the centrepieces.

At the western end of the garden you'll find the large tomb which Truc built for himself, complete with a sculpted dog at its foot, and nearby there's a tiny chapel, not much larger than an outside lavatory. There's also an extraordinary tower, 8m tall, which you can climb up (at your own risk) for an incredible view out over the Luberon. Finally, look out for a monument to the 1989 bicentennial of the French Revolution, and a Lorraine cross, a testimony to Truc's Gaullist leanings.

Unfortunately, the garden hasn't been maintained since Truc's death in 1991, and it's beginning to get a bit tatty. So (with apologies to Milton) although it's still far from being *Paradise Lost*, it's to be hoped that one day it'll nonetheless be *Paradise Regain'd*.

Le Paradis isn't open to the public as such, but you can visit, if you can find it (no mean feat), if you arrange it in advance with Léopold's son, René Truc.

The *Santa Maria*

This is a sad story. The writer Pierre Arnoux (he's published a dozen books, my favourite of which is *La Vigne au Loup*, a story of ruined French 19th-century winegrowers who try to make a go of it in Mexico) is also a bit of a model-maker. After his wife gave him a model of the *Santa Maria*, the ship Christopher Columbus sailed over to the West Indies and back in 1492, he decided to do it justice by making a full-scale version, in his garden, near Dijon.

His first task was getting planning permission (no mean feat, for a 20m-long, 6m-wide 15th-century sailing ship), and his second was persuading the Le Creuset foundry, more used to turning out pots and pans, to make the iron plates needed for the hull.

The job took Arnoux five years, and cost him all his saved royalties, but it was worth it. The *Santa Maria* was absolutely magnificent, and a perfect model of the original, right down to having antique canons (a gift from the town of Toledo, in Spain), copies of all the original furniture inside, blazons from Castille and Aragon, an original Spanish 15th-century chair, and lovely stained glass windows. There was even a gilded wooden Virgin Mary in a chapel in the prow, and 40 medallions on the ceilings designed by Arnoux himself.

But in 1998, vandals broke in and damaged the interior, before making off with some of the original canons and firearms. The following year, even worse damage was done, and in the year 2000 the ship was completely destroyed by cretinous teenagers. It's a real tragedy, and it's hard to believe that Arnoux was able to pick himself up, dust himself off, and start on a new project, a full-sized windmill, which was completed in 2002.

Shell garden

In the triangle formed by Laon, Saint Quentin and Compiègne, just outside the town of Chauny is the village of Viry Noureuil, where Bodan Litnanski, almost 90, lives with his wife Emilie. Here, he created the marvellous **Jardin du Coquillage** – though in reality there are many more 'found' objects than seashells.

Litnanski, born in 1913, came to France as young Russian immigrant in the 1930s, and worked as a tailor, a jeweller, and a builder. In the 1950s, he bought the house in Viry, restored it, and covered the walls with broken crockery (as you do). He then set to work on the garden. First he built a wall two metres tall separating the house from the road, and then covered this with found objects such as broken toys, household appliances, TV sets, dolls and plastic animals, all collected on his travels around the neighbourhood by moped. He embedded seashells (leftovers from local restaurants) into the wall, and later built other sculptures and structures along the same lines. As a whole, it makes for a devastating comment on the consumer society.

The garden, and Litnanski himself, starred in the excellent documentary film *The Gleaners and I*, which was made in the year 2000 by Agnes Varda, one of France's most talented directors, with more than 30 movies to her credit.

It's not open to the public as such, but if you're lucky Bodan or Emilie Litnanski will show you round.

Le Village d'Art Préludien

The life of Roger Chomeaux, better known as plain Chomo, was an extraordinary one, even by the standards of most artists. He was born into a poor family in 1907, but showed early promise as a painter and sculptor, winning a number of prizes at the Beaux-Arts in Paris. As the breadwinner for a growing family, however, he made a living designing carpets until World War II, when he was deported to Poland, but faking deafness he was fortunately repatriated on health grounds.

Back in France, he retired from the world, moving in 1946 to a piece of land his wife had bought in the Fontainebleau forests, and he lived a hermit-like existence there for the rest of the 20th century. For the first 15 years of his self-imposed exile, his only contact with the outside world was the radio he listened to at night.

During the day, he worked incessantly on building his Village d'Art Préludien. He created sculptures using only 'found' materials, such as chicken wire, dead branches, plastic and glass bottles, scrap metal, rocks and stones, dead cars, old bicycles, children's' toys, and the local sand. Nothing was ever deemed complete or unchangeable, and Chomo spent as much time updating existing sculptures as creating new ones. By the time of his death, there were over 30,000 works of art in the woods, many of them only protected by improvised shelters.

From the 1960s onwards, word spread about Chomo and his art, and he showed visitors around his 'village' on weekend afternoons, living on the offerings they left behind. He placed phonetically written signs at strategic points instructing visitors to *'Fet un rêve avec Chomo'* (create a dream with Chomo), or warning that *'Nous n'allons pas vers l'apocalypse; nous sommes l'apocalypse.'* (We're not heading for the apocalypse; we are the apocalypse.)

Chomo died in June 1999, at the age of 92, and as with so many other wonders in this chapter, the future of his work remains uncertain. Visits have been suspended, and there's been worrying talk about selling off the land. You can call the town hall in Achères le Forêt for more information, or write a letter to Chomo's widow, who was still showing occasional visitors on request around the 'village' in the year and a half after her husband's death.

L'Ys

In the heart of the Vosges, somewhere between Dijon and Nancy, a remarkable work of art is being created in more or less total secrecy. The artist is a monumental sculptor called Yves Humblot (the sculptures are monumental; Humblot isn't unusually outsized himself), and the work of art is called L'Ys.

It all started after Humblot, who was born in the late 1940s, returned from a long trip to India, and decided to retreat from the world and live as a hermit in the woods, far from all mod cons (including electricity). He built himself a Tibetan temple to live in, and started cutting huge blocks of stone out of the local quarry.

These he turned into giant sculptures (weighing up to 10 tonnes apiece), representing different themes, such as cosmic energy (fire for man; water for woman), symbiosis (two bodies with a single head), the shadow of the evening, and the big bang. He's now built a series of even larger sculptures, with various different religious themes, and it's to be hoped that some day his work will go on show. So far, only one can be seen by the general public, the monumental *Children's Corner* in Epinal, between Nancy and Belfort.

TRAVEL INFORMATION

Barry follow the D26 north out of Bollène about 2km, and then turn off to the right. The troglodyte village is at the end of the road, another 3km further up; tel: 04 90 40 51 45 (Bollène tourist office).

Bitche 70km north of Strasbourg; tel: 03 87 06 16 16 (Pays de Bitche tourist office).

La Bohème just outside Yviers, a village 5km west of Chalais, in the Charente; tel: 05 45 98 02 65 (Mireille Favreau-Dussuel) / 05 45 98 02 71 (Chalais tourist office); open by appointment only; free.

Le Cactus Eze; tel: 04 93 41 19 02.

Cardo Land on the D951 from Vézelay, at Chamoux, on the road to Clamecy; tel: 03 86 33 28 33; web: http://perso.wanadoo.fr/sacy/cardoenglish.html; open Sun Apr–Nov, daily Jun–Sep; € 5.

Chapel of the Espace Bernadette Nevers; tel 03 86 71 99 50 (tourist office); web: www.ville-nevers.fr/indexstb.htm.

Le Château de la Chévre d'Or Eze; tel: 04 10 92 66 66; menus at € 68 and € 122, and a lunch menu at € 54.

Condom 40km southwest of Agen; tel: 05 62 28 00 80 (tourist office); web: www.condom.org.

Désert de Retz just outside Chambourcy, 20km west of Paris; tel: 01 39 65 46 93 (Société civile du Désert de Retz); web: www.geocities.com/rwkenyon/ (excellent independent site run by Ronald Kenyon); the Désert de Retz is currently closed to visitors.

Eze 10km east of Nice; tel: 04 93 41 26 00 (tourist office); web: www.eze-riviera.com. The **Cactus Garden** is usually open daily, although the hours are irregular – call the tourist office for details.

El Dorado City Ensues la Redonne, just west of Marseilles (take the Carry le Rouet exit off the autoroute to Fos); tel: 04 92 79 86 90; web: www.eldoradocity.fr; open weekends and school holidays Apr–Oct, daily in summer; € 12 (free if you happen to be under one metre tall).

La Ferme aux Crocodiles Pierrelatte, between Montélimar and Orange; tel: 04 75 04 33 73; web: www.lafermeauxcrocodiles.com; open every day of the year; € 8.

Forêt aux Champignons et Insectes Géants a kilometre out of the old village of Saint Antoine l'Abbaye, 8km west of Saint Marcellin, on the main road from Grenoble to Valence; tel: 04 76 36 44 77; web: www.insectes-geants.com; open weekends Mar–Nov, daily Apr–Sep; € 7.

Hélice Terrestre de l'Orbière Saint Georges des Sept Voies, northwest of Saumur; tel: 02 41 57 95 92; open daily in summer, afternoons in winter (call ahead to check times); € 5.

Jardin du Coquillage 15 rue Jean Jaurès, in Viry Noureuil, near Chauny; tel: 03 23 39 35 17; not open as such – call ahead to ask if you can visit; free.

Jardin de Nous Deux Civrieux d'Azergues, 20km northwest of Lyon; tel: 04 78 43 04 17 (Civrieux d'Azergues town hall); currently closed (contact the local town hall for an update).

Jardin Sculpté south of Saint Jean d'Angély, on the D129, which runs north from Ecoyeux to Varaize, about 20km north of Saintes; tel: 05 46 95 92 12 (Nantillé town hall); town hall open Mon and Fri mornings, and Tue afternoons – sometimes also on Thu mornings; free.

Jardin Zoologique just outside Thorée les Pins, about 40km south of Le Mans and 10km east of La Flèche; tel: 02 43 45 61 81 (Thorée les Pins town hall); closed.

Llívia between Bourg Madame and Font Romeu; tel: +34 972 89 63 01 (tourist office – Spanish number!); web: www.llivia.com.

Lourdes tel: 05 62 42 77 40 (tourist office); web: www.lourdes-france.com.

Musée de la Forêt Renwez, in the Ardennes, not far from Charleville-Mézières; tel: 03 24 54 82 66; open daily, though by prior arrangement only in the winter months, and on afternoons only in the spring and autumn; € 4.

Musée du Préservatif Condom; tel: 05 62 28 00 80 (tourist office); web: www.condom.org; open daily, summer only; € 4.

OK Corral just east of the village of Cuges les Pins, 20km east of Marseille; tel: 04 42 73 80 05; web: www.okcorral-france.com; open weekends and school holidays Mar–Oct, daily in summer; € 15.50 (free if you're under a metre tall); € 220 buys you three days in the park and two nights in a tepee, for two adults and four kids.

Le Paradis head up out of Cabrières d'Avignon (itself 20km east of Avignon, off the main road to Apt) towards Les Cédres, turn left up the Chemin des Cabannes, and Le Paradis is about half way up, on the left hand side, hidden behind a brand new house; tel: 04 90 76 81 22 (René Truc); not open to the public as such, but if you're lucky René Truc or his wife will show you round; free.

Parc-Exposition de Raymond Moralès Port de Bouc, on the main road from Martigues to Fos; tel: 04 42 06 26 29; open daily except Tue (though it's possible it will soon be made visitable by appointment only, or closed to the public altogether, so call ahead to check); € 4.

Pessac Zoo 3 chemin du Transvaal, Pessac, just west of Bordeaux, take J12 off the Bordeaux ring road; tel: 05 56 36 46 28; open daily; € 7.

Rochemenier 20km west of Saumur; tel: 02 41 59 18 15; web: http://perso.club-internet.fr/troglody; open daily Apr–Oct, weekend afternoons Feb, Mar, Nov, closed Dec, Jan; € 5.

La Roque Saint Christophe between Les Eyzies and Montignac, about 40km southeast of Périgueux; tel 05 53 50 70 45; web: www.roque-st-christophe.com; daily; € 5.50.

Santa Maria Arceau, about 20km northeast of Dijon; tel: 03 80 37 00 68 (Pierre Arnoux); destroyed by idiot vandals – but you can go and see Arnoux's windmill instead; free.

Trôo 40km north of Tours, 20km west of Vendôme; tel: 02 54 73 55 00 (town hall – there's no tourist office); web: www.troovillage.com.

Le Village d'Art Préludien just outside the commune of Achères le Forêt, a few kilometres from Ury, and about 40km south of Paris; tel: 01 64 24 40 11 (Achères le Forêt town hall), or write to Chomo's widow (Marie Chomeaux, 24 Paris Foret, 77760, Achères le Foret) to request a visit – but don't be surprised if you don't succeed.

L'Ys Firmly off limits – Humblot has asked in no uncertain terms not to be disturbed by readers of this book (or indeed any other), so please respect his privacy.

Eccentric Hotels and Restaurants

After 25 years of searching out and paying for my own accommodation in France, I'm sorry to have to report that the overwhelming majority of hotels are charming and/or quaint, luxurious, calm, well-situated, good value, plain or pretty, but simply not eccentric at all. I've listed a handful here, but I'd be delighted if anyone wants to write in with more for the next edition.

The same is true for restaurants. There are more than 100,000 places to sit down and eat in France, but they almost all serve up the same monotonously wonderful regional and local food, at extremely fair prices. Service and value for money are both generally better outside Paris than in, but if you're splashing out you can still expect to be treated like royalty in the capital – even if you're a mere movie star.

Hotels and restaurants are listed in this chapter with the nearest major city in brackets in the title, and practical information such as contact details and prices in the text rather than at the end of the section. Listings start with Paris and then run (roughly) from north to south.

ECCENTRIC NIGHTS IN – HOTELS
Paris
Hôtel du Septième Art
Movie buffs should probably check straight into the Hôtel du Septième Art which is in the heart of the Marais, and totally dedicated to the cinema-goer's passion. There are framed pictures of stars everywhere, old posters in the bedrooms, and a small memorabilia shop. The 25 rooms are clean, comfortable and popular, and at €60–120 a pop, they get snapped up well ahead.

20 rue Saint Paul, 75004, Paris; tel: 01 44 54 85 00; fax: 01 42 77 69 10; M Saint Paul.

Hôtel Esméralda
The Hôtel Esméralda, right by the Shakespeare & Company bookshop (see page 162) is in an unbeatable location, and the best rooms have views of the twin towers of Notre Dame cathedral, across the river.

It's idiosyncratically basic, with authentically creaky and uneven stripped-pine floors, and everything else wildly wallpapered (including the ceilings), but it's probably as near as you'll get to the original garret experience in the Latin Quarter these days. Which means you shouldn't peer too closely into the bathrooms, or worry about when the wallpaper was last cleaned (never). Some of the rooms are pretty dingy and genuinely too small to swing the hotel cat in (which the hotel cat's grateful for, at least), so be careful what you're getting into. Rooms go from a modest €40 for the rather unpleasant singles to around €100 for doubles with en suites and those famous views.

4 rue Saint Julien le Pauvre, 75005, Paris; tel: 01 43 54 19 20; fax: 01 40 51 00 68; M Saint Michel.

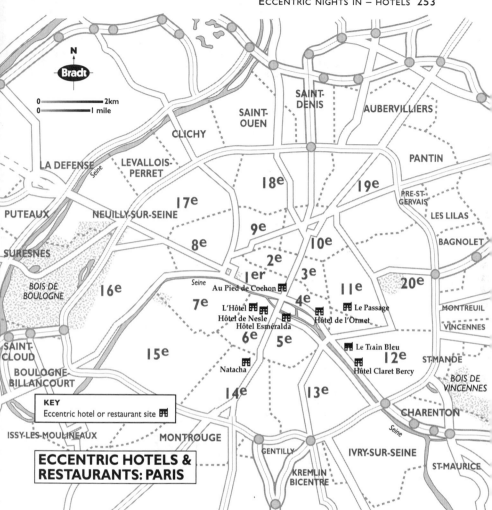

ECCENTRIC HOTELS & RESTAURANTS: PARIS

L'Hôtel

L'Hôtel trades busily on its morbid heritage. Oscar Wilde (see page 175) and Jim Morrison (see page 123) both shared a bed here in room #16 – though when Oscar Wilde died in 1900, it was still the Hôtel d'Alsace, and way downmarket, and Jim Morrison was only briefly a resident before falling drunkenly (if harmlessly) out of the window, 71 years later.

It's a suitably swanky establishment now, with prices to match (Oscar Wilde's room goes for a princely € 600 a night; cheaper doubles come in at € 260–350; and the lovely Cardinale apartment, with its own rooftop terrace, is a snip at € 700 – but you may find Robert de Niro's slipped in ahead of you, as it's said to be his room of choice in Paris these days). It certainly wouldn't be recognisable to either Wilde or Morrison – but the legends live on.

13 rue des Beaux Arts, 75006, Paris; tel: 01 44 41 99 00; fax: 01 43 25 64 31; M̲ Saint Germain des Prés, Louvre.

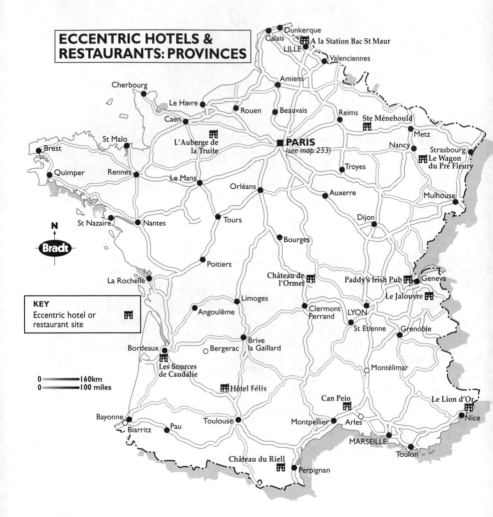

Hôtel de Nesle

If you want eccentric, then the Hôtel de Nesle has been decorated with just you in mind. Each of the 20 rooms (∈ 70–100) has a different theme, and features graphic murals and furnishings to create just the right atmosphere for colonial, oriental, historical or writerly nights in. On the downside you'll find it hard to get a room (booking doesn't always seem to be an option), there are no mod-cons, and the beds are pretty small – but it is clean and cosy, does have a garden, and it's in a fabulous location on the Left Bank.

7 rue de Nesle, 75006, Paris; tel: 01 43 54 62 41; fax: 01 43 54 31 88; web: www.hoteldenesle.com; M̲ Odéon, Saint Michel.

Hôtel Claret Bercy

A word of warning: the Hôtel Claret Bercy has been recently done up. So no longer, sadly, is each room named after a different Bordeaux *cru*, no longer are the room keys attached to giant corks, and no longer are the rooms decorated not just with a poster-sized wine label but with a bottle of the wine itself as well. It used to be that you could even try each of the different reds in the bar downstairs, by the glass – but it's all gone, presumably in the cause of efficiency. The newly decorated rooms are nice enough, and even reasonable value at € 115–135, but simply no longer eccentric.

44 boulevard de Bercy, 75012, Paris; tel: 01 46 28 41 31; fax: 01 49 28 09 29; web: www.hotel-claret.com; M̲ Bercy, Dugommier.

Provinces
Château de l'Ormet (Clermont Ferrand)
If you're a train enthusiast, then you simply have to meet Pierre Laederich, who has created a railway paradise in the grounds of his 18th-century château, about 50km north of Clermont Ferrand. Upstairs there are three really lovely bedrooms (from € 55–75) with a view out over the surrounding countryside and Laederich's three model railways.

Each evening, Laederich (who is also editor-in-chief of the railway enthusiasts' magazine *Connaissance du Rail*) runs electric 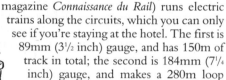 trains along the circuits, which you can only see if you're staying at the hotel. The first is 89mm (3½ inch) gauge, and has 150m of track in total; the second is 184mm (7¼ inch) gauge, and makes a 280m loop which you can ride on(!); and the third is a full 60cm gauge, running over a 500m-long network, which was recovered from an old quarry. There's room for up to 12 passengers if you squeeze up tightly.

The **Château de l'Ormet** is between the lovely villages of Valignat and Veauce. Leave the A71 at junction 12, and head north towards Vicq, before turning left onto the D183. The hotel is open all year round, but welcomes neither pets nor smokers (and especially not pets which smoke).

RD 183, 03330, Valignat; tel: 04 70 58 57 23; fax: 04 70 58 54 36; web: http://ormet.multimania.com.

A la Station Bac Saint Maur (Lille)
Bac Saint Maur, hard up against the Belgian border, west of Lille, may no longer have a railway, but it still has a railway station, called A la Station Bac Saint Maur. More importantly, there's a First-Class 1930 sleeping-car, in perfect condition, complete with mahogany, mother-of-pearl inlay and velvet furnishings, to accommodate you. It offers Orient Express comfort at far from Orient Express prices, and you don't have to travel anywhere, or worry about your murderous fellow passengers (I sincerely hope not, anyway).

The wagon is one of the original PLM (Paris–Lyon–Méditerranée) cars, and has six sleeping compartments, each with a hand-basin, two separate showers and loos, and a tiny dining room for that intimate candlelit dinner. Compartments cost from € 30–40 per night, or for under € 200 you can take the whole wagon, which sleeps up to nine. It's open from April to October, and reservations are absolutely essential.

At the station itself there's also the nearest thing you'll find to a French tavern, which serves up excellent traditional food with a Flemish flavour, in surrounds which are suitably railway-dominated. The Maître d' is the station-master, the waiter is the conductor, and menus are either first or second class, unless you opt for the lunchtime express. It's open year-round except Tuesdays, and closes down for a month around Christmas.

A la Station Bac Saint Maur is 20km west of Lille – take junction 9 off the A25. 77 rue de la Gare, 62840, Sailly sur La Lys; tel: 03 21 02 68 20; fax: 03 21 02 74 37; web: http://perso.wanadoo.fr/station-bac-saint-maur.

Les Sources de Caudalie (Bordeaux)

For a health farm with a real difference, you simply can't beat Les Sources de Caudalie at Martillac, just 10km south of Bordeaux. For a start, it's suspiciously close to the prestigious Smith Haut Lafitte vineyards, and boasts a Michelin-starred restaurant. Add in a bar called 'The French Paradox', with 10,000 bottles of the world's most precious wines on offer, the *'Tour des Cigares'* where you can swirl a post-prandial Cognac around in its balloon while smoking a serious Havana, and the world's only *Vinothérapie* anti-aging and slimming clinic, and I think you'll begin to get the picture.

Quite apart from the simply lovely accommodations and the gourmet food, the *Vinothérapie* cures offer you a unique chance to be pampered by naturally hot water pumped from 500m underground and mixed with 'the health- and beauty-enhancing properties of grapes and vines featured in the Caudalie range of cosmetics' (it says here). Only in France.

None of it's cheap, but then what did you expect? Double rooms and suites go for € 200–450 a night, meals come in at € 40–100 per person, and you can spend anything from € 200–600 per person per day for the various *Vinothérapie* cures.

Chemin de Smith Haut-Lafitte, 33650, Bordeaux-Martillac; tel: 05 57 83 83 83; fax: 05 57 83 83 84; web: www.sources-caudalie.com.

Hôtel Félix (Toulouse)

Head 60km or so north of Toulouse, and between Castelsarrasin and Moissac you'll find the most extraordinary hotel. It wouldn't be out of place in the good ole US of A, but in France there's nothing else quite like it, as the Hôtel Félix is neither more nor less than a reconstructed town from the Wild West.

Surrounding a vast and dusty gravel car park, the motel-like rooms have each been done up as a different Western-style building, so you can sleep in the bank, the prison, the general store, or the mission church. The main building is the saloon, complete with six-shooters for door handles, and the décor is everything you'd expect – the blacksmith's room has an alarming Clint Eastwood mural, while in the tepee an Indian chief stares enigmatically across at the TV.

It's all running slightly to seed, but represents good value at € 50–65 for double rooms. And while the restaurant menu's made a slight nod towards American cuisine, the best dishes are very French and mostly duck-based, as you'd expect in this part of the world.

Fleury, RN 113, 82100, Castelsarrasin, tel: 05 63 32 14 97; fax: 05 63 32 37 51; web: www.restaurant-felix.com.

Château de Riell (Perpignan)

The 19th century was a great time for Gothic follies in France as well as in Britain, and fortunately some have survived – and in one case survived in the shape of a

Gothic hotel, the Château de Riell. Situated in Molitg les Bains, near Prades, some 50km west of Perpignan, the hotel overlooks the impressive Mont Canigou to the south, and has a wonderful situation.

As a Relais & Châteaux member, its eccentricities have necessarily been largely ironed-out, but the 19 Gothic rooms (€ 150–230) still have their individual fireplaces (which you won't be needing, as it's only open from April to October), and plenty of authentic and creaky old furniture. Two swimming pools, a large private park and a gourmet restaurant round out the general air of baronial smugness, but the fillet of sole with caviar and oysters was simply scrummy.

Les Thermes, 66500, Molitg les Bains; tel: 04 68 05 04 40; fax: 04 68 05 04 37.

ECCENTRIC NIGHTS OUT – RESTAURANTS
Paris
Le Goût du Noir

You can no longer eat at the Goût du Noir, as it was never intended to be a restaurant, but instead to teach you what it's like to be blind, and to think twice before you next frogmarch a blind person across a street they didn't even want to cross. The concept was an excellent one, and proved hugely successful – so much so that it's likely to be repeated. So (assuming you're sighted) keep your eyes peeled for the next time such a place opens up.

The Goût du Noir was in a basement in the heart of the Les Halles district in Paris. On arrival (old clothes *de rigueur*) you would be led downstairs into the unlit basement, and fed a three-course meal in pitch darkness. You wouldn't know who your fellow diners were until you'd struck up a conversation with them, or what you were eating until you'd got it in your mouth (far, far harder than you'd think). Put your glass down an inch from where you'd remembered, and the next thing you know there's wine all over the table. Wander over to the buffet, and you'll never find your seat again, unaided.

The staff were all blind themselves, and so had a huge advantage in serving and clearing up the mess, not to mention in translating the Braille menus. The diners, meanwhile, were quick to forget their table manners – it really is a whole lot easier to eat with your hands, if you can't see. It was all a truly humbling experience.

The restaurant was set up by the **Paul Guinot Association for the Blind** (tel 01 53 98 74 97; web: www.guinot.asso.fr), which has been working in helping blind people back into the community since 1920. Since you can't eat at the Goût du Noir, why not make a donation?

Au Pied de Cochon

You've doubtless been wondering all this time when I was finally going to get around to pigs' trotters (*pieds de cochon*), but now your wait is happily over. Au Pied de Cochon is one of the best-known restaurants in Paris, the last hangover from the days when Les Halles was a regular market rather than a shopping mall, and it's open 24 hours a day, every day of the year.

The onion soup here is among the best in Paris, while the pigs' trotters are as tasty as any you'll find in the capital, but the restaurant itself is heaving and way too noisy most of the time, with wall-to-wall tourists until the small hours every morning. It's not the best place for a romantic *tête-à-tête* (or more appropriately *pied-à-pied*), and you won't even get a table any time before 3am if you haven't booked. Expect to pay € 30–50 a head.

If you want the real thing, however, at half the price and a quarter of the hassle, head for Sainte Ménehould (see below), the world's undisputed pig trotter capital.

6 rue Coquillière, 75001, Paris; tel 01 40 13 77 00; M̲ Châtelet Les Halles.

Le Passage

Two thirds or more of your experience at Le Passage or more properly Le Pas'Sage (ie: foolish) will be *andouillette* and wine-related. The *andouillette* range is as wide as you could hope for (∈ 12–25), and the wine list has to be seen to be believed. More than 300 varieties are marked as ready for drinking, and hundreds more are catalogued as on their way up – but you may prefer to go straight for the dozen or so really first-class bottles already open, which you can order by the glass. If you don't like *andouillette*, however, you should probably eat somewhere else.

18 Passage de la Bonne Graine, 75011, Paris; tel: 01 47 00 73 30; fax: 01 47 00 65 68; M̲ Ledru-Rollin.

Le Train Bleu

If the journey is more important than the destination, then Le Train Bleu might just be for you. Not that the food's in any way inferior, but the setting is simply sumptuous. It's the station buffet to beat all station buffets, with the original 1901 Belle Epoque stucco and murals, and heavy leather chairs, frosted glass and extravagant chandeliers.

It's not the best meal in Paris by a long shot, but it's easily the best food I've ever eaten at a train station (and the most expensive – the main menu is ∈ 40, not including wine). On the other hand, ironically, it's definitely not the place to go if you're hoping to actually catch a train – the service, like the décor, is geared for a different era, when the lunchtime diner only needed to be aboard the Train Bleu to Nice in time for the early evening departure.

Upstairs at the Gare de Lyon, 75012, Paris; tel: 01 43 43 09 06; fax: 01 43 43 97 96; M̲ Gare de Lyon (natch).

Natacha

Most diners at trendy Natacha would be lying if they said they'd come for the food alone, which is based around good, upmarket pasta dishes (expect to pay ∈ 30 for a simple meal). But watch eyes roving the tables and turning to the door to scope out new arrivals, and you'll soon cotton on to the fact that this is where models and film-stars come to see, be seen and hold court. It's not really my kind of thing – but here at Bradt Travel Guides we do try to keep an open mind.

17 bis rue Campagne Première, 75014, Paris; tel: 01 43 20 79 27; fax: 01 43 22 93 97; M̲ Raspail.

Provinces
Sainte Ménehould (Reims)

Sainte Ménehould, a small town 60km east of Reims, is deservedly the world capital of pigs' trotters (*pieds de cochon*), and tradition has it that the exquisitely glutinous version of the dish was invented here when someone once left the pot cooking overnight by mistake.

For more than 200 years, Sainte Ménehould chefs have been jealously guarding their individual recipes, and if pigs' trotters are your thing, this is the best town in the world for porking out. Indeed, why restrict yourself to mere trotters alone, when you can equally find pigs' ears and pigs' tails on the menus here?

There are a number of restaurants in town specialising in the dish, starting with the **Auberge du Soleil d'Or** (tel: 03 26 60 82 49), which is also home to the local Confrérie Gastronomique des Compagnons du Pied d'Or (gastronomic brotherhood of the golden trotter). Next door is **Le Cheval Rouge** (tel: 03 26 60 81 04; web: www.lechevalrouge.com), which has 20 rooms upstairs if you've really pigged out; but if that's full there's also the homey **Restaurant de La Poste** (tel: 03 26 60 80 16) and the fine **Restaurant Le Saint Nicolas** (tel: 03 26 60 80 59).

For a little something to take home (surprise your friends!), look no further than the local boutique, **Au Pied de Cochon** (tel: 03 26 60 17 71).

Le Wagon du Pré Fleury (Nancy)

At the old station at Magnières there's a fine restaurant called Le Wagon du Pré **Fleury**, which has been set up in a railway carriage. Not one of your swanky Wagon-Lits dining cars, either, but a standard SNCF passenger car, converted into a cosy dining room. It's a lovely environment, and helped by excellent menus featuring fine food from the Vosges. Magnières is about 30km southeast of Nancy, and less than 15km west of Baccarat.

Rue de la Gare, 54129, Magnières; tel: **03 83 72 32 58**.

L'Auberge de la Truite (Rouen)

There's nothing like a bit of fairground-organ music to drown out the conversation of a dull dinner partner. So if you're anxious about being bored to death by a loved one or wearied by a tiresome business colleague, why not suggest dining out at the Auberge de la Truite, in Montreuil l'Argillé, about 60km southwest of Rouen? You'll receive a warm welcome, wholesome local food at good prices, and a fair earful from the owner's excellent personal collection of around a dozen original fairground organs.

Rue Grande, 27390, Montreuil l'Argillé; tel: **02 32 44 50 47**.

Paddy's Irish Pub (Geneva)

Nothing special about an Irish pub in France, you'd think (there are, after all, many hundreds of such establishments), but none I've supped Guinness at is anything like as authentic as Paddy's Irish Pub in Ferney Voltaire, the small town on the French-Swiss border where Voltaire (see page 146) spent the last 19 years of his life.

The pub was the direct result of a nasty smash-up in 1993, which put two sailing friends, who'd been in the car together, into hospital. Questioning the meaning of life, as you do in such circumstances, David (Irish) and Patrick (French) both quit their Swiss jobs, and went to Ireland on crutches, with the idea of creating the perfect Irish pub in France.

They scoured more than 100 Irish cottage pubs looking for what made each one distinctive, and working out how they could recreate some of that famous Irish welcome. They toured the distilleries and breweries, bought furniture, brass fittings, mirrors, frosted glass, stained glass, and even flagstones in Ireland, and then shipped the whole 35-tonne load over to France, where they installed it in a place they'd found next door to a vintners.

By October 1995, it was ready, and seven years on it's very much part of the local scene – which happens to include not just an unusually large number of Irish and English ex-pats, but also more than 100 other nationalities. The pub acts as a focal point, and is popular with the local French people too – hardly surprising as there's no better pint of Guinness to be found in France, the live Breton and Irish music is a draw, and the fish and chips are first-rate.

La Poterie, 01210, Ferney Voltaire; tel: 04 50 40 77 47.

Le Jalouvre (Geneva)

Up in the French Alps, at 1,100m, in the charming mountain village of Mont Saxonnex, you'll find the Jalouvre, where the owner has been serving up pretty much the same Sunday lunch since 1948. I discovered it by accident about 15 years ago, and have dropped in from time to time ever since.

You'll start with slices of the locally cured mountain ham with big chunks of bread and a slab of butter. Next up is a *feuilleté*, filled with mushrooms, which is followed by the main event, roast guinea-fowl (*pintade*), served with the best *frites* in France and a cauliflower gratin. Salad, cheese, and a portion of home-made apple tart round things off very nicely.

Twice, I've made the mistake of saying that it's so nice to be served the same meal, only to have my wrist severely slapped. It's never the same meal at all. You might get seafood in sauce instead of the mushrooms in the *feuilleté*, for instance, and on occasion the cauliflower gratin will actually be a cabbage gratin.

Booking is essential, as *madame* only cooks up enough for those who've confirmed they're coming. And heaven help you if you arrive at 12.31 for a 12.30 booking – *madame* will have given your table (and your *pintade*) away by the time you arrive.

Mont Saxonnex is about 50km east of Geneva, and sits high up above the Arve valley which runs up to Chamonix Mont Blanc – it can be reached from either Bonneville or Cluses, via a narrow and winding road, and up above the village there's some excellent walking to be found. The Jalouvre also has half a dozen simple but clean rooms upstairs.

Le Bourgéal, 74130, Mont Saxonnex; tel: 04 50 96 90 67.

Can Peio (Nîmes)

Closer to Provence than Catalonia, you'll nonetheless find one of France's best Catalan restaurants, Can Peio in a refurbished railway station dating back to 1882. Run by the zealously cheerful Peio Rahola and his wife, the dining room is the former waiting room, the terrace is on Platform One, the serving hatch is the ex-ticket office, and the kitchen is in the old station-master's office.

Amongst railway memorabilia, you'll find an interesting collection of insects and butterflies testifying to Rahola's former career as an entomologist – though it's unlikely to distract you from the lively Catalan food (I had squid with artichokes, an excellent combination) and mostly Spanish wine list. If you're into tapas, Peio will knock you up a whole meal's worth, but don't expect him to do children's menus, as he doesn't approve – he'd rather they dipped into whatever you're eating, to improve their palettes.

Can Peio is at the old train station of Junas-Aujargues, 20km west of Nîmes, 2km before Sommières, and it's usually open every day except Sunday evenings and all day Wednesday. It's a sound idea to reserve ahead, and expect to pay € 30–40 a head, including wine.

Route Aujargues, 30250, Junas-Aujargues; tel: 04 66 77 71 83; web: http://membres.lycos.fr/canpeio/.

Le Lion d'Or (Nice)

Almost on the Italian border, in Menton, right by the market hall, is the Lion d'Or, which for most of the year simply serves up a seafood storm in one of the liveliest and most cheerful settings imaginable. It's also the only place I've ever been offered full-sized *Cigales de Mer* (a local crustacean related to lobsters and langoustes, but without claws). Grilled in an olive-wood-fired pizza oven, and served with mayonnaise and baked potatoes, there's simply nothing to compare it to.

Every New Year's Eve, for the past 15 years or so, the owners have thrown a terrific drag party, and the extravagant photos of past years' events can be seen all over the restaurant. Indeed, the flamboyant service and camp asides from the staff give you a pretty clear indication of not-so-well-hidden stage talents. It's a huge amount of fun – and if that's not enough to sell you on the restaurant, a slice of its magnificent *Tarte Tatin* certainly should be. Gabriel Santucci, the owner, is planning on retiring in the next few years, however, so catch it while you can.

7 rue des Marins, 06500, Menton; tel: 04 93 35 74 67.

Nuts and Bolts

It's beyond the remit of this book, but there are plenty of guides which will tell you how to get to France, how to get around, where to stay, what to eat and what to see – and indeed how much it's all going to cost you. You may nonetheless find some of the following information useful.

GETTING AROUND

There's no point in pulling punches here. With the exception of the places mentioned in Paris, and the occasional in-town attraction, the great majority of things you can see, do and visit from this book simply aren't easily accessible on public transport. Essentially, therefore, that means driving, biking or cycling.

By plane/train/bus

You can cut out some of the hard work by taking efficient (if expensive) local flights, or by jumping onto France's excellent fast-train (TGV, *Train à Grande Vitesse*) network, and renting a car when you get there. If you're going to be using the TGV, however, it's important to book ahead at any time (not just during holiday periods) and to make sure you also have a seat reservation (obligatory).

Ordinary trains cover the rest of the rail network, and are a great way to see the country if you're not in a hurry, but still won't take you to most of the places in this book. And don't forget that your ticket's not valid on any French train until you've punched it in the orange *composteur* on the station platform.

Buses fill in the gaps in the rail network, and tend to be cheaper, but slower, when they're available.

By bicycle

France is still one of the best countries in the world for cyclists. Towns and villages are rarely very far apart, there's a huge network of country lanes to keep you off the busy arterial roads, and motorists are more cycle-aware and cycle-friendly than anywhere else I've cycled.

There's a bicycle-culture throughout the country which makes it a real pleasure to pedal through, and hotels and restaurants will treat you kindly if you roll up on a bike. The railways are more accommodating than they used to be, too, with a variety of trains now accepting cycles on board – even some TGVs.

By car

If you *are* driving, the main things to remember are that France is still a pretty dangerous place for motorists (over 8,000 people were killed in French road accidents in 2001); the speed limits are 130km/h on motorways (*autoroutes*), 90km/h on normal roads and 50km/h in towns (and anywhere suburban where there are streetlights); the other driver flashing his lights is more likely to be an 'I'm coming through' signal than a courtesy call; and you should avoid the seasonal migrations if you possibly can.

In summer, all of France goes on holiday (and mostly within France), and while factories no longer close down for the whole of July or August, Saturdays in season (and especially those closest to 14 July, 1 August and 15 August) can be hellish (*Un Saison d'Enfer*, indeed, as Rimbaud, see page 142, would have it) – as that's the changeover day for every weekly rental in the country.

There's an excellent organisation in France, however, called the Bison Futé (the canny bison) which not only marks jam-avoiding routes across the country, but also helps you steer clear of the worst of the problems by classifying the various days of the year according to traffic intensity, with green for normal, orange for busy, red for chock-a-block, and black for avoid-at-all-costs. The **Bison Futé** website (www.bison-fute.equipement.gouv.fr) has the full details, with local problems highlighted, and updates every hour or so (although it's available only in French).

Essentially, if you can avoid travelling on Saturdays in summer, do so, and especially if you're heading in or out of Paris. Bottlenecks form around many major (and some minor) cities, tempers flare, and accidents happen. If you must travel on a summer Saturday, be on the roads very, very early, set off after lunch, or resign yourself to the long-term close-quartered company of your fellow passengers.

In summer you'll also see lots of traffic police about, doing their bit to curb over-excited French drivers, and pulling people in at random to check that everything's in order. Fines can be quite steep, and foreigners are expected to pay up on the spot. It's worth knowing, too, that driving offences which are considered serious include: not coming to a complete halt at stop signs; not buckling up (driver and all passengers); overtaking across solid white lines; having faulty lights of any kind (carry spare bulbs); not carrying a warning triangle (check, if you're renting a car); and stopping out of town without getting your vehicle right off the road.

Speeding and drink driving are rightly treated with the severity they deserve, and random breath tests (the alcohol limit is low, at 0.5g/l) are widely applied, especially around festive occasions like Christmas and New Year – though I've yet to see a breathalyser in operation if there's a wedding in town. None of this of course will stop you being flashed repeatedly by the bloke behind you on the motorway, if he wants you to get out of the fast lane RIGHT NOW, even though you're already going over the speed limit yourself – but it's worth knowing the rules.

Finally, refuel at hypermarkets if you can, as they're significantly cheaper than roadside petrol stations, and far, far more economical than autoroute service stations.

In Paris

Paris is great. You can flag down a reasonably priced taxi, jump into it, state your destination, and sit back and relax. Chances are, however, you'll then get stuck in traffic, watching the euros mount up on the meter, and wondering why on earth you didn't simply head underground like everyone else. For Paris's *métro* is magnificent. Stations are closely spaced, lines are incredibly regularly serviced, and it's cheap as chips (actually it's a good deal cheaper, *frites* being notoriously over-priced in the capital).

As you head towards the outskirts the *métro* gives way to a well-organised RER (*Réseau Express Régional*) suburban train system which interconnects you with a myriad bus network, so unless you're madly determined (or it's August, when everyone's out, and parking is generally free), leave your car somewhere else. You don't need it in the city.

Finding your way around

After spending a good part of the year in Croatia, researching and writing the eponymous Bradt Travel Guide (see www.bradt-travelguides.com), I came back home in the summer of 2002, and realised that the signage around France is simply brilliant. Knowing your road numbers is a definite help, but even without them you can get a long way by following the *Toutes Directions* (anywhere but here) and *Autres Directions* (anywhere but there) signs through town, until you see your destination indicated.

Motorways are signed in blue, and labelled A (for *autoroute*), while all other roads are signed in green (and why is it the opposite in Switzerland, could a kind reader please tell me?). Roads maintained at the national level are N roads, while those at the departmental and communal level are D and C roads – the size and quality however depending more on the throughput than the labelling.

If you're lost, or just needing directions, your best bet is to stop at a garage or restaurant/brasserie/café/bar and you'll find locals willing not only to help, but to provide you with some sort of sustenance for the journey as well. People are naturally proud of their local heritage and colourful characters (even if they might admit *'il est un peu spécial'* – he's an odd one, he is), and will go to great lengths to help you find what you're looking for.

Careful planning, of course, can take a lot of the hassle (and fun) out of the game, especially now that you can get really detailed route and location maps from **Michelin on-line** (at www.viamichelin.com – which works irritatingly well for trips in the UK, let alone in France). Just bear in mind that the journey times quoted on the site are best-possible no-stops times, so add in refuelling, rest-breaks and potential traffic jams to your own estimates. And don't be competitive.

Another very useful tool is the **French phone book**, which is online at www.pagesjaunes.fr. Switch it into English and head for the white pages, and you can find everyone in France who doesn't have an unlisted number. For people in the bigger cities you can even pull up a map of exactly where they live. If you're looking for tourist offices, type in *tourisme* or *syndicat d'initiative* and you'll quickly come up with a number you can call. When there isn't a tourist office, try the *mairie* (town hall), where you'll invariably find helpful staff (albeit frequently monolingual – and their one language ain't English).

Maps

There are any number of different maps of France, but only two companies map the whole country seriously, the IGN (*Institut Géographique National*), which is the equivalent of the National Survey in the UK, and Michelin, which broadly equates to the AA (Automobile Association), even though it makes tyres rather than operating a breakdown service as its original core business.

The IGN maps (which come in 1:250,000, 1:100,000, 1:50,000 and 1:25,000 varieties) are on the whole nicer looking, and much better for hiking, cycling and the outdoors, while the Michelin maps (mainly 1:1,000,000, 1:200,000, 1:150,000) are clearly easier for drivers. Michelin has the advantage too of tying in with its famous red guide, with towns underlined on the regional maps being listed for accommodation or restaurants in the guide itself. If you know where you're going, but not where it is, then you can look it up ahead of time at www.viamichelin.com, and even tap into the relevant section of *Le Guide Rouge* online.

HOTELS, RESTAURANTS, BARS AND CAFÉS

As the most-touristed country on earth (more than 75 million people a year visit France, compared to 50 odd million to the USA or Spain, 40 million to Italy and a mere 25 million to the UK), there's an abundance of hotels and restaurants in France, and a huge guidebook industry to point you in the right direction, whatever your niche speciality might be. It's not for me, therefore, to recommend (or indeed not recommend) specific guides to France, but if you're heading anywhere near Paris or Lille you could do worse than pick up Laurence Phillips' excellent *Bradt Guide to Eurostar Cities*. Check out, too, the few places I've listed in *Chapter 11*.

Hotels

It's a source of constant wonderment to me, after 25 years of travelling around the country under my own steam, that France is still such extraordinary value for money as far as accommodation's concerned. Sure, you can pay a small fortune if you want to mix with the models and the movie stars in Paris or Cannes, but then that's true anywhere in the world. But what France still seems to have in spades is an abundance of affordable, friendly, family-run establishments.

Even in Paris, there are hundreds of hotels which aren't prohibitively expensive, and where you can expect a warm welcome and a clean room. Head out into the provinces, however, and you'll be amazed (particularly if you're coming from the UK) at how keenly hotel rooms are priced – it's a wonder, sometimes, that the places stay in business at all.

Beyond the family-owned hotels, you'll also find several hotel chains in operation, often close to motorway junctions, and while these might at first sight seem unappealing, they're at least practical, flexible, and especially good value if you're travelling *en famille*. At the other end of the scale there's an ever-increasing number of châteaux and manor houses being done up as top-end accommodation, and while it's all very attractive and luxurious, you should expect to pay accordingly.

Finally, with such a huge number of rooms available, you'd think you should be able to rock up and check in on arrival, but increasingly you can't – especially in season. It's far safer therefore, to book ahead, and to secure the booking with a credit card number and a brief fax (still far more reliable than the Internet). It may take some of the spontaneity out of your journey, but trudging round an unknown city with heavy bags looking desperately for a room is tiresome at best and heartbreaking at worst.

When you do reserve, check what the price includes. In the majority of cases the rate will be for the room, rather than the person, and won't include breakfast – which is generally no bad thing, as a coffee and a croissant (or even a full continental breakfast) is going to be far better value at the café next door. In season, however, you may find yourself obliged to stay *demi-pension*, in which case the price quoted will be per person, rather than for the room, and will cover dinner, bed and breakfast. If you're staying at a swanky restaurant with a few rooms upstairs, this can represent phenomenal value.

Restaurants

If there's one thing you should have no problem with at all in France, it's finding somewhere to eat – there are more restaurants per capita here than anywhere else in the world. That said, if you're used to an urban English environment, or even a cosmopolitan American one, you'll find the number of restaurants impressive but the variety thin. The French overwhelmingly like French food, and they expect you to do so as well. Asian and African variety tends to come in pale reverse-colonial Vietnamese, Moroccan and Caribbean dishes, and strong spices are spurned across the nation.

Vegetarians – this, in the 21st century! – will still have a surprisingly dull time of it, too, especially outside major cities. An incredible number of little restaurants will assume that being vegetarian, there's something slightly wrong with you, and that you'll therefore be happy with a meat-eater's meal, without the meat. I've seen vegetarians sadly served with a plate of boiled potatoes and peas, followed by a green salad, while the people at the table next door scoff their way through a seven-course dinner. As a vegetarian, however, you'll find pizzerias aplenty, and any bar will knock you up a cheese sandwich. Vegans, on the other hand, are in for a really rough time.

If you're on a tight budget, make lunch your main meal, as almost every restaurant in the country offers a special lunchtime fixed-price menu, often including a quarter-litre of the house wine, which is never undrinkable. Selecting a restaurant is pretty easy, too, as you'll find menus posted up outside (you can eschew the places which don't), and the usual maxim of eating where other people are having a good time holds as well here as anywhere else. Dishes of the day and fixed-price menus will generally be better quality than rarely ordered speciality items, and on the whole shorter menus are going to have more attention given to each dish than places where the choice is more extensive (we're not talking pizzerias, here, however).

Finally, most restaurants offer menus *service compris*, which means you should just leave a few coins or round up to the nearest note if you want to leave an extra tip. If service isn't included, then you should add 10–15% to the bill (and most places which aren't *service compris* will do this for you, anyway).

Bars and cafés

A good part of France's social life is associated with the local bar or café, and it's here that you'll often get the best feel for what a place is really like. Through the day the atmosphere will change, as people first stop in for a coffee (and, in the country, a small glass of wine, too) on their way to work, then come back in for a simple lunch or a sandwich, and finally come by on their way home for a drink.

You can take children with you into bars, though of course they can't be ordering alcoholic drinks for themselves (you have to do that for them – only kidding), and you can usually get a sandwich and a drink very reasonably priced at the bar. Sitting at tables will generally cost a little more than drinking at the bar, and if there's a terrace (especially in Paris) you should expect to pay more again.

The vast majority of bars and cafés are friendly and have a warm atmosphere, but if you're the only woman in a place full of men, you can expect to be the centre of attention. It's extremely unlikely to go any further than staring, but that can be unpleasant enough.

PRACTICAL INFORMATION
Opening times/prices

Throughout this book I've tried to give an idea about when you'll find places open, but given the eccentric nature of many of them, you should call ahead, especially where it says so specifically in the text. Many of the collections and museums described here are in private hands, so be warned that the owners are under no obligation to open up and show you around, or even to keep their collections intact.

You'll also find, as time goes on, that some of the things in the book are no longer visitable – people die, their families lose interest, and the local community can't always step in to preserve the eccentric heritage. So checking ahead is common sense as well as courteous.

If you find a place no longer in the state it's described in here, do please drop me a line for the next edition – your feedback will be greatly appreciated.

Prices quoted through the guide are as up to date as possible, but inevitably you'll find that prices creep up over time; on the other hand there's a quiet trend (as in the UK) towards making some of the national heritage available for free – it used to be that the Musée Carnavalet, in Paris, for example (where you can see Proust's bedroom and Natalie Barney's portrait, see page 140 and page 161), charged visitors, but since 2002 entry has been free.

Formalities
Visas

Visitors from EU countries, the USA, Canada, Australia and New Zealand, and a considerable number of other countries, don't need a visa to come to France on holiday – but if you want to check up, there's an excellent website which gives the full details, for all countries in the world, at www.france.diplomatie.fr/venir/visas.

Papers

In France you're legally obliged to carry a national identity card with you at all times, and this is the first thing the police will ask you for if they stop you for any reason. For countries (like the UK and Australia) which don't issue national identity cards, you will need to keep your passport with you at all times. You should therefore make a photocopy of this and keep it safe in case of loss or theft of the original.

If you're driving you must also have with you (in the car at all times) your driving licence, the registration documents for the car (*carte grise*, in French), and international insurance (a green card). You'll be heavily fined if you leave the papers at your hotel and you're then stopped by the police.

Health

The World Health Organisation recently rated French healthcare number one in the world, well ahead of countries like the UK and the USA, so you shouldn't worry about whether you'll be properly treated here if you fall sick. Hospitals will treat you first and ask questions about payment later, but you'd be unwise not to have extra travel and health insurance anyway. At doctors' surgeries you'll be expected to pay (about €20) in cash at the end of the consultation.

For simple problems, and as a first port of call, you should definitely consider asking at one of France's ubiquitous pharmacies. Staff expect to deal with minor health issues, and are well-informed and helpful. The same is true, extraordinarily, if your dog falls sick – French pharmacists also stock dog medicine. Finally, any pharmacy will be able and willing to tell you on the spot whether the mushrooms you've been collecting will send you into transports of culinary delight or straight into the nearest emergency ward.

Communications
Telephone
In towns and cities across France you'll find (assuming you have a roaming agreement with your local operator, and that you're using GSM) your mobile phone works fine. Head into the country, however, and coverage is still surprisingly patchy. I rented a *gîte* in the southwest of France in 2002, in the middle of a small village, where the nearest effective phone reception was a good 100m from the house.

Payphones, on the other hand, can be found everywhere, and take phone-cards which can be bought at newsagents, *Tabacs* (cigarette shops, usually also selling lottery cards), and post offices. Phone charges are reasonable, though not, of course, if you're calling long-distance from your hotel room.

Call **15** for the SAMU (the ambulance service), **17** for the police, and **18** for the *pompiers* (fire brigade).

Post
The postal service in France is pretty quick and efficient, though letters (especially with *'lettre'* written on the envelope) travel far more swiftly than postcards, even though they're no more expensive to send. Drop your stamped letter in one of the yellow post-boxes you'll find all over the country and it should normally be in the UK within three days, or delivered to America within the week. You can buy stamps at post offices (of course) and also at *Tabacs*.

Internet
In spite of having better broadband Internet connections to the home (ADSL is easily available) than either the USA or the UK, France is surprisingly weak when it comes to Internet access for visitors. There are cyber-cafés in some but by no means all towns, and you may find the local tourist office has an access point you can use if you're lucky – but there are whole tracts of the country which the Internet doesn't yet appear to have reached. Most people, especially in the provinces, see no real use for it, and email is considered a novelty by many (but then that's true of some people I know in the UK too).

That said, an increasing number of hotels (and especially those used to foreign visitors) do have an access point, and will help you pick up your email and send home those gratifyingly instant digital pictures.

Toilets
Finally, a word about toilets. While France's hotels and restaurants have universally (almost) adopted modern and clean loos, thousands of cafés, bars and service stations across the country are still fighting a rearguard action to save the dreaded long-drop (or Turkish toilet) from extinction.

It's quite an art for the inexperienced, but at some time or another, especially if you're travelling in the provinces, you'll

probably have to learn for yourself. Stand (or indeed crouch) firmly on the footplates provided, and concentrate clearly on your balance. When you're done, stand well back before flushing, to avoid an unpleasantly vigorous *douche* experience.

Even in places which have finally given up, and installed a standard WC, you're surprisingly likely to find the apparatus seat-less – and there's still a nationwide shortage of lavatory paper, so come prepared with a few sheets of your own.

Eccentric Itineraries

Given the themed-nature of the subjects in this book, and the way eccentric attractions are spread right across the whole country, this chapter pulls together the different things you might want to go and see which are located within fairly comfortable reach of 29 of France's key towns and cities.

Apart from the Paris/Ile de France section, you'll need your own wheels if you're going a-visiting, and you should generally call ahead, as most of the museums, collections, etc are privately-owned, and opening times will be variable. You should also remember that France is a big country (over four times the land area of Great Britain) and that you probably shouldn't therefore attempt more than two or three of these places in any one day.

The information here has been culled from *Chapters 2* to *11* inclusive – the festivals and fairs haven't been included, as they only happen at-most once a year. Check under the relevant month in *Chapter 1* to see if there's anything on near you. You'll also find that where a place falls between two of the towns listed below, it's been listed under both.

Finally, given the geographical remoteness of the majority of the places detailed here, it's well worth planning ahead (using a tool like www.viamichelin.com, if you have internet access), and making sure you have a good map with you when you set off (see page 264).

PARIS/ILE DE FRANCE

There's a wealth of eccentric things to do and see in and around the capital, and most of them can be reached on perfectly uneccentric public transport. See also *Chapter 11* for places to stay and eat.

In Paris

Arc de Triomphe (see page 228), Musée Carnavalet (see page 177), Catacombs (see page 194), Cité de la Musique (see page 136), Conservatoire Nationale des Arts et Métiers (see pages 73 and 234), Musée de la Contrefaçon (see page 196), Curie Museum (see page 58), Espace Salvador Dalí (see page 100), La Défense (see page 229), Eiffel Tower (see page 229), Musée de l'Erotisme (see page 196), Père Lachaise Cemetery (see pages 76, 107, 124, 126, 176 and 226), Musée d'Orsay (see pages 103 and 112), Musée Edith Piaf (see page 124), Picpus Cemetery (see page 198), Police Museum (see page 199), Pompidou Centre (see page 232), Musée Rodin (see page 98), Sewers (see page 200), Shakespeare & Company (see page 162), Statue of Liberty (see page 233), Musée de la Vie Romantique (see pages 122 and 144), Yves Saint Laurent Centre (see page 116).

Around Paris

Musée de l'Air et l'Espace, Le Bourget (see pages 45, 46 and 73), Villa des Brillants, Meudon (see page 98), Désert de Retz, Chambourcy (see page 243), Fragonard

Museum, Maisons Alfort (see page 201), Maison Picassiette, Chartres (see page 223), Saint Denis Basilica (see page 81), Erik Satie house and grave, Arcueil (see page 127), Musée Utrillo-Valadon, Sannois (see page 110), Van Gogh house and grave, Auvers sur Oise (see page 112), Château de Versailles (see pages 87 and 89), Le Village Préludien, Achères la Forêt (see page 248).

NORTHWEST
Rennes
Rothéneuf Rock Sculptures (see page 226), Christian Dior house, Granville (see page 115), Arthurian Forests, Paimpont (see page 76), Strawberry Museum, Plougastel (see page 186), Vélo Parc, Plouay (see page 202), Musée du Vieux-Château, Laval (see page 107), La Frênouse, Cossé le Vivien (see page 223), Maison Sculpté, l'Essart (see page 224).

Caen
Christian Dior house, Granville (see page 115), Maisons Satie/Musée Eugène Boudin, Honfleur (see page 127), Forbes Balloon Museum, Balleroy (see pages 34–7), Camembert Museum, Vimoutiers (see page 181), Sistine Chapel, Saint Vincent la Rivière (see page 227), L'Auberge de la Truite, Montreuil l'Argillé (see page 259).

Rouen
Joan of Arc Museum, Rouen (see page 83), Nungesser and Coli Museum, Etretat (see page 45), Maisons Satie/Musée Eugène Boudin, Honfleur (see page 127), Rothéneuf Rock Sculptures (see page 226), Broken Crockery House, Louviers (see page 219), L'Auberge de la Truite, Montreuil l'Argillé (see page 259).

Tours
Cointreau Museum, Angers (see page 188), Maurice Dufresne Museum, Marnay (see page 205), La Cave aux Sculptures, Dénezé sous Doué (see page 221), Maison Picassiette, Chartres (see page 223), Loire Châteaux (see page 231), Rochemenier Troglodyte Village (see page 241), L'Hélice Terrestre de l'Orbière (see page 241), Trôo Troglodyte Village (see page 241), Le Jardin Zoologique, Thorée les Pins (see page 246).

Bourges
Château de Nohant, Nohant Vicq (see page 144), Château de Saint Sauveur en Puisaye (see page 151), snail farm, Montigny (see page 185), Witches Museum, Concressault (see page 215), La Cathédrale, Neuvy Deux Clochers (see page 220), La Fabuloserie, Dicy (see page 221).

Angoulême
It's all about food, round Angoulême – though don't forget the Comic Strip Museum (see page 8). Otherwise it's foie gras, Thiviers (see page 183), snails, Vaunac (see page 186), and truffles, Sorges (see page 187).

NORTHEAST
Lille
There ought to be more to do and see which is eccentric around Lille – so please write in with your ideas for the next edition. In the meantime, there's the Beaux-Arts, in Lille (see page 98), the Latham Statue, at Sangatte (see page 41), the Caudron Brothers Museum, in Rue (see page 47), and A la Station Bac Saint Maur (see page 235).

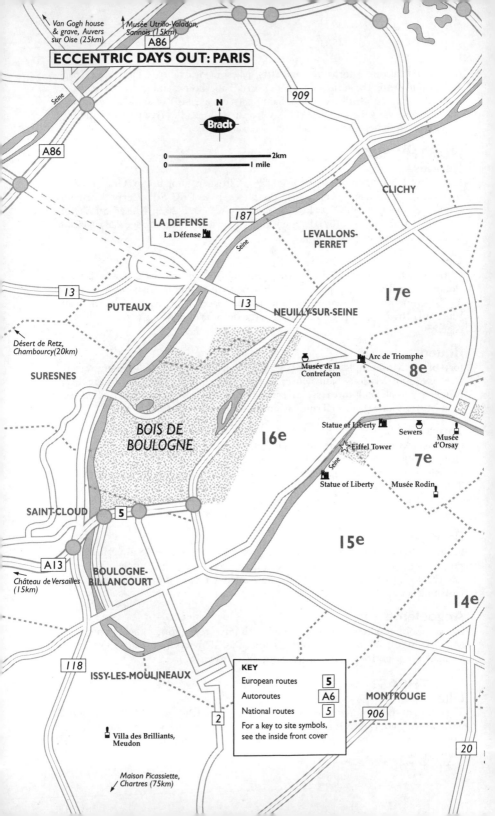

ECCENTRIC DAYS OUT: PARIS

Van Gogh house & grave, Auvers sur Oise (25km)

Musée Utrillo-Valadon, Sannois (1.5km)

A86

A86

909

Bradt

N

0 — 2km
0 — 1 mile

187

CLICHY

LA DEFENSE
La Défense

LEVALLONS-PERRET

13

13

NEUILLY-SUR-SEINE

17e

PUTEAUX

Désert de Retz, Chambourcy(20km)

SURESNES

Musée de la Contrefaçon

Arc de Triomphe

8e

BOIS DE BOULOGNE

16e

Statue of Liberty

Sewers

Musée d'Orsay

Eiffel Tower

7e

Statue of Liberty

Musée Rodin

SAINT-CLOUD

5

15e

A13

Château de Versailles (15km)

BOULOGNE-BILLANCOURT

14e

118

ISSY-LES-MOULINEAUX

MONTROUGE

906

2

20

Villa des Brilliants, Meudon

KEY

European routes	5
Autoroutes	A6
National routes	5

For a key to site symbols, see the inside front cover

Maison Picassiette, Chartres (75km)

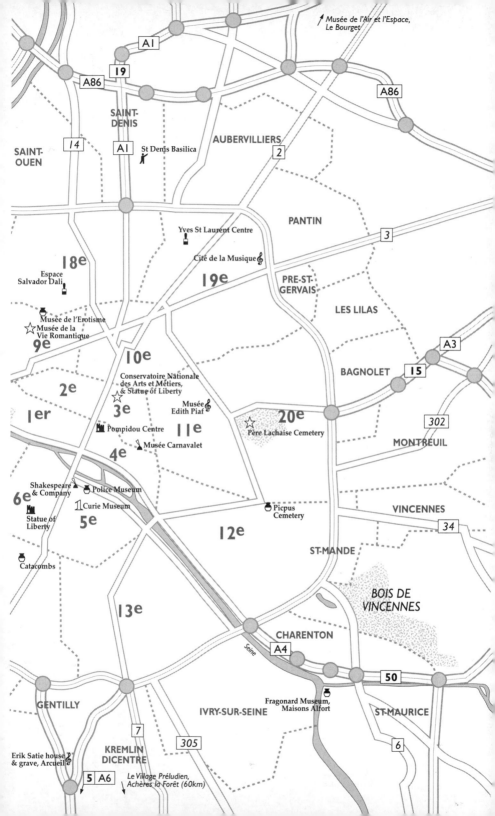

ECCENTRIC DAYS OUT: NORTHWEST

N

Bradt

0 ___ 160km
0 ___ 100 miles

NORD-PAS-DE-CALAIS
DUNKERQUE
CALAIS
Dover
Latham Statue, Sangatte
Strait of
Boulogne sur Mer
St Omer
40
15
402
Le Touquet Paris Plage
Caudron Brothers Museum, Rue
Abbeville
402

PICARDIE
AMIENS
44
44
Creil
Gournay en Bray
BEAUVAIS
46
402

ILE DE PARIS
St Denis
PARIS
St Germain
Van Gogh, Auvers sur Oise
Musée Utrillo-Valadon, Sannois
Vernon
Étampes
Creil
Evry
MANTES LA JOLIE
Château de Versailles
Désert de Retz
Chambourcy
Rambouillet, Erik Satie, Arcueil
Villa des Brillantes, Meudon
Le Village Préludien, Achères la Forêt
Maison Picassiette, Chartres
5

HAUTE-NORMANDIE
ROUEN
Joan of Arc Museum
Neufchâtel en Bray
Dieppe
44
402
Broken Crockery House, Louviers
Elbeuf
Seine
5
EVREUX
Dreux
Maison Picassiette, Chartres
CHARTRES
50
Châteaudun
Fécamp
44
46
L'Auberge de la Truite
402
LE MANS
Nungesser and Coli Museum, Étretat
LE HAVRE
Maisons Satie, Honfleur
Musée Eugène Boudin, Honfleur
Lisieux
Sistine Chapel, St Vincent la Rivière
Camembert, Vimoutiers
Argentan
Alençon
402
50
Musée du Vieux-Château, Laval

BASSE-NORMANDIE
CAEN
401
Bayeux
Forbes Balloon Museum, Balleroy
Flers
3
46
St Lô
3
Valognes
46/3
Cherbourg
Pte de Barfleur
Baie de la Seine
Coutances
401

Cap de la Hogue
Pte de la Hague

C h a n n e l

E n g l i s h   C h a n n e l

Alderney
Guernsey
Sark
Jersey

Golfe de St Malo

Christian Dior, Granville
Rothéneuf Rock Sculptures
St Malo
401
50
RENNES
Maison Sculpté, l'Essart
Arthurian Forests, Paimpont

BRETAGNE
Paimpol
St Brieuc
Lannion
50
Morlaix
Roscoff
50
60
BREST
Strawberries, Plougastel
Ile d'Ouessant
Douarnenez
Quimper
60
Velocipèdes, Plouay
Pte de Penmarch
Pte du Raz

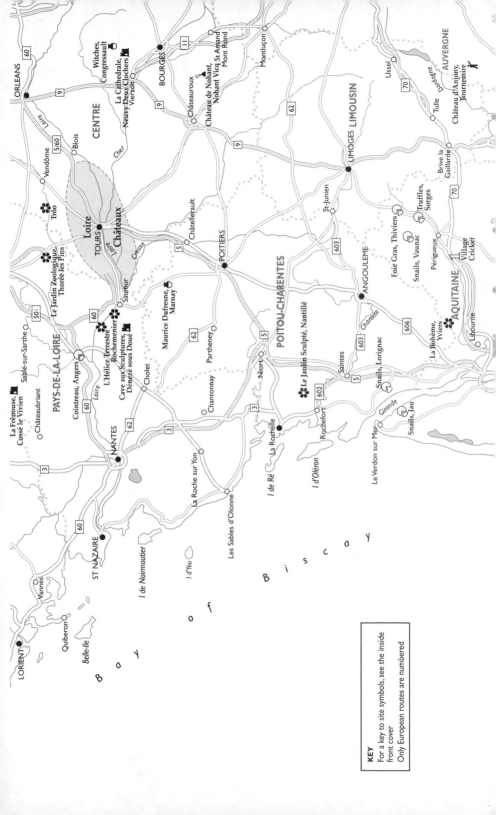

KEY
For a key to site symbols, see the inside front cover
Only European routes are numbered

ECCENTRIC DAYS OUT: NORTHEAST

KEY
For a key to site symbols, see the inside front cover
Only European routes are numbered

0 ____ 160km
0 ____ 100 miles

N

Bradt

Strait of Dover

Boulogne sur Mer

Le Touquet Paris Plage

DUNKERQUE
CALAIS
Latham Statue, Sangatte
402
40
St Omer
15
402

NORD-PAS-DE-CALAIS
A la Station Bac St Maur
Roubaix
Beaux-Arts
LILLE
42
BÉTHUNE
LENS
17
Bruay la Buissière
Arras
DOUAI
19
Cambrai
15
19
VALENCIENNES

Caudron Brothers Museum, Rue

Abbeville
402
Neufchâtel en Bray
Dieppe
5
Seine
Elbeuf
ROUEN
Joan of Arc Museum
HAUTE-NORMANDIE
402
Gournay en Bray
BEAUVAIS
46
Broken Crockery House, Louviers
Vernon
Musée Utrillo-Valadon, Sannois
Van Gogh, Auvers sur Oise
Antvers sur Oise
St-Denis
EVREUX
DREUX
MANTES LA JOLIE
St Germain
Désert de Retz
Château de Versailles
Chambourcy
Rambouillet
Villa des Brillantes, Meudon
Le Village Prélludien, Achères la Forêt

AMIENS
44
Albert
St Quentin
17
19
Roye
Chauny
Laon
17
PICARDIE
Creil
Oise
Compiègne
Château de Pierrefonds
Soissons
Shell Garden, Vitry Noureuil
17
Snails, Olizy Violaine
50

Musée de la Forêt, Renwez
44
Rimbaud Museum, Charleville Mézières
Woinic the Pig, Bogny sur Meuse
Sedan
46
Aisne
Auberge Verlaine, Juniville

Aix la Chapelle/Aachen

Musée de l'Air et l'Espace, Le Bourget
Maux
Marne
PARIS
ÎLE DE FRANCE
Créteil
Evry
Érik Satie, Arcueil
Melun
54

REIMS
Champagne
Château Thiery
Champagne, Epernay
Ste-Ménehould
Châlons sur Marne
17
Marne
Pargny sur Saulx
52
CHAMPAGNE-ARDENNE
17
St-Dizier
Tiles, Pargny sur Saulx
Verdun
44
BRIEY
Joan of Arc birthplace, Domrémy la Pucelle

THIONVILLE
25/50
Forbach
50
METZ
21/23
NANCY
Lunéville
LORRAINE

Kronenbourg STRASBOURG
Bitche
25
ALSACE

FRANCE

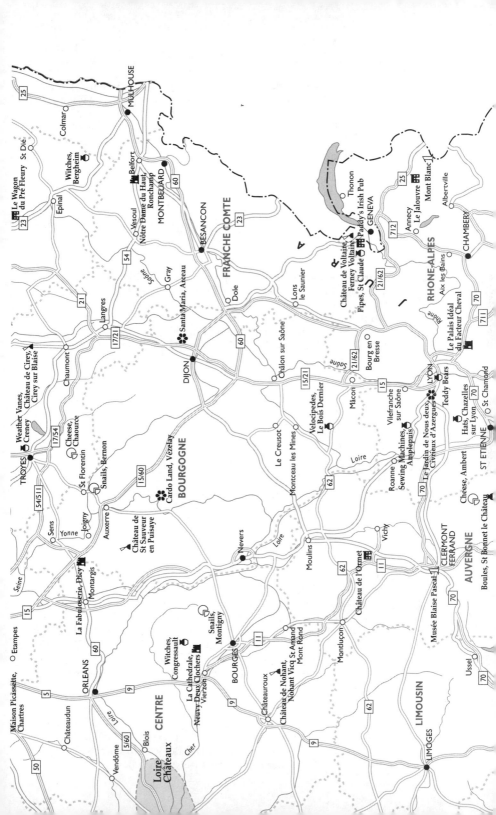

Reims

Rimbaud Museum, Charleville Mézières (see page 143), Auberge Verlaine, Juniville (see page 146), Château de Pierrefonds (see page 65), Musée de la Forêt, Renwez (see page 245), Tile Museum, Pargny sur Saulx (see page 214), Shell Garden, Viry Noureuil (see page 248), snail farm, Olizy Violaine (see page 185), Woinic the Pig, Bogny sur Meuse (see page 227), Pigs' Trotters at Sainte Ménehould (see page 258), and Champagne, at Reims and Epernay (see page 189).

Troyes

Château de Cirey, Cirey sur Blaise (see page 148), Château de Saint Sauveur en Puisaye (see page 151), Cheese Museum, Chaource (see page 179), snail farm, Bernon (see page 185), weather vanes, Creney sur Troyes (see page 214).

Nancy

Joan of Arc birthplace, Domrémy la Pucelle (see page 84), Château de Cirey, Cirey sur Blaise (see page 148), Le Wagon du Pré Fleury (see page 259).

Strasbourg

If you're not into Kronenbourg, in Strasbourg itself (see page 188), then you'll have to make do with the town of Bitche (see page 237), and the Witches Museum, in Bergheim (see page 215).

Dijon

Musée du Vélo, Le Bois Dernier (see page 202), Notre Dame du Haut, Ronchamp (see page 232), Cardo Land, Vézelay (see page 242), Santa Maria, Arceau (see page 247).

SOUTHWEST
Bordeaux

Village cricket (see page 71), snail farm, Jau (see page 185), snail farm, Lorignac (see page 186), Old Vegetables, Sadirac (see page 187), Matches, Clairac (see page 210), La Ferme-Musée Barret, Pineuilh (see page 222), Le Jardin Sculpté, Nantillé (see page 246), Pessac Zoo (see page 244), La Bohème, Yviers (see page 245), Les Sources de Caudalie (see page 256).

Bergerac

Tobacco, Bergerac (see page 214), La Ferme-Musée Barret, Pineuilh (see page 222), village cricket (see page 71), Château des Millandes (see page 132), chestnuts and mushrooms, Villefranche du Périgord (see page 181), foie gras, Frespech (see page 183), La Roque Saint Christophe Troglodyte Village (see page 241), Musée du Vélocipède, Cadouin (see page 202), Prune Museum, Granges sur Lot (see page 184), matches, Clairac (see page 210), Horse-drawn Hearse Museum, Cazes Mondenard (see page 208), Hôtel Félix, Castelsarrasin (see page 256).

Clermont Ferrand

Musée Blaise Pascal, Clermont Ferrand (see page 60), Château d'Anjony, Tournemire (see page 94), Cheese Museum, Ambert (see page 179), Hat Museum, Chazelles sur Lyon (see page 208), Pétanques and Boules Museum, Saint Bonnet le Château (see page 211), Château de l'Ormet (see page 255).

Biarritz

Biarritz is astonishingly uneccentric. In fact the only things you can do are food-related. Visit the Chocolate Museum in town (see page 182), or the Gâteau Basque Museum in Sare (see page 179).

Pau

Bee Museum, Saint Faust (see page 183), Rizla+ Museum, Mazères sur Salat (see page 204), Tile Museum, Blajan (see page 213), Lourdes (see page 240), Vignemalle (see page 56).

Toulouse

Condom en Armagnac (see pages 24, 31, 188 and 237), Foie Gras Museum, Roquettes (see page 183), Foie Gras Museum, Samatan (see page 183), Pigeon Eco-museum, Lombers (see page 184), Sugar Museum, Cordes sur Ciel (see page 186), Horse-drawn Hearse Museum, Cazes Mondenard (see page 208), Rizla+ Museum, Mazères sur Salat (see page 204), Palais de la Berbie, Albi (see page 110), matches, Najac (see page 211), Tile Museum, Blajan (see page 213), Montségur Castle (see page 78), Carcassonne (see page 78), Llivia (see page 239), Hôtel Félix, Castelsarrasin (see page 256).

Perpignan

Montségur Castle (see page 84), Château de Quéribus (see page 84), Château de Peyrepetuse (see page 84), Carcassonne (see page 84), Bee Museum, Valcebollère (see page 183), crops and whips, Sorède (see page 205), Palais des Naïfs, Bages (see page 226), Llivia (see page 239), Château du Riell (see page 256).

Montpellier

Robert Louis Stevenson trail, from Monastier to Alès (see page 174), Sainte Enimie (see page 80), Roquefort (see page 181), Insect Museum, Saint Léons (see page 209), snail farm, Auxillac la Canourgue (see page 186), Musée du Vélo et de la Moto, Château de Bosc (see page 203), Can Peio (see page 260), Château d'Arpaillargues, Uzès (see page 139).

SOUTHEAST
Saint Etienne

Robert Louis Stevenson trail, from Monastier to Alès (see page 174), Montgolfières, Annonay (see page 34), Cheese Museum, Ambert (see page 179), Hat Museum, Chazelles sur Lyon (see page 208), Pétanques and Boules Museum, Saint Bonnet le Château (see page 211).

Lyon

Teddy Bears Museum, Lyon (see page 213), Hat Museum, Chazelles sur Lyon (see page 208), Sewing Machine Museum, Amplepuis (see page 212), Musée du Vélo, Le Bois Dernier (see page 203), Montgolfières, Annonay (see page 34), Le Palais Idéal du Facteur Cheval (see page 224), Le Jardin de Nous Deux, Civrieux d'Azergues (see page 246).

Geneva

Okay, okay, so I know Geneva's not in France. But these French places are all closer to Geneva than any major French town: Château de Voltaire, Ferney Voltaire (see page 148), Paddy's Irish Pub, Ferney Voltaire (see page 259), Pipe Museum, Saint Claude (see page 212), Le Jalouvre, Mont Saxonnex (see page 260), Mont Blanc (see page 54).

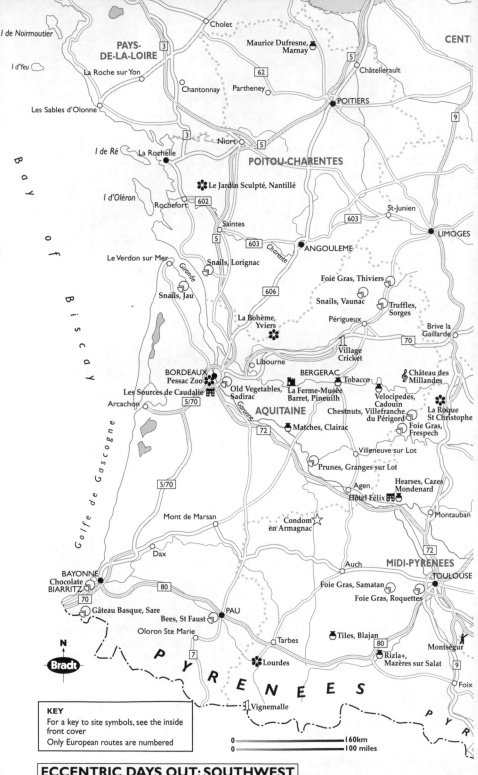

I de Noirmoutier

PAYS-DE-LA-LOIRE

I d'Yeu

La Roche sur Yon

Les Sables d'Olonne

Cholet

Maurice Dufresne, Marnay

Châtellerault

CENT

POITIERS

Chantonnay
Partheney

Niort

I de Ré
La Rochelle

POITOU-CHARENTES

Bay of Biscay

I d'Oléron
Rochefort

Le Jardin Sculpté, Nantillé

St-Junien

LIMOGES

Saintes

ANGOULEME

Charente

Le Verdon sur Mer

Snails, Lorignac

Foie Gras, Thiviers

Gironde

Snails, Jau

Snails, Vaunac

Truffles, Sorges

Périgueux

Brive la Gaillarde

La Bohème, Yviers

Libourne

Village Cricket

BORDEAUX
Pessac Zoo
Les Sources de Caudalie

Old Vegetables, Sadirac

BERGERAC

Tobacco

Château des Millandes

La Ferme-Musée Barret, Pineuílh

Velocipedes, Cadouin

Arcachon

Garonne

AQUITAINE

Chestnuts, Villefranche du Périgord

La Roque St Christophe

Matches, Clairac

Foie Gras, Frespech

Villeneuve sur Lot

Prunes, Granges sur Lot

Agen
Hôtel Félix

Hearses, Cazes Mondenard

Montauban

Golfe de Gascogne

Mont de Marsan

Condom en Armagnac

Dax

Auch

MIDI-PYRENEES

TOULOUSE

BAYONNE
Chocolate
BIARRITZ

Foie Gras, Samatan

Foie Gras, Roquettes

Gâteau Basque, Sare

Bees, St Faust

PAU

Oloron Ste Marie

Tarbes

Tiles, Blajan

Montségur

Rizla+, Mazères sur Salat

Lourdes

Foix

P Y R E N E E S

Vignemalle

P Y R

N

Bradt

0   160km
0   100 miles

ECCENTRIC DAYS OUT: SOUTHWEST

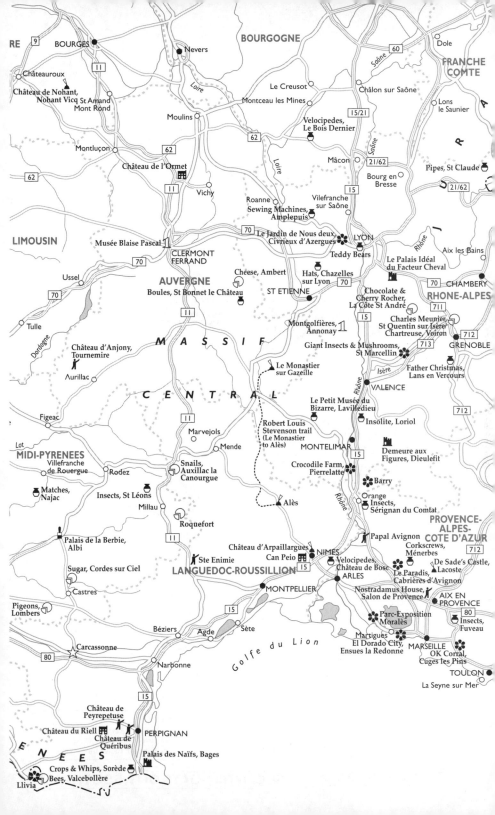

ECCENTRIC DAYS OUT: SOUTHEAST

BOURGOGNE

FRANCHE COMTE

Dole

60

Saône

23

Le Creusot

Montceau les Mines

Châlon sur Saône

Lons
le Saunier

15/21

JURA

Thonon

Velocipedes,
Le Bois Dernier

62

AUVERGNE

Mâcon

Loire

Saône

21/62

15

Bourg en
Bresse

Château de Voltaire,
Ferney Voltaire
Pipes, St Claude

21/62

Paddy's Irish Pub
GENEVA

Roanne

Vilefranche
sur Saône

712

25

Sewing Machines,
Amplepuis

70

Le Jardin de Nous deux,
Civrieux d'Azergues

LYON

Rhône

Annecy
Le Jalouvre

Mont Blanc

Teddy Bears

Aix les Bains

Albertville

Cheese, Ambert

Hats, Chazelles
sur Lyon

Le Palais Idéal
du Facteur Cheval

70

CHAMBERY

ST ETIENNE

70

Boules,
St Bonnet
le Château

St Chamond

711

RHONE-ALPES

MASSIF

Montgolfières,
Annonay

15

Chocolate &
Cherry Rocher,
La Côte St André

Charles Meunier,
St Quentin sur Isère/
Chartreuse, Voiron

AUVERGNE

Giant Insects & Mushrooms,
St Marcellin

713

712

GRENOBLE

Le Monastier
sur Gazeille

Isère

Father Christmas,
Lans en Vercours

Briançon

CENTRAL

Rhône

VALENCE

Le Petit Musée du
Bizarre, Lavilledieu

712

Robert Louis
Stevenson trail
(Le Monastier
to Alès)

Insolite, Loriol

Gap

MONTELIMAR

15

Demeure aux
Figures, Dieulefit

Crocodile Farm,
Pierrelatte

Barry

Digne-les-Bains

Alès

Rhône

Orange

Insects,
Sérignan du Comtat

PROVENCE-ALPES-COTE D'AZUR

LANGUEDOC-
ROUSSILLION

Papal Avignon

712

Musée Jean
Cocteau, Menton

Château d'Arpaillargues
Can Peio

NIMES

Corkscrews,
Ménerbes

Le Lion d'Or

Eze

15

Velocipedes,
Château de Bosc
ARLES

Le Paradis,
Cabrières d'Avignon

De Sade's Castle,
Lacoste

Promenade des Anglais, Nice

Josephi

Escoffier, Villeneuve Loubet

Baker's G

MONTPELLIER

Parc-Exposition
Moralès

Nostradamus House, Salon de Provence
AIX EN PROVENCE

80

CANNES

Monac

Chez Félix, Antibe

Sète

15

Insects,
Fuveau

80

Golfe du Lion

Martigues
El Dorado City,
Ensues la Redonne

OK Corral,
Cuges les Pins

MARSEILLE

Hyères

TOULON

La Seyne sur Mer

Iles d'Hyères

N

Bradt

0 — 160km
0 — 100 miles

KEY
For a key to site symbols, see the inside
front cover
Only European routes are numbered

Grenoble

Palais du Chocolat, La Côte Saint André (see page 182), Cherry Rocher Museum, La Côte Saint André (see page 190), Charles Meunier, Saint Quentin sur Isère (see page 188), Chartreuse Cellars, Voiron (see page 190), Father Christmas Museum, Lans en Vercours (see page 206), Le Palais Idéal du Facteur Cheval (see page 224), giant insects and mushrooms, Saint Marcellin (see page 244).

Montélimar

Crocodile farm (see page 242), Musée de l'Insolite, Loriol (see page 209), Le Petit Musée du Bizarre, Lavilledieu (see page 203), Insect Museum, Sérignan du Comtat (see page 209), La Demeure aux Figures, Dieulefit (see page 221), Barry Troglodyte Village (see page 242), Robert Louis Stevenson trail, from Monastier to Alès (see page 174).

Arles

Barry Troglodyte Village (see page 242), Insect Museum, Sérignan du Comtat (see page 209), Musée du Vélo et de la Moto, Château de Bosc (see page 203), Papal Avignon (see page 93), Le Paradis, Cabrières d'Avignon (see page 247), Corkscrew Museum, Ménerbes (see page 204), Marquis de Sade's Castle, Lacoste (see page 143), Nostradamus House, Salon de Provence (see page 92), Château d'Arpaillargues (see page 139), Parc-Exposition Moralès (see page 245), El Dorado City, Ensues la Redonne (see page 245).

Marseille

Papal Avignon (see page 93), Le Paradis, Cabrières d'Avignon (see page 247), Corkscrew Museum, Ménerbes (see page 204), Marquis de Sade's Castle, Lacoste (see page 143), Nostradamus House, Salon de Provence (see page 92), Parc-Exposition Moralès (see page 245), El Dorado City, Ensues la Redonne (see page 245), Insect Museum, Fuveau (see page 209), OK Corral, Cuges les Pins (see page 245).

Nice

Josephine Baker's grave, Monaco (see page 130), Musée Jean Cocteau, Menton (see page 149), Le Lion d'Or, Menton (see page 261), Eze (see page 239), Promenade des Anglais, Nice (see page 134), Escoffier Museum, Villeneuve Loubet (see page 206), Chez Félix au Port, Antibes (see page 166).

Appendix

FURTHER READING/REFERENCES

Aboville, Gérard d' *Alone: The Man Who Braved the Vast Pacific – And Won*, Arcade Publishing, 1993. D'Aboville's astonishing account of rowing across the Pacific. It's currently out of print in English, but you can pick up second-hand copies – or read the original in French.

Applefield, David *The Unofficial Guide to Paris*, Hungry Minds Inc, 2002. This covers pretty much everything you need to know about the capital, but is also great if you've never been to France before. (See also *Phillips*, below.)

Baldwin, James *Giovanni's Room*, Penguin Twentieth-Century Classics, 1956. My personal favourite among Baldwin's novels.

Baldwin, James *The Fire Next Time*, Penguin Twentieth-Century Classics, 1963. A staggering paean against racism, essential reading, even 40 years on.

Baudelaire, Charles *The Flowers of Evil (Les Fleurs du Mal)*, Oxford Paperbacks, 1998. Excellent edition, with the original French on the facing pages.

de Beauvoir, Simone *She Came to Stay*, Flamingo, 1943 (first published). De Beauvoir's first novel, a thinly disguised account of life with Jean-Paul Sartre and Olga Kosakiewicz, the lover they shared in a ménage à trois in 1933.

de Beauvoir, Simone *The Second Sex*, Vintage, 1949 (first published). Enormously influential tome which helped kick-start post-war feminism.

Beckett, Samuel *Samuel Beckett: The Complete Dramatic Works* Faber & Faber, 1990. The complete English texts. If your French is up to it, Beckett is better in the language he wrote in.

Bellos, David *Georges Perec: A Life in Words*, Harvill Press, 1999 (new edition). Engaging biography of the quiet man who composed the world's longest palindrome and wrote the only full-length novel which doesn't contain the letter 'e'. Bellos translated much of Perec's work into English, which makes the books themselves even more enjoyable.

Berger, John *Ways of Seeing: Based on the BBC Television Series*, Penguin, 1990 (re-issue). Wonderful book which shakes up the way you look at art and advertising, and still remains pretty radical thirty years after its original publication.

Berger, John *G*, Bloomsbury, 1996 (re-issue). Winner of the Booker Prize in 1972, this tale of migrant workers and a latter-day Don Juan in pre-World War I Europe is still well-worth seeking out.

Berger, John *Into Their Labours*, Bloomsbury. I could go on and on about John Berger's wonderful books, but instead I'll just recommend that you read this trilogy, which comprises *Pig Earth* (1979), *Once in Europa* (1983), and *Lilac and Flag* (1990), which deals with peasant life in France.

Bernhardt, Sarah *My Double Life: The Memoirs of Sarah Bernhardt*, State University of New York Press, 1999. New translation of the 1907 original, which interweaves fact and fiction seamlessly into a thoroughly entertaining whole. The stories are great, but not necessarily to be believed.

Bombard, Alain *The Bombard Story*, Grafton, 1986. A truly terrifying glimpse of what it's like to try and live on plankton and raw fish for a couple of months. Available fairly easily secondhand.

Bouchet, Peggy *Ma Victoire Sur L'Atlantique*, Actes Graphiques, 1999. Peggy Bouchet's account of her solo row across the Atlantic. Available only in French.

Bovard, Didier *L'Atlantique à Mes Pieds*, Editions Le Vieil Annecy, 2002. This wittily-titled book (it means 'The Atlantic at / by my feet') covers the first of Didier Bovard's audacious transatlantic pedalo expeditions. It's an excellent read, though available so far only in French.

Buñuel, Luis *My Last Breath*, Vintage 1994 (reissue). Wonderful, funny, witty and delightful (if not always factually 100% accurate) autobiography by one of cinema's true iconoclasts. His recipe for a Martini is unbeatable – but remember that Buñuel did die of cirrhosis of the liver.

Brandon, Ruth *Being Divine: A Biography of Sarah Bernhardt*, Secker & Warburg 1991. The most interesting if not the most comprehensive of a number of biographies of the legendary actress.

Camus, Albert. All of his works are available in good translations in English. His essays and non-fiction can be quite hard-going, but his three novels, *The Outsider* (1942), *The Plague* (1948) and *The Fall* (1957), are all excellent.

Cocteau, Jean *Opium: The Diary of a Cure*, Peter Owen Limited, 1957. Cocteau's most interesting book; particularly good, and particularly hard to find.

Colette, Sidonie. Many of Colette's books are easily available in translation, and they're surprisingly racy and accessible, even a century on.

Duncan, Isadora *My Life*, Liveright Books 1995 (reissue). Great and frequently poignant autobiography by Isadora Duncan, up to the time she left for Russia in 1921.

Einhard, Abbot of Seligenstadt, and Balbulus Notker, *Two Lives of Charlemagne*, Penguin 1969. The first life here, by Einhard (*Vita Caroli Magni*) is excellent; the second, written nearly a century later and a great deal more anecdotally, is interesting – but Charlemagne was already well on the way to epic sainthood by this time. You can also pick up *Vita Caroli Magna* easily off the web, in English or Latin.

Ford, Mark, *Raymond Roussel and the Republic of Dreams*, Faber & Faber, 2000. Excellent new biography of the most eccentric man in early 20th-century literature, and arguably the inventor of the RV.

Gauguin, Paul *The Intimate Journals of Paul Gauguin*, Heinemann 1952. In 1923, Emile Gauguin published a limited edition of this excellent book, which was then republished by Heinemann in 1952. It's hard to find but well worth the effort – and a far better book than *Noa Noa*, which was published during the painter's lifetime.

Greene, Graham. Graham Greene's books have been translated into more than 25 languages and over 30 million copies have been sold – so you shouldn't have any problem finding something to read, either new or secondhand.

Hemingway, Ernest *The Sun Also Rises* and *A Moveable Feast*, Vintage, 2000 (re-issues). These are as close as you're going to get to Hemingway's Paris of the 1920s – which isn't actually all that close. Nonetheless, good reads, both.

James, Henry *A Little Tour in France*, Oxford University Press, 1984 (centenary re-issue). Amazingly enough, this charming little book isn't currently in print – but it's relatively easy to find secondhand. It was published in book form in Boston in 1900 (the source for the quotes on page 168–9), with an illustrated edition coming out in London later the same year, with a longer 'Introductory' and British spelling and punctuation. The text of this version was republished in 1984, for the centenary edition. As the text is out of copyright, it's also available at several places on the web.

Krupskaya, Nadezhada K *Reminiscences of Lenin* International Publishers 1970 (originally published in Russian in 1933). Gripping reading throughout, by Lenin's wife, which contains some chapters about the life of Lenin and co in Paris from 1908 to 1912.

Lord, James *Giacometti, A Biography*, Faber & Faber 1986. Definitive life of Giacometti by an American who knew the artist in Paris and spent 15 years researching and writing the biography – a great book about a wonderful sculptor and painter.

McBrien, William *Cole Porter, The Definitive Biography*, HarperCollins 1998. As it says, the definitive biography. As a bonus, it's well-written.

Maugham, Somerset. Maugham's most famous novels – *Of Human Bondage, The Moon and Sixpence, Cakes and Ale*, and *Up at the Villa* – are easily available, as are various collections of his finely-turned short stories.

Meyssonnier, Fernand *Paroles de bourreau: Témoignage unique d'un éxécuteur des arrêts criminals*, Imago 2002. The executioner speaks, and goes into plenty of detail about his career in Algeria, lopping the heads off convicted criminals with a guillotine. It's a grisly read (and perhaps fortunately, for sensitive readers, only available in French).

Miller, Henry *Tropic of Cancer* and *Tropic of Capricorn*, Flamingo, 1993 (re-issues). Henry Miller's fictionalised accounts of his years in Paris were banned in his native America and the UK for 30 years after publication, which helped their huge popularity in the 1960s and 1970s. They're still an interesting snapshot of 1930s Paris, but still more profane than many may wish – and oddly, in the light of that, somewhat dated to a modern reader.

Monnet, Philippe *Le Monde à l'Envers* (The World Backwards), Glénat, 2000. Great account of sailing round the world the hard way (in French only).

Nin, Anaïs *Diaries*, Harcourt, 1966 (new editions published since 1985). Anaïs Nin's mammoth diaries have now been retro-fitted to re-include the excised relationships with Henry Miller and Otto Rank after the death of Hugo Guiler in 1985, so try and buy recent rather than older editions. Her best-selling works, however, remain the erotica she wrote for a dollar a page in the 1930s to make enough to print the first edition of Henry Miller's *Tropic of Cancer*.

Paris, Reine-Marie *Camille*, Aurum Press, 1988. Excellent, moving, but increasingly hard-to-find biography of Camille Claudel.

Pascal, Blaise *Pensées*, Penguin Classics, 1995. Profound and bleak by turns, Pascal's 'thoughts' are as relevant and enlightening today as when they were penned in the middle of the 17th century.

Perec, Georges *Life: A User's Manual*, Harvill Press, 1996 (new edition). One of the most interesting works of 20th-century fiction, and Perec's literary masterpiece. The novel describes the lives within a Paris apartment building in more than 100 interwoven tales. Perec's work is easy to find in translation, and well worth the effort.

Phillips, Laurence *Paris, Lille, Brussels – The Bradt Guide to Eurostar Cities*, Bradt Travel Guides, 2002. This guide is terrific if you're going to Paris or Lille (we won't discuss Brussels here), and includes an astonishing number of hotels and restaurants, with detailed reviews of all, as well as covering pretty much everything you can do and see in both cities.

Piaf, Edith and Cerdan, Marcel *Moi Pour Toi, Lettres d'amour*, Le Cherche Midi, 2002. Wonderful correspondence between Edith Piaf, the singer, and Marcel Cerdan, the boxer, leading up to his tragic death in a plane crash in 1949. In French.

Piron, Didier *Philippe Monnet, Biographie*, Mango, 2000. Excellent biography of the first man to sail round the world backwards. It's a pity it's only available in French.

Proust, Marcel *In Search of Lost Time*, Penguin, 1996 (seven volumes). Enormous but marvellous work of literature which ebbs and flows its way through the mind of Marcel Proust. A truly staggering achievement. Can be read in bite-sized, ordinary novel-length chunks.

Raspail, Jean *Le Camp des Saints* (The Camp of the Saints) Sphere, 1977. A good deal easier to find in French than English, this is Jean Raspail's most controversial novel, dealing as it does with the moral implications of a clash between the developed and developing worlds.

Raspail, Jean *Blue Island*, Mercury Hose, 1991. A powerful allegory of France's fall to the Nazis; akin, in its way, to William Golding's *Lord of the Flies*.

Rimbaud, Arthur *Collected Poems*, Oxford Paperbacks, 2001. This excellent bilingual edition contains almost everything Rimbaud wrote in his incredibly short career. Even if you don't understand French it's really worth reading the poems aloud in French (after you've read the English) as the rhythm adds a lot which is lost in translation.

Sade, Marquis de *120 Days of Sodom*, Arrow, 1991. I'm not recommending this; it's just here for completeness.

de Saint-Exupéry, Antoine *Southern Mail / Night Flight*, Penguin, 2000. Combined edition which describes the dangers and bravado of flying the mails. *Southern Mail*, originally published in 1929, features a thinly-disguised subplot about the author's failed love affair with Louise de Vilmorin.

de Saint-Exupéry, Consuelo *Tale of the Rose: The Passion that Inspired the Little Prince*, Random House, 2001. Taken with a pinch of salt, these racy memoirs by Saint-Exupéry's widow make for a great read. Due out in paperback in early 2003.

Sand, Georges *The Story of My Life: The Autobiography of Georges Sand*, State University of New York Press, 1991. At close to 1,200 pages, this doorstop tells you as much as you could possibly want to know about what Georges Sand herself was thinking. It's quite a challenging read.

Sartre, Jean-Paul *The Roads to Freedom (The Age of Reason; The Reprieve; Iron in the Soul)*, Penguin, 1945-49 (first published). Superb trilogy which chronicles the fictional lives of various French people through World War II and expounds a great deal of existentialist philosophy along the way. Highly recommended.

Stein, Gertrude *The Autobiography of Alice B Toklas*, Penguin, 2001. Originally published in 1933, this is actually the autobiography of Stein herself rather than that of her long-time companion, and (not to put too fine a point on it) remains the least inaccessible of her works. Cubism and literature really, really don't mix, don't mix, really.

Stevenson, Robert Louis *Travels with a Donkey in the Cevennes*. Robert Louis Stevenson's account of his hike through the Cevennes is as charming today as it was when it was written, over a century ago. Originally published in 1879, there are lots of different editions, but incredibly none is currently in print. That said, it's easy to find second-hand.

Toklas, Alice B *What is Remembered*, Michael Joseph, 1963. Toklas' memoirs are a good deal more readable (thank heavens) than Gertie Stein's – though they're currently out of print and not so easy to find, even secondhand. Her *Cook Book*, published in the 1950s, and reissued by various publishers, is still remarkable for its range of recipes, including the one for Haschich Fudge.

Van Gogh, Vincent *The Letters of Vincent Van Gogh*, Flamingo, 1983. Wonderful insight into the real state of mind of the mad painter, via his letters to his brother Théo.

Verlaine, Paul *Collected Poems*, Oxford World's Classics, 2001. Fine bilingual edition of the best of Verlaine's work.

Volta, Ornella *Erik Satie: Correspondance Presque Complète*, Fayard, 2000. Over the years, Ornella Volta has published an astonishing 12 books about Erik Satie, and this one, at 1,234 pages should keep you busy for quite a while. Some of the books have been published in English and if you can't find them new you should definitely track them down second-hand, as there's nobody more interesting (or indeed more eccentric) than Satie.

White, Edmund *Proust*, Weidenfeld & Nicholson, 1999. Excellent short biography of Proust, rating Proust himself as *the* writer of the early 20th-century, if focusing (unsurprisingly) on the author's (both authors') gay credentials. A fine read, full of charming detail, and highly evocative about the stuffiness of turn of the century France – not to mention Proust's over-heated bedroom.

WEBSITES

Arc de Triomphe www.monum.fr/m_arc/
Brigitte Bardot www.fondationbrigittebardot.fr/uk/ (in English)
Bernadette (Lourdes) www.ville-nevers.fr/indexstb.htm
Bicycles http://museeduvelo.free.fr, http://perso.wanadoo.fr/musee.velo-moto, www.veloparc.com. See also Cycling.
Louis Blériot www.bleriot.com

Didier Bovard www.didierbovard.com (partly bilingual)
José Bové www.la-vache-folle.com (ie: mad-cow.com). An excellent little game, where you can play at being José Bové – first you have to eliminate mad cows and cut down GM crops, after which you get to trash McDonald's and throw cheese at riot police.
Cardo Land http://perso.wanadoo.fr/sacy/cardoenglish.html
Coco Chanel www.chanel.com
Chartreuse www.chartreuse.fr
Château d'Amboise www.chateau-amboise.tm.fr
Château Chambord www.chambord.org
Château de Chenonceau www.chenonceau.com
Cherry Rocher www.cherry-rocher.fr
Cité des Abeilles http://citedesabeilles.com
CNAM (Conservatoire Nationale des Arts et Métiers) www.arts-et-metiers.net
Cointreau www.cointreau.com
Condom www.condom.org
Crocodiles www.lafermeauxcrocodiles.com
Cycling www.letour.fr, www.velo101.com, www.velo-club.net. In the UK there's also the excellent www.cyclingnews.com. See also Bicycles.
Guy Delage www.guydelage.fr
Désert de Retz www.geocities.com/rwkenyon/
Maurice Dufresne www.musee-dufresne.com
Eiffel Tower www.tour-eiffel.fr
El Dorado City www.eldoradocity.fr
Epernay www.epernay.net
Escoffier www.fondation-escoffier.org
Eze www.eze-riviera.com
La Fabuloserie http://fabuloserie.chez.tiscali.fr/
Father Christmas www.magiedesautomates.com
La Frênouse http://pointcomlaval.free.fr/musee
Gâteau Basque http://perso.wanadoo.fr/musee.gateaubasque/
Giant Mushrooms and Insects www.insectes-geants.com
Garden Gnomes: Mouvement d'Emancipation des Nains de Jardin www.menj.com.
    Front de Libération des Nains de Jardin membres.lycos.fr/flnjfrance
La Grande Arche de la Défense www.grandearche.com
Hats www.museeduchapeau.com
Insects www.micropolis-cite-des-insectes.tm.fr
Henry James www.underthesun.cc/classics/james/
Christine Janin www.achacunsoneverest.com
James Joyce www.robotwisdom.com/jaj/
Benoit Lecomte www.theswim.com (in English)
Llívia www.llivia.com
Lourdes www.lourdes-france.com
Lyon www.lyon-france.com
La Maison Sculptée www.rom.fr/lucas
Lee Miller www.leemiller.co.uk
Philippe Monnet www.70degresud.com
Mont Blanc www.chamonix.com, www.ohm-chamonix.com
Napoleon www.napoleonguide.com
Ocean-going rowing www.oceanrowing.com
OK Corral www.okcorral-france.com
Palais Idéal du Facteur Cheval www.aricie.fr/facteur-cheval/
Palais des Naïfs www.palais-des-naifs.com

Papal Palace, Avignon www.palais-des-papes.com
Parc des Mini-Chateaux www.mini-chateaux.com
Pigeons www.pigeons-du-mont-royal.com
Pompidou Centre www.cnac-gp.fr
Jean Raspail http://jeanraspail.free.fr
Reims www.tourisme.fr/reims/
Rochemenier http://perso.club-internet.fr/troglody
La Roque Saint Christophe www.roque-st-christophe.com
Antoine de Saint-Exupéry www.saint-exupery.com and www.lepetitprince.com
Snails www.charentes-escargots.com, http://membres.lycos.fr/escargotdumedoc/,
    http://pro.wanadoo.fr/escargot.perigord/, http://perso.wanadoo.fr/escargot.lozere/
Spectacles www.lunetiers-du-jura.com
Sugar http://thuries.fr/musee_du_sucre
Strawberries www.musee-fraise.infini.fr
Théâtre Ver à Pieds http://perso.libertysurf.fr/verapied/
Tobacco www.france-tabac.com/musee.htm/
Trôo www.troovillage.com
Vegetables www.ohlegumesoublies.com
Ville Souterraine http://perso.wanadoo.fr/delalande/sommaire.html
Vincent Van Gogh www.vangoghgallery.com
Witchcraft www.musee-sorcellerie.fr
Whiskies www.thelin.net/whisky/
Yves St Laurent www.ysl-hautecouture.com

Index

Abbé Pierre **65–6**
Abbé Saunière 78
Abélard **74–6**
Aboville, Gérard d' **49**
absinthe 188
Agostinelli, Alfred 141
Agoult, Marie de Flavigny, Comtesse d' **138–9**
Alkan, Charles-Valentin **119–21**
Amboise 231
Anderson, Sherwood 167
Anginot, Philippe 184–5
Anjony d' **94–6**
Anquetil, Jacques 6
Apollinaire, Guillaume 108, **157**, 161
Aragon, Louis 154, 156, **157**
Arc de Triomphe **228–9**, 244, 246
Armagnac **31–2, 188**
Armstrong, Lance 6
Armstrong, Louis 134, 160
Arnoux, Pierre 247–8
Arouet, François Marie 146–8
Arthurian forests, Brittany **76–7**
Asso, Raymond 125
aviators 34–48
Avignon popes **93–4**
Avril, Jane 109
Aznavour, Charles 125

bachelors' fairs 13–14, 27
Baïse, Condom 237
Baker, Josephine **130–2**, 133, 161
Baldwin, James **160–1**
balloons, hot-air 18
Balmain, Pierre 116
Balmat, Jacques **54–7**
Balzac, Honoré de 124, 144, 169
bande dessinée 8
Bardo, Alain 206–8
Bardot, Brigitte 131, **132**, 197, 242
Barnacle, Nora 169
Barnes, Djuna 161
Barney, Natalie 141, 150, **161–2**, 163, 174, 196, 267
Baron, Frédéric 223
Barret, Franck 222

Barry **242**
bars and cafés 266
Bartholdi, Auguste 233–4
base-jumping 53
Basque, Gâteau 179
Bastié, Maryse **46–7**
Baudelaire, Charles **139–40**, 144, 145
Beach, Sylvia 161, **162–4**
bear festival 9–10
Beardsley, Aubrey 176
Beaubourg **232–3**
Beauvoir, Simone de 103, **154–6**
Beckett, Samuel 103, 162, **164**, 170
Becquerel, Henri 58
bed-racing championships 22
bees **183**
Belboeuf, Marquise de (Missy) 150
Belfort Lion 233
Bergé, Pierre 117
Berger, John **165–6**
Berlioz, Hector 83, 130
Bernadette, Saint 240
Bernhardt, Sarah **132–3**, 150, 176, 201, 230
Beuret, Rose 99–100
bicycles **202–3**, 213
Bienenfeld, Bianca 155
Billy, Charles 246
bird festival 15
biscuits 179
Bitche **237**
Bizarre, Petit Musée de 203–4
Blaikie, Thomas **62**
Blanc, Jean 211
Blériot, Louis 30, 40, 41, **42–4**, 203, 205, 234
boeufs 10–11
Bogart, Humphrey 196
Bohème, La **245–6**
Boissière, Yves 183
Boivin, Jean-Marc **52–3**
Bombard, Alain **49**
Bonnat, Léon 109
Bordeaux–Paris cycle race 5, 69
Bosie (Alfred Lord Douglas) 161, 163, 176
Boswell, James 147
Boucher, Alfred 99
Bouchet, Peggy **51**

boudin contest 11–12, 18, 25
Boudin, Eugène 97
Boule Bleue, la 211–12
boules and pétanques **211–12**
boules carrés 27
Bourbonnais, Alain and Caroline 221–2
Bourrit, Marc-Théodore 54–5
Bourvil 242
Bovard, Didier **50–1**
Bové, José **66–7**
Braque, Georges 108
Bras, Christian Le 136
Brassens, George 246
Breton, André 101, 154, 156, **157–8**, 159, 222, 225, 244
briar pipes **212**
Bricktop 127, **133–4**
Broken Crockery House **219**
Brooks, Romaine 162, **163**
Bruant, Aristide 106, 109
Brunel, Isambard Kingdom 63
bûcherons, fête 22
Buisset, Gérard 202
bulls 10–11
Buñuel, Luis **97–8**, 101, 156

cactus garden 239
cafés and bars 266
Cage, John 129
Calaferte, Louis 136
Calvados 188
Camembert **181**
Camille Claudel sculpture festival 15
Camus, Albert **148–9**, 165
Candide (Serge Tekielski) 203–4
capercaillies 16
Capote, Truman 161
Carcassonne 78
Cardin, Pierre 144
Cardo Land **242**
carnival giants 7, 14–15
Carrère, François 226
Cartier Bresson, Henri 104
Cartier, Louis 37
Casque d'Or (Amélie Hélie) 196
Catacombs (Paris) **194–5**
Cathars **77–9**
Cathédrale, La **220**

Catherine de Medici 82, 92, 221, 231
Caux, Françoise 226
Cave aux Sculptures, la **221**
Cerdan, Marcel 125, 126
Chambord 231
champagne **189**
Champignons et Insectes Géants, Forêt aux **244**
Chanel, Coco **114–15**
Channel tunnel **62–4**
Chapeau, Musée du 208
charcuterie festival 19–20
Charlemagne **79–80**
Charles VII, King 83, 95
Charles IX, King 82, 92
Charles, Jacques 35–6
Chartreuse 188, **190**
Châtelet, Marquise de 146–7
Chausson, Ernest **121**
Chavannes, Puvis de 111
cheese **179–81**
Chenonceau 231
Cherry Rocher **190**
chestnuts 181–2
Cheval, Ferdinand 224–6
chocolate **182**
Chomeaux, Roger (Chomo) 248–9
Chopin, Frédéric 119, **122–3**, 124, 144–5
cigarette papers **204**
Claudel, Camille 15, **98–100**, 107
Claudel, Paul 99–100
Cloetta, Yvonne 166–7
Closerie des Lilas, la 168
cockerels, fishing 14
Cocteau, Jean 106, 115, 125, 126, 129, **149–50**, 151, 156, 161
Cointreau 188
Colbert 87
Colette **150–51**, 161
Coli, François 46
Coluche 246
Columbus, Christopher 247
comic strip festival 8
Condom en Armagnac 24, 31, 188, **237–9**
conscription museum/ conscripts' festival 8–9
Contrefaçon, Musée de la **196–7**
coqs de pêche 14
Corbillard, Musée du 208–9
Corbusier, Le 232
Corday, Charlotte 199
corkscrews **204–5**
Cortot, Jean-Pierre 228
Coupole, la 156
Cousteau, Jacques 208
Couzigou, Serge 182

Craig, Gordon 134
cricket 71
crise de foie 189
Crocodile Farm **242–3**
crops and whips **205**
Cruège, Robert 183
Cunard, Nancy 164
Curie, Marie **58–9**
cycling 5, 262
Cyrano de Bergerac **80**

Dagobert, King 81
Dalí, Salvador 97, **100–1**, 156, 157, 158
Daudet, Alphonse 19
Davis, Miles 160
Debussy, Claude 121, 127
Défense, la 229
Delacroix, Eugène 122, 144, 145, 222
Delage, Guy **51–2**
Demeure aux Figures, la **221**
Deneuve, Catherine 97, 117
Denfert-Rochereau 195, 233
Deschevaux-Dusmesnil, Suzanne 164
Désert de Retz **243–4**
Deutsch-Archdeacon prize 39, 42
Deux Magots, les 155, 156, 168
Diaghilev, Sergei 129, 149, 156
DiCaprio, Leonardo 143
Dior, Christian **115–16**
directions, maps 264–5
Disney-Ffytche, Lewis 243–4
Doisneau, Robert 135
donkeys 21
Dorval, Marie 144
Douanier Rousseau **107–8**
driving **262–3**
Dubois, Daniel 209
Dubuffet, Jean 221–2
Ducuing, Jean 244
Dufresne, Maurice **205–6**
Duncan, Isadora **134–5**, 161
Dürer, Albrecht 202
Durrell, Lawrence 163, 172
Dutel, Roland 221

Easter eggs 11, 13
écorchés (Fragonard) 201–2
Edison, Thomas 230
Edward VII, King 196, 230
egg festival 13
egg in its finery 11
Egouts, Musée des **200**
Eiffel Tower 105, **229–30**
Eiffel, Gustave 230, 233
El Dorado City 245
Eliot, TS 161
Ellington, Duke 134
Eluard, Paul 101, 156, 157, **158**

Emmaus 65–6
engineers 62–5
Enimie, Sainte **80–1**
Epstein, Jean 97
Erotisme, Musée de l' **196**
Escoffier, Auguste **206**
Esenin, Sergei 135
espadrille festival 25–6
Etex, Antoine 228
European procession of carried giants 7, 14–15
Explorimages festival 30–1
Eze **239**

Fabre, Jean-Henri 209
Fabuloserie, La **221–2**
Facteur Cheval 224–6
Fakes Museum **196–7**
Fanny 211–12
Farman Henri **39**
Father Christmas **206–8**
fattened bulls festival 10–11
Faure, Jacques 41
Favreau, Lucien 245–6
Femme et de l'Automate, Musée de la **197**
Fenn-Smith, Louise 43
Ferber, Ferdinand **39**
Ferlinghetti, Lawrence 163
Ferme-Musée Barret, la **222**
Fernandel 242
fishing cockerels 14
Fitzgerald, F Scott 134, 161, 162, 167
Flamme d'Armagnac 31–2
Flaubert, Gustave 144
Flavigny, Marie de **138–9**
Flore, Café de 160, 168
foie gras 4, **183**
Foire du Gras 4
Fontanges, Mademoiselle de 95
food and drink 4–5
Forbes, Malcolm 37
Forêt, Musée de la **245**
Forget, André 24
Fougeirol, Luc 243
Fougère, Serge 22, **23**, 26
Fouré, Adolphe-Julien (Abbé) 227–8
Fragonard, Musée **201–2**
Franck, César 121
François I, King 231
Franklin, Benjamin 35, 36, 243
Frênouse, La **222–3**, 224
Freud, Sigmund 157, 173
Frézier, Amédée François 186
frog festival 20–1
fruits, forgotten 30, **187**

Gabriel, Albert 246
Gala (Helena Ivanovna Diakonova) 101, 158

Gamond, Aimé Thomé de **63–4**
garden gnomes **67–8**
Garin, Maurice 70
Garnerin, André-Jacques
Garros, Roland **44-5**
Gastaud, Jean 239
Gauguin, Paul **101–3**, 113, 171, 222
Gaulle, Charles de 65, 131, 160, 190, 246
Gauthier-Villars, Henri 150
Gellhorn, Martha 151, 168
Giacometti, Alberto **103–4**, 156, 157, 196
giants, carnival 7, 14–15
Gibbon, Edward 147
Gide, André 48, 141, 161, 176
Gielgud, John 133, 134
Ginsberg, Allen 163
Girouettes, Musée des **214–15**
goat-eaters' festival 32
Golding, Mike 52
golf, snow 11
Goudeket, Maurice 151
Goulue, la 109, **110**, 196
Grande Arche de la Défense **229**
Grant, Cary 196
Greene, Graham **166–7**
Grenouille, Fête de la 20-1
Grévy, Jules 23
Guggenheim, Peggy 159
Guiler, Hugo 172, 173
Guillaume le Conquerand 18
guillotine **68**, 198, 199. 205, 210
gypsies' pilgrimage 16–17

Hahn, Reynaldo 141
Hare, David 159
Harel, Marie 181
Hassell, Bernard 160
hats **208**
Haussmann, Baron 121, 229
Haxton, Gerald 170–1
hearses, horse-drawn **208–9**
Hébuterne, Jeanne 107
Hélice Terrestre de l'Orbière, l' **241**
Hélie, Amélie (Casque d'Or) 196
Héloise **74–6**
Hemingway, Ernest 134, 151, 161, 162, 163, **167–8**, 169, 170, 174
Henry II, King 82, 231
Henry IV, King **81–3**
Henry V, King of England 82
Hepburn, Audrey 200
herring fair 31
Herrings, Battle of the 83
Herzog, Maurice 53, 184

Hicks, Wynford 71
Hinault, Bernard 6, 72, 213
hippo 244
honey **183**
hot-air balloons 18
hot water bottles **197–8**
hotels **252–7**, 265
Howe, Elias 212–13
Huguenots 82
Humblot, Yves 249
Hunt, Walter 212–13

ice sculpture 7
Indurain, Miguel 6
Indy, Vincent d' 121, 127, 129
insects **209**, 244
Insolite, Musée de l' **209–10**
Irving, Henry 134
Isidore, Raymond 223–4

Jacob, Max 108
James, Henry **168–9**, 174
Janin, Christine **53–4**
Jardin de Nous Deux, le **246**
Jardin du Coquillage **248**
Jardin Sculpté, le **246**
Jardin Zoologique, le **246–7**
Jeanne d'Albret 82
Joan of Arc **83–4**, 95, 197, 204, 222
John, Elton 200
Joliot, Frédéric and Iréne 59
Josephine (Napoleon) 91
jousting, water 18–19, 21–2, 26
Jouvenal, Henry de, Bertrand de 151
Jouvenal, Pierre 182
Joyce, James 161, 162, 163, **169–70**

Kahlo, Frida 157
Kelly, Grace 131, 208, 210
Kennedy, Jackie 200
King, Martin Luther 131
Komir the hippo **244**
Kosakiewicz, Olga 155
Kronenbourg 188

Lacroix, Christian 204
ladle-throwing festival 29
Laederich, Pierre 255
Lafargue, Laura 85
Lafayette 198
Lafon, Bernard 14, 30, 187
Lamba, Jacqueline 157, **158**
Lambert, Bertrand 30
Lambert, Count Charles de 42
Landru, Henri 199
Lanier, Paul 212
Lanzmann, Charles 156
Laroche, Baronne de **39–40**
Lascaux 241, 242

Latham, Hubert **41–4**
Launet, Gilbert 24
Lawrence, D H 133, 173
Lawson, Nigella 206
Lecomte, Benoit **52**
Legros, Fernand **104**
Lenin **84–5**
Leplée, Louis 124–5
Létinois, Lucien 145–6
Leyat, Marcel **59**
liars' festival 24
Lilienthal, Otto 39
Linard, Jean 220–1
Lindbergh, Charles 46
Lion of Belfort 233
Lister, Anne **56**
Liszt, Franz 119, 138–9, 144
Litnanski, Bodan and Emilie 248
Llívia **239–40**
Locke, John 146
Loire Châteaux **231–2**
Lord Alfred Douglas (Bosie) 161, 163, 176
Lorraine pâté festival 28
Lotar, Elie 104
Louis XIII, King 86, 87
Louis XIV, King **86–7**, 88, 95, 123
Louis XV, King 87, 228
Louis XVI, King 26, **87–9**
Lourdes **240**
Lovers' Wall **223**
Luberon wines 59–60
Lucas, Jacques 224
Lully, Jean-Baptiste 86, **123**
lumberjacks' festival 22
Lunettes et Lorgnettes, Musée des **200–1**, 213
Lustig, Victor **105**, 230

Magie des Automates 206–8
Maison à Vaisselle Cassée, la **219**
Maison Picassiette **223–4**
Maison Sculptée **224**
Man Ray **105–6**, 156
Manceau, Alexandre 145
Manent, Max 209–10
Manet, Edouard 140
manifestations 1–4
Mansfield, June 171–2
maps, directions 264–5
Marais, Jean 126, 149
Marat, Jean-Paul 199
Marchal, Captain **39**
Marchois, Bernard 126
Marechal, Pierre 40
Marianne 23
Marie-Antoinette 36, 62, **87–9**, 197, 243
Marly, Pierre 200–1

Martha, Saint 19
Massenet, Jules 121
Mata Hari 89–90, 161
matches 210–11
Mathieu, Mireille 197, 246
Mathieu-Favier, Albert 63
Maugham, Somerset 163,
170–1
Mayle, Peter 60, 144, 149, 165,
204
Mazarin, Cardinal 86
Medici, Catherine de 82, 92,
221, 231
Melba, Dame Nellie 206
Merckx, Eddy 6
Meunier, Charles 188
Meurisse, Paul 125
Meyssonnier, Fernand 68–9
Michaud, François 22–3
Micropolis 209
Miller, Henry 162, 163, 171–2
Miller, Lee 105–6, 149, 156–7
Mini-Châteaux, Parc 232
Missy (Marquise de Belboeuf)
150
Mitterand, François 208
Modigliani, Amedeo 106–7
Molière 123
Monnet, Philippe 52
Mont Blanc 54–7
montagnards 52–8
Montand, Yves 125
Montgolfier brothers/festival
18, 34–6
Montségur 78
Monville, François Racine de
243–4
Moralès, Raymond, Parc-
Exposition 245
Morny, Duc de 132, 150
Morris, William 65
Morrison, Jim 123–4, 176, 253
Moulin Rouge 109, 110, 196
mountaineers 52–8
mourre championship 17
Mur des Je t'aime 223
mushrooms 181–2, 244
Musset, Alfred de 144
Mussolini 154

Napoleon 62, 63, 83, 90–2, 228
Napoleon III 63–5
nativity, living 33
Newton, Isaac 146
Nietzsche, Frédéric 239
Nin, Anaïs 171, 172–3
Niro, Robert de 253
Nollet, Jean-Antoine 60
Nostradamus 92–3
Notre Dame du Haut,
Ronchamp 232
Nungesser, Charles 45–6

Obut 211
Oeuf en Habit de Fête 11
Oh! Legumes Oubliés 14, 30,
187
oiseau, fête 15–16
OK Corral 245
Oliver, Jamie 206
Orwell, George 172
Osborne, Fanny 174–5
ours, fête 9–10
oyster shucking contest 25

Paccard, Michel-Gabriel 54–7,
62
Palais des Naïfs 226
Palais Idéal du Facteur Cheval,
le 224–6
palindromes 92, 152
Palmer, Eva 161
Pansart 12
Paradis, le 247
Paradis, Maria 55
Parc Animalier de Sainte Croix
20
Paris-Nice cycle race 5
Paris–Roubaix cycle race 5–6
Parker, Dorothy 134
Pascal, Blaise 60–1
Pasternak, Boris 156
pastis 188
Pécheux, Catherine 136
penitents' processions 6
Penrose, Roland 106
Père Noël 206–8
Perec, Georges 151–2
Perez, Armand 26
Perlès, Alfred 171
Pernod, Henri-Louis 188
Pessac zoo 244
pétanques and boules 211–12
Petiot, Marcel 199–200
Peyrepertuse 78
Pfeiffer, Pauline 167
Philby, Kim 166
Piaf, Edith 124–6, 149, 196,
242
Piano, Renzo 233
Picasso, Pablo 108, 129, 134,
149
Picpus Cemetery 198–9
pigeons 184
piglet race 20, 25
pigs' trotters 257, 258–9
pig-squealing championships
24–5
Pilâtre de Rozier 36
Pills, Jacques 125
pipes, briar 212
plucking contest 32–3
Plumy, Alain 196
Poe, Edgar Allan 140, 174
Pole, Rupert 173

Police Museum 199–200
polo, snow 8
Pompidou Centre 232–3
Ponceau, Daniel 26–7
Porsche tractor 209
Porter, Cole 126–7, 134, 196
Post, Peter 6
Pottok Fair 8
Pougy, Liane de 161, 196
Pound, Ezra 161, 162, 167, 169
Préservatif, Musée du 237,
238–9
Proust, Marcel 140–2, 153,
161, 184, 189, 267
prunes 23, 184
prune-stone spitting 23–4
Publivores 12
pyramid, Paris 226

Quatre Jours de Dunkerque 5
Quercy, Yvan and Mary-France
208–9
Quéribus 78
Quimby, Harriet 40
Quinault, Philippe 123

Rabelais, François 92
Radiguet, Raymond 149, 150
Rank, Otto 173
Raspail, Jean 152–3
records' festival 26–7
redingote anglaise 238
Renard, Maurice and Olivier
215
Renaudin, Jacques 110
René, King 19
restaurants 257–61, 266
Reynaud, Claude 203
Richard, Hugues 231
Richardson, Hadley 167
Richelieu, Cardinal 86, 87
Rimbaud, Arthur 142–3,
145–6, 149, 150, 188, 263
Ritz, César 206
Rivera, Diego 157
Rizla+ 204
Robert the Devil 18
Robespierre 198, 244
Rochemenier 241
Rodin, Auguste 98–100
Rogers, Richard 233
Roque Saint Christophe, la
241–2
Roquefort 66, 181
Rostand, Edmond 80
Rothéneuf rock sculptures
226–7
Rousseau, Henri 'Douanier'
107–8, 222
Roussel, Albert 129
Roussel, Raymond 153–4
Rousset-Rouard, Yves 205

Rude, François 228–9
Ruskin, John 65, 141
Russell, Count Henry 57–8
Sade, Marquis de 143–4
Saint Exupéry, Antoine de 47–8
Saint Laurent, Yves 116–17
Saint Pansart 12
Sainte Croix animal park 20
Sand, Georges 119, 122–3, 144–5, 169
sand-yachting 30
Santa Maria 247–8
Santos-Dumont, Alberto 37–8, 41, 44
Sara-la-Kâli 16–17
Sarapo, Théo 125–6
sardines 184–5
Sartre, Jean-Paul 103, 154–6, 159
Satie, Erik 111, 127–30, 149
Saunière, Abbé 78
Saussure, Horace Bénédict de 54–7, 55
Savignac, Jean-Claude 187
Sax, Adolphe 130
scarecrows 26
Schweitzer, Albert 155
scientists 58–61
seafarers 48–52
Searle, Alan 171
sea-shanty festival 24
Senft, Didi 27
Seurat, Georges 172
sewers 200
sewing machines 212–13
Shakespeare & Company 162–4, 252
Shell Garden 248
shrimp festival 28
Signoret, Simone 196
Simpson, Tommy 6
Singer, Isaac Merritt 212–13
Singer, Paris 134–135
Siohan, François 69–70
Sistine Chapel, Normandy 227
ski-joëring 9
skylark whistlers 28
Sleziak, Eric 227–8
Smith, Ada 127, 133–4
Smith, Albert 55–6
snails 15, 185–6
snow golf 11
snow polo 8
snow sculpture 7
Soufflacul festivals 13
spectacles 200–1, 213
square bowling 27
stags, troating 20
Statue of Liberty, Paris 233–4, 244

Stein, Gertrude 108, 161, 162, 167, 173–4
Steinbeck, John 134
Stern, Daniel 138–9
Stevenson, Robert Louis 174–5
stonecutting days 22–3
strawberries 186
sugar 186
Sun King 86–7
Suncin, Consuelo 47–8
Surrealism 97, 101, 103, 105, 129, 149, 154, 156–9, 225, 244, 245

Tapie, Bernard 70–1
Tarasque festival 19
Tarn, Pauline 161
Tartarin de Tarascon 19
Tati, Jacques 124, 135–6
Tatin, Robert 222, 224
teddy bears 213
Tekielski, Serge 203–4
Terry, Ellen 134
Thatcher, Margaret 197
Thévenet, Bernard 72
Thimonnier, Barthélémy 212–13
Thomas, Linda Lee 127
Thompson, Hunter S 190
Thuriès, Yves 186
tiles 213–14
Tire-Bouchon, Musée du 204–5
Titanic 40
tobacco 214
Toklas, Alice B 161, 173–4
Tougourdeau, Emile 246–7
Toulouse-Lautrec, Henri 108–10, 111, 188, 196, 222
Tour de France 5–6, 27, 70
Tour Eiffel 229–30
Tournemire family 94–6
transhumance festivals 17–18
tripe 15, 29–30
troglodyte villages 240–2
Trôo 241
Trotsky, Leon 158
Truc, Léopold 247
truffles 5, 186

U2 239
Utrillo, Maurice 111, 112, 222

Vadim, Roger 132
Valadon, Suzanne 109, 110–12, 128, 130, 222
Van Gogh, Théo 102, 112–14
Van Gogh, Vincent 102, 109, 112–14, 188, 222
Varda, Agnes 248

Vasseur, Robert 219
Vastine, Henri 245
Vauban 237
vegetables, old 14, 29, 187
Ver à Pieds, Théâtre 136
Verlaine, Paul 142–3, 145–6, 149, 150, 188
Versailles, Château de 87, 89
veterinary science 201–2
Vets, Irial 227
Vignemale 56–8
village cricket 71
Village d'Art Préludien, le 248–9
Ville Souterraine 232
Vilmorin, Louise de 47
Vinci, Leonardo da 231
Viollet le Duc 64–5
Vivien, Renée 161
Voisin brothers 38–9
Volta, Ornella 129–30
Voltaire 146–8, 240, 259
Vuillemenot, Roland 71–3

Wagner, Richard 121, 138
waiter racing 16
Warminski, Jacques 241
water jousting 18–19, 21–2, 26
Waugh, Evelyn 134
weather vanes 214–15
Weber, Louise-Josephine (La Goulue) 109, 110
Weil, Simone 159–60
Weinberg, Albert 197–8
Wellcome, Syrie 170–1
whips and crops 205
whiskies 190–1
Whitman, George 162–3
Wild West parks 245
Wilde, Dolly 161–2
Wilde, Oscar 124, 133, 161, 175–6, 188, 253
William the Conqueror 18
Willy (Henri Gauthier-Villars) 150
Winchell, Walter 131
wine 187–8
wine festivals 5
witchcraft 215
Woinic, the pig 227–8
wolves, howling 20
Wright brothers 34, 37, 38, 39, 41, 42, 44

Y's, l' 249
Yourcenar, Marguerite 161

Zborowski, Leopold 107
Zola, Emile 144, 167, 230
zoo, Pessac 244